EXTREME SURVIVAL

EXTREME SURVIVAL

WILDERNESS • TERRORISM

Akkermans • Cook • Mattos • Morrison

AIR • SEA • LAND

HERMES HOUSE

© 2014 by Anness Publishing Ltd
Illustrations © 2014 by Anness Publishing Ltd

Publisher: Joanna Lorenz
Editorial Director: Helen Sudell
Text Contributors: Anthonio Akkermans (Bushcraft),
Bill Mattos (Surviving on the Move and Surviving Nature),
Bob Morrison (Survival in the Home and Surviving Terrorism and Conflict),
Harry Cook (Self-defence in the Urban Jungle)
Project Editors: Sarah Ainley, James Harrison
Photography by Helen Metcalfe and Tim Gundry
Illustrations by Patrick Mulrey and Peter Bull Studios
Designer: Nigel Partridge
Production Manager: Ben Worley

ISBN: 978-1-4351-5828-3

Manufactured in China

2 4 6 8 10 9 7 5 3 1

COPYRIGHT HOLDER'S NOTE

CONTENTS

Introduction by Debra Searle MBE 6

PRINCIPLES OF BUSHCRAFT 10
Mental and emotional survival 12
Signalling for help 14
Finding your bearings 16
Taking care of yourself and
    others 18
Natural hazards 20
Natural remedies 21
The importance of hygiene 22
Making soaps and toiletries 24

SHELTER 26
Choosing a place to shelter 28
Building a debris hut 30
Building a stacked debris wall 32
Building a long-term shelter 34
Snow shelters 38
Building a quinze shelter 40
Snow caves and other shelters 42
Finding shelter in the desert 44
Building a desert shelter 46
Building a jungle shelter 48

FIRE 50
Fire for survival 52
Firelighters and fuels 54
Lighting fires using friction 56
The bow drill 58
The hand drill 62
The pump drill 64
Jungle fire 66
Arctic fire 67
Building a fire 68
Keeping a fire going 69
Building a fire for cooking 70
Using hot rocks for cooking 72
Cooking food in a covered pit 73

WATER 74
The importance of water 76
Finding a safe water supply 78
Natural sources of water 80

Filtering and purifying water 82
Further ways to find and treat water 84

FOOD 86
Nutrition for survival 88
Edible plants 90
Wildlife food sources 92
Tracking animals 94
Identifying animal footprints 95
Stalking animals 96
Setting animal traps 100
Fishing techniques 102
Making and using a throwing stick 104
Skinning and butchering an animal 106
Preserving meat and other animal
    products 108
Making buckskin for clothes 109

TOOLS AND EQUIPMENT 112
Basic food bowls and
    containers 114
Weaving a basket 116
Crafting simple pottery 118
Making a bow for hunting 120
Making arrows 122
Making basic stone tools 124
Working with bones and sticks 126
Working with natural resins
    and oils 128
Making cordage 130

**SELF-DEFENCE IN THE URBAN
JUNGLE 132**
Identifying the risk of
    attack 134
Attacks on women 136
Learning to defend yourself 138
Using improvised weapons 142
Frontal attack 144
Attack from behind 146
Attacks with knives and other
    weapons 148
Strangulation 152
Head butt 155
Bag snatching 156
Sexual assaults 158

SURVIVAL IN THE HOME 162
Guarding against break-ins 164
Enhancing your security 166
Dealing with an intruder 168
Fire in the home 170
Gas leaks 172
Flooding 173
Emergency escape 174
Emergency home shelter 176

SURVIVING ON THE MOVE 178
Safeguarding yourself and your
    possessions 180
Surviving city streets 181
Coping with dangerous road
    situations 182
Dealing with mechanical failure 184
Getting out of a skid 186
Fire in a vehicle 188
Drivers' survival strategies 189
Choosing a safe seat 190
Transport accidents on land 192
When things go wrong in the air 194
Surviving an air emergency 196
Abandoning ship 198
Survival at sea 200
Survival at the seashore 202
Travelling abroad 204

**SURVIVING TERRORISM AND
CONFLICT 206**
Being street smart 208
Being taken prisoner or hostage 210
Survival in captivity 212
Transport hijacks 214
Bombs and explosives 216
Toxic gases and poisons 218
War zones 220
Survival in the workplace 222

SURVIVING NATURE 224
Surviving acts of nature 226
Surviving wild animal attacks 232
Surviving arctic conditions 236

LIFE-SAVING FIRST AID 238
First-aid essentials and assessment 240
Moving an injured person 242
Rescue and resuscitation 244
Dressing wounds 246
Burns, shock and extreme
    temperatures 248

Useful knots 250
Survival resources 251
Index 252

INTRODUCTION
by Debra Searle MBE

Survival is necessary only when the environment becomes unfamiliar to us and we are far beyond our comfort zone, battling with situations outside the realms of our previous experience. I'm sure that I am not the only person who sometimes struggles with motivation. Mentally, I just don't always feel up to going to work, doing the washing up or the weekly food shop, but surely a life or death situation is something that none of us would struggle to motivate ourselves over? You would think so, but it's not quite as simple as that. Few of us have a death wish, but if we should ever find ourselves in one of the situations described in this book we may not feel able to fight to survive if the circumstances seemed overwhelming, or we were pitched against Mother Nature – the ultimate battle. When we are sapped of all of our energy and reserves the only thing we have left to fight with is our minds.

THE WILL TO SURVIVE

Over the years much research has been conducted into why it should be that some people can survive a life-threatening situation when others in the same situation are overwhelmed. Often it is not the strongest or those with the best equipment who make it, although these things undoubtedly make a big difference. Unequivocally, the same conclusion is always reached: the difference between living or dying lies in the mind. The power of the mind, the resilience of the human spirit, an unshakable optimism and a mental readiness to handle the unexpected are vital in the ultimate survival situations.

Naturally some people have these qualities in abundance, but not all. Happily there are skills that can be learned to help us achieve the necessary mental strength. Just as we can repeat movements, like the running action or biceps curl, to make our bodies physically fitter, so the same principle can also be applied to the mind. But as with getting our bodies fitter, we have to work at it and repeat the action to increase our performance.

Rowing solo across the Atlantic, as I did, is certainly a test of your mental strength. You may find yourself in numerous survival situations that you have not anticipated. In my case, I had to have my rowing partner rescued

▼ *Debra Searle has honed her mental survival skills both as a sports psychologist and as an extreme sports participator.*

▲ *Bushcraft skills can employ modern tools like a well-designed steel utility knife, but should also be based upon utilizing — and respecting — what nature has to offer.*

two weeks into the journey and consequently I rowed the Atlantic alone for three months in an 8m/24ft plywood rowing boat. During the voyage I had to survive many hazardous situations, such as hurricanes, attack by sharks and almost being run over by a supertanker.

The conclusion I have drawn from my experience on that and many other expeditions is that training the mind allows us to cope with situations that take us way beyond any mental or physical pain threshold we may have set ourselves, and that these mental skills, once learned, can be applied to all survival situations. It therefore makes sense to look at these now, at the start of this book, before you read on.

The two most important mental strength-building skills that can be developed can be summed up in two words — visualization and attitude.

VISUALIZATION

It may sound like psychobabble at first, but visualization is certainly not just for elite athletes. The idea is that by mentally imagining doing an action we can train our bodies to carry out that action without actually moving or completing it for real; therefore a thought alone can produce a physical response. An example of this that we can all experience is imagining sucking on a slice of lemon. When we do we get a rush of saliva to the mouth yet there is not a real lemon in sight! Our minds have just induced a physical response to the thought. Visualization is the most powerful survival tool we

can ever develop because often we cannot replicate an actual situation in order to practise surviving. However, if we can use our minds to rehearse mentally how we will respond, our minds and bodies will be trained and automatically know what to do if and when the situation arises.

I spent time before, and even more time during, my row across the Atlantic doing mental risk assessments of all the things that could go wrong and be potentially fatal. Running these "movies" in my head allowed me to rehearse life-threatening situations, such as fixing the watermaker in a big storm or surviving a collision with a whale, in which the key was to respond positively and correctly. Practising the physical response to a threatening situation without fail every time I visualized it meant that I did not even have to think about what to do when such a situation really arose. My body instinctively seemed to know exactly what to do. Visualization increased the speed of my reactions and provided me with an effective response.

Not only can visualization help us achieve the right physical response, it is also incredibly powerful for eliminating fear. Let's face it — any survival situation is likely to be terrifying, but if we can remain calm we are likely to be able to analyse, prioritize and plan a response amid the chaos and confusion. When visualization is used in this way it is like watching a scary movie for the second time. The first time you put the DVD

▲ *The* Troika Transatlantic *was Debra Searle's (formerly Veal) home for 3½ months as she made a solo crossing of the Atlantic. She faced the mental challenge of survival alone on such a long journey, as well as the fear of the boat being hit by whales or supertankers, or of being attacked by sharks.*

in the machine and press Play you find yourself jumping at the scary bits because you don't quite know when they are going to happen. But when you put the DVD in for a second viewing and press Play you don't jump when you get to the scary bits, because you have seen it all before and know that it is coming.

▼ *A positive mental attitude and ability to dig deep for inner strength are key to survival, as well as being able to adapt.*

▲ *If a fire broke out in your home, would you know how to get everyone out safely? Using visualization to help you to anticipate escape scenarios will enable you to cope that much better in a live situation.*

We often feel fear because we don't know what is going to happen next, but if we can visualize some of the possibilities by running our own "movies" in our heads we can eliminate some of the fear. We simply press Play when the situation arises.

THE POWER OF VISUALIZATION

Perhaps one of the most powerful ways to use visualization is as a means of developing that eternal optimism and hardness of human spirit that is so vital for survival. It is also possibly the simplest form of visualization to develop, for all you really need to do is visualize that one thing that is worth living for.

We all have something to live for – something we love more than anything else. Maybe it would be to hold your child again, drive your car, watch your favourite football team win a home game…Whatever it may be you just have to visualize it using every sense in your body and imagine how amazing it will feel to do that again. For me it was

the moment when I was finally going to row into a marina on the other side of the Atlantic and see all my friends and family waiting there to greet me. I used to imagine it in so much detail, using every sense in my armoury. I could see myself walking up to my mum and giving her a huge hug. I would imagine her familiar smell, then what I would say to my twin sister and what she would say to me, and I would imagine seeing my brother in those scruffy shoes that he always wears. It

used to take me an hour to imagine that moment, though in reality it was going to last only a few minutes. When I was lonely, scared or in pain it made the time go faster and it stopped me from giving up.

CHOOSE YOUR ATTITUDE

The one element common to many of the scenarios in this book is that we don't have a choice about being in these life-threatening situations. We can attempt to avoid them but some are unavoidable. For example, we have little choice about being involved in a kidnap, a terrorist attack or a natural disaster. Often the situation will be totally out of our control. If this is the case then it is vital to be able to recognize those things that you do have a choice about, rather than wasting time and energy worrying about those things that you have no control over. You may not be able to change the situation but you can always change the way in which you are responding to it. You can always "choose your attitude".

"Choose your attitude" is more than just a motto – it is a way of life. For this Atlantic rower it was a case of picking an attitude over breakfast every morning at sea, but it had to be a positive one. Negative attitudes had

▼ *Vigilance is the new buzzword of urban survival following the wave of terrorist alerts on public transport.*

DEBRA SEARLE MBE

Debra and her then husband Andrew took part in the Ward Evans Atlantic Rowing Challenge at the end of 2001, but the sudden onset of her husband's phobia meant that he had to be rescued, leaving Debra to face the 5,000km/3,000-mile challenge alone. This she did with incredible bravery, completing her voyage in Barbados after 112 days and gaining universal respect. Her transatlantic adventure became the talk of the media and an inspiration for other people battling against the odds in every area of life.

▲ *Terrorism has changed the way in which we view our chances of survival and how we can prepare ourselves against the unexpected. An obvious example after 9/11 is airport and airline secuirty.*

been banned from on board the rowing boat. So optimism might be the attitude of the day, and a list of all the things there were to be optimistic about had to be formulated. The result was a pretty upbeat feel about what the day might bring, which in reality was

▼ *Fortunately, we can learn survival skills such as self-defence for use out on the street when we find ourselves most vulnerable.*

crazy considering the situation. There was in fact every reason to have a rotten attitude at sea – being desperately lonely, scared and not sleeping for more than 20 minutes at a time for fear of collision with a ship or attack by sharks. Rowing for three days might achieve about 50km/30 miles, but then overnight a storm would hit and push the boat back 60km/40 miles. Lack of toilet paper was just another negative. But the key to survival was

refusing to dwell on how bad the situation was, and choosing a positive attitude, because that was the one thing about which I had a choice.

So as you read this book, don't just let the words flow over you. Instead, visualize yourself in the situation and imagine how you would respond. Live the survival situation now in the safety of your own home, just in case you ever have to face it for real. And remember: choose your attitude.

THE KEYS TO SURVIVAL

What do we need most to survive? Many people will answer "food", when asked about what they feel is a priority in a survival situation. It makes sense that we should think this way, because, of the four basic requirements for life, we can take three of them for granted in our modern lifestyle. Water comes from the tap on demand, our houses are our shelters from the elements, and few of us need to light a fire when we feel cold. Food is the only need we put more thought into. We cook every evening, and we notice instantly when food runs out. However, we can actually survive for a long time without food. It is water intake

that is vital, because without water we would die in three to five days.

This book is divided into two sections: the first section looks at the principles of bushcraft and the four cornerstones of survival. It shows you how to ensure that you can live in a hostile wilderness environment by building a shelter, making fires, finding food and water and keeping yourself safe. The second section shows you how to survive hostility in an urban environment, covering everything from street assaults to kidnapping, terrorist alerts, natural disasters and emergency first aid for when you are on your own.

PRINCIPLES OF BUSHCRAFT

Learning bushcraft skills allows us to live off the land naturally, travel light, and survive most terrain when equipment is scarce or not available. Even if we are not in a survival situation, bushcraft skills provide a profound way of connecting with our ancestors and allowing us to revive our link with the earth. In fact, bushcraft skills are really earth-living skills, managing without modern tools or aids. Acquiring these skills requires diligent practice and maintenance, but once learned they open a world of possibilities. Most importantly, these skills belong to anyone and have been passed on by those who travelled the wilderness trails before us. They should be preserved intact for the next generation.

Mental and emotional survival

By far the biggest problem people face when thrust into a survival situation is not how to find food or water, but how to cope mentally with the situation. Suddenly they have to rely on their instincts, and a whole range of powerful and conflicting emotions can surface. Psychologists generally agree that there is a classic sequence of reactions to any traumatic event: shock, denial, fear and anger, blame, depression, acceptance, and moving on – or variations of those emotions.

EMOTIONAL RESPONSES

• **Shock** You are unprepared for what's just hit you. You have difficulty processing the information.
• **Denial** As a survival mechanism, you may now acknowledge your situation, but you refuse to believe it is true. You continue to say, "No, this can't be happening to me."
• **Anger** You become enraged over your situation. You are upset that things aren't the way they were, and you're scared that you'll never get back to normal.
• **Blame** Blaming others for your

▼ *The most inhospitable environment can yield clues for survival. Green shrubbery indicates a water source in a desert.*

situation makes you feel better but makes little rational sense.
• **Depression** This is internalized anger. You search for some way to make your stress more manageable.
• **Acceptance** Now you are getting "real". You are facing reality, however wild and remote it appears to be.
• **Moving on** Mentally you begin to

▲ *Solve each problem as it arises. Once a problem has been fully resolved, you are free to move on to the next issue.*

redress the balance and think about your situation and how you are going to survive, not just for the next few hours but the next few days and weeks.

DON'T PANIC

In a survival situation, feelings of helplessness can turn into depression and loneliness very quickly. One of the greatest and most difficult emotional states to deal with is panic. Panic can cause you to perform irrational actions that can worsen the situation you're in. In extreme circumstances, failure to remain calm can even endanger your life, just because you didn't have the presence of mind to make the right decisions. Most of the time, you won't even realize you're panicking.

The first step to beating panic is to recognize the fact that you may panic if you don't take steps to prevent it. When you are in an unnerving situation it is important to take things step by step and to give yourself a chance to assess your situation properly.

ONE STEP AT A TIME

Don't fall into the trap of adding all your problems one on top of the other until they become one gigantic problem. Sit down for a moment, take a few deep breaths, and think about your most urgent difficulty. Then concentrate on solving this particular problem. After this first issue is resolved, you can move on to the next. Take it one step at a time.

There is an apt story of the man who found himself having to paddle a kayak back to shore during a storm on the ocean. If this man had thought about all the waves he would have to survive, he might well have drowned. Instead, he took it one wave at a time, taking care to steer his kayak right into each wave as it came and never thinking about the next problem until the current one was solved. He battled against the waves for hours, but made it to calmer waters and the shore in the end.

STAYING UPBEAT IS A SKILL

Many people feel that maintaining an upbeat mentality is something you read about and then remember when it really matters. This isn't the case.

Controlling your mindset is as much a skill as making fire by friction. You can practise your mental skills by applying a calm, positive approach to events in your everyday life. Whenever things start to get tough, just do one thing and then turn to the next on the list. Not only will this prepare you for any survival situation, you will also find that it makes day-to-day life a lot more enjoyable and less stressful.

You can ensure an upbeat mentality by making sure you have the skills to provide for yourself and others. Well-honed skills will boost your confidence and will help keep panic at bay.

SURVIVAL IN A GROUP

There is safety in numbers and obvious physical advantages in having someone else there if you are injured or weak. But there are other advantages to being in a group when you are in a survival situation. The greatest is that there are more individuals to take care of the necessary tasks of day-to-day living. Not only do many hands make light work, but the various individuals in the party are bound to have different strengths and weaknesses. If you are

▲ *In a survival situation with another person or a group, a lot of emotional comfort can be shared between individuals.*

someone who is very good at building a shelter but less proficient at finding wild edibles, for instance, being part of a group allows you to put all your efforts into providing an effective group shelter, while feeling secure that other people in the group will provide other necessities, such as food, water and fire.

There are also a few disadvantages, however. Now you have to provide not only for yourself, but for the whole group. If all the other group members have a certain amount of outdoor skills and there are plenty of resources around, this may not be a difficulty, but if you are the only one with any survival skills or if there aren't many supplies available, it can be very hard to ensure that the whole group is well hydrated, fed and comfortable. It may also happen that one member of the group is injured and needs taking care of. After all, the chain is only as strong as its weakest link.

SURVIVING ALONE

If you are on your own, one of the most difficult problems to overcome is loneliness, which can quickly lead to feelings of hopelessness, panic and then desperation. To counteract this, use visualization skills to overcome fears. Imagine yourself rescued and work towards making that happen. Make a list of priorities and stick to it. Keep focused on the task in hand and drive away negative thoughts whenever they creep into your head. Take strength from each task you complete. A strong mental attitude will pull you through.

GROUP PRIORITIES

Follow these steps to ensure that your group is well prepared to face the challenges ahead.
- Choose a leader. This should be the person with the greatest skill, who must be able to carry the responsibility, acting as chairperson rather than as dictator. As leader, you must take responsibility for the situation and organize any tasks that need to be completed; listen to all the ideas the group bring forward and help them come to any decisions that need to be made. Sometimes this may not be possible, and you will have to make decisions and assign tasks, for instance in the case that only one of your group has the relevant knowledge.
- List all the tasks needed to ensure immediate survival and share them out among the group members.

- Find out what each individual's strong points are, so that tasks can be put in the most able hands. Some tasks will have to be done by everyone working together, such as building the group shelter.
- Keep each other up to date on the progress the group is making, and make sure everybody is still OK. Promote a feeling of mutual dependence within the group, so that everyone is there for the whole group and no one feels left out. Make sure that people who have difficulty with certain tasks get help.
- Make an inventory of all the items in everyone's possession. In the case of a crash, try to rescue as much from the wreckage as possible: anything from electrical wires (to use as cordage) to the stuffing in the seats (for insulation).

Signalling for help

It cannot be stressed enough that whenever you go on a trip in the wilderness people back home should know where you're headed and what time you expect to arrive at your destination. This way there will be people in the outside world who will miss you (and your fellow travellers) if something does go wrong.

If you have found yourself (alone or with a group) in a survival situation and it was not by choice – if your vehicle has crashed, for instance – there is another issue to consider. With every decision you make, whether it is in siting your camp or leaving it to find food and water, you need to ensure that any rescue teams who reach the area will be able to find you.

LEAVING SIGNS FOR RESCUERS

It is all too common for people to leave a crash site without any indication where they were headed. It is best to remain near the crash site, but if the site cannot sustain you it may sometimes be necessary to move away. In this case, it is vital that you leave

clear signs behind, indicating the number of survivors, whether any are wounded and where you have gone.

Once you have arrived at a site that can sustain you well and you decide to settle and wait for rescue, make sure your site is clearly visible from the air. You can do this by making large signs on the ground with sticks or any other easily distinguishable material. If a sign is at any distance from the actual camp, make sure it indicates where the camp is by means of an arrow.

Another idea is to throw green plants and leaves on to the camp fire during the day, as smoke is a good indicator of where you are. During the

▼ *If you draw signs on a beach it is very important that they are above the high tide mark, so they are not washed away in the surf. Rather than drawing in the sand, use rocks or branches, which show up clearly.*

▲ *Using stones, you can lay out signs on or beside the trail for rescuers to follow. These signs are mainly useful when leaving the site of an accident.*

night you may want to have a large fire, depending on your resources. If you have got plenty of fuel, one thing you can do is to construct three fires in a triangle with the corners approximately 10m/33ft apart.

▼ *When abandoning a crash site you must leave signs that make it clear there are survivors, and show where you have gone.*

LEAVING TRAIL SIGNS

	STRAIGHT AHEAD	TURN RIGHT	TURN LEFT	DO NOT GO THIS WAY
ROCKS				
PEBBLES				
STICKS				
LONG GRASS				
NUMBER OF PACES IN DIRECTION INDICATED		9 →	I HAVE GONE HOME	

There are many ways to leave telltale signs for would-be rescuers that you have passed by this trail and to show your onward direction. Use rocks if possible, otherwise wood or even rooted grass and foliage.

ESSENTIAL SIGNALLING TO AN AIRCRAFT

▲ *Stretch out both arms as if to embrace the aircraft to ask the crew to fly towards you to pick you up.*

▲ *Stretch out both arms sideways, to signal to the pilot to hold the aircraft in a hover pattern.*

▲ *Palms down, arms outstretched, moving your arm up like a bird's wings, tells the aircraft to descend.*

▲ *Lower your outstretched arm as part of the bird-like movement to make it clear to the pilot it's safe to descend.*

▲ *With left arm outstretched, wave your right arm to make it clear that the pilot needs to move to your left.*

▲ *Continue waving your right arm deliberately and keep your left arm outstretched to maintain this signal.*

▲ *Placing both hands behind your ears indicates that your receiver is working.*

▲ *This signal indicates to the pilot that mechanical aid is needed.*

▲ *This tells the pilot that the safe direction to exit is to your left.*

▲ *Stretch out your arms in a particular direction and bend your knees, to show the area that is a safe landing zone.*

▲ *Moving both outstretched arms parallel above you from side to side says: "Do not try to land."*

▲ *Stretching your arms out in front of you and waving them up and down signals the word "yes".*

Finding your bearings

Getting your bearings is essential for survival in the wild – that doesn't just mean finding the direction of north or south but, rather, being aware of your surroundings. As one wilderness instructor has put it: "You cannot get lost unless you have a place to go to and a time to be there." There is good sense in this saying.

In many cases when you accidentally find yourself in a survival situation, you may not know exactly where you are. You may not know what civilization lies closest to you. In such instances, knowing where north or south is may not really be an advantage. It is more important to learn as much as you can about your surroundings. Find a stream or river and follow it down – you will

often come to some sort of civilization this way. You may also want to listen very carefully for any sounds of modern day life, such as trains, factories or traffic noise.

If you do need to establish the direction, it can be time-consuming if you have to rely solely on natural resources. There may be times when it is simply impossible to say for sure which way you're facing. For example, though it is often true that mosses grow on the north side of trees, it is not always the case – moss can grow all around a tree, so it is not a very good idea to rely on this kind of method. However, there are some techniques that can work for you if you need to find the cardinal directions.

NAVIGATIONAL STARS

North Star Also known as Polaris or the Pole Star and located above the North Pole, it is a key reference for north. It is the only star that appears to remain static in the sky.
The Plough Also known as the Big Dipper, it forms part of the large Great Bear constellation.
Orion Also known as the Hunter, this rises above the equator and can be seen in both hemispheres.
Southern Cross This indicates south in the southern hemisphere.
Milky Way A hazy band of stars stretching across the sky. The dark patch in it is called the Coalsack.

DIRECTION-FINDING WITH A SHADOW STICK

1 If you don't have a compass you can use the sun to get your bearings. Find a stick at least 50cm/20in long and drive it vertically into flat, even ground.

2 Find a number of small pebbles, and place one on the tip of the shadow the stick is casting on the ground. Now wait 10–20 minutes.

3 You will find that the tip of the shadow has moved. Take another pebble and place this where the tip of the shadow now reaches.

4 Wait another 10–20 minutes. The shadow of the stick will have moved even farther round. Take a third pebble and once again place it on the tip of the shadow.

5 The pebbles you have placed on the ground will form a line. This line goes from east to west. To find the north–south axis, place a stick at right angles to the line of pebbles.

6 This stick will point north and south. If you follow the direction of the stick with the sun at your back, you will be walking north; walking towards the sun will take you south.

USING THE STARS TO FIND DIRECTION

▲ *The North Star lies above the North Pole and can be found by running a line into the sky from the far side of the Plough's pan.*

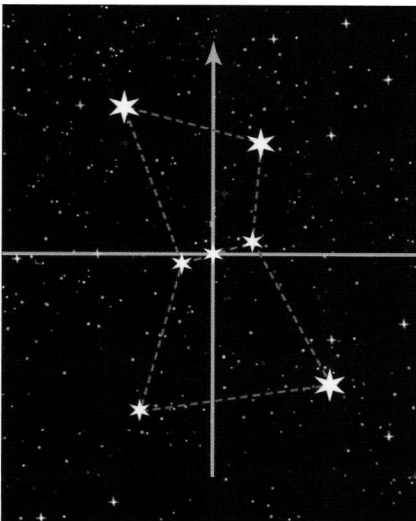

▲ *An imaginary line drawn across the middle of Orion lies roughly east–west in the northern hemisphere.*

▲ *The Southern Cross will help you to find south in the southern hemisphere. Note the false cross of dimmer stars to the right.*

▲ *Keep a button compass handy as part of your travel kit for emergencies. It will pinpoint your direction accurately.*

FINDING NORTH BY THE STARS

To find a northerly direction in the northern hemisphere on a clear night, look for the constellation of the Plough or Big Dipper and draw an imaginary line from the two stars farthest from the "handle". This line will intersect with the North Star, also known as the Pole Star (five times the distance between the two "guiding" stars). Once you have located the North Star, push a stick in the ground then insert a second stick, lined up so that when you look over the first stick you can see the second one directly under Polaris. If you leave the two sticks in the ground, they will act as a reminder of the direction in daylight.

In the southern hemisphere, the best celestial signpost is the Southern Cross, which circles the South Pole. This constellation, located near the dark area known as the Coalsack in the Milky Way, has four bright stars in the shape of a cross and two "pointer" stars beside it. Imagine a line through the longer part of the cross and another line bisecting the two bright pointer stars – these two lines intersect at the celestial South Pole.

USING THE SUN TO MEASURE TIME

1 To see how much light is left, extend your arm towards the sun. Each finger's width represents about 20 minutes.

2 Bend your wrist so your hand is horizontal and lower your hand so that it appears to "rest" on the horizon.

3 The sun is visible above three fingers. This means that it is about one hour after sunrise or before sunset.

Taking care of yourself and others

Although you should learn how to do without it, it is advisable to carry a small survival kit with you at all times. A few basic items will make some tasks a bit easier for you or allow you to get vital chores done using less energy.

ESSENTIAL SURVIVAL KIT

A knife will be your most useful tool in most survival situations, but the other items listed here won't take up much space and could be very helpful.

- Penknife
- Waterproof matches
- Candle
- Fishing line
- Fish hooks of various sizes
- Two small fishing lures
- Snare wire
- Water purifying tablets
- Whistle
- Cord
- Safety pins/needles
- Surgical adhesive tape
- Sticking plasters (Band-Aids)
- Dental floss or strong thread
- Compass
- Tweezers
- Paracetamol (acetaminophen)

Pack these into a small tin (which can also act as a pot to boil water) and seal it with duct tape to keep it dry. Keep your survival kit in your backpack or in your jacket on every trip.

▲ *If you take care in picking the items for your survival kit, they should all fit into a container small enough to fit in a pocket. Take items that you would find hard to make alternatives for in the wild, such as a sharp knife, waterproof matches, a candle, a whistle, safety pins, a needle and strong thread, a hook, some wire and a compass.*

PREVENTION IS BETTER THAN CURE

Common sense will tell you that the best way to treat illness or injury is to prevent it. You don't want to wound yourself by being careless with a knife, for instance, especially when in an accidental survival situation, since adding to your problems will cause your situation to deteriorate faster.

There are a few important guidelines you should follow when out in the wild. The most important is to wash your hands thoroughly after going to the toilet. In a survival situation, a lot of tasks will be done with your bare hands (such as skinning wildlife or gathering water) and you must avoid

any cross-contamination, which could make you or others in your party ill.

Ensure that sharp implements are used and stored correctly so you don't accidentally stab yourself. When using tools such as knives or axes, it is vital that your body is never in the path of the tool or a splinter of stone or metal.

▼ *Take a first-aid course before you go on a major trip or trek. It will help you to assess a survival situation coolly and clearly.*

◄ *Avoid situations that might create self-inflicted injuries, such as lifting too much at once, or placing your feet without looking.*

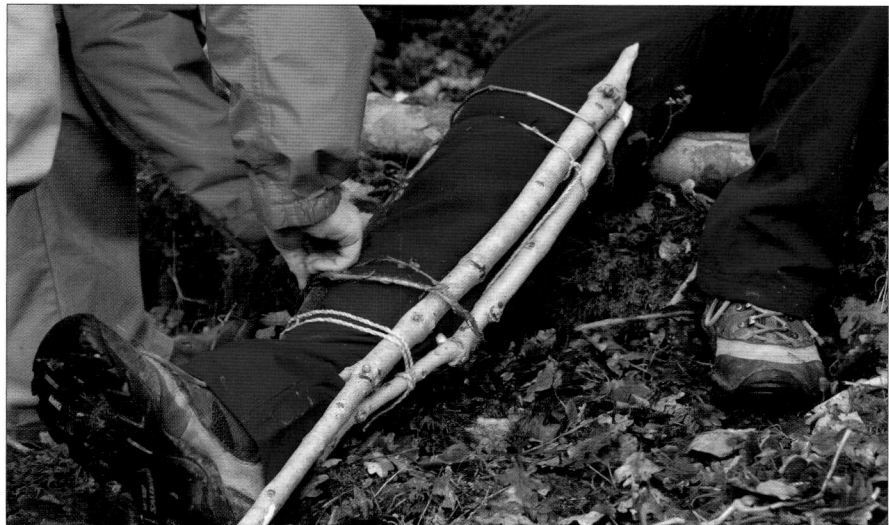

When gathering wood, never break branches over your knee or by jumping on them. It is easy to underestimate the strength of the wood and hurt yourself. Always do the work with sharp tools or by burning them to the right length in a fire (which is a more efficient use of your energy anyway).

Be careful where you put your feet when hiking, and take as little risk as

▲ *When bleeding is controlled and shock has been dealt with, it is time to tend to non-life-threatening wounds like fractures.*

possible. Sometimes it's better to go around difficult terrain than to cross it. Safety should always be uppermost in your mind when there is no one on hand to give you medical treatment if you are ill or injured.

▲ *When you are shaping wood, carve smoothly and slowly, with the blade facing away from your body.*

▲ *Never turn the blade of the knife towards your hand or body, and make sure the path of the knife is clear of obstruction.*

▲ *Never break a branch of wood over your knee in case it is stronger than it looks and you hurt your leg.*

▲ *Jumping on a piece of wood could damage your ankle. If you can't cut it, burn it through to achieve the correct length.*

RESPECTING NATURE

There is a balance to strike between reducing your impact on the environment as much as possible, and staying alive. For example, if your life is not in immediate danger, you can build your shelter using only dead material, but if your life depends on it the conservation rules have to give way. If you have to survive the night and there is not enough debris to shelter you, you shouldn't hesitate to cut down live branches and leaves to use as insulation.

In a non-life-threatening situation, it is important to take care of the environment you live in. You do not, for instance, have to eat every single bulrush or cattail root. Approach your environment much as a gardener would. If you have to cut down particular trees or plants for use in your shelter or for other purposes, always try to find those trees that are in competition with others, so that your action benefits them. Try to pick trees and plants growing in places where they seem less likely to thrive. This kind of "caretaker" attitude could actually improve the area where you find yourself.

A second important rule is not to harvest any plants or kill any animals in the immediate vicinity of your camp. Move at least 100m/110yd away from your camp before looking for what you need. This way, you are not only leaving your immediate area intact, you are also creating an emergency cache. If you were to fall ill, it would be a relief to find edible plants growing right outside your shelter. Always follow a different path to and from your camp, making sure you don't trample too much brush.

If survival forces you to kill an animal for food then use everything there is to glean from that particular animal – meat for food, bones for tools, hide for clothing – leaving nothing to waste.

Natural hazards

Wherever you are in the wild, it is important to watch out for dangerous animals and habitats. For more information on surviving wild animal attacks – including those by bears, canines, crocodiles and alligators, big cats and snakes – see page 232. The general rule is to be wary at all times.

AVOIDING DANGEROUS WILDLIFE
You actually need to alert potentially dangerous animals of your presence and should certainly not surprise them. Use whistles or bang tins to let them know you are there. They won't want anything to do with you, provided you don't threaten them or their young. It's only the presence of food that may make them view you as a competitor.

When you enter bear country you threaten the animals' status at the top of the food chain. They have an acute sense of smell, so an obvious precaution is to hide food and waste well away from your camp. Keep food at least 300m/330yd from your sleeping area tied up in a bear baggy (for instructions

on how to make one, see page 232). Burn all toilet paper and feminine hygiene products. Bury your waste at least 15–20cm/6–8in deep.

TICKS AND OTHER INSECTS
Insects can be very harmful. In the tropics, mosquitoes are mainly responsible for passing on illnesses, but even in temperate regions there are insects that can pass on viruses and infections. The most common (and most often ignored) danger in temperate climates comes from ticks. They carry various diseases but Lyme disease is the one to watch out for. In most places the risk is low, but up to one third of ticks in the USA carry it.

Once on your body, the tick will dig into your skin to feed on your blood. After about 12 hours it will release its barb by injecting saliva to dissolve the tissue around the bite. It is this saliva that may contain bacteria or viruses.

If you contract Lyme disease you may or may not find a "bull's-eye-like" rash, which is usually not itchy, and you may have flu-like symptoms such as headache, fever, stiff neck and sore joints. If the infection spreads, it can affect the heart, nervous system and joints. If untreated, it could go on to affect your short-term memory and ultimately be fatal. Treatment is with antibiotics; there is no vaccine.

Remove a tick as soon as you spot it and don't leave it to fall off by itself. In

If confronted by a bear, remain calm and quiet, fall to the ground and protect your neck and stomach by clasping your hands over your neck, and laying face down. Playing dead during an attack has been documented in survival cases. Climbing a tree is not a good option. Grizzly bears can stand over 2m/8ft on their hind legs and climb trees. Fighting back is a last resort.

high-risk areas, check for ticks every 12 hours. Burning it off with a cigarette will only encourage the tick to inject saliva. Instead, grab it with tweezers and pull it straight out.

▼ *Remove leeches with a hot flame or salt. Remove the whole animal. Clean thoroughly with antiseptic.*

ESCAPING QUICKSAND

In tropical conditions walk with a strong stick or pole – then if you sink in quicksand (sand saturated in water), you can lie on your back on the pole and "relax". Keep your hips on the pole and your body will float as it is less dense than the sand. If you struggle you will sink deeper. Quicksand is rarely deeper than a few feet. Spread yourself out and backreach for dry land.

▼ *Well-camouflaged crocodiles are ambush hunters and kill by gripping, rolling and drowning their victims back in the water.*

Natural remedies

If you haven't any first aid supplies with you in the wilderness, don't panic: it does not mean you can't do anything to help yourself or others. There are some common ailments that can be treated in a wilderness survival situation using the plants and wildlife you may find around you. There are many plant remedies that can take care of ailments that are widespread over the globe.

MINOR CUTS

By far the most widespread plant of this kind, with many uses, is plantain. Many people use the crushed leaves to relieve the irritation of insect bites. Historically, however, plantain leaves were chewed into a pulp and used to treat minor cuts. Plantain tea is also very helpful for soothing a cough. It is made by putting approximately 10ml/ 2 tsp of dried leaves in a mug of boiling water and leaving them to infuse for 10 minutes.

COLDS WITH FEVER

Elder is a common shrub, or more rarely a tree, that grows in many areas with temperate climates; it is familiar as the source of elderberry wine, which is said to prevent winter colds. The flowers, fresh or dried, can be made into an infusion, in much the same way as plantain leaves, which will help to cool a fever and alleviate the symptoms of a cold. Elder leaves help to repel biting flies and mosquitoes, and an infusion of the leaves can be dabbed on the skin for this purpose.

DIARRHOEA

Oak bark is traditionally used to alleviate chronic diarrhoea and dysentry (see page 23). You need to collect the bark of young twigs in the spring; this can be dried and stored. For the treatment of diarrhoea it can be made into a decoction by putting about 10ml/2 tsp of dried oak bark in 0.5 litre/1 pint of water and boiling it for 3–5 minutes before drinking. The liquid has antiseptic and astringent properties, and can also be used on a compress to treat slow-healing wounds, or as a gargle to help with problems such as infected gums or throat.

▲ Mosses can be used to bandage wounds and control bleeding. Some, such as sphagnum moss, have antiseptic properties.

▲ Plantain can be chewed to a pulp and applied to a wound to help the healing process; it also soothes insect bites.

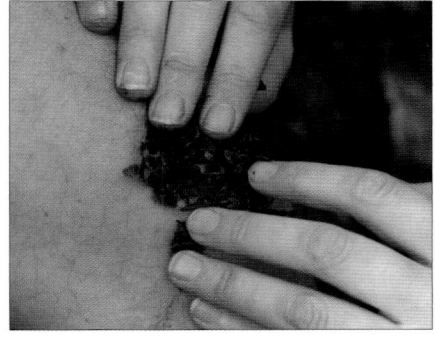

▲ Wounds need to be tended to and direct pressure to wounds needs to be applied if there is any bleeding.

MAKING A NATURAL COUGH MIXTURE

1 Dried plantain can be used to brew a good anti-cough tea. Put a handful of dried plantain leaves in a bowl.

2 Boil some water and pour it over the leaves. Then let the leaves steep in the hot water for about 10 minutes.

3 Remove the plantain leaves from the bowl and the cough mixture is ready for use.

The importance of hygiene

In any kind of survival situation personal hygiene is critical, especially in avoiding the possibility of cross-infection. It is a common misconception that primitive peoples are less clean that we are, when in fact, in many so-called primitive societies, cleanliness and hygiene are as important as they are in Western society.

There are a host of natural alternatives to soap, shampoos, brushes and toothpastes that are used by primitive societies the world over, and knowledge of these can be useful in a survival situation. A little preparation is needed to produce many of these items, so they may not be a priority for you. In a long-term situation, however, it is well worth spending some time and effort making toiletries.

TOILET PAPER
"What can I use instead of toilet paper?" is probably the question most frequently asked regarding hygiene. There are many things in nature that can be used for this purpose. In fact, anything you can find around you will work when you really need it. A good solution is a combination of dried and wet moss. Use the wet moss first to clean yourself and then use the dried moss to dry off. Some people prefer it the other way around, which, they say, works in a refreshing way.

When there is not a lot of moss around, or in an emergency, you can pick some large leaves from nearby plants. Again, use fresh green leaves first, followed by some barely dead leaves. You should always make sure the

leaves you choose are not poisonous or irritating to the skin. Some people use the inner bark from trees, but getting it entails quite a lot of work.

DEALING WITH HUMAN WASTE
Whatever method you prefer for dealing with waste, observe the following basic rules:
• Always make sure you dig your toilet facility at least 25m/27yd away from your fresh water source, so that there is no chance of contamination.
• Dig the hole to a minimum depth of 45cm/18in.
• Always cover your waste with soil immediately, and when your pit is full, or if it starts to smell even after a layer of soil has been added, fill in the rest of the pit and make another one.

▼ *A good example of a discreet latrine, sited well away from the living area.*

▼ *Make sure your toilet hole is deep so that waste will not be detected by animals.*

▼ *Wash your hands to help prevent unhealthy bacteria entering your body.*

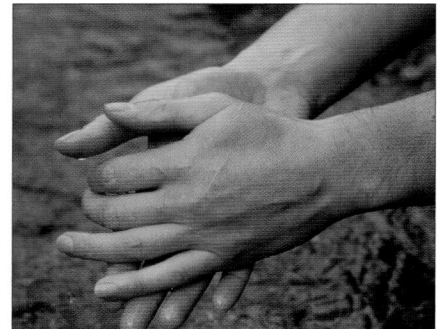

DIGGING A LATRINE

1 If you are staying in an area for a while, dig a latrine at least 25m/27yd away from your fresh water source, to a minimum depth of 45cm/18in.

2 You can make the latrine more comfortable by placing a log or two over the pit. Gather mosses and leaves so that "toilet paper" is always at hand.

3 Each time you use the latrine, add a layer of soil to keep smells at bay. Adding some charcoal from the fire will also help to mask any smells.

▲ *In a survival situation you must stay well hydrated. Food is important in the long term, but is not needed as much as fluids.*

• When using paper, always burn the paper afterwards. Paper can lie around for many years to come and will spoil the environment quickly.
• Make sure none of the items you keep in your pockets can accidentally fall in. Having to fish your knife out of your latrine is very unpleasant.
• As always, wash your hands and wrists when you have finished.

DIAPERS AND MENSTRUAL CARE
Most native peoples use dried moss for feminine hygiene, but very soft, well tanned animal hides have also been used for this and for babies' diapers. Some native peoples make pads from cloth filled with absorbent material such as moss or bulrush (cattail) fluff. Hygiene is important because menstruating women may otherwise attract unwelcome attention from bears.

▲ *Never use soaps or shampoos when washing in streams, lakes or rivers, even if they are labelled as biodegradable. Contrary to the manufacturers' claims, these products will not degrade completely and even a small percentage of soap in the water may destroy the environment.*

A NATURAL DIARRHOEA REMEDY

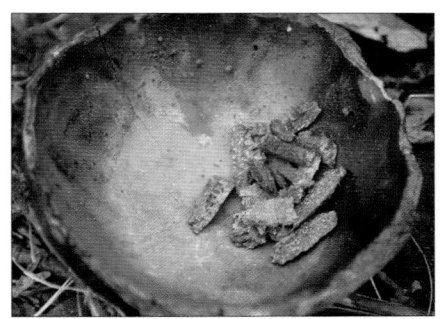

1 A decoction of oak bark is a good remedy for diarrhoea, slow-healing wounds, or throat and gum infection.

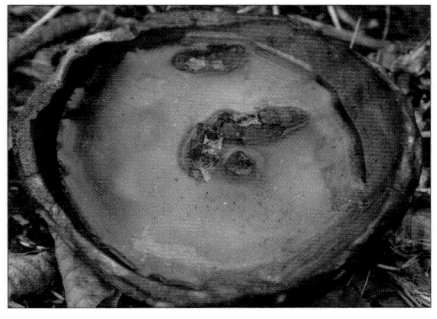

2 Pound the bark and put it in a bowl, then cover it with fresh water, put it on the fire and bring it to the boil.

3 When it has boiled for 3–5 minutes, remove from the fire and allow to cool before drinking like a tea.

MAKING NATURAL SANITARY TOWELS

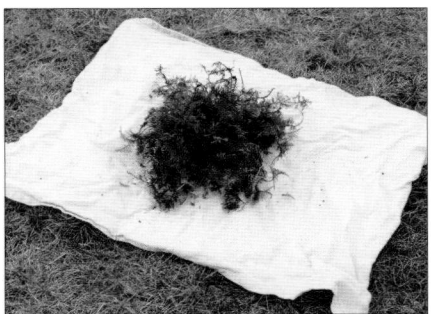

1 Diapers or absorbent sanitary pads can be made by collecting a supply of dry, springy moss.

2 Put a pile of moss into the middle of a clean piece of cloth or soft, thin buckskin and fold in the edges.

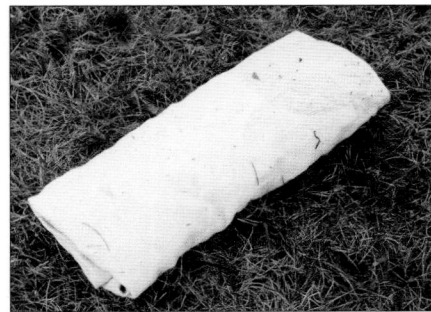

3 This makes an absorbent pad that has many uses. The cloth or buckskin can be washed and re-used.

Making soaps and toiletries

One of the things most often forgotten on trips and outings, but often needed, is soap. It is quite easy to make in the wild and can be a great aid to hygiene, especially in a survival situation.

If you do have biodegradable soaps or shampoos with you, you should be aware that they need soil in order to degrade. So dig a pit at least 25m/27yd away from the water source, to avoid contaminating it, and pour all your washing water into this.

The ingredients you need to make a basic soap are as follows:
• Wood ash or charcoal (which contains alkali).
• Water.
• Oil or fat (either animal or vegetable fat will do).
• Pine resin or needles (these are not essential but will make the soap slightly antibacterial and give it a nice smell).

You will also need some kind of strainer or filter, such as a piece of cloth, to strain the ash out of the water. Always use a stick rather than your hand to stir the ash in the water, since wood ash and water create a very strong alkaline solution that can burn your skin.

Once all the water has boiled off the mixture you will have a good, serviceable soap. You can make it stronger or weaker by changing the percentages of ash, oil and pine resin.

YUCCA-BASED SOAP

Another common way of making soap is by pounding the roots of yucca plants. You get a froth when pounding the plant, which contains a lot of saponin, a lathering substance. The soap that comes from this froth is best used as a shampoo.

TOOTHPASTE

If dogwood or birch are growing in the area, you can chew on one of their fibrous twigs to create a toothbrush. You can use water mixed with wood-ash as toothpaste, but rinse your mouth very well after use to ensure that this doesn't irritate your gums.

A very effective mouth rinse can be made by pounding pine needles in water, then filtering it. The water will smell of pine and be slightly antiseptic.

NAIL AND HAIRCARE

Other aspects of hygiene that are taken for granted are cutting nails and hair. The easiest method of keeping your nails short is to file them regularly on a smooth stone. The stone should have the texture of an emery board. Filing nails may take a long time, but it is preferable to breaking them when they

MAKING A BASIC SOAP

1 First wait until the campfire has cooled down, and collect some charcoal from its centre.

2 Grind down the pieces of charcoal using a stone until you have a fine black powder.

3 Mix the charcoal with water. Stir well, and then strain it through a filter and reserve the water.

4 Heat up some oil or fat and mix the filtered water into it. Bring the mixture back to the boil.

5 Pound a handful of pine needles and add them to the mixture. Boil until all the water has evaporated.

6 Take the mixture off the fire, allow it to cool down and you are left with a good, mildly antiseptic soap.

are too long. Unless you have access to a very sharp, hard stone such as flint or obsidian, it may be easiest just to leave your hair to grow.

If you do have access to obsidian, sharp flakes can even be used for shaving. However, it is important to be extremely careful if you try this, as obsidian can be far sharper than a metal blade and the flakes can cut you easily, since they are not protected as in a modern razor and are often irregular. It may be better not to shave than to run the risk of cutting yourself.

▶ *If you have any small cuts or wounds, you can keep them clean and help them heal by making an oak bark compress. Simply make a decoction of oak bark by boiling it in water, and soak a wad of moss in the liquid when it's cooled down. Secure this over the wound using cordage or a bandage made from cloth or buckskin.*

MAKING AN ANTISEPTIC MOUTHWASH

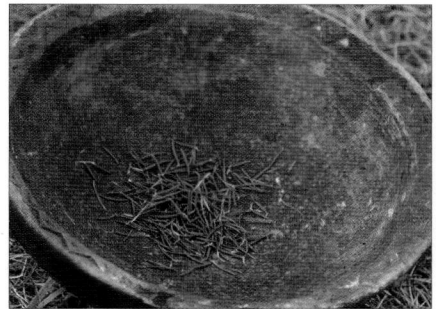

1 Gather a handful of fresh pine needles and put them in a bowl.

2 Use a clean stone to pound and grind the pine needles.

3 Add boiling water, leave to infuse for five minutes, then strain.

MAKING A NATURAL SHAMPOO

1 Dig up a yucca root and trim off the shoots. Scrape off all the soil and cut the root into short sections.

2 Collect a clean rock to use as a mortar and a smaller clean stone to use as a pestle. Then pound the root.

3 Pounding the yucca root produces a lather, which is perfect for use as a shampoo as well as a regular soap.

SHELTER

The first basic requirement of survival is shelter, to protect yourself from the elements. Whether it is to help you survive a single night or for a longer period, a shelter offers you a place in which you can feel safe physically and, just as importantly, psychologically. A good shelter will provide protection against rain, snow, heat and unwelcome wildlife, while allowing you to conserve your body heat and energy and to rest, recuperate and recover. Though the principles of erecting shelters in the wilderness are simple, building one can be hard work. If you try to take shortcuts, your well-being and perhaps your survival may be compromised. If you build your shelter soundly, you will be safe and secure night after night.

Choosing a place to shelter

Finding a place to shelter from the elements should be your first priority in any survival situation. Fire can also give some protection from the elements, but it may be hard to make a fire if you are unequipped. Take the hypothetical example of trekkers in the wilderness who have forgotten this and spend most of the day trying to get a fire going with a bow drill. When they finally realize that their first priority should have been shelter rather than fire, they have spent too much time and energy on trying to make a fire, and no longer have time to build a shelter. They have to spend the night freezing without either a fire or shelter.

SHELTERING NEEDS AND WANTS

If you consider for a moment what you have in a modern house, the list can be overwhelming. Amenities such as flowing water, electricity, toilets and so on make modern life pleasant, but you can survive without them – you don't really *need* them. When thinking about a natural shelter, it is important to distinguish your needs from your wants.

An emergency shelter will normally be small enough to conserve your body heat, and it should be thickly insulated

▼ *If you are travelling across the frozen Arctic tundra, knowing how to build a snow shelter could save your life if you lose your way or there's a sudden snowstorm.*

so heat can't escape and rain can't get in. Conversely, in a hot climate it will need to provide shade from the sun and should be slightly larger with lighter insulation.

When erecting an emergency shelter it is important to preserve energy and time. Ask yourself first, "What are my needs?" The answer is that whatever the environment you find yourself in, you need protection from its extremes. This could mean any of the following:
• cold
• heat
• the sun
• wind
• rain
• dangerous animals

In some circumstances, you may need protection from all of the above. Think about where you site your shelter, and the direction in which it faces, so as to minimize exposure to such extremes.

SHELTER FOR EMOTIONAL SURVIVAL

A shelter can be built entirely with your bare hands, without the need for tools or cordage. A good shelter can keep you alive by conserving your body temperature, so it is not essential to keep a fire alight through the night. Apart from physical safety, it is also emotionally important to have a shelter. It is a place you can call home, where you can sit down to think about your

▲ *If you have no tools, it's possible to make a shelter entirely with your bare hands.*

situation. It is a refuge where you can stay safe in a wild environment. It also gives you a base from where you can venture out to get food, water and fuel.

USING A NATURAL SHELTER

There may be situations where you are forced to find some sort of natural shelter. You may not have time to build anything late in the evening, or you may be ill or weak from hunger.

A natural shelter can be anything in nature that will protect you from the elements. A fallen tree that still has all its leaves and branches can protect you

▼ *The roots of a fallen tree will give some shelter from rain and wind, and can be used to support your own construction.*

from the worst of the wind and rain. Big clumps of vegetation may offer you the opportunity to quickly bend the stems and leaves over yourself. In some environments, you may find caves or natural hollows that can be stuffed with vegetation to insulate them.

If you are stranded in a sandy desert, you might have to bury yourself in the sand to protect your body from the sun during the day. In most situations, however, especially in cold weather, you should try to insulate yourself from the ground in any way you can, as it can quickly sap all your body heat.

It is likely that spending the night in a natural shelter will be the most uncomfortable night you ever spent, but the main objective is to stay alive. You can improve on your shelter, or build a new one, the next day.

FINDING THE RIGHT LOCATION

Consider the points on this checklist when deciding where to build a shelter.

- Ensure that there are plenty of shelter-building materials around you. Dragging them over a long distance can cost hours of unnecessary labour and waste your precious energy.
- Make sure you are close to water, but not in the floodplain of a stream. To avoid contaminating the water, build your shelter at least 30m/33yd away from the bank of a river or stream. This also prevents too much dew from falling on your shelter in the morning.
- Check for any dead branches in overhanging trees, which could fall on your head or damage your shelter. Check for the possibility of an avalanche or rockslide.
- Ensure you are not building your shelter on top of an anthill or other animal shelter.
- Try to find areas that are naturally protected from severe weather, but avoid building deep in the woods. Deep woods take a long time to dry out, and don't get much sun. Try to stay on the leeside, or sheltered side, of woods, mountains and other such protective features in the landscape.
- If you intend to have a fire, ensure you look out for fire hazards such as overhanging boughs, peat-like soil or dry grasses.

WHERE TO FIND A NATURAL SHELTER

▲ *Woodland offers some protection from wind and rain, and there will be plenty of debris to insulate your shelter.*

▲ *Try to make sure there is no heavy dead wood above the site. Remove it and pile it up for firewood, or move to a safer location.*

▲ *Natural caves are always a good option, though you must be careful of other creatures that may have the same idea.*

WHERE TO BUILD A SHELTER

▲ *When looking for a site to build a shelter, try to find a place where there is plenty of raw material within easy reach.*

▲ *Make sure the site is not below a possible landslide. If you have no choice, let the slide happen before you build.*

▲ *You will need access to water, but beware of choosing a low-lying site in case rain upstream causes the water level to rise.*

Building a debris hut

In many wilderness environments, there is plenty of debris such as dead leaves and brushwood available, and a debris hut is the ideal short-term shelter. It is small and well insulated to conserve heat and protect you from the rain. The debris hut is such an effective shelter that it can keep you warm in temperatures well below freezing. It can also be built entirely with your bare hands, so no tools or cordage are needed. The debris doesn't have to be dry, and in a survival situation green material could be used instead.

The debris hut creates a maximum amount of dead air to keep heat in the shelter. It forms a cocoon around you, ensuring that your body is not heating up unnecessary empty space.

AN ADAPTABLE HUT

A debris hut can be adapted to suit the most difficult scenarios as long as you stick to the guidelines shown here. You need to gather as much debris as possible in the shortest amount of time – when your life is on the line, every minute counts. You'll need a thickness of about 1m/3ft around the sides (except the opening) – use a stick to help you judge the amount of debris you've added and pack it down as much as possible.

Fill the interior with the driest, fluffiest material you can find. If there is a lot of fern or bracken around, use

it as a top layer inside the shelter. It smells nice, and does not poke into your body. Make sure you pack it in well. When you bed down in the shelter, you will automatically squeeze the excess debris into the corners and the foot-end, forming a cocoon around your body.

Put some branches over the shelter to stop leaves blowing away. Slabs of bark or a layer of moss will help to stop rain getting through. You will also need to fashion a door by weaving a "bag" from flexible stems and filling it with leaves. You can pull this bag into the entrance behind you to seal it. Trying to seal the entrance with a pile of leaves

▲ *The debris hut takes the form of a dome, which is perfect for shedding water.*

is really cumbersome, and ineffective. Once the bag of leaves is in place, use debris from inside to plug any holes.

Don't worry about cutting off the fresh air supply by plugging the door. There will still be plenty of air flowing in through the leaves. Just make sure you go to the toilet before you crawl in and get snug, as it takes a long time to get in and out of this shelter.

▼ *In order to retain heat, make the entrance of the shelter just big enough to shuffle into backwards, lying flat on your belly.*

▼ *For the framework of the debris hut you will need a strong ridge pole, about 2.5m/8ft long, and two strong Y-sticks, like this one, each about 60cm/2ft long.*

BUILDING A DEBRIS HUT

1 Lie down on the ground and mark out a line around your body, about a hand's width away from you.

2 Dig a pit about 30cm/12in deep in the marked area. If the weather is very cold, try to dig down even more.

3 Create a "floor" over the ground by laying branches along the bottom of the pit, running from head to foot.

4 Create another layer by placing a second row of branches crossways over the first layer. Keep it sturdy and even.

5 Fill up the hole with the driest debris you can find. This layer should be at least 15cm/6in deep.

6 For the frame, plant two Y-sticks at the two corners of the head end, leaning them against each other.

7 Rest a long ridge pole on the Y-sticks, extending to the foot end.

8 Add branches to each side of the frame, lining them up vertically.

9 Fill up both sides of the framework with sticks, then pile debris over them.

10 Pile the debris over the shelter to a depth of about 1m/3ft on all sides, leaving the opening clear.

11 Fill the interior with the driest, fluffiest material you can find. Fern or bracken makes an aromatic top layer.

12 Use pliable green shoots to make a 1m/3ft tunnel for the entrance and cover them thickly in debris.

Building a stacked debris wall

The stacked debris wall is a shelter component that can be used in many different ways. It is simply a double row of poles driven into the ground and woven together with brushwood, with a thick wad of insulating debris between them, so it can be straight or curved, tall or short.

You can use this technique to build a small survival shelter for one person or adapt it to a large construction for a group, perhaps building a number of shelters around a central fire, which will help to retain and reflect heat. It can also be used in other ways – as a hide for hunting, for example. A small semicircular version can be built around the back of a fire as a heat reflector.

THE RAW MATERIALS

To build this kind of wall you'll need plenty of poles. Their length will depend on how high you need the wall to be, but for a shelter they should generally be about 120cm/4ft long.

You'll need a heavy rock to hammer the poles firmly into the ground. You will also need a lot of material to weave the sides, such as semi-flexible brushwood, though in a survival situation you might need to use fresh, green material if there is no dead wood available. You'll also need plenty of debris, which can be of any kind, wet or dry, as long as it creates air pockets.

CONSTRUCTING THE WALL

Having decided on the site for the wall, hammer the first line of poles as deeply as possible into the ground, about 30cm/1ft apart. The second row should be parallel with the first, about 50cm/20in away to allow for plenty of insulation. You might want to put an extra pole at each end of the wall so you can weave around the ends too.

Weave brushwood loosely along the rows to make the sides of the walls. Now all that remains is to pack the space in between with debris.

As a possible variation, you could weave one side of the wall tightly for strength, for example if it is to form the inside of the shelter. If you also weave the outer side tightly you can plaster the wall with "survival cement" (a 50:50 mix of dry grass and sticky mud) or clay. Another option is to build two side walls at each end of the wall, thereby giving you protection from wind blowing in from the side. You could also add a roof using Y-poles to support the front where it's not resting on the wall.

The stacked debris wall is an amazingly strong construction when it is built properly, and a tightly woven wall can last for years. If you ensure that the roof slopes gently you won't even need too much debris to make it more or less waterproof.

▼ *Building a stacked debris wall rather than a complete shelter may save time, but you will need a fire to keep you warm all night.*

BUILDING A STACKED DEBRIS WALL

1 Lay two long branches on the ground or mark two lines indicating where the poles are going to be driven in.

2 Hammer strong, straight poles into the ground 30cm/12in apart, following the first line.

3 When the first row is completed, make a second one parallel with it, about 50cm/20in away.

4 Hammer in a pole between the rows at each end of the wall to stop debris spilling out when you pack the wall.

5 Weave flexible shoots or brushwood between the poles to give the structure stability and hold the debris inside.

6 To neaten the inside of a shelter, or if you intend to plaster the wall, make the weaving really tight.

7 Once all the weaving is completed, fill the whole cavity with debris.

8 Pad the debris down well, checking that there are no large gaps.

9 Plastering the wall with survival cement will help it reflect more heat.

10 To construct a roof over the wall, place Y-sticks in front of the two ends and inside each end of the wall.

11 Place a ridge pole along the top of the wall and a second in front of it; lay sticks across the two ridge poles.

12 Place a good thick layer of debris over the top. A layer 50cm/20in thick should keep out moderate rain.

Building a long-term shelter

All over the world, primitive shelters are built in the round. There are several good reasons for this. When a fire is lit inside (in the centre) the heat can reach everywhere in the shelter, and the walls will reflect all of it right back. In a square shelter, the distribution of heat tends to be uneven, resulting in cold corners. If there are several people in a round shelter, everyone gets an equal share of heat. Round shelters are also stronger than square ones, and they are easier to build.

UPGRADING YOUR SHELTER

Once all the basics of survival are taken care of and you have supplies to last you for a week or more, if you have time and materials available you can consider making your existing shelter more comfortable. Remember though, that you don't want to waste resources

and energy building a shelter that is larger than you need.

To improve on your shelter use the stacked debris wall technique. This

▲ *A long-term shelter can make life a lot more comfortable. Because this can take a long time to build, it is important that all essentials should be taken care of first.*

BUILDING A LONG-TERM SHELTER

1 First make the fireplace. Dig four trenches to carry air to your fire pit and build a hearth with large stones.

2 Cover the trenches with sturdy sticks, so that soil will not fall through and eventually block the tunnels.

3 Pack a layer of soil over the sticks, so that you can walk over the floor without disturbing the oxygen tunnels.

4 Use a line and two sticks, planting the first stick in the central fireplace, to mark out the perimeter of the shelter.

5 Place two markers where the doorway will be. When building the wall, leave this space open.

6 Start the wall by driving 120cm/4ft poles into the ground, following the circle, keeping them 30cm/1ft apart.

means you'll need to collect plenty of poles and weaving material. In this case the roof will be supported by four Y-sticks in the centre, each a good 2m/6ft long. They will need to be very thick and sturdy: the poles shown here are about 12.5cm/5in in diameter. You will also need four sticks to connect the Y-poles in the centre, creating a square. These will also need to be very strong and about 1m/3ft long.

PLANNING THE SHELTER

Think a little about how large you really need your shelter to be. If you are on your own you should go for a diameter of about 3m/10ft: this gives plenty of space for one person and will be easy to heat. Don't overestimate the space you need: a group of six might plan a shelter about 5m/16ft across, but this could accommodate nine.

Before you start building the walls you should construct the fireplace. The fire will burn better if oxygen reaches it from underneath, and you can achieve this by digging four trenches in the floor, one from each direction, from the walls to the centre.

The easiest way to mark the line of the wall is with a line and two sticks. Drive one stick into the centre of the site and tie a cord to this. Measure the required radius and attach the second stick at this point. Now walk around the centre, keeping the line taut and drawing a circle on the ground with the point of the stick.

Next, decide where you want the door. Traditionally, doors face east to catch the morning sun, and this makes sense because it is a mental and physical boost to be woken up by the sun shining through the doorway (assuming you can leave this open). It also allows the sun to dry out any dampness inside the shelter during the morning. If your shelter faces west you may find you wake up a lot later because it seems darker inside.

BUILDING AND FURNISHING

When the poles for the walls have been pounded in you will get a much clearer idea of the size of your shelter. You might even want to build some basic furniture in the shelter now, before the walls and roof are finished, because it is harder to bring materials inside once the shelter is complete.

Consider making a low platform for your bed. Otherwise, if you intend to sleep on the ground, put down a layer of rushes or twigs, then throw about 20cm/8in of debris over this, to keep you well insulated from the ground.

Once you are happy with the interior, you can complete the debris wall by weaving flexible material through the two rows of poles and filling the space between them with debris. You should make sure that the wall is about the same height as your head when you are sitting inside the shelter – about 120cm/4ft – to enable you to sit against it with a straight back.

7 Once the first circle is complete, hammer in the second circle of stakes about 30cm/1ft outside it.

8 Hammer in the four Y-pole roof supports to form a central square; try to orient them on the entrance.

9 Weave brushwood between the poles to create two circular walls with an empty space between them.

10 Fill the area between the woven walls with debris, making sure it is packed in tightly.

11 Use four stout branches to connect the central Y-poles: these must be strong enough to support the roof.

12 Lay sturdy poles from the wall to the central square: these will support a thick layer of debris for the roof.

Before you begin to add the debris, hammer a number of sturdy Y-shaped poles into the ground between the two woven walls. You can connect these with strong branches later on to act as the outer supports for the roof. If you don't do this, the sides of the shelter will gradually sink as the weight of the roof compresses the debris wall.

BUILDING THE ROOF

When the wall is finished, you can connect the four Y-poles in the middle with the four strong branches you selected for this. Make sure that these branches are really sturdy: they should be capable of carrying three times the weight of the roof when you first assemble it. In the lifespan of the shelter, you will be adding more debris as it compresses, and it will also get very wet regularly when it rains. These factors can add a tremendous amount of weight to the roof of your shelter.

Now you can start building the roof by laying thick, sturdy poles from the wall to the Y-pole square in the centre of your shelter. Make sure the poles stick out a little on both the square and the wall. However, you should leave a large enough hole in the centre for smoke from the fire to escape. Depending on how much wind is

FIRE HAZARD

A note of warning. A shelter built of debris is basically one giant bundle of tinder. Take great care to keep your fire under control and watch that embers don't suddenly burst into flame. Even if you come out of it unharmed, if your shelter burns down hours of hard labour will have been wasted.

likely to reach your shelter, your smoke hole should be around 20-30cm/8–12in wide at least.

At the doorway, lay some extra sturdy poles at each side of the door, then lay a very thick branch across the entrance so you can put roof poles there too. When you cannot fit any more poles on to the square of branches in the centre, fill up any remaining gaps in the roof with smaller sticks and branches, until all the major holes are covered.

DEBRIS FOR THE ROOF

All you have to do now is add a thick layer of debris to the roof. Depending on the angle of your roof and the size of the material you are using for this, you may have to weave a layer of supple twigs through the poles to stop debris from sliding down the roof.

A good 60cm/2ft layer of debris on top of the poles and twigs will be needed to stop the rain soaking through into the shelter. Ensure the debris goes all the way from the smoke hole across the whole width of the wall (this is why the roof poles should overhang the wall).

If you find the roof is too high for you to reach the centre in order to pile on the debris, you can leave out the poles at the entrance temporarily, to

▲ *Once all the roof poles are laid, you can finish the roof by placing a thick layer of debris on top, leaving the smoke hole open.*

enable you to throw the material on to those difficult spots from there. Once the roof is completely covered with debris, smooth it out and add some heavier branches to stop the material from blowing away in the wind.

FINISHING OFF THE SHELTER

There are a few things you can do with a primitive shelter to make it more comfortable. Obviously all the building materials you've gathered will be full of small creatures, so one of the most important tricks is smoking out your shelter before you move in, to get rid of all the insects that are now inside it.

You can create a lot of smoke by placing a few embers in a fireproof container and then throwing on some damp, green materials that will produce a thick, pungent smoke. Try using fresh pine needles or sage if they are growing in the area. When the container is smoking furiously, place it inside the shelter for about half an hour. Keep the entrance closed so all the smoke goes through the debris.

Once you are living in your shelter you will want any smoke from your fire to escape through the central smoke hole. You can help to direct it out of the hole by weaving a little square "lid" the same size as your smoke hole. Place this upright next to the smoke hole, facing into the wind. The contraption will act like a funnel, allowing the smoke to escape from your shelter before it's caught by the wind, and stopping the wind blowing smoke back into the hole.

The smoke-hole cover can be made in many different ways. The easiest is to use an animal skin, if you have one, stretching it over a square framework of flexible branches woven together. Keep in mind that the hide will shrink as it dries and expand when it gets wet.

In heavy rain, the cover can be used to close the smoke hole, though you will not be able to have a fire inside the shelter if you do this, as the smoke will have no way out.

▲ *If you are carrying cordage and a tarpaulin, you can rig up a hammock between two trees. This way you can sleep off the ground, which will help you to keep warmer overnight if you haven't got the time to build a proper shelter. Once you've built your shelter, a hammock provides a comfortable alternative on warm, dry nights.*

SMOKING OUT INSECTS AND BUGS

1 Put a few burning embers in a fireproof container.

2 Add a handful of fresh spruce needles or sage to encourage smoking.

3 Put the container in the hut and seal the entrance for about 30 minutes.

MAKING A SMOKE-HOLE COVER

1 Cut some flexible branches to the size of the opening you need to cover. Plant a row of them in the ground about 7.5cm/3in apart.

2 Weave more flexible branches from side to side to construct a sturdy frame. You can make it stronger by tying the corners with some cordage.

3 Finish the cover by tying an animal skin or some large leaves over the frame. In this case, a rabbit skin was just the right size for the smoke hole.

Snow shelters

In winter conditions snow can be used to build an emergency shelter. It has long been used to build shelters by the military of northern countries. The Swedish army, for instance, has built large snow shelters for vehicles and also for use as field hospitals.

When you are trekking in this kind of climate, having the skill to build a proper snow shelter can save your life in the event of a snowstorm. If you lose your way or your equipment fails – for example if your skidoo gets broken – building a snow shelter enables you to protect yourself from the cold.

▼ *In Antarctica this perfect four-person shelter was built from a hundred blocks hewn with the most valuable tool – a saw.*

Protection from the wind is most important, since a high windchill factor can create dangerously cold conditions that quickly lead to death.

When selecting a site for a shelter in a snow-covered environment, keep in mind that the easiest way to build a shelter is by digging into the snow rather than building it up in walls. Look out for places where snow has drifted, or dig around trees and other natural "funnels" where the snow has concentrated and is at its deepest. Of course, there may be situations when you are forced to build rather than dig to create a shelter.

There are three main types of snow shelters, each suited to particular kinds of snow: the igloo is designed for hard snow, the quinze for powdery snow, and the snow cave, or "drift cave", for drifts. While a lot of different designs and variations are possible, there are a few important things to keep in mind in all cases.

PROVIDING AN AIR SUPPLY

You need to ensure you are protected from the cold, and you want to be insulated, but you also have to make sure there is sufficient ventilation to allow fresh air inside your shelter. When the heat from your body warms the shelter the surface of the snow will melt slightly, forming an airtight seal, so you must cut vents and check them regularly to prevent a build-up of carbon dioxide in your shelter.

WINDCHILL									
Wind speed in MPH	Air temperature in °F								
	40	30	20	10	0	–10	–20	–30	–40
	Comparable windchill temperature								
0–4	40	30	20	10	0	–10	–20	–30	–40
5	37	27	16	6	–5	–15	–26	–36	–47
10	28	16	4	–9	–21	–33	–46	–58	–70
15	22	9	–5	–18	–36	–45	–58	–72	–85
20	18	4	–10	–25	–39	–53	–67	–82	–96
25	16	0	–15	–29	–44	–59	–74	–88	–104
30	13	–2	–18	–33	–48	–63	–79	–94	–109
35	11	–4	–20	–35	–49	–67	–83	–98	–113
40	10	–6	–21	–37	–53	–69	–85	–100	–116

Little effect on windchill, little danger of frostbite

Increasing danger of frostbite

Great danger of frostbite

▲ *Once an igloo is completed, melting snow inside will make the joints airtight. The entrance should be a tunnel under the wall, allowing cold air to sink and flow away.*

▲ *Wind can make the air feel much colder than the recorded temperature, and as its strength increases the effect is multiplied.*

KEEPING DRY

When you are building a shelter with snow there is a great danger of your clothes getting wet. When the weather is very cold this is unlikely, but at temperatures higher than –15°C/5°F it can be a serious problem. In all temperatures mittens get wet easily. You should also try not to work yourself into too much of a sweat. It is one thing trying to keep warm when you are dry, but quite another to stay warm when wet.

IGLOOS

If you are in the high Arctic, tundra or other open snow-covered terrain where the temperature is below –5°C/23°F, it is relatively easy to dig or cut snow for a shelter, and the low temperature will ensure that the walls of your structure will stay safely in place. If you are stranded on hard-packed snow you can cut blocks and build an igloo. This makes a comfortable, long-term shelter, though you should bear in mind that it will take time to build and you need a saw or knife to cut the blocks.

Start by marking out a circle on a flat area of compacted snow. For a two-person igloo you will need a circle of about 2.5–2.8m/8–9ft diameter. As you cut the snow blocks, lay them on their long edges in a rising spiral, stepping them slightly so that most of the weight of each block is on the blocks beneath it. When you have completed the dome shape, the inside should be smoothed so that the "steps" inside do not start to drip water as the inside temperature rises. The outer wall should be covered with loose snow to fill all the cracks and make the igloo windproof. It is best to dig a tunnel under the wall for the entrance, but if this is not possible it can be cut straight through the wall and covered with a rucksack or a block of snow.

BUILDING AN IGLOO

1 Cut blocks of hard-packed snow 60 x 40 x 20cm/24 x 16 x 8in and use them to form a circle around the hole you cut them from.

2 Cut away the tops of the first few blocks at an angle to the ground and build up the walls in a spiral. Cut an entrance hole under the wall.

3 Make the blocks lean into the igloo a little more in each row, to create a dome. Trim the last block from inside to fit exactly into the central hole.

Building a quinze shelter

The quinze shelter looks a little like the better-known igloo, but it is constructed in a different way and is suitable for areas of powdery snow. Obviously when snow is in this condition it has no structural strength and it would be impossible to cut the kind of blocks you would need to build an igloo.

The quinze is made by collecting snow into a pile, which is then left to harden by recrystallizing before the structure is hollowed out from the inside. Making a snow pile of a usable size takes about an hour. You then need to wait for about another hour if the temperature is at least −10°C/14°F. At higher temperatures up to two hours will be needed.

PLANNING THE QUINZE
For a two-person quinze the snow pile should be about 1.8m/6ft high, 2.5m/8ft wide and 3m/10ft long. If you need to accommodate more people, add another 80cm/2ft 6in per person.

Unless time is short because night is falling, the work of piling the snow should be done quite slowly to avoid the diggers getting overheated and sweating. A shovel is ideal for the purpose, but in an emergency situation snowshoes, a billy can or a frying pan can be used to scoop up the snow.

Before you start to make the pile, mark out the area of the shelter and tread the floor to compact the snow.

▲ *If the snow is loose, as it is in northern forests, taiga, boreal forest and coniferous forests, and the temperature is below −5°C/23°F, you can build a quinze.*

CREATING THE SHELTER
On to this floor, arrange rucksacks and any spare gear, bushes and any other bulky material you can find, forming a compact heap. This will help to create the basic dome shape, and will reduce the amount of snow you need to shovel on to the pile. The gear can be removed later. Cover the heap with a layer of snow at least 1m/3ft thick and leave it to harden.

Once the snow has recrystallized, your gear and any other material you have used can be dug out again from the side. You can then enlarge the shelter by digging out from the inside, but you must be very careful that you don't dig away too much and weaken

◄ *Very cold conditions present the dangers of frostbite and hypothermia. If you feel cold, do not fall asleep at any cost. Try to stay warm by moving around, sing songs and keep busy attending to your equipment.*

USING A QUINZE

1 The temperature inside should be below freezing, so the snow is dry. Do not make a fire inside a quinze.

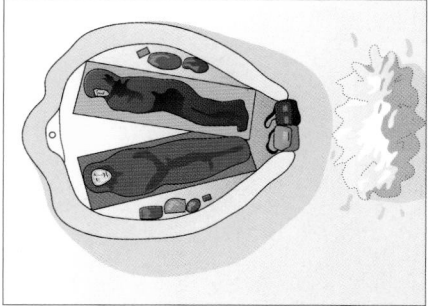

2 Make a small shelf for a candle in the wall near your head. As long as the candle burns there is enough oxygen in the quinze.

the walls. To avoid this, find some sticks and trim them all to the same length – at least 30cm/12in. Poke them at regular intervals into the outside of the snow pile. When you come to dig away the snow from the inside, you will hit the ends of the sticks and know that it is time to stop digging. When the main shelter is complete, you can add a tunnel, digging a trench where

the entrance tunnel is going to be so that the cold air sinks below the level at which you are sitting or lying. It is important to make the entrance just large enough to crawl through. You can use the snow you have dug out of the shelter to create a windbreak outside the entrance. The door should be plugged with snow or a rucksack before you go to sleep.

VENTILATION

The snow walls will be airtight, so you must cut a hole in the roof for ventilation to avoid the possibility of carbon dioxide poisoning. Keeping a candle burning inside the quinze will tell you that there is enough oxygen. The best place for the candle is a small niche in the wall at the end of the shelter, near the sleepers' heads.

BUILDING A QUINZE SHELTER

1 Work out the rough dimensions by lying down and drawing a circle around the users (this is a three-person quinze).

2 Tread down the floor to compact it, then make a pile of powdery snow at least 3m/10ft wide and 1.8m/6ft high.

3 When the pile is complete, tap down the surface with the flat of the shovel to compact the snow.

4 Wait an hour for the snow pile to recrystallize so that it is hard enough for you to begin hollowing it out.

5 Meanwhile, cut some 30cm/1ft long sticks and poke them into the snow to an equal depth all around the pile.

6 When the snow is hard enough, cut out a small doorway. Pile up the snow on the windward side of the hole.

7 Hollow out the shelter, bringing the snow out through the door. When you meet the ends of the sticks, stop digging – the wall is 30cm/12in thick.

8 The roof should be dome-shaped. Make a 10cm/4in diameter ventilation hole in the roof to avoid the danger of carbon dioxide poisoning.

9 Close the doorway using snow or a rucksack, or a plastic bag filled with snow or clothes. You can also make a little shelf for a candle in the wall.

Snow caves and other shelters

If weather conditions worsen suddenly or the light is failing, there may be very little time available to build a snow shelter. In these situations look for natural hollows, perhaps with overhanging trees, that will offer some protection from the wind, or a large drift into which you can dig to make a cave. Tools for cutting snow and ice are an essential part of your survival equipment when you are travelling in arctic terrain, but in an emergency other items, such as skis or cooking pots, can be used to dig a trench or cave. Keep things simple – smaller shelters tend to retain their warmth longer and take less time to build.

SNOW TRENCH

The simplest one-person snow survival shelter is the snow trench, also known as a "snow grave". Its main purpose is to keep out the wind. At its most basic, it involves digging a slit trench in the snow with whatever tools are available, adding a roof and then covering it with an insulating layer of snow.

Having dug the hole, dig down another 60cm/2ft at one end. When you make the roof from branches and snow, site the entrance opening above the deeper part of the pit. Lay branches and other material on the higher part of the shelter to form an insulated seat.

If the bottom of your pit reaches the ground, you can light a fire here, but if the snow is very deep this won't be possible. Even without a fire, the cold air will sink down into the deeper part of the shelter, leaving the higher part, warmed by your body, slightly warmer.

▲ *In coniferous forest there is plenty to build an improvised shelter with. A lean-to of spruce branches, with a fire in front of it, makes a good shelter. Make sure that there are logs or foliage insulating you from the ground, and that your fire doesn't melt snow on overhanging branches.*

BUILDING A SNOW TRENCH

▲ *For a quick survival refuge, dig a trench about 1m/3ft deep and wide and 2m/6ft 6in long. This one has a roof made of packed snow blocks.*

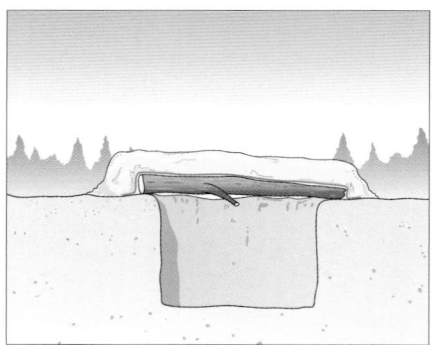

▲ *If wood is available, lay some branches over the trench, leaving one end open, and cover the roof with 30–60cm/1–2ft of snow.*

▲ *By adding brushwood to the sides and piling up the snow you dig out on either side, you can make an insulated shelter in which you can sit.*

▲ *When trekking in arctic conditions, it's vital to carry an emergency survival kit containing a snow saw, ice axe and shovel.*

SNOW CAVES

A snow cave requires a depth of snow of at least 2m/6ft. While the simplest of trenches can be built in under half an hour, a snow cave takes far more time and effort to complete – allow at least three hours to build a basic cave. You'll need digging tools, and because digging will make you perspire, you should remove one of your inner garments before you start digging so that you have something dry to put on when you have completed your shelter.

▲ *Digging your snow cave near the top of a slope means the snow you dig out will naturally fall away from the entrance.*

In a large bank of drifted snow, dig a cave starting about 2.5m/8ft above the bottom of the drift: this saves energy as the shovelled snow simply drops down the hill. You should then tunnel slightly uphill so that your snow cave is higher than the door. In a small drift you may have to hollow out a shallower cave and close up the front with blocks of snow.

As with all shelters, don't forget the ventilation – your survival depends on it. Also, erect a clear marker outside so that potential rescuers can find you.

▲ *If the snow is very deep you can dig directly down and then tunnel sideways under the snow surface.*

▼ *If you are in a group you can dig a number of snow caves in a large drift.*

BUILDING A SNOW CAVE

▲ *Make a temporary shelter in a shallow drift by hollowing out the snow, then closing the entrance with snow blocks and making an airhole.*

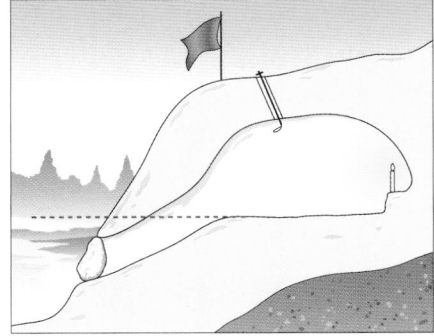

▲ *On a slope, the sleeping area in a drift cave should ideally be higher than the entrance tunnel so that the warmer air stays inside.*

▲ *Despite the flat terrain, the snow here is deep enough to be able to dig down then sideways to make the cave. Ventilation will need to be added.*

Finding shelter in the desert

Deserts pose their own unique problems. Most of these are due to the immense heat present in many deserts during the day. This leads to a lack of vegetation, so that there are few materials to work with when you need to build a shelter. So what do you do when there are no resources in the area around you? What if there is nowhere to dig, nowhere to find wood or scrub, no water and no food? The answer sounds very stark, but it is very simple. If you cannot get to an area where there are resources, you will die.

Deserts actually force you to deal with two extremes: apart from the searing heat of the day, the second is the intense cold of the night, when the temperature can fall very rapidly.

DAYTIME SHELTER

During the day, your main concern will be shade. If you have the materials to hand, a roof or canopy will help you to keep cool. The story is rather different at night, when you need insulation. Most of the time in the desert, however, you'll be travelling

▼ *A desert rock face makes a natural windbreak and radiates heat at night.*

through the night. This means that you will only need shelter during the day, to protect you from the sun while you sleep. In many situations, it is not necessary to build anything.

Shade can often be found under trees or, if there are no trees in the area, you may be able to find caves to hole up in. Just remember that animals

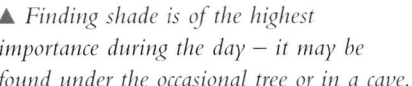

▲ *Finding shade is of the highest importance during the day – it may be found under the occasional tree or in a cave.*

need the same things you do, and may also be sheltering in these nice cool spots. Always check for scorpions, snakes and the like. When you rest in the shade of trees or shallow caves, keep in mind that the sun moves through the day, so be careful about falling asleep in a shady area that may not be so shady any more in an hour's time. It's easy to get burned while you are asleep. As a last resort during the day, you can dig yourself in under the sand, which may be slightly cooler.

SITES TO AVOID

Take great care in choosing a safe site for your shelter. In many desert areas, flash floods can occur during the rainy season, because the rain falls so heavily that the hard, dry ground does not have time to absorb it all. The water will then just run off the surface and collect in rivers.

These floods can become very large in no time, appearing with little or no warning, often as a result of rain falling far away. Sometimes you will find a

▲ *A shallow cave may provide just enough shelter from the sun. Keep in mind that the shade in such a cave may not last all day.*

▼ *A heat-stress index combines the effects of high temperature and humidity to show how much stress your body might be under.*

river where five minutes before there was only cracked earth. These "temporary" rivers can have amazingly strong currents, so it is a good idea to stay away from areas that resemble river beds, the bottoms of canyons, places right at the foot of cliffs and other low-lying areas. It is also important to keep away from areas where rock falls and landslides may occur, as these can be quite common.

USE THE NIGHT-TIME

Heat and lack of water can wear you down very quickly, so you should try to travel at night and rest in the shade during the day. This way you will at least avoid exercising in extreme heat, which will only worsen your physical condition further. Unless it is absolutely necessary, it is advisable even to build your shelter and find your firewood during the night, or at least in the evening and early morning, while it is relatively cool. If in doubt, have a look at what the local animals are doing: where do they find shelter, when do they use their shelter, when do they come out to feed, and where do they find water?

The table below explains the stress placed upon the body in different types of heat. The higher the number, the more stress your body is under and the more dangerous your position is. For instance, if the temperature is 40°C/105°F and the humidity is 50 per cent this means that your body has a stress factor of 135, which is very high. This number is located in the "Extreme danger" zone, meaning that heatstroke is very likely if you continue to be exposed to the heat. Exercise in such conditions heightens the risk.

HEAT-STRESS INDEX

Temp in degrees F	Relative humidity														Heat-stress index
	10%	20%	30%	35%	40%	45%	50%	55%	60%	65%	70%	75%	80%	90%	
70	65	66	67	67	68	68	69	69	70	70	70	70	71	71	
75	70	72	73	73	74	74	75	75	76	76	77	77	78	79	I Caution 80–89°F
80	75	77	78	79	79	80	81	81	82	83	85	86	86	88	
85	80	82	84	85	86	87	88	89	90	91	93	95	97	102	II Extreme 90–104°F
90	85	87	90	91	93	95	96	98	100	102	106	109	113	122	III Danger 105–129°F
95	90	93	96	98	101	104	107	110	114	119	124	130	136	•	
100	95	99	104	107	110	115	120	126	132	138	144	•	•	•	
105	100	105	113	118	123	129	135	142	149	•	•	•	•	•	
110	105	112	123	130	137	143	150	•	•	•	•	•	•	•	IV Extreme danger greater than 130°F
115	111	120	135	143	151	•	•	•	•	•	•	•	•	•	
120	116	130	148	•	•	•	•	•	•	•	•	•	•	•	
125	123	141	•	•	•	•	•	•	•	•	•	•	•	•	
130	131	•	•	•	•	•	•	•	•	•	•	•	•	•	
135	•	•	•	•	•	•	•	•	•	•	•	•	•	•	
140	•	•	•	•	•	•	•	•	•	•	•	•	•	•	

• Beyond the capacity of the atmosphere to hold water

I Caution 80°F	**Effect**: fatigue possible with prolonged exposure and/or physical activity
II Extreme 90–104°F	**Effect**: heat cramps and heat exhaustion possible with prolonged exposure and/or physical activity
III Danger 105–129°F	**Effect**: heat exhaustion, heat cramps likely; heatstroke possible with prolonged exposure and/or physical activity
IV Extreme danger greater than 130°F	**Effect**: heatstroke highly likely with continued exposure

Building a desert shelter

When you need a shelter in the desert and a suitable natural feature such as a cave is not available, you will have to build something.

Remember that "small is beautiful" and avoid spending energy on any unnecessary space even if you feel you really want it. Try to make sure the shelter can be well sealed, whether you are occupying it or not, as dangerous animals may try to spend the day there too, especially if you build an underground shelter. This means trying to create a door that fits the entrance snugly, and making sure there are no exposed openings.

USING HOT ROCKS

The most basic method of surviving the cold hours is to find a slope facing the sun, with plenty of rocks lying about. Pick up the hottest rocks you can find, and build some sort of wall around the site where you are going to spend the night. To get most benefit during the night, you should build the wall in such a way that the side of the rock that has been baking in the sun faces you when the wall is complete. The rocks will radiate their heat for much of the night.

If you are in a sandy area, you can dig down into the sand slightly and build the rock wall inside the hollow. Such a shelter could see you through the night. However, it would have to be broken down in the morning and built again in the evening to make it work a second night. You can use the same technique, however, as a natural central heating system in a more permanent shelter.

PIT SHELTERS

In an area of sand or soil you can construct an underground pit shelter. It needs to be about 1m/3ft deep, but don't make it larger than you need: you should just have space to lie down.

You may have to support the sides of your shelter by building walls inside the pit, so you will need to find branches or rocks. You will also need two sturdy beams at the sides of the pit to support the roof. There will be a considerable amount of weight on top of the roof, and you need to make sure your shelter won't cave in during the night.

Use clothing, shrubs or flat rocks to fill all the gaps between the sticks, before adding a deep layer of sand. The main problem with this shelter is fashioning a door to prevent heat escaping and animals coming in.

BUILDING A ROCK WALL SHELTER

1 When building a rock wall shelter to keep you warm overnight, find a south-facing slope.

2 A shallow cave like this is ideal. As it is south-facing, the walls of the cave will retain the heat of the sun.

3 Use any rocks you find strewn about on the slope, which will have been baking in the sun for most of the day.

4 Build a wall using these rocks, leaving just enough space for you to lie. Make sure the hot side of each rock is facing into the shelter.

5 Try to enclose the entire hollow apart from an entrance, which can be located either at the foot or the head end of the shelter.

6 It is important to make this shelter as small as possible, so that your body nearly touches the hot rocks and there is less space to heat.

BUILDING A SAND PIT SHELTER

1 You need to be in an area where there is sand or soil that you can dig and some wood or shrub.

2 Mark out an area for the pit, which should not be more than 30cm/1ft longer and wider than your body.

3 Start digging the pit, using any tools you have or your bare hands. It will need to be about 1m/3ft deep.

4 If the soil is sandy, you may have to build retaining walls inside the pit to prevent the sides collapsing.

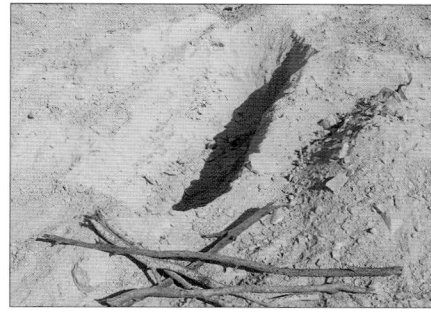

5 Even if the soil is not sandy, you will need to lay two beams alongside your pit for the roof to rest on.

6 Gather some strong branches and lay them across the pit to begin constructing the roof.

7 Leaving an opening near the head-end, pile flat rocks on the sticks.

8 Cover the rocks with sand or soil to form the ceiling.

9 Try to eradicate all the gaps, so sand can't fall through into the pit.

10 Place a good layer of sand over the rocks as insulation. Form a slight dome over the area, so any water can run off.

11 Make sure you leave an opening that runs the entire width of the shelter and is large enough to squeeze through.

12 The shelter needs to be easy to spot, both for yourself when out roaming, and for potential rescuers.

Building a jungle shelter

In the jungle, the main concern is often rain. The shelter you will make has to withstand the rain, offering you a well-protected, dry spot inside. Palms are usually very abundant in rainforests, making their leaves the ideal material for your shelter. Bamboo is another natural tropical material you can adapt to build a workable shelter. The shelter shown here uses cohune palm leaves.

MAKING THE LEAN-TO FRAME
You will need six poles, each about 2–3m/6–10ft long, to make the frame on which the roof will rest. Drive two poles into the ground about 2–3m/6–10ft apart. Another pole is then tied to the top of these uprights. You can use any kind of vine as cordage to tie the frame together; the bark of various

▲ *A woven palm-leaf structure makes an ideal roof and walls. The shelter will be more comfortable if you raise the floor surface to avoid the jungle damp and the myriad insects.*

COVERING A ROOF WITH PALM LEAVES

1 Locate a suitable palm tree. The cohune palm has large divided leaves that can be arranged like thatch to channel water off the roof.

2 Use a machete to chop down the stems of the palm and trim the fresh leaves. You will need enough leaves to set closely together on the frame.

3 Split each palm leaf in two all the way down its length, starting from the tip. If you try to split it from the thick end it may break.

4 The next stage is to collect enough vines to use as cordage. This will then be used to tie the frame together and to tie on the leaves.

5 Starting from the bottom of the frame, lay the halved leaves crossways with the fronds hanging down, and alternate the direction of the leaves.

6 The last palm leaf to go on the frame should be unspliced. This will provide an "eave" to channel the raindrops away from the front of the shelter.

forest species is also suitable. The three remaining poles are arranged at an angle from the ground to the crossbar to form a lean-to frame.

WEAVING THE PALM LEAF ROOF
Cut down some palm leaves from a tree (you'll need quite a few) then splice the palm leaves in half: this is easy to do by splitting the tip of the stem and working your way down. Splice most of the leaves before you start attaching them to the frame.

The split palm leaves are laid on top of the wooden frame, starting at the bottom. Arrange them so that the

▲ *Tropical rainforest provides an abundance of raw materials with which to build shelters. The main challenge is keeping dry.*

fronds hang down, directing the water to the back of the roof. Use alternate sides of the leaf each time to create a good watertight "cross-hatching". Once a full row of palm has been placed on the frame, tie it to the bars and add the next layer, until you have covered the whole structure. If you wish you can extend the top of the roof a little in front of the uprights when building the frame, to keep the rain off the front of the area.

You can use the same palm leaves to make yourself a comfortable mat to sleep or sit on inside the shelter. Lay them in alternate directions, as before, for maximum comfort.

▲ *A machete, or parang, is a sharp slashing bushcraft tool for the jungle. Look for handles with riveted plate grips and always sheath the blade when not in use.*

▲ *Bamboo is one of the jungle's most versatile plants. It is a rich source of food and its exceptionally strong wood is used to construct everything from chairs to bridges.*

BUILDING A TROPICAL A-FRAME SHELTER

1 Lash two branches or bamboo poles together to make an A-frame and erect it against a tree for support. Set up a second A-frame about 2.5m/8ft away.

2 Secure a long branch in the V-shaped tops of the A-frames. Tie two poles to the sides and lash a groundsheet around them to make a raised bed.

3 Spread a tarpaulin over the top of the frame to protect the bed from the rain, and keep the roof taut by tying the corners to surrounding trees.

FIRE

Creating a fire without recourse to matches or a lighter is one of the most crucial survival skills you can master. Once a fire is built and lit it gives warmth, provides light during the long dark hours of night, enables you to cook food, sterilize water and make tools, and helps to keep your spirits up. Starting a fire using friction is not an easy task, and the various techniques require a lot of skill. Even then, being able to conjure a burning ember by rubbing sticks together is only half the skill. Tinder does not burn for long, so it is equally important to know how to build a fire that lights with the smallest flame and stays lit.

Fire for survival

Of the four basic building blocks of survival, the need for fire may seem least urgent, but you will often need to start a fire even before you can think about water. The reason for this is that even in the most remote places on earth, water may not be safe to drink unless it is purified first. In addition to bacteria, viruses and other natural contaminations, there may also be chemical pollutants in the water. These could have come from a plane dumping its fuel, farmers spraying insecticide on their fields, illegal dumping or the discharge of chemical waste farther up a watercourse. There are many possible ways for water to be contaminated, but many of the risks can be reduced or eliminated by boiling water before you drink it.

Apart from this vital procedure, fire allows you to create containers in which to carry water, and can help you shape tools to take care of your other needs. Fire will help you stay warm and comfortable. It will also ward off potentially dangerous wildlife and generally make the camp feel safer.

▼ *Knowing how to make a fire may be vital to survival, as water is often contaminated and needs to be purified by boiling.*

SITING A FIRE

Before you can even begin trying to make a fire, you have to consider the best location for it. There are a few important rules to remember:

• To make sure the fire starts easily and burns without too much smoke, you need to build it on dry ground. This is not always possible, however, and if the area is wet it is best to create a dry base using bark or large stones. Once the fire has caught and is burning brightly, the dampness or rain should not matter too much.

• If you can find a feature such as a large rock or a small dip in the ground, the natural surroundings will act as a windbreak and help to reflect the heat of the fire. If it is very windy but there are no natural windbreaks or hollows, you will need to site the fire below ground level in a trench, downwind from your shelter.

• As when choosing a site for your shelter, it is always a good idea to build a fire where there is plenty of material to use for fuel. You don't want to have to walk a long distance each time you need more wood for the fire.

• Before lighting a fire you must ensure that there are no flammable materials on the ground, such as dry leaves. In

▲ *Not only is a fire warming, but getting it to light can make you feel you have achieved something important. A fire also creates a sense of increased security.*

extremely dry regions, the roots of trees or accumulated underground debris could easily start smouldering and might eventually start a fire far away from the original site of the camp fire. When there are flammable materials on the ground you should clear an area at least 120cm/4ft across. Try to build the fire at least 2m/6ft 6in away from your shelter to make sure it stays safe: a debris hut can act like a gigantic tinder bundle.

• If the ground is wet or contains flammable materials such as tree roots, and you need to line the fire pit with stones, make sure they are not waterlogged otherwise you could end up having to protect yourself from exploding rocks (*see panel opposite*).

• Do not make the fire any larger than necessary, both to avoid accidents and to conserve fuel. Placing a circle of stones around the edge of the fire helps to define its size.

• Finally, make your fire in a location where you can watch it at all times.

CLEARING UP YOUR FIRE

When you go into the wilderness to practise your survival skills, it is important to leave the natural beauty of the area intact when you depart. This means that when you have finished with your fire you should remove all visible traces of it.

If you want to preserve the embers for the duration of your journey so that you can make a new fire somewhere else, scoop them up and put them into a non-flammable container, such as an old tin can. Make sure the fire is completely extinguished by dousing it with a lot of water, then check whether there is any warmth or smoke still emanating from it. If there is still a trace of heat or smoke, douse it again.

Ideally, all wood should have been burned away before extinguishing the fire, but if this has not been possible, remove and bury any half-burned

pieces of wood. Remove the ashes and scatter them around the area. Then remove any stones you used to border the fire, and fill in the pit with the soil you dug out of it. Camouflage the area

SUCCESSFUL SMALL FIRES EVERY TIME

Here are some tips to help you make a small fire that will burn efficiently and keep you warm and comfortable.

- When you dig a pit for the fire, try to give it gently sloping sides. This will help to keep the burning materials gathered in the centre of the fire, making them burn longer and hotter.
- Build a horseshoe-shaped wall on the opposite side of the fire to where you are sitting. You should make this wall as smooth as possible, preferably using stones, to help it reflect the heat back towards you. Keep the wall about 60–90cm/2–3ft away from the fire and about 90cm/3ft high.
- Another wall, or a natural feature you can sit against, will reflect the heat passing you. A grassy bank, a pile of logs or a stump would do fine instead of a solid wall.
- If you are in a larger group of people, you might want to build both walls far enough away from the fire for you all to sit inside them and keep your backs warm.

so it fits in with the landscape, for example by drawing the forest debris back over it. This way, the area will look pristine when another person passes through in the future.

PREPARING A SAFE, EFFICIENT FIRE

1 Locate a suitable piece of ground that is free of debris, or clear the site, then dig a shallow pit about 15–25cm/ 6–10in deep, with sloping sides.

2 Place rocks on the bottom of the pit, to help reflect any heat upwards. You can also line the far side of the pit to reflect the heat towards you.

3 Gather all the resources you need to start your fire and maintain it. In a desert area there may not be much available, but at least it will be dry.

4 Build a simple reflecting wall about 1m/3ft from the fire using rocks, logs or whatever you can forage, to reflect the heat back towards you.

5 A wall behind you will reflect any heat that passes you back in your direction. This is a highly efficent way of channelling the available heat.

EXPLODING ROCKS

Select the rocks you use at the bottom of a pit with care. You should never use stones that may have water trapped inside them, as this can turn to steam when the stones are heated up, leading to an explosion. To avoid this, never collect rocks from stream beds or from the bottom of valleys. It is not necessary to find completely dry stones, so long as they are not waterlogged.

Firelighters and fuels

All over the world people use numerous different fuels – including dried grasses, wood of many different trees and dried animal excrement – to start and maintain fires.

The first rule when gathering fuel is that it must be dry. This sounds obvious, but it may be very hard in some survival situations. It is also a good reason to gather plenty of fuel at the outset. You should have enough to last at least the whole night, as you don't want to have to go out to find more dry fuel in the dark or when it has started to rain.

▶ *Firewood needs to be as dry as possible, though larger pieces will burn even if damp once the fire is well established.*

▲ *Always try to collect dead wood that is still hanging in the trees to burn in your fire, as it will be drier and less smoky. For kindling purposes, the dead twigs in the left hand above are better for starting a fire than the leaves, even though they are dead.*

▲ *Use a flint or sharp stone to lift the bark off dead wood. The dry inner bark can be shredded into loose fibres to use as tinder.*

KINDLING FOR GETTING FIRES STARTED

▲ *Dry grass may burn well, but is not great as a fire starter because it will remain whole after burning, cutting off vital oxygen.*

▲ *Dry seed heads are excellent for catching a spark. They will allow your ember to grow before you place it in the tinder.*

▲ *The high oil content of dry gorse or furze means it catches light easily and burns well when used as kindling.*

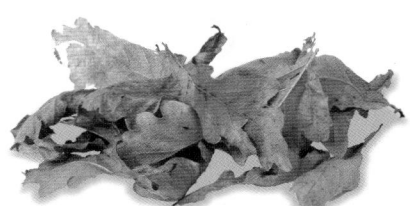

▲ *Dry leaves burn brightly but, just like grass, remain intact, often smothering the fire. Never use leaves to light your fire.*

▲ *Dry plant stalks can be shredded to form excellent tinder or can be used as kindling, though they often burn away fast.*

▲ *Dry sticks are the material of choice to build your fire with. If they are thin they also make excellent kindling.*

THE IDEAL WOOD FOR FIRE

If possible, try to gather dead wood exclusively from standing trees, because when it has been lying on the ground for a while it will probably have soaked up moisture, with the result that it will create too much smoke when burned.

Five different grades of fuel are needed to make a fire, from tinder, to catch the first spark, to large logs.

TINDER

In a survival situation in which you need to light a fire by a friction method, and not with a flame from a match or lighter, tinder is the first and most important component. Basically, it is any soft, fluffy, dry material that will ignite from a spark.

You can use any fine, dry plant material, such as fluffy seed heads or the dry inner bark of dead wood. Fibre that you would normally use to make cordage is usually a great source of tinder. The best way to learn what works well is to experiment.

Having collected the material, you need to break it down with your hands into separate plant fibres, teasing and fluffing it up until you have a soft, dry ball about the size of a grapefruit.

KINDLING

Though a larger firelighter than tinder, kindling is still small: you should be looking for twigs about as thick as a pencil. It also has to be totally dry. Just as with tinder, you always need far

▲ *Sticks ranging from thin twigs to boughs as thick as a wrist are generally referred to as small bulkwood. They make up most of the wood that is used in a fire once it is lit.*

more than you think – if you gather three or four times as much as you think you will need, that should be enough. Always bear in mind that if you do not select your tinder and kindling carefully, all your fire-making efforts might come to a frustrating halt.

As an alternative type of firelighter, you can try making a "fuzz-stick" (*see below*). This is a larger stick carved in thin slivers down to the dry wood: the slivers should be left attached like many small "branches" on a tree.

SQUAW WOOD

Named after the Native American women who gathered this wood in large quantities, squaw wood ranges in size from the thickness of a pencil to that of a finger. If you don't mind a lot of smoke, you can use this wood when it is slightly damp.

▲ *Bulkwood is used to keep a fire going. Though it burns for a long time, it needs small bulkwood to keep it going, and may be smoky if the fire isn't hot enough.*

SMALL BULKWOOD

This is the kind of wood you will mainly be burning. The thickness ranges from marker-pen size to the thickness of your wrist. This is the most important size, as the wood is large enough to give off the heat you need, but small enough to burn on its own without failing. You will need to get your fire established using this size of wood before you can get larger pieces of bulkwood to burn.

BULKWOOD

This is the type of fuel that is too big to break. You would want to use it only to make a large fire, or to keep the fire burning overnight. Never waste energy trying to cut wood this size – just let the fire break it for you. This size of wood can be wet if you don't mind the smoke.

MAKING A FUZZ-STICK

1 If you have a blade suitable for carving you can make this firelighting aid. Select a dry stick, preferably of birch or another resinous wood.

2 Carve deep cuts into the stick, layering them like the scales on a fish. Don't cut right through the wood, but leave the slivers hanging on it.

3 By carving these "scales" you are essentially enlarging the surface area of the wood. This means the fire has more wood to "get at" to ignite.

Lighting fires using friction

There are many ways to light a fire besides using matches or a lighter, and they have been around a lot longer than these artifical methods of creating a flame. Learning the so-called "primitive" ways will enable you to light a fire when your matches get wet, run out or if you don't have any.

Ancient peoples all over the world used these methods. Their very lives depended on their skill, and it is still truly awesome to watch somebody learn this age-old skill, seeing that look on their face when they first manage to get an ember after hours of trying. It is always a special feeling when the ember forms itself, even after you have started hundreds of fires.

The friction method (which applies to all of the techniques described in this chapter apart from the Arctic fire) depends on the fact that two pieces of wood rubbed together at speed will generate enough heat to produce carbonized particles and sparks, which will ignite a ball of dry tinder. The trick lies in not only getting the correct technique but also having the right mindset. You will probably come to understand this when you learn to make fire, and it is also true of other techniques of survival.

THE FIRE PLOUGH

A simple firelighting technique using the friction method that works quite well in some circumstances is the fire plough. As a sharpened stick is rubbed up and down in the groove of a fireboard, small fragments of wood dust collect at the bottom of the groove, and will eventually ignite into an ember when there is enough heat. You must take care not to scatter the dust by an erratic stroke of the plough. This procedure can be fairly laborious, and the friction techniques described on the following pages are usually preferable if there is an option.

THE DRILL METHOD

The bow drill, hand drill and pump drill (*see pages 58, 62 and 64 respectively*) are traditional ways of generating enough friction to create a spark. Each technique relies on a stick being spun at speed in the notch of a "hearth-board" to create embers. The Native Americans have a neat way of describing the process: they tell their children that making a fire resembles making a baby. They liken the drill to the male reproductive organ, while the hearth-board is the female. The ember is created in the notch, like the embryo forming in the womb.

MAKING A FIRE PLOUGH

1 Find a strong stick of hard wood and carve the tip to make a sharp edge like that of a screwdriver.

2 Split a thick branch of softer wood or shave off one side to make a flat fireboard about 60cm/2ft long.

3 With a sharp stone carve a groove about 45cm/18in long for the plough to move along.

4 Place the plough in the groove, and start moving it back and forth. At first nothing will seem to happen.

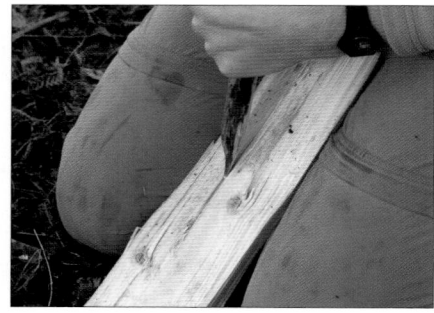

5 After a while, you will notice smoke coming off the fireboard and plough, and the groove will darken.

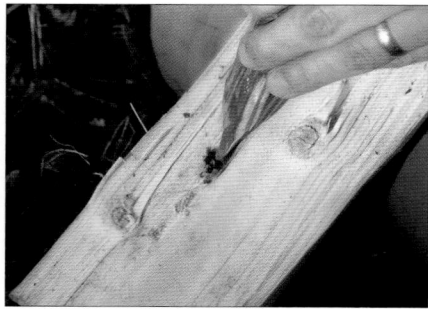

6 Wood fibres collect at the bottom and with a lot of speed and pressure, they will ignite into an ember.

SOURCES OF WOOD FOR LIGHTING FIRES BY FRICTION

▲ *Alder is a medium-hard wood, often used for carving reasonably efficient drill sets.*

▲ *Cedar bark makes excellent kindling and the wood is good for making bow drills.*

▲ *Poplar can be used to make successful drill sets, and it is also slow-burning.*

▲ *Elder branches have a soft, pithy centre, which works well to help extend an ember.*

▲ *Stout, woody mullein stalks also have a pithy centre and make good hand drills.*

▲ *Burdock is another large herb with rigid, woody stalks that are good for fire-making.*

DRILL-MAKING MATERIALS

You need medium-hard wood to make a drill, and some of the best species for this purpose are shown above. If you're not sure what kind of wood you have, it's quite easy to test its hardness by running your thumbnail down the length of the stick.

Apart from wood, to make a bow drill you will need a length of cord about 60–90cm/2–3ft long, and you can make this by braiding plant or tree fibres. The best fibres come from stinging nettles stems, but many other plants are also suitable. The dry stems need to be pounded with a rounded stone to separate the fibres, which can then be twisted or braided together.

Another solution is to use spruce roots, which also work extremely well. To find spruce roots, simply dig around the base of a spruce tree. When you come across a root, follow it through the ground, carefully extracting it as you go along. The roots are usually quite close to the soil surface and grow straight out from the tree. When you have collected a few roots, rub them over a branch to get rid of the bark. The roots can be quite long and it is better to use them as single lengths, because they are more likely to break if they are tied in knots.

TESTING WOOD FOR HARDNESS

1 Find a dry stick of the material you intend to use for your bow drill. Cut down the stick to expose a flat area.

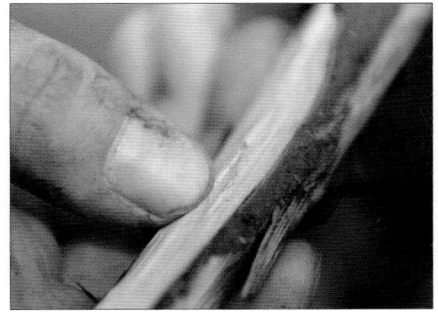

2 Run your nail from one end of the stick to the other. You do not have to follow the grain.

3 If the line is crumbly the wood is too soft or rotten. If there is no line or it's only barely visible, it's too hard.

The bow drill

The bow drill is the staple means of lighting a fire by friction. It works on the same principle as all other methods, but is the easiest to use. It is efficient and works even in damp conditions.

SELECTING AND CARVING THE WOOD

To make a bow drill set you will need some suitable pieces of wood from which to make the three carved components, a slightly curved stick (which does not have to be flexible) for the bow, and some cordage. You will also need a knife or stone tool for carving. The set consists of several different parts: a spindle, a hearth-board, a handhold and a bow, and for each of these you should select wood that requires a minimum of shaping.

The first component to carve is the spindle, which should be as long as the distance between the tip of your index finger and the tip of your thumb when you hold your hand outstretched. The top of the spindle needs to have a long point, while the bottom should have a shallow point. The spindle should be perfectly round, and the points need to be sharp and even.

The hearth-board, made from the same wood as the spindle, should be of about the same thickness and twice the width. It should be about 30cm/1ft long so that you can hold it steady with your foot, and should have a flat bottom so that it does not wobble.

The handhold can be made of any material as long as it is as hard or harder than the wood from which the spindle is made. The handhold should fit comfortably in your hand, with a thickness at least that of the drill.

The bow is best made with a slight bend, though a completely straight stick will work. It is best to learn to use the drill with a bow about 1m/3ft long. Once you have mastered the technique, you can try longer or shorter bows: even a bow as little as 20cm/8in long may work.

A piece of cordage is attached to the bow and you have to try to get just the right tension when the spindle is twisted into the cord. It should not be so loose that you can pull the spindle up and down while holding it in your hand, but it should not be so tight that you cannot twist the spindle at all: ideally, you should just about manage to twist the drill with effort. The correct tension will also depend on how flexible your bow is, and the cord is bound to need tightening during use, so you will need to make adjustments. For this reason, you should tie a permanent knot at one end, but a semi-permanent knot that is easily undone at the other.

MAKING A BOW DRILL

1 Gather three pieces of wood: the pieces for the hearth-board and the spindle should be about 2.5cm/1in thick. The handhold should be thicker.

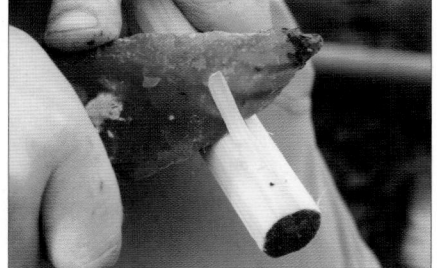

2 First carve the spindle: it needs to be straight, perfectly round and smooth, about 2.5cm/1in in diameter and 20–23cm/8–9in long.

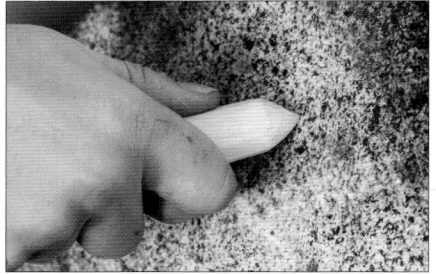

3 Carve or abrade (scrape away) one end to a fairly deep point, about 2.5cm/1in long. This point will become the top of the drill.

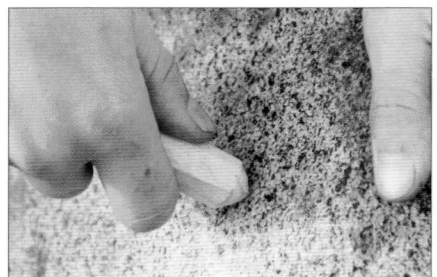

4 Abrade the other end into a much shallower point, about 6mm/¼in deep. This end will be the bottom.

5 After use, both points may look very similar, so to make sure you remember which is the top, carve a notch.

6 The finished spindle should be straight, with a shorter and a longer point, and a notch around the top.

7 To prepare the hearth-board, carve a small hole a spindle's width from the edge. This is where the bottom end of the spindle will go.

8 Make a similar hole in the handhold, positioning it above the line on the palm of your hand running up from your wrist, clear of your fingertips.

9 Fasten the string to the bow. Use a permanent knot at one end and one that is easily undone at the other, as you may need to tighten it frequently.

10 Twist the spindle into the string, ensuring that the string is between the bow and the spindle (the spindle is on the outside of the bowstring).

11 With your left foot on the hearth-board, wrap your arm around your left leg, and place the spindle in the holes in the hearth-board and the handhold.

12 Start to move the bow back and forth vigorously. The action will drill round impressions in the hearth-board and the handhold.

13 When the whole diameter of the drill has been drilled into the hearth-board, you can stop. By now, there should also be a hole in the handhold.

14 Grease the handhold so the spindle rotates smoothly. The notch will stop you accidentally putting the greased end of the spindle in the hearth-board.

15 Carve or abrade a wedge shaped notch in the hearth-board, nearly, but not quite, reaching the centre of the hole you have drilled.

PREPARING THE BOW DRILL SET

Before you can start making fire you must drill holes to take the spindle in both the hearth-board and the handle. This is done by using the spindle itself to enlarge small guide holes made with the point of your knife or another sharp tool. The drilling action is the same as that used for making fire, and for this you need to practise getting into the right position to make the drill work efficiently.

GETTING INTO POSITION

These instructions are written for a right-handed person – if you are left-handed you will need to reverse them.

Kneel down on your right knee, while placing your left foot over the hearth-board. The arch of your left foot should be right beside the hole where the drill is going to be once it's in place. Your left knee should be bent at a right angle. Now you are ready to twist the spindle into the cord on the bow so that it is outside the string, meaning that the string is between the spindle and the bow.

Rest your chest on your left knee, and wrap your left arm, holding the handle, around the outside of your thigh and across your shin. Your wrist and thumb pad should be pressing against your leg with the handhold facing down. Position the drill with the top in the handhold and the bottom in the hole on the hearth-board.

THE RIGHT STROKE

The spindle should now be standing perfectly upright between the handhold and the hearth-board. If this is not the case, try to adjust the angle of your left knee slightly until the drill is pointing straight down into the hearth-board. Once your angles are nice and straight, grasp the bow with your right hand.

To get the most out of each stroke, grip the bow as far back as you can. Move it slowly backwards and forwards while keeping the bow parallel with the ground. Once you get a feel for the technique and once your strokes are steady and regular, you can try to speed up a bit with the bow.

If your technique is correct – with the right pressure on the handhold, keeping the spindle steady and vertical and the bow horizontal and going at the right speed – you should start to get some smoke and black dust around the edges of the hole in the hearth-board even if you are not going too fast with the bow. Don't worry if you are not getting any smoke at first. It takes a bit of practice to get it right. The usual problem is not holding the drill steadily enough and at the same time not applying enough downward pressure. You should be spending about 25 per cent of your energy holding your wrist tight against your left leg, 50 per cent pushing down and 25 per cent moving the bow back and forth.

Once there is plenty of smoke, you can increase the speed of the bow a

little while applying more downward pressure. You can stop drilling once the whole diameter of the spindle is in the hearth-board.

COMPLETING THE BOW DRILL

At this point, it is time to grease the handhold to reduce the friction there, and to carve a notch to collect the black dust and eventually the ember.

The hole in the handhold can be greased with the oil from crushed pine needles, animal or vegetable fat, the oil from your skin or hair, or anything else you have available. But don't use water – it will not lubricate the top of the spindle and it will make the wood swell, shrinking the hole and thus creating more friction. Once you have greased the top of the spindle, you must never put the greased end into the hole on the hearth-board because you need friction there.

▲ *Use medium-hard woods for your DIY wood-burning kit, such as hazel, cedar, poplar or sycamore, and look for pieces that require minimal shaping.*

The notch in the hearth-board is important as it will collect all the dust created by the friction, and the size of the notch makes a big difference in performance. It should be a perfect eighth of the hole and should stop just short of the centre of the hole. Divide the circular hole into 16 segments and then carve out the two segments closest to the edge of the hearth-board. Make sure the sides of the notch are smooth.

Now your set is ready to create an ember. At this point you should construct your fire and prepare the tinder to receive the spark. The tinder bundle, made from fine, dry fibres, should be fluffy and in the shape of a shallow bird's nest.

USING A BOW DRILL

1 Place a piece of wood, a leaf or a dry flat stone under the notch in the hearth-board, so that any dust that gathers will not fall on damp ground.

2 Place the spindle in the hole, and start moving the bow at a slow but steady speed, increasing the speed and pressure as smoke starts to build.

3 When you are successful, there will be an ember in the dust in the notch. It may not be visible at first, but there will be sustained smoke from the dust.

► *The trick of using a bow drill lies in applying enough pressure with your left arm while holding the spindle steady and upright and ensuring the bow is going at the right speed, level with the ground.*

MAKING AN EMBER

Place the hearth-board with the notch on a piece of dry bark or some thick dry leaves to prevent the hot dust from falling on the ground and getting damp or cooling down. This base will also help you later when transferring the ember to your tinder bundle. Some people like to dig a little hole in the ground underneath the notch to hold the tinder, but this can cause the tinder bundle to get squashed or damp.

It doesn't matter too much whether the notch is facing you or away from you. Check the wind direction and make sure there is enough room to hold your foot down on the hearth-board. Taking up the same position you used to drill the holes, start off again with gentle strokes to warm up the hearth-board. Often it will sound squeaky at this point – this means you are going too fast with the bow or applying too little pressure.

Don't put too much pressure on the spindle just yet. Once the set starts to smoke, you can speed up and apply

more pressure. Continue until there is a lot of smoke coming from the bottom of your hearth-board and until it seems that smoke is coming from below the dust in the notch. Then carefully lift off the drill and very carefully remove the hearth-board to see if you have an ember. You will tell from the smoke – if it continues to pour from the black dust you have an ember. Sometimes you can also see a red glow at this

point. Once you have reached this stage, you can take a breather to allow the ember to grow. You can also help the process by gently wafting a little air towards it with your hand, but be gentle as the ember is only just forming and is very frail.

Once the ember has settled a little and you've had a few seconds rest, carefully pick it up and transfer it to your tinder bundle.

TURNING AN EMBER INTO A FLAME

1 Hold the tinder bundle slightly higher than your face to prevent too much smoke going in your eyes and start blowing on it gently. Once the ember starts to spread into the tinder you can blow a little harder.

2 When the tinder bundle is nearly too hot to hold in your hands, give it all the oxygen you can. The tinder should go up in flames. You don't have a lot of time to place your tinder bundle in the fire before it burns out, but be careful.

3 If you squeeze the bundle too much, you may extinguish the flames. If you are worried that you don't have enough tinder, place the bundle inside the fire as soon as it's glowing well, and blow it into flames there.

The hand drill

Though the technique and materials are different, the hand drill works on the same principle as the bow drill. The hand drill consists of a straight stick, 30cm–1.5m/1–5ft long and as thick as an average pen, and a hearth-board about the same thickness as the drill and twice as wide. This means that the hand drill involves a lot less material and less preparation than the bow drill. The downside is that the hand drill does not work well in damp conditions, whereas the bow drill will work under most circumstances.

Medium-hard woods are needed for the apparatus. The spindle is often made from hollow straight shoots of plants such as elder, mullein or burdock. The hearth-board should be made from woods such as poplar and cedar. This time the spindle is not pointed at the top or bottom. The only preparation it requires is smoothing and the removal of side branches and knots.

MAKING A HAND DRILL

1 To prepare the spindle, select a straight shoot or branch about 1.2cm/¹⁄₂in thick.

2 Make sure the stick is perfectly smooth by cutting away any side branches, knots and perhaps even bark.

3 Round the bottom of the spindle to stop it creating excess friction at the side of the hole in the hearth-board.

4 Press the tip of the drill into the hearth-board, about 6mm/¹⁄₄in from the edge, to make a round indentation.

5 Carve out the indentation carefully. The resulting hole should be exactly the same diameter as the drill.

6 Holding the hearth-board with one foot, spin the drill slowly between your hands starting at the top of the spindle.

7 Once you are confident the hole has been burnt deep enough to prevent the spindle slipping, stop.

8 Carve a notch in the hearth-board, cutting a segment of one eighth of the circle, which just enters the hole.

9 If the drill is hollow you may cut the notch all the way to the centre. The hand drill set is now ready for use.

▶ *The hand drill method requires minimal preparation but is a reliable technique only in dry or hot regions.*

CREATING AN EMBER

Place the hearth-board on a stable surface and steady it with your foot, as far away from the hole as possible. If you kneel, as with the bow drill, your left arm should be on the inside of your leg. You may be flexible enough to sit, steadying the board with the side of your foot. This gives more space to move your hands, but it may be harder to apply enough downward pressure.

With the spindle in the hole, hold it at the top between your flat palms. While pressing down, move your hands back and forth across the drill to make it twirl. Work slowly and gently until there is plenty of smoke coming from the bottom of the spindle, then speed up and apply more pressure.

Embers produced with the hand drill are generally frail and burn out quickly.

It may help to have an "extender" to hand to help strengthen and enlarge the ember before you place it in the tinder bundle. This can be any dry, fluffy material that helps the ember grow. Good materials include bulrush (cattail) down, shredded cedar bark or pulverized, dead softwood.

USING A HAND DRILL

1 Place the end of the drill in the hole in the hearth-board. Orient the notch so that it is protected from wind.

2 Start by slowly rubbing the stick back and forth between your hands until you notice the first puff of smoke.

3 Your hands will move down the drill; when you reach the bottom, move up as fast as possible for another run.

4 Try to ensure you use the whole hand, including your fingers, so that there are more revolutions per stroke.

5 Once the notch has filled with dust, and smoke pours from it when you stop drilling, you may have an ember.

6 The ember is generally small and can break very easily or run out of fuel. Try to use it as soon as it's made.

The pump drill

In a survival situation you need to get an ember going fast, and this takes energy and muscle power. If you find yourself surviving in a more permanent shelter where there is not much room to move about you can try the pump drill method. The apparatus is harder to make, but it is easier to use in a confined space such as inside a shelter, and will light many fires without too much effort. It can also be used for drilling holes for other purposes.

MAKING THE SPINDLE
For the spindle of the pump drill, you'll need a straight branch about 60cm/2ft long and about 3cm/1¹/₄in in diameter. If the branch is at all bent you'll have to straighten it, or find another branch, otherwise the drill will not work properly.

Clean off all the bark, and abrade the stick so that it tapers slightly: the thicker end will eventually be the bottom of the pump drill. Once this is done, carve or drill a notch in the thicker end of the stick to enable you to insert a stone blade or a chuck later on. The thinner end of the spindle is also notched. It will later hold a string.

MAKING THE FLYWHEEL
The next component to be made is the flywheel. To make the two halves match exactly, make them from a single piece of wood about 7.5cm/3in wide and 45cm/18in long. Drill, burn or carve a hole right through the middle. The hole must be slightly less than the diameter of the spindle at the bottom end. Split the wood in half so you have two matching pieces, each with a hole through the centre.

To weight the flywheel, find two round stones of the same weight. These will be sandwiched between the two half sticks. Carve a few notches in the ends of the sticks to make it easier to tie the rocks securely into place. When tying the pieces together, make sure you line up the central holes perfectly.

Once the flywheel is assembled, you can slide it on to the spindle. If you

have made the holes the correct size, it should fit snugly when it is about 2.5–7.5cm/1–3in from the bottom of the spindle.

THE HANDHOLD
The handle of the pump should be about 60cm/2ft long and 7.5cm/3in wide. You may be able to split a branch to get a plank with these measurements. You need to drill a hole in the centre of this piece, which should be large enough for the handle to slide freely right down the spindle to meet the flywheel. Carve notches at each side of both ends of the handle to take the string.

Now all you need to complete the apparatus is a piece of cordage, which should be about 1m/3ft long. Tie one end of the cord around one end of the handle, securing it in the notches, and the other end to the second set of notches on the other end. Slide handle down over the spindle, and insert the middle of the cord into the notch you made on the spindle.

PREPARING THE FIRE PUMP
The pump drill can perform a number of functions, but in order to use it to start a fire by friction, it needs to be fitted with a wooden bit that can

▲ *The fire pump is especially useful when you need to make fire regularly while inside a confined space such as a long-term shelter.*

be twirled in a hearth-board. Select a piece of medium-hard wood such as poplar or cedar for this purpose. The bit should be carved to look much like the bottom of a bow drill spindle, though the top end will need to be shaped to fit into the notch you made in the bottom of the pump drill spindle. The diameter of the bit can be a little smaller than that of the bow drill spindle – 12mm/¹/₂in or slightly thicker works very well. Insert the bit into the spindle and tie it securely so there is no sideways movement.

Make a hearth-board like that for the bow drill. Carve a little hole into it, and insert the tip of the pump drill. Wind the handle up to twist the cord around the spindle, then push it down. Once it's fully down, the flywheel will take over the motion and bring the handle up automatically. Push down again and keep this motion going until you have drilled a sizable hole into the hearth-board. Carve a notch and you are ready to start lighting fires with your pump drill. The technique of balancing pressure and speed is exactly the same as in the other methods.

MAKING A PUMP DRILL

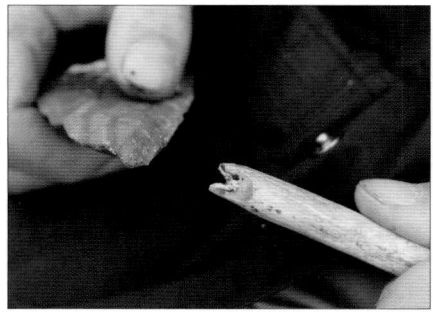

1 The spindle should be about 1m/3ft long and 2.5cm/1in in diameter. Carve a notch in the top (the thinner end).

2 Drill a hole in the thicker end to hold a chuck, and wrap cord around the spindle just above the hole.

3 Find a piece of wood 7.5cm/3in wide and 45cm/18in long. Drill a hole through the centre then split the stick.

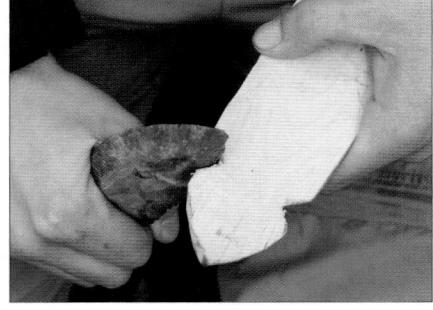

4 Find a piece of wood about 60cm/2ft long for the handle and carve notches in each end to hold the string.

5 Drill a hole in the centre of the handle. It should be large enough for the spindle to move freely through it.

6 To weight the flywheel find two large stones of about 1–1.5kg/2–3lb and several lengths of cordage.

7 Wrap cord around both pieces of the flywheel to reinforce the centre and prevent splits when pressure is applied.

8 Sandwich the two stones between the pieces of wood and tie them in securely to make the flywheel.

9 Slide the flywheel over the thin part of the spindle. It should stick 2.5–5cm/1–2in above the hole in the bottom.

10 Tie a 1m/3ft piece of string around the notches at both ends of the handle.

11 Thread on the handle and insert the string in the notch on the spindle.

12 Twist the handle up to the top then push it down to start the pump action.

Jungle fire

A method that works extremely well in tropical environments is the fire saw, which is usually made from a piece of dead bamboo, about 60cm/2ft long and with a diameter of 4–5cm/1¹/₂–2in.

The bamboo is split in half and the hearth-board is prepared by laying one piece flat on a stable, dry surface with the convex side facing up. If you are by yourself, you will need to anchor the hearth-board very securely to the surface it's lying on, otherwise get another person to hold it down. Cut a small hole in the convex surface to keep the saw on one spot.

The saw is prepared by carving off any joints in and outside the stick and scraping one of the split sides to smooth it and even it out. This saw is then placed perpendicular to the hearth-board, with the smoothed edge over the hole.

USING THE FIRE SAW

Just as with the other friction methods, you should start slowly, sawing back and forth over the hearth-board until it starts smoking. The pressure and speed should then be increased until there is a lot of smoke or until you can't go on any longer. The ember will form under the hollow of the hearth-board.

This ember tends to be fairly frail, so be careful to extend it with some dry, fluffy, easily flammable material and be sure to handle it gently.

THE FIRE THONG

Instead of the saw, a piece of dry, flexible rattan about 90–120cm/3–4ft long can be used, though then the hearth-board is held upside down, and you saw upwards. This method, known as the fire thong, is very efficient with a little practice.

FIRE PISTON

Conditions in the jungle can often be too wet to light a fire by friction. An ingenious method developed by indigenous people is a device known as a "fire piston". This rapidly compresses air in a small, very smoothly bored cylinder, which makes it very hot. The end of the piston is hollowed out to hold tinder, and the compressed air gets hot enough to ignite it.

The tube itself, closed at one end, is traditionally made of hardwood, bamboo or even horn. The piston can be made of wound thread, fibre or leather, to ensure a proper seal to create the compression successfully.

MAKING A FIRE SAW

1 Split a length of bamboo in half. One half will become the hearth-board and the other half will be the saw.

2 Using a knife or sharp stone, make a little hole in the convex side of one piece of bamboo, just piercing it.

3 Prepare the saw by cleaning up the edge of the other piece of bamboo. It should be rounded, not too sharp.

4 Hold the saw in the hole, keeping it at a slight tilt so as not to saw both sides of the split at once.

5 Move the saw back and forth while applying a lot of pressure. It should start smoking quite rapidly.

6 When the set is smoking profusely, lift the saw. If the smoke persists, there is an ember under the hearth-board.

Arctic fire

By far the most amazing way to light a fire is by using ice. Being able to create an ember using this fire kit is something special indeed, since it is the only natural method that doesn't depend on generating friction between pieces of wood. In fact, no wood is needed at all, apart from the fuel that is to be used in the fire. In polar regions even the fire may be built using different materials – fuels such as dried dung and animal fat are commonly used in such extreme terrain.

To make an ice lens you'll need a block of ice about 10cm/4in thick and about 5cm/2in long and wide. It should be free of cracks and other imperfections that will distort the lens. Carve the block into a round shape, before carefully carving away the edges to create the lens. Don't carve too much material away from the centre,

but make the edges nearly sharp. Once you are approaching the right shape, put your knife or stone tool down, and continue shaping the lens by using body heat to melt the ice where it is not needed. This will prevent you from accidentally breaking the lens. Test the lens by looking through it at a nearby object, and go on shaping until you achieve a clear magnified image.

MAKING AN EMBER

You'll need some very fine tinder to make an ember with the lens. Crushed bark works well, but only if it's fibrous. Hold the lens between the sun and the piece of tinder and move it back and forth until the light is focused on the tinder. This should start smoking very rapidly. By blowing on it gently you should be able to get an ember in about 30 seconds.

MAKING FIRE FROM ICE

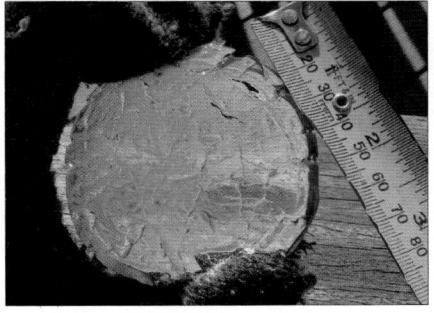

1 The ice needs to be about 10cm/4in across and 5cm/2in thick. Carve a circular shape, then pare the edges.

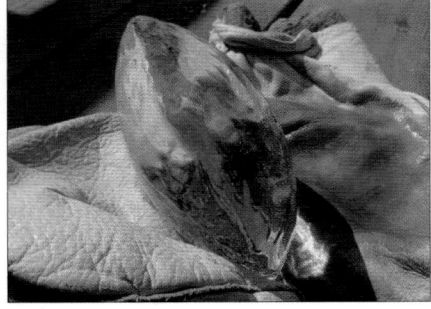

2 The profile of the ice lens shows its shape clearly. The final shaping is best done by rubbing with the fingers.

3 You should strive for a clear, magnified image when shaping the lens: test it by looking through it.

4 When you find the lens's focal point by trial and error, it will quickly char a sheet of paper by focusing sunlight.

5 It is better to hold the lens only with gloves after it has been completed, otherwise it will soon melt away.

6 When the sunlight is focused on a piece of tinder, in this case cedar, it will start to smoke in a matter of seconds.

Building a fire

Having decided where you will site your fire and how you will light it, you need to build it using dry, carefully selected fuel so that it lights easily and burns steadily, otherwise all the effort you put into igniting your tinder will be wasted. Different situations require different sorts of fires. However, the tipi fire is probably one of the best constructions to use in a survival situation. It has several advantages:
• maximum heat
• maximum light
• efficient use of fuel
• smoke and sparks travel straight up
• it is resistant to water and snow.

To build the fire you need a shallow fire-pit, which (in damp or dangerously dry conditions) you should line with dried bark, grasses or stones. Then add the fuel, starting with the smallest type of wood, the kindling. Try to fashion a neat pyramid, but be sure to leave an opening near the ground, because that is where the tinder is going to be put as soon as it's alight.

Aim to put the thinner pieces of kindling nearer to the inside and the bigger pieces to the outside of the fire. Do not pack the wood too tightly at this stage. Leave space for oxygen to reach the centre of the fire, and if there is any wind, line up the opening with the direction it is coming from – it will help drive the flames up into the tipi. If you have any available, it is a good idea to add pieces of resinous bark, such as birch bark, which will combust very, very easily.

Next comes the squaw wood, which is built up in the same manner. At this point, you can also add some pieces of small bulkwood to the fire if you wish. The only problem is that the fire may collapse as the smaller wood burns away from underneath the bulkwood. It is important in any case to feed smaller pieces of wood into the bottom of the fire rather than just piling wood on top. This is especially important if you are using bulkwood, otherwise the fire sometimes hollows out, making it hard to keep alight.

MAKING A TIPI FIRE

1 Dig out a shallow pit with sloping sides to keep the embers in the centre.

2 If the ground is damp or extremely dry, line the pit with bark or stones.

3 To contain the fire, place a ring of large rocks around the side.

4 Break a bunch of kindling in half and arrange it in a pyramid shape.

5 Add slightly larger wood but leave an opening to insert the lighted tinder.

6 You can add a few larger pieces of wood at this point, but not too many.

7 Add the tinder as soon as it is alight, because it doesn't burn for long.

8 Once the fire is lit, you can maintain it by adding larger pieces of wood.

Keeping a fire going

There may be many times when you want to ensure that your fire survives through the night, so you don't have to go through the process of relighting it in the morning. There are various ways to make sure that some embers survive all night, but you must be very sure that there is no danger of the fire spreading and getting out of control while you are asleep.

Once you are pretty much ready to go to sleep for the night, you can prepare the fire to last until the morning by adding some large pieces of green wood. The best wood to use

for this would be fresh branches of hardwoods such as oak. However, green wood will cause a lot of smoke, which may be undesirable.

If the fire is sheltered and the smoke will not disturb you, just throwing on a large amount of green wood should make it glow through the night. If the fire is less protected from the wind, you can also throw some soil over the glowing embers once you have placed the green wood on the fire. The soil will prevent too much oxygen from reaching the embers, thereby reducing the speed at which they burn out.

Make sure that the soil does not contain dry leaves, grasses or other such material, because this may flare up unexpectedly.

The next morning, to get the fire going again, all you have to do is carefully remove the soil from the fire. There should be plenty of embers still there, though they may be buried beneath a layer of ash. Use a bit of tinder and plenty of kindling wood to build a small new fire on top of the embers. By blowing at the embers, you should be able to get the fire to light again in a matter of seconds.

DAMPING DOWN A CAMP FIRE

1 While you are getting ready to go to sleep in the evening, leave the fire until it has pretty much burned down. Place a number of thick green sticks on the fire, which will smoulder slowly through the night.

2 Cover the fire with soil, making sure you are not using really wet soil, to reduce the flow of oxygen. In the morning, remove the soil from the fire and carefully scrape the ash away so the embers are exposed.

3 Using some tinder and plenty of kindling, build a small fire over the embers and blow on it to get it going. Once the first flames have started to appear, add more wood, and build your fire up again as usual.

MAKING A MATCH TO CARRY FIRE

1 Collect a good amount of tinder such as bulrush (cattail) down and other small fibres, and find a piece of bark 10cm/4in wide and 30cm/12in long.

2 Roll the tinder into the bark like a cigar. Make sure the tinder is not too tightly rolled, but not too loosely either. A bit of testing is often required.

3 Tie up the bundle with cord and put the ember in the top. The trick is to give it just enough oxygen to let it slowly smoulder down the match.

Building a fire for cooking

A fire for cooking needs to be built in a way that will create plenty of hot embers. When you are roasting meat or cooking food in a vessel such as an earthenware pot, you don't want too many flames. A good bed of hot coals will give a more sustained heat and the temperature will also be more regular, so that your food will cook properly without charring.

Often such a fire is built between two heavy logs, which both contain the fire and provide support for any pots or sticks to rest above the embers. Of course these two logs will burn as well and will eventually have to be replaced. One way round this is to line the inside of the logs with a layer of clay, which will prevent them from burning. The fire will be somewhat hemmed in by the logs, so if there is a prevailing wind, lay them in that direction to ensure a good supply of air.

A tipi fire is initially built between the logs. Once this is lit and burning profusely, thicker squaw wood is added, laying it in the same direction as the two logs. Once these are burning well, more branches are laid crossways and left to burn. The fire will burn down rather quickly, but will leave a lot of embers suitable for cooking on.

From now on, the trick is to keep a good amount of embers in the fire. It helps to add only one stick at a time. This will flare up, but turn into embers

▲ *The best fire for cooking provides a good bed of embers and should be built with stable supports for bowls and pots.*

quickly, because there is no additional wood to support the flames. Just keep adding sticks one after the other.

Cooking fires have many other uses. When you light one, be ready to make some glue, strip some spruce roots, or do any other tasks that require a fire without flames. You should light the fire for such activities during the day, as the embers do not provide much light to see by.

HANDLING EQUIPMENT
Apart from some fireproof containers, you also need to make some equipment to get the containers off the fire when the food is ready. Make suitable tools

before you start cooking, as it can be very frustrating if food or hot water gets lost in the fire because you drop a container or knock it over.

The most useful tool would be a pair of tongs, though separate tools often need to be fashioned for each container you use, since the shapes of cooking pots can vary so much. Try to incorporate features such as handles that sticks can slide through when you are making the pots. For further advice on tools and equipment, see page 112.

COOKING WITHOUT UTENSILS

▲ *Cook fish by laying it out flat on a hot rock, or hang it on a stout log placed next to the fire.*

▲ *Thread meat and vegetables on to straight sticks to make kebabs, then roast them over ash-covered embers so they don't burn.*

▲ *Simple small loaves of unleavened bread are delicious when baked on a flat stone heated by a wood fire.*

CONSTRUCTING A SHALLOW OPEN FIRE FOR COOKING

1 Dig a shallow fire-pit so the embers stay together. Don't make the pit any wider than your cooking pot.

2 Line the pit carefully with either bark or stones. If you use stones, make sure they are collected from a dry area.

3 Place two thick logs on either side of the pit, close enough together to support the pot over the fire.

4 Break a few handfuls of kindling in half and arrange them in the middle of the pit in the shape of a tipi.

5 Leave an opening on one side of the fire so you can place the burning tinder bundle under the wood.

6 Add some slightly larger pieces of wood, again leaving one side open. The fire will now resemble a lean-to.

7 Add small bulkwood if you wish, but take care not to choke the fire.

8 As it is hemmed in, you may need to blow on the fire to get it to light.

9 Once the fire is lit, add squaw wood and small bulkwood to the open side.

10 As the fire takes hold, add larger pieces of wood until a good bed of embers is forming below the fire.

11 Go on adding wood for about half an hour, so that you end up with a good thick layer of embers.

12 After the base of embers is established, keep adding the odd stick, so fresh embers are produced.

Using hot rocks for cooking

As well as cooking your food in or over the fire, you can try an alternative method using rocks, which retain heat well and can be used in various ways. You'll need to gather some large, smooth rocks and place them inside a hot fire that is already well established. Leave them for a few hours, until they are red hot.

CHOOSING THE RIGHT ROCKS

When finding rocks or stones to put in your fire, never collect them from streams, marshes or other waterlogged areas. Always collect them from higher ground where they won't have soaked up a lot of water. When waterlogged rocks are heated, it may be too hard for the expanding water to seep back out, causing the rock to explode. Rocks that appear damp due to rainfall are

usually fine as long as they are collected from a higher elevation. Even then, it's usually a good idea to stay away from them for half an hour when they first go into the fire, just to be safe.

▲ *Tempting though it might be, never remove waterlogged rocks from a stream to use on your fire.*

BOILING WATER

One of the most useful ways of using heated rocks is to boil water. You can use them to heat water stored in containers, such as wooden bowls or animal bladders, that would burn if placed over the fire. A few fist-sized rocks can easily bring several litres of water to the boil. If necessary you can keep it boiling by adding more rocks.

HEATING ROCKS TO BOIL WATER

1 Collect dry rocks and place them in a hot fire. Make sure they are placed right in the hottest part of the fire.

2 Keep adding wood, and use your fire as normal. The stones are ready when they appear to be red hot.

3 Take a rock out of the fire with a pair of improvised tongs and carefully immerse it in water. The water should start bubbling immediately.

4 Add more rocks to boil large amounts of water, or to keep the water boiling. Stirring the water will help to distribute the heat of the rocks evenly.

COOKING ON ROCKS

If you can find large flat rocks, you can heat them in the fire until they are red hot and then use them in much the same way as a griddle or frying pan. This technique is most successful if you have some oil or fat to prevent the food sticking to the stone. It can be used to fry or bake flat bread.

If you have two thin flat rocks you can even cook food such as meat or fish between them. This makes the food taste good as well as speeding up the cooking time.

ROCKS AS HEATING DEVICES

Having cooked your meal, you can also use hot rocks to keep you warm. You can place them inside your shelter to warm up the space, or use them as personal body warmers (though you should make sure they are not too hot).

Cooking food in a covered pit

Another great way of cooking is in a pit, heated with rocks from the fire. You simply put your meal in the pit, let it cook throughout the day, and have a nice meal ready for you when you come back home in the evening. The pit needs to be 30–60cm/1–2ft deep, and the hot rocks are put on the bottom. Wait a little to allow the rocks to dry out the pit, otherwise the food may taste rather earthy.

Once the pit has dried out, put a thick layer (about 20cm/8in) of green grass or large edible leaves over the rocks. Place your food in the pit, cover it with more grass or leaves, and fill the pit with debris and soil. All you have to do is dig your food up again a few hours later. If you put in plenty of rocks, it should be thoroughly cooked. It's worth experimenting with this to see just how many hot rocks you need and how long the food should stay in the pit for the ideal meal.

MAKING A COVERED PIT FOR COOKING

1 Collect plenty of rocks, making sure they are not waterlogged, and place them in the fire to heat up.

2 Dig a pit about 60cm/2ft deep and wide enough to place all the food you want to cook in a single layer.

3 Once the rocks are red hot, place them in the bottom of the pit. The more rocks you have, the better.

4 Leave the rocks for a while so that the pit dries out. Cover the rocks with leaves to stop them burning the food.

5 Wrap the food in large edible leaves and place the wrapped food bundles at the bottom of the pit.

6 The heat from the rocks will rise up to cook the food bundles. Large pieces of meat do not need to be wrapped.

7 Cover the food with more grass and edible leaves. Adding a layer of bark will also help to protect it from debris.

8 Fill up the pit with debris and soil. Mark the pit in some way to remind you where you buried your food.

9 Leave the food to cook for 3–7 hours (depending on its size) then dig it up carefully and enjoy your meal.

WATER

Even in ideal circumstances, human beings can survive for only three to four days without water, and if you are exerting yourself or having to contend with high temperatures, this time will be much shorter. So as soon as your shelter is taken care of, you must make sure you have access to a supply of fresh water. That's easier said than done and if you don't have a modern water filter, then you will need to purify the water by boiling it (this, in turn, makes fire more important in the big scheme of survival). Purification of drinking water could turn out to be your biggest headache in a survival situation. It is essential, however, otherwise you might survive other adverse conditions only to fall prey to waterborne diseases or the chemical pollution that infiltrates many water sources.

The importance of water

About 60–70 per cent of the human body consists of water, and the brain consists of about 85 per cent water. This means that the average person contains about 50–60 litres/11–13 gallons of water. Clearly, water is therefore very important for survival. Every cell in the body depends upon water in order to function properly. We need a supply of water daily, because we cannot maintain reserves of it in our body as we can with food. Numerous disorders are caused by insufficient water, as well as by drinking water containing micro-organisms or polluted by chemical effluent.

In order to maintain the various bodily functions in a temperate climate, the average person should consume about 3.8 litres/6½ pints of water a day. In hot climates, or when working hard, the average person may need to consume over 10 litres/17½ pints of water per day.

WATER LOSS

The table below shows the effects of losing only a moderate amount of water without replenishing it. Looking at this table, it becomes clear that in a temperate climate you would start to feel some unpleasant effects of dehydration after just one day without water. The second row pretty much coincides with the end of a second day without water. This table represents loss of water only in a moderate climate – in extreme situations, the loss of water can be a lot faster.

KEEPING FLUID LOSS DOWN

If you can't acquire water immediately, or if the supply is limited, it is clearly important to try to minimize your loss of fluid so that you need to replace less.

Humans have the capability to sweat away as much as 1.5 litres/2½ pints of fluids per hour when engaged in strenuous exercise in temperate conditions. Couple physical exertion with a hot environment, and you could lose even more. In moderate circumstances, when at rest, the average person sweats about 1 litre/1¾ pints per day. This means that by keeping sweating down, you can stop a lot of fluid from being lost from the body.

In a survival situation, you will have no choice but to exert yourself quite

▲ *Natural caches often contain water but it is important to purify it as the water may have been stagnant for a long time.*

regularly to satisfy your daily needs, and this can cause sweating. However, there are a few ways in which you can reduce this loss of fluid.

The first necessity is to master all the skills you need to survive. Spending only 30 seconds to light a fire using a bow drill set, for example, will cost you a lot less effort, and therefore a lot less sweat, than having to spend 30 minutes to get a fire lit. Mastering survival skills also includes learning to be as efficient as possible when gathering the materials you need, again saving on fluid loss through sweating.

THE EFFECTS OF DEHYDRATION		
Loss of water	**Effects**	**Survival chances**
Up to 4 litres/ 7 pints	Thirst, vague discomfort, impatience, nausea and loss of efficiency.	3 days in moderate climate
Up to 8 litres/ 14 pints	Dizziness, headache, breathing difficulty, tingling in the limbs, increased blood concentration, absence of salivation, purplish discoloration of the skin, indistinct speech and inability to walk.	2 days in moderate climate
Up to 15 litres/ 26 pints	Delirium, spasticity, dimming of vision and death.	1 day in moderate climate

SIGNS OF WATER – SIGNS OF LIFE

▲ *Although rivers are often not visible during the dry season, they may still be running below ground. Patches of vegetation can indicate their courses.*

▲ *Often there is water below the ground at the bottom of deep canyons like this one. This may or may not be confirmed by the presence of vegetation.*

▲ *Coarse vegetation is usually found farther away from the underground water source, while the presence of grasses indicates water just below the surface.*

The second way to prevent excessive sweating is to take care of as many of the tasks requiring physical activity as you can during the cool hours of the day. In extremely hot climates, that may even mean working during the night and resting during the day when it's scorchingly hot.

The third method is the simple precaution of avoiding overheating by removing layers of clothing when you get hot. On the other hand, in some climates adding layers can help keep the heat down. A good example is set by various nomadic desert peoples, who are often covered from head to toe in several layers of loose clothing to keep them cool. Covering the head with a turban or other headdress to protect it from the sun is another example.

A lot of moisture is lost through breathing. Again, keeping your core temperature and expenditure of effort down is one way to prevent excessive loss by this means. Another way to minimize loss of moisture is to focus on breathing through the nose, rather than through the mouth. This might seem extreme, but concentrating on small things like this can make all the difference in a survival situation.

Water is also needed to break down food, so when water is short, avoid eating as far as possible. You should also be careful what you drink. Don't consume alcohol, as it will take more water to break down the alcohol than is added by drinking the alcoholic

beverage. Coffee is another liquid to avoid when there is little water available, as it has a diuretic effect.

RATIONING YOUR WATER

A common misconception is that you need to ration water when it is short, much as you would ration food. It is important not to do this. The negative result far outweighs the positive result of saving water for later. Sometimes, dehydration can overcome your body too fast to realize something is wrong. A state of unconsciousness can often occur with little warning when you are

dehydrated. There are recorded incidents of people having been found dead due to dehydration even though they had a full water bottle at their side. Even when you are short of water, therefore, it is important to continue to drink as normal.

Don't guzzle what you have, however – take it in sips. Be methodical. If you do become dehydrated and then find a source of water, you should replenish your body fluids slowly, otherwise the stomach may go into convulsions, losing even more fluid by vomiting.

CONSERVING WATER

1 When you do have a supply of water, store it out of the sun to avoid excessive loss by evaporation.

2 Suspending a water bag under a tree will keep it cool. Take only as much as you need, to conserve your supply.

Finding a safe water supply

There are many ways to gather water and the ideal source to look for is clear, fresh, running water. Gathering is the first part of the exercise, for which you need manufactured or natural containers. You should then always filter and purify water, but it is a good idea to get it from the cleanest source.

WHAT TO LOOK FOR

Look for relatively fast-flowing rivers and streams, with healthy vegetation on their banks. In stagnant pools of water, it is generally easier for bacteria and viruses to survive and multiply. It is harder for fast-flowing water to sustain much bacterial growth.

One indication of water quality is to see whether many animals come to drink from it or if they favour a different source. This method is not always foolproof, however, as many wild animals build up a certain amount of resistance to waterborne bacteria and viruses that may cause serious illness in humans. The same is true for water sources frequented by the local human population. It is often the case that Western people become ill after drinking water that local people have been drinking all their lives.

If you find what appears to be a good, clean source, check it out as far upstream as you can. It is possible that an animal carcass or some other pollutant may be located just upstream, making the water unsafe.

▲ *Only when you are absolutely certain the water is safe to drink should you drink straight from a stream.*

DANGERS IN DRINKING WATER

Common infections that may be contracted from unclean water include cholera, hepatitis A and giardiasis.

Cholera is the relatively friendly one. It is a bacterial infection that causes mainly diarrhoea, and is treated by continually replacing lost fluid by drinking clean water. (Continuing to drink infected water will make the situation far worse.) Approximately one in 20 of those infected will have severe symptoms characterized by profuse

watery diarrhoea, vomiting and leg cramps. In these people, rapid loss of body fluids often leads to dehydration and shock. Without treatment, death can occur within hours, and such victims may require fluids to be replaced intravenously.

Hepatitis A is rather less friendly; it is a disease of the liver caused by a viral infection. Symptoms do not always occur but may last for up to two months and include fever, tiredness, loss of appetite, nausea, abdominal discomfort, dark urine and jaundice (yellowing of the skin and eyes). Older people are generally more susceptible to the disease than children. Luckily,

▼ *A watering hole on the African savanna may be a hazardous source of water as it will attract many dangerous creatures who come to drink there.*

▼ *Animals drinking water is not always a sign that it is safe for human consumption: many animals are resistant to infections and diseases that can make humans ill.*

▼ *Some wells have a mechanical method of lifting water while others require you to haul it up manually. Never pollute a well by washing yourself or your equipment near it.*

COLLECTING WATER

▲ *One of the commonest ways of collecting water is by cupping your hands and drinking directly from a stream. Do so only if you know the water is absolutely safe.*

▲ *If you have plenty of containers, rainwater can be collected as it falls and does not need to be purified, though it may contain low concentrations of chemicals.*

▲ *If you have a tarpaulin or poncho, set it up on four poles with a weight in the centre to collect rainwater. Keep one edge low to allow the water to run off into a container.*

the disease is not life-threatening, though medication is often required, and once you have recovered, your body will have made antibodies that prevent a recurrence of the disease.

Giardiasis is caused by a one-celled, microscopic parasite that lives in the intestines and is ingested in water contaminated by sewage. Due to its tough outer shell, it can survive outside the body for a long time. Giardia is currently one of the most common waterborne diseases. Infection can

▼ *For a few days after rain has fallen you can often find water in natural hollows in the landscape.*

cause a variety of intestinal symptoms, which include diarrhoea, greasy stools that tend to float, stomach cramps and nausea. These symptoms may lead to weight loss and dehydration. Symptoms may last from two to six weeks or longer, though some people with giardia have no symptoms at all. The disease is generally treated by alleviating the symptoms and allowing the parasite to be flushed out of the body.

ALWAYS PURIFY

If you find a water source where animals appear to drink, where the water flows fast and cold and no dead animals have been found higher up the stream, you can be reasonably sure the source is fairly clean of bacterial and viral infections. Even then, you should be sure to purify water for drinking, as any infectious agents will not be apparent until it's too late.

CHECKING FOR CHEMICAL POLLUTANTS

Even when the water is free of viral and bacterial contamination, the source may have been polluted by chemicals. The only ways to minimize the danger of drinking chemically contaminated water are to walk all the way upstream, or to check the plant life in and around the water source carefully.

Ask yourself questions such as: "Are there many algae in the water?" (None could be a bad sign, but so can too many, as some algae thrive on phosphates and the like.) Another question might be: "How healthy do the plants growing around the water source look?" Often, when water is chemically contaminated, it affects the health of the flora around the polluted area. "Are there many healthy looking fish living in the stream?" is another question worth asking yourself.

The problem with chemical pollutants is that many will not "boil" away when the water is purified. Filtering through charcoal and the like may filter out some chemicals, but not others. So if in doubt about pollution, try to find an alternative source before relying on your purifying techniques.

Natural sources of water

In most regions, it is fairly easy to obtain enough water to sustain yourself. In a moderate climate there are generally plenty of rivers and streams from which you can take water. However, if you find yourself in an area where there are no watercourses nearby, or where riverbeds have dried up, you need to know how to locate alternative sources.

NATURAL WATER CACHES

After rain has fallen, you may find water that has collected in natural caches such as hollows in rocks. Ideally, you should use this kind of standing water within a few days of the rainfall. A small cache of water that remains for a long period of time can become the perfect breeding ground for bacteria and viruses.

Useful caches of water can often be found in uneven ground. A good example is where rainwater has collected in little holes and hollows in a rocky surface. These sources will often be fairly safe, but even so you should not neglect to treat any water you collect, just in case of some form of pollutant being present.

It is also important to collect as much water as possible from such sources, as the water may be around for only a day or two. Sometimes it may even disappear within hours.

COLLECTING MORNING DEW

Even where no rain falls, changes of temperature at night result in moisture condensing out of the atmosphere and being deposited on the landscape in the form of dew. In the morning you can collect it by wiping it from vegetation and rocks with an absorbent cloth, then wringing it out into a container.

A very successful Australian native method of collecting this kind of water is to tie absorbent materials to your legs and walk through the grass when there is a layer of dew or raindrops clinging to it. It is possible to gather a large amount of water using this method.

▲ *Water may be found in streams such as this, but make sure it is safe to drink by checking for obvious signs of pollution.*

RAINWATER

An excellent source of drinking water, rainwater has the additional advantage that it is free of bacterial and viral infection. It may, however, contain traces of chemical pollution in heavily industrialized regions.

Rainwater can be gathered using the dew collection method, though it may be easier to collect it while it is actually raining if you have plenty of containers to spread over an area.

COLLECTING DEW

1 If you have some spare clothes made out of material such as cotton, they can be used to collect water. Simply tie the material around your feet.

2 Walk through areas of fairly long grass or other plants, allowing the cloth around your ankles to soak up as much dew as possible.

3 Wring the water out of the soaked material into a bowl. Don't forget to purify it, even though dew is not very likely to contain pollutants.

▲ *Birch sap can be tapped from the trunk and drunk as it is, or boiled down to a sweet liquid not unlike maple syrup.*

▲ *Slow-moving streams are often dangerous to drink from as bacteria and viruses can more easily reproduce in sluggish water.*

▲ *Useful liquid can be found in the fruits of many trees, such as the palm. Coconuts have more liquid inside when unripe.*

GETTING WATER FROM PLANTS

In the jungle a common way of getting water is by retrieving it from water vines, which are easily identified by their round stems, 7.5–15cm/3–6in thick. To produce clear water you simply cut off a piece of stem about 1m/1yd long. If the vine produces a cloudy, bitter liquid, you have picked a different species: don't drink that sap. The liquid from a water vine will have a neutral or fruity taste. The downside

is that it cannot be stored. Some vines irritate the skin, so gather the liquid in a container rather than putting the stem straight to your mouth.

In Australia, the water tree, desert oak and bloodwood grow roots near the surface that can be prised out of the ground. Remove the bark and suck out the moisture or reduce the root to a pulp and squeeze it over your mouth or a container. Green bamboo thickets are an excellent source of fresh water.

Bend a stalk over, tie it down, and cut off the top. Place a container under the cut, and you can collect quite a lot of water in a few hours.

In deserts, most species of barrel cacti contain water. If you cut off the top you can mash the pulp and suck it dry, though it is not edible. However, unless you have a large tool such as a machete, it is impossible to get through the defensive spines and cut the flesh, and doing so will kill the plant.

PLANTS THAT STORE WATER

▲ *This pitcher plant contains fluid that is drinkable in small doses but beware of insects trapped inside: you need to filter and sterilize the fluid first.*

▲ *Succulent desert plants such as aloes and agaves hoard fluid to help them survive periods of drought. The fleshy leaves can be cut or broken off to obtain the liquid.*

▲ Opuntia microdasys, *a prickly pear cactus also known as "bunny ears", has thousands of barbed spikes that can irritate, but contains moisture in its fleshy pads.*

Filtering and purifying water

Whatever water you get, it is a good idea to purify it. You can never tell for sure where the water has been, and what may be in it.

You should start by filtering the water if it contains debris and larger particles. To do this you will need to make some kind of sieve or strainer. A hollow log stuffed with grass can do a good job of removing larger particles from the water, but if you have a sock you can make a finer filter. The first resort is to fill it with grass, as with the hollow log, but if you have access to sand you can use this to fill the sock filter. Start with the finest sand you can find, and fill the sock with coarser and coarser sand until you reach the top.

Suspend the filled sock over a container, pour in the water you have collected, and leave it to filter through.

BOILING WATER
Filtered water may look clean but it is by no means safe to drink. To purify water, you have to boil it (or use a modern filter or purifying agent if you have access to either of these options).

There are different opinions on how long water should be boiled to get rid of bacteria. It is safer to stick to a time of about 15–20 minutes. This may sound like a long time, but you just cannot afford to risk drinking water that is still contaminated.

PURIFYING AGENTS
Modern methods of purifying water include the use of purifying agents such as household bleach, iodine and water-purifying tablets. Modern commercially available filters purify the water as well as filtering it. The purifying agents are used in the following ways:

Bleach: Add 10 drops of household bleach to 4.5 litres/1 gallon of water and mix it well. Then allow it to stand for 30 minutes. A slight smell or taste of chlorine indicates that the water is fit to drink.

Iodine: This can be used in much the same way as bleach.

▲ *Use a sock, filled with sand if possible, to filter silt and debris out of your water before you purify it. Ideally, use fine sand at the bottom and coarser sand at the top.*

Water-purifying tablets: If you use commercial tablets, ensure you follow the package directions. They will make the water taste of bleach, but it will be very safe.

With all these agents, be sure to shake the container so that the purifier reaches every part of the water, to ensure that no bacteria are left behind. Bacteria often lurk in the screw top of a bottle, for example.

FILTERING WATER

1 To filter out pieces of debris and small aquatic creatures floating in water, hollow out a piece of dead wood by burning it almost through.

2 Create a form of sieve or strainer by stuffing the cavity with grass to catch the larger particles. The charcoal on the log will also help to clean the water.

3 Pour the water you have collected through the filter and collect it in a container placed underneath. The water will now need to be purified.

DESALINATING SEA WATER

1 When all you have is salt water, it's possible to make drinking water by distilling it. Bring it to the boil in a fireproof container.

2 Place a clean piece of cloth over the container so it catches all the steam. If you don't have any cloth, you can use moss instead.

3 From time to time, wring out the cloth or mosses and catch the liquid in another container. This water will be pure and ready to drink when cooled.

The problem with some of the above methods is that water treated in this way can make you feel unwell if you drink it over an extensive period of time. Many makers of commercially available tablets will advise you not to use their product continuously for longer than a few weeks. And, of course, tablets and tinctures eventually run out, so use them to extend the time before you have to gather clean water and purify it using more primitive methods.

COMMERCIAL FILTERS

The second option is to use a commercial filter. Such filters are an ideal way to clean large amounts of water over a long period. There are many different types of filters on the market, and many are small enough to fit in your pocket.

Filters are available for different conditions. Make sure that your filter can take care of chemical as well as viral and bacterial pollution, as it is possible to buy filters that filter out only one type of pollutant. Read the instructions carefully, as some filters require you to clean them regularly with iodine or similar fluids. Some filters have a shelf life too, meaning they can only filter a certain amount of water before "running out". If this happens you will have to fall back on the boiling method.

VITAL SALT

You can't drink salt water, but your body does need a regular intake of salt in order to retain water. So when you desalinate salt water, keep and use the salt that remains behind when the liquid has evaporated.

RESTORING THE TASTE OF BOILED WATER

1 When water has been purified by boiling for 15–20 minutes, it loses its taste. It will be perfectly drinkable, but will simply taste flat.

2 Adding a tiny amount of charcoal greatly improves the taste. You will need to let the water stand for a little while after adding the charcoal.

3 Another way of refreshing the water is to blow air through it using a straw. Alternatively, you can pour the water from container to container.

Further ways to find and treat water

Even in the most inhospitable, apparently arid terrain, it may be possible to find enough water to sustain life.

SEARCH FOR TRAILS

In the desert, it is often worthwhile following local wildlife to their water source, though you should keep in mind that a lot of desert animals do not drink, but get their liquid from the food they eat.

There is an important saying among the natives of desert regions: "The path is wiser than the person who walks it." Animals and native people use the same trails, and these paths often twist and meander across the land. If you come across such a trail it is better to follow it than to walk in a straight line to "cut off a corner". The trails follow courses where there are the least obstacles. Furthermore, they often run from shadow to shadow, and from water source to water source. If you find a well-used trail in the desert follow it, and stick to it.

UNDERGROUND WATER

In a dry region, look for dried-up river beds or canyons where water can be found by digging. Any vegetation will generally lead you in the right direction. The first plants you find will be thorny brush, farthest from the invisible water source; when the vegetation changes to grass-like plants you will be near the underground

▲ *Placing a clear bag over a leafy branch with one corner weighed down will collect water as it evaporates from the leaves and condenses on the bag.*

▲ *Some water filters can be complicated and contain a number of components (as with this tower water filter) and this may cause difficulties in extreme conditions.*

▲ *The tube of a portable filter goes into the unpurified water and clean water comes out of the spout once the pump is primed.*

▲ *Purifying agents can be used to eliminate any bacteria in water; their main drawback is their unpleasant taste.*

water. A ribbon of vegetation is often the only indication of a streambed in the desert, but it shows that there is water below ground. If the water is very hard to get at, you may be able to reach it with a filter straw, if you are carrying one. This very small, light device enables you to drink directly from an impure water source in an emergency, filtering and purifying the water as you suck it up.

In some deserts indigenous peoples have built extensive waterworks that capture any rainfall that does occur. In the Negev desert in Israel, for instance, there are areas where channels built in the rocks catch any rainwater that runs

down the hills and guide it to deep water pits. These systems are so effective that there will be water in the pits all year round. This may be valuable information if you land in a survival situation in a desert region where such pits exist.

COLLECTING CONDENSATION

An easy way to get water when the temperature is high and there is plenty of vegetation is to "capture" a branch with plenty of leaves, and tie a transparent plastic bag around it. Make sure you choose a tree that is non-poisonous, as the poison may find its way into the water. Then you must

MAKING A SOLAR STILL

1 To desalinate or purify water, build a solar still by digging a pit 60cm/2ft wide and 60cm/2ft deep. (Don't try to use a solar still to procure water in the desert, as it takes too much effort for too little return.)

2 Place an empty container in the middle of the pit to act as a collecting bowl. If you have a plastic tube at least 60–90cm/2–3ft long, place one end in the container, and allow the other end to come out of the side of the pit.

3 Place whatever water and vegetation you have found beside the collecting bowl. Place a sheet of clear plastic over the pit, secured by sand and weighted in the middle. Any condensation that forms will drip into the bowl.

---

tie one corner of the bag down, so the water doesn't escape near the branch where you tied the bag closed.

After a day, you can often procure a substantial volume of water by this means. Remember to change the location of the bag regularly to prevent leaves drying out completely, thereby stopping the process. A bag placed on a branch in the sun will produce more water than a bag placed in shadow.

The water produced by this method will be absolutely clean and safe to drink without any purification, though you may find that a lot of debris from the branch has dropped into the water. A quick filtering should sort that out.

WATER FROM SNOW AND ICE

In arctic regions, your main source of water may be the snow and ice around you. The snow is always as clean – or as dirty – as rainwater: that is, it may contain chemicals but not micro-organisms, though if it has been lying on the ground for an extended period of time it may have picked up pollutants from the environment. The saying "Never eat yellow snow" is one to be heeded.

Snow should always be pre-melted, as it takes too much of your body's energy to melt it in your mouth or in your stomach. This may not only cause you to lose vital heat, but can also lead

to dehydration, as you cannot get sufficient water into your system quickly enough.

Ice can be a great source of water, though again it will need to be melted. In arctic regions the problem is that a lot of ice is formed from salt water. Ice that is opaque or grey is often formed from salt water. More crystalline ice, with a bluish cast, has little or no salt in it. The water from salt water ice will need to be desalinated for drinking.

Don't forget that ice is no cleaner than the water it was formed from, and will often require purification. Some bacteria and viruses are able to survive for many years in a frozen state.

USING A FILTER STRAW

1 If you find a dried-up watercourse, you can dig down and use a filter straw to obtain the water directly.

2 It is possible to drink water direct from an inaccessible source if you have some kind of filter straw.

3 Before taking water from a pool try to clean the surface of the water or you will clog up your filter.

FOOD

When you begin to fend for yourself in the wilderness, it immediately becomes obvious how much is taken for granted in the modern urban environment. The food you normally eat probably comes with very little effort, whereas providing yourself with food in the wild is an activity and a chore that may consume a large part of the day. One thing is for sure: gathering all your food from the wild for a few days will make you appreciate your nourishment a lot more. Another facet you may notice is that you will have to adjust your taste buds. You become so used to the tastes of the foods you buy and cook that it can take a while to assimilate the different tastes and textures of the food that is available for free in the wild. However, when you are eating to survive you will quickly learn to appreciate your new-found sustenance.

Nutrition for survival

Food is our body's fuel. It supplies us with energy not only to work but to generate the heat that maintains our body temperature. Food also provides the body with the material needed to make and repair cells.

Activities such as hiking or climbing use huge amounts of energy, and if your energy levels are not topped up regularly, the body will start to use its reserves of energy, stored in the form of fat. This too will eventually run out, depending on how much fat your body contains. If your fuel supplies are still not topped up, your body will be less able to expend energy as it tries to maintain the supply to your vital organs. When all stored energy runs out, death soon follows.

THE CALORIES YOU NEED
The amount of energy you need in the form of food is measured in calories. A calorie is a unit of energy – the amount needed to raise the temperature of 1g of water by 1°C. Because this is a very small amount of energy, the kilocalorie (1000 calories) is more commonly used to measure food requirements, often expressed as a Calorie (with a capital C).

The amount of food you need each day varies with age, gender and the amount of energy you are expending.

▼ *Roots and tubers, such as these cultivated yams, provide essential nutrition. Your survival might depend on what grows below the ground when other foods are scarce.*

To function properly when working moderately, the average woman needs about 1500 Calories per day and the average man needs about 1800 Calories per day. However, in a survival situation you may be using as many as 4000–5000 Calories per day if you are working very hard (building your shelter, for instance) or trying to keep the body warm in extreme weather conditions. Foods rich in carbohydrates, such as fruits, vegetables and grains, normally supply the bulk of the body's energy needs.

VITAMINS
The body needs a regular supply of various organic substances, collectively known as vitamins, which are essential to break down foods into chemicals that can be absorbed and to sustain chemical processes within the cells. Deficiency diseases resulting from an absence of vitamins include scurvy (caused by a lack of vitamin C) and pellagra (a disorder of the nervous system caused by a lack of vitamin B3).

There are two different groups of vitamins. Those in the first group, notably vitamins B and C, are water-soluble and cannot be stored in the body, so they need to be replenished daily. The vitamins in the second group are fat-soluble and can therefore be stored in the body to be used over a longer period of time. They include vitamins A, D, E and K. These also need to be restored regularly, though not necessarily daily.

Like other essential nutrients, most vitamins can be obtained naturally by eating a balanced diet that includes fruit, vegetables, meat, grains and dairy products. This list can create problems in the wilderness, as you may not be able to get your hands on meat, grain or dairy products for a long time, while fruits, an excellent source of vitamins, are seasonal. The only vitamin manufactured in the body is vitamin D, which is essential for the absorption of calcium from the diet. This is created under the skin when in direct sunlight.

▲ *While locusts can destroy any vegetation they land on, they can also save your life as they make ideal food.*

▼ *Plantains are a staple food in the tropical regions of the world. They can be eaten green or ripe, raw or cooked.*

A BALANCED DIET

In normal circumstances, your daily diet should include foods from four groups, in the following proportions:
- Vegetables and fruits: 5–9 servings.
- Grain products, such as bread and cereals: 6–11 servings.
- Dairy products: 2–3 servings.
- Protein-rich foods such as meat, fish and beans: 2–3 servings.

▲ *In a survival situation you will have to work hard to keep yourself alive, so you need to find nourishing food to keep up your energy levels.*

CELLULOSE FOR SURVIVAL

Grain products such as bread and cereals provide cellulose, otherwise known as fibre, in your ordinary diet. Your body is unable to break down cellulose, so it has no value as a nutrient. It travels through the body unchanged until it is eliminated as a waste product. It does, however, aid in the digestion of food, and is therefore an essential part of the diet. Deprived of cellulose, the body's system works too slowly and the result is constipation. When grains are not available, you should replace them by eating more vegetables, which also contain a certain amount of fibre.

▼ *Eggs are a good source of "complete" protein, an essential part of a balanced diet, but are only available in some seasons.*

KILLING TO SURVIVE

The two sources of food in the wild are plants and animals. Between them they provide the nutrition for survival. Plants are easy to gather but tend to be fairly low in food value, while animals take a lot of catching but are high in food value. For some, the idea of killing a living creature for food is completely at odds with their moral values, and even the most ardent meat-eater could find the experience of performing the *coup de grâce* on an animal fighting for its life a gruesome prospect. In a survival situation, though, you need to be able to deal with such issues from day one. Even then, the hunter must act responsibly and not cause unneccesary suffering.

PROTEIN AND CALCIUM

About 20 different amino acids are needed by the body to build other proteins that are not obtained from food. Of these, 12 are manufactured by the body and the remainder have to be obtained from food. Foods such as meat, fish, eggs and milk are known as "complete" proteins because they contain all eight of the essential amino acids we need.

Dairy products are an important part of a modern diet because they not only provide complete protein but are also a source of calcium. However, they are most likely to be unobtainable in a survival situation. Calcium can also be derived from water so milk can be replaced with extra water.

BALANCING A SURVIVAL DIET

In a survival situation where no grains or dairy products are available, the "balanced" diet (*see box opposite*) needs to be adjusted to include 11–20 portions of vegetable or fruit and 4–6 portions of protein-rich food, such as meat and fish, per day. Grains should be included if the opportunity arises.

Clearly, such a diet can bore the taste buds rather quickly, so it is important to learn to identify as many

▲ *Meat can be the hardest food to come by in the wilderness, since you need some kind of tool or trap, but animals provide a lot of protein and are an essential food.*

edibles in the area as you can to create a more diverse diet. You should also seize every opportunity to collect seasonal items, such as fruits. When autumn arrives, spend as much time as possible gathering berries, for instance. Preserve them for winter by turning them into jams or drying them.

While you are gathering wild edibles, make a mental map of where you spot animals such as rabbits near their burrows. Consider where good trapping areas may lie, such as on an animal trail between a feeding and bedding ground and a water source. Just before dusk is a good time to locate them, or early in the morning.

▼ *Vegetables and fruits are most important in the wild, as they replace many of the foods we would normally eat.*

Edible plants

Since nearly three-quarters of your balanced diet in the wilderness will come from vegetables and fruit, your chances of survival will be improved by learning to recognize as many edible plants as possible. You also need to be able to recognize suitable plants at any time of the year, as many species look completely different in different seasons. For example, in a long-term survival situation you may be able to identify a tree that you know will bear fruit later in the year.

Some plants completely disappear in the winter except for the roots, which may provide essential nutrition when other foods are scarce. For this reason it can be important to locate particular plants while they are growing during the summer, or to recognize their likely habitat, so you can find the roots when you need them in the winter.

PLANT FOOD

Whenever you gather plants for food, whatever the species, keep the following points in mind:
- The plants should be clean and growing in a healthy looking area. Never collect plants close to roads, quarries and other disturbed areas.
- Never gather more than a third of a particular species in your area. You don't want the species to disappear, and you should keep some for real emergencies.
- When picking leaves and stems, try to find the youngest plants. In general they are easier to digest.
- Go for leaves that haven't been eaten away by other insects or animals. Always try to get the best quality food you can.
- Avoid accidentally gathering parts of other plants that are growing alongside those you are picking.
- Whatever plants you gather, eat them sparingly at first. People react differently to certain plants, and they may disagree with you.

TASTE TEST

Although about 80 per cent of plants are edible, and another small percentage are inedible but not poisonous, the remainder can be very dangerous. To avoid the toxic ones it is vital that you leave alone any plants you don't recognize. However, where there is no other option but starvation, you can do a taste test as a last resort.

Before you begin you should have eaten nothing in the previous eight hours. Divide up the plant so that the leaves, stem, roots, buds and flowers are separate, and test only one part of the plant at a time.

Start by smelling the first part of the plant: if it has a strong or acid odour, don't eat it.

Put the plant part against your skin for about 15 minutes (your elbow will do here). If there is no skin reaction, prepare it in the way you plan to cook it (boiling is a preferred method).

When the plant is cooked, place a small amount against your lip for a few minutes. If no itching or burning sensation occurs, place it under your tongue for about 15 minutes. If no

▶ *Doing a taste test is not recommended, but in an emergency it may be the only way to find edibles if your local knowledge is limited, and you will have to take the risk.*

▲ *Most people are aware of the tasty berries produced by plants such as blackberries and cranberries. However, other parts of the plants, such as the leaves, are also edible.*

burning or itching occurs, chew it well and keep it in your mouth for another 15 minutes. If there is still no irritation, you can swallow it.

Now you should wait for another eight hours to see if you still feel normal. If you start feeling sick or get an upset stomach, try to induce vomiting, and drink plenty of water. If

POISONOUS FUNGI

Fungi are rich in protein, high in vitamins, tasty and free to pick. There are over 1,000 edible species but you must only ever eat those you can definitely identify and know to be safe, as some contain deadly toxins, which can cause symptoms up to 14 hours after eating. It's a tough call when you're desperate for food but it's not worth death by liver failure.

Some poisonous species are easy to confuse with common edible mushrooms. A case in point is the yellow stainer, which will make you very ill, unlike its edible lookalike the horse mushroom (*Agaricus arvensis*). The yellow stainer colours yellow when pressed or cut, whereas the horse mushroom's cap keeps its natural buff colour. You should always make a positive identification before eating any fungus, rejecting any unfamiliar species, and all fungi should be cooked before eating.

crowded gills, brown bruises

inrolled margin

Brown roll-rim (*Paxillus involutus*)

olive or yellowish cap; white, unchanging gills

white, bag-like volva

Death cap (*Amanita phalloides*)

yellow bruise forms when touched or rubbed

Yellow stainer
(*Agaricus xanthodermus*)

Fly Agaric
(*Amanita muscaria*)

pure white, slightly pointed cap

white, bag-like volva

Destroying angel
(*Amanita virosa*)

all stays fine, prepare a little more for eating – you could try a quarter of a portion, for instance. Eat this and wait another eight hours. If there is still no adverse reaction, you can eat this part.

The problem with the test is that certain plants can make you seriously ill with just one leaf, while it is safe to eat others in small amounts, though they carry toxins that gather in your body,

making you ill after you have eaten a large amount over several days. This is why it is best not to use it unless you have absolutely no other option.

While you are learning, your first few meals may be a little bland, but as you gain experience and expand your plant knowledge, you will soon be able to create tasty and satisfying meals in your "wilderness kitchen".

▼ *Pick only the plant you mean to pick: it's easy to grab leaves of a neighbouring plant, which could be dangerous, by accident.*

▼ *Be as picky as you would be when buying vegetables in a shop. Pick only young fresh leaves, and leave the half-eaten ones.*

▼▲ *In temperate climates wild foods such as rowan berries (above) and blackberries (below) are abundant in summer and autumn.*

Wildlife food sources

There is hardly any animal that cannot be eaten. However, for safety reasons it is important always to cook meat and fish thoroughly when you are taking your food from the wild, since this will kill bacteria, parasites and any other harmful organisms residing in the meat.

FISH AND SHELLFISH

If you have the time and energy to make some simple fishing tools or traps (*see page 102*), and there is flowing water close at hand, then fishing is a perfect way to get easy food. Fish are often plentiful and all freshwater fish are edible.

If you are on the coast, look in tidal pools and wet sand for marine edibles. Rocks on beaches or reefs leading into deeper water often bear clinging shellfish. Shellfish must always be caught alive, and should be cooked and eaten straight away. Avoid eating mussels in tropical zones in winter as they can be poisonous, and don't collect any fish in polluted areas.

▶ *Though crab meat is delicious, it must be eaten as soon as the crab is caught, as it goes off very quickly.*

▶ *Steam, boil, or bake shellfish in their shells. They make very good stews in combination with greens.*

▼ *Fishing can be an excellent way to gather fresh food. Especially when you can build fish traps that can be left unattended, fishing can be done with a minimum of effort.*

SMALL MAMMALS

If fishing is not an option, then you may need to catch smaller animals such as squirrels and rabbits. Rabbits can be found throughout the world and are relatively easy to catch – a snare or trap (*see page 100*) outside a burrow or along a rabbit run is usually enough to catch one. If you can make some tools for hunting, such as a throwing stick (*see page 104*) you can get larger animals such as deer this way. The only thing to look out for when getting food from land mammals is the danger an animal

▲ *Snails can be eaten, as long as they are boiled or cooked thoroughly. They are full of calcium, magnesium and vitamin C.*

may pose if it is not hunted correctly, or when it is wounded. Nearly all mammals will fight if they are cornered or protecting their young.

Hunting involves a host of different wilderness skills, including tracking, stalking and camouflage, and these are covered on the following pages. Learn these skills because in a survival situation you won't have the luxury of a rifle or ready-made bow and arrows.

Although most animals can be eaten, not all of them will necessarily be tasty or easily digested. Try to go for young animals, since their meat is usually the most tender. The flesh of some animals, although edible, may have a strong smell that can make it unpalatable. Though you will want to avoid such animals when possible, you should not disregard them as a viable food source.

INSECTS

The same goes for insects. In general, insects carry about 70 per cent of their weight in protein, while regular meat normally consists of about 20 per cent protein. The downside of eating insects is that you have to gather a fair number to get the same amount of meat as you would from, say, a rabbit. However, large quantities of insects can be found

GUTTING AND FILLETING A FISH

1 Insert the point of a knife or a sharp stone into the anal vent and slit the fish up the belly to just behind the gills. Carefully remove the internal organs.

2 Cut through the flesh just below the gills to separate the head, then open out the body and work the flesh away from the bones using your fingers.

3 Pull the head and bones away from the flesh in one piece, severing the spine at the tail end. The bones and head can be used to make stock.

by looking under stones, or in places where a lot of insects live in colonies, such as in rotten wood or anthills.

The only insects that you should steer clear of are adults that sting or bite, hairy or brightly coloured insects, and caterpillars and insects that have a pungent odour. You should also avoid spiders and common disease carriers such as ticks, flies and mosquitoes.

The idea of eating insects is enough to turn most people's stomachs. The best way to eat any unappetizing creature is to cook them in a stew, and try to forget they are even there.

FORAGING FOR FOOD

Although you will certainly be making "normal" meals in your camp, you should try to use your energy efficiently and this may mean eating on the move, snacking on local edibles while you are finding materials for your shelter or tools. During the first few days, especially, it will be hard to make time to gather enough food for a proper meal – as long as you drink enough, you shouldn't worry about that. It is then best to feed by nibbling at nettles, berries and whatever else may be easy to find. Only when all

essential tasks have been taken care of should you take time to forage properly for food. If you have been prowling around the area for a few days, you should already have a good idea of where to go for what foods.

If you can source a regular supply of food, try to make your main meal around noon, when it is light enough to cook. In the evening, you can snack on leftovers or items that don't require cooking. Ordering your meals this way is also healthier for your body. A good meal in the morning will raise your energy levels, ready for the coming day.

▼ *Most frog species are edible, but avoid brightly coloured ones or those with a cross on their back. Most toads are poisonous.*

▼ *Worms may appear unappetizing, but nearly all are edible. Put them in clean water for a few minutes, then mix into a stew.*

▼ *Rodents such as squirrels are abundant and will probably be the main part of your meat diet until you fashion hunting tools.*

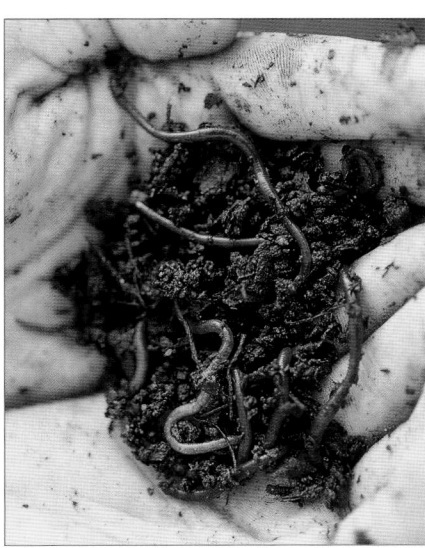

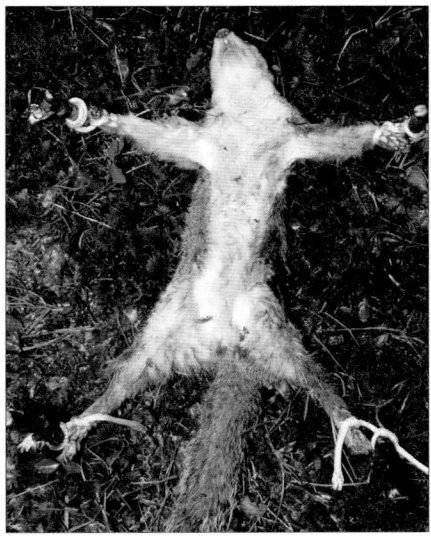

Tracking animals

When you start hunting animals for food the first thing you have to realize is that mammals and rodents – your potential meals – are not evenly spread about the whole wilderness. They gravitate close to where food, water and shelter are available. The middle of a dense forest, for instance, provides no water, light or food, so there will be few animals dwelling there. The edge of a forest is likely to provide food, water and shelter.

TRAILS AND RUNS
To find out which animals live in a particular area you must seek out their trails and runs. These are the most obvious signs of wildlife. Trails are used by many different species and generally lead towards water, food or shelter. Runs are smaller than trails, and are used by a particular animal species. They connect the trails with the shelter areas and sometimes connect water and food areas to the trails as well. Runs often change location, and sometimes a run becomes a trail over time. You can often guess by the width of the run who travels there.

SLEEPING AND FEEDING AREAS
The other signs that can help you establish your "virtual map" of animal life are sleeping, resting and feeding areas. Sleeping areas differ according to

▲ *A deer lie, or sleeping area, will be used for many nights, until the season changes or the area is threatened repeatedly.*

▼ *Clues such as these scrape marks on a mossy log help you to build a "virtual map" of an area's animal life.*

species. Many small animals sleep in burrows, while larger animals often sleep out in the open. If a sleeping area is out in the open you can usually detect the outline of the animal's body on the ground. These areas are often bordered by scrub that is dense enough to stop predators walking through, though not so dense that the animal can't look through the brush. They will have three or more escape routes.

Resting areas have less cover and generally offer animals a good view of their surroundings. They are often found near feeding and watering areas and are infrequently used.

Feeding areas are also likely to be different for different species, but they are often grassy areas with a good variety of plants.

IDENTIFYING SPECIES
Once you have these signs mapped out, you can try to find smaller signs to narrow down the species that live in the landscape. By looking more closely you can often find scat throughout the trails, runs, resting areas and even feeding areas. If there are hoofed animals, you can often find exposed roots and branches on the ground with scrape marks all over them. In feeding areas, you can observe how the grass and other plants are eaten. Rabbits, for instance, neatly scissor through grass,

whereas hoofed animals rip it up, creating jagged breaks. In resting and sleeping areas you will no doubt find hairs belonging to the residents.

Next, you can look for actual animal footprints, narrowing certain runs and feeding areas down even further. Quite often, you won't actually find such clear prints as those shown opposite, but more of an outline. The tracks that you do find, whether they are outlines (compression marks) or full prints, should be combined with all the other information you have found on the trail or run, to give you a clear picture of which animal uses it.

THE COUP DE GRACE

When hunting you should always aim to kill with the first strike. If the animal is only wounded, once you've found it you need to finish it off swiftly. For an animal that's still dangerous, you will probably want to use your weapon again, but the most efficient method if the creature is safe to touch is to slit its throat either side of the windpipe. The best way to put a bird or small animal out of its misery is to break its neck by pulling the head away from the body with a sharp twist.

IDENTIFYING ANIMAL FOOTPRINTS

Being able to read animal footprints is a great survival skill. Footprints reveal the identity of an animal, the direction in which it was heading and when it last used the track – all crucial information when hunting animals for food or keeping out of the way of animals such as bears or wild cats.

▲ *Grey fox: front foot 4 x 3.5cm/1⁵/8 x 1³/8in, rear foot 3.8 x 3.2cm /1¹/2 x 1¹/4in.*

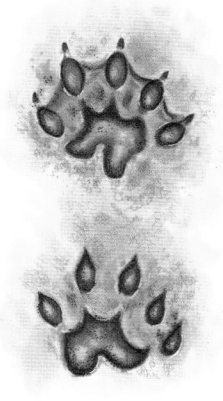

▲ *Otter: front foot 6.7 x 7.5cm/2⁵/8 x 3in, rear foot 7.3 x 8cm /2⁷/8 x 3¹/8in.*

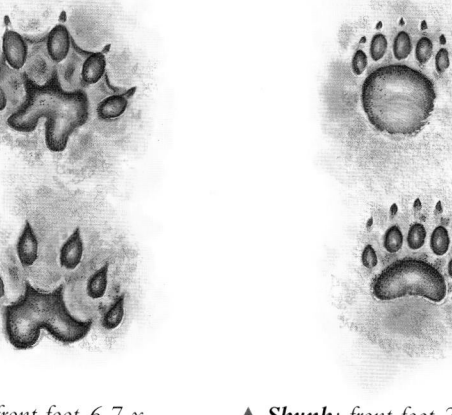

▲ *Skunk: front foot 2.2 x 2.8cm/⁷/8 x 1¹/8in, rear foot 3.8 x 3.8cm /1¹/2 x 1¹/2in.*

▲ *Marten: front foot 4.5 x 4.5cm/1³/4 x 1³/4in, rear foot 3.5 x 4cm /1³/8 x 1⁵/8in.*

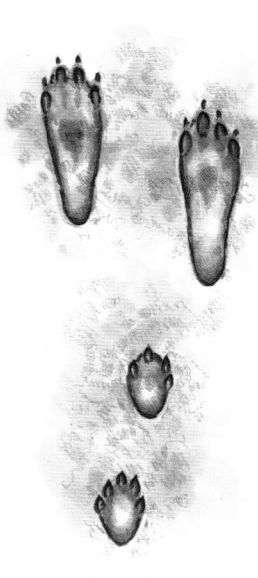

▲ *Hare: front foot 3.8 x 2.8cm /1¹/2 x 1¹/8in, rear foot 7.5 x 5cm/3 x 2in.*

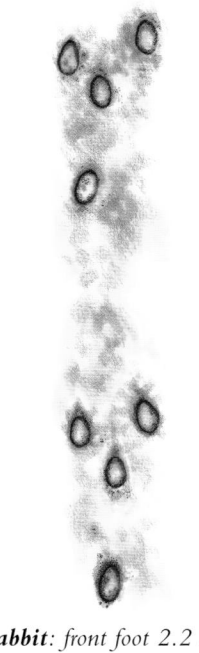

▲ *Rabbit: front foot 2.2 x 1.5cm/⁷/8 x⁵/8in, rear foot 7 x 2.8cm/2³/4 x 1¹/8in.*

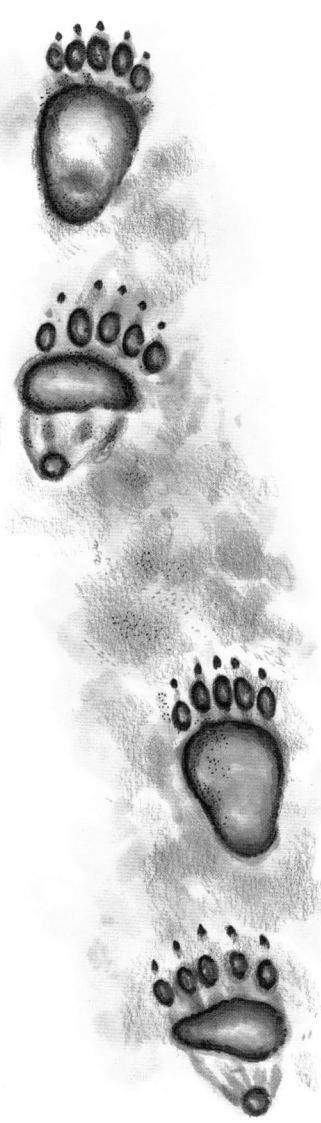

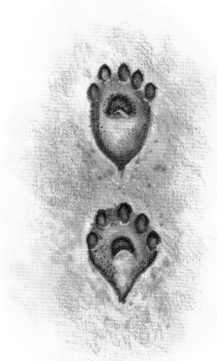

▲ *Weasel: front foot 2.8 x 1.2cm/1¹/8 x ¹/2in, rear foot 3.8 x 2cm /1¹/2 x ³/4in.*

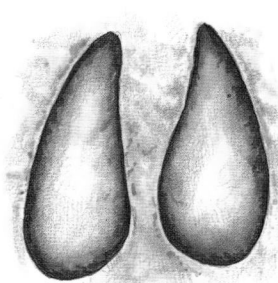

▲ *White tail deer: (one foot shown) front foot 7.5 x 4.7cm/3 x 1⁷/8in, rear foot 6.7 x 3.8cm/2⁵/8 x 1¹/2in.*

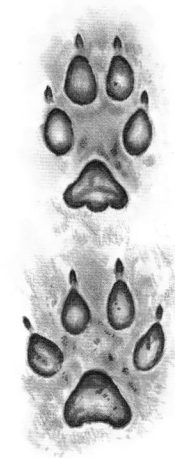

▲ *Grey wolf: front foot 12 x 10.8cm/4³/4 x 4¹/4in, rear foot 11.5 x 10.5cm /4¹/2 x 4¹/8in.*

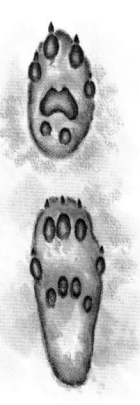

▲ *Grey squirrel: front foot 5 x 3.5cm/2 x 1³/8in, rear foot 6.7 x 3.2cm /2⁵/8 x 1¹/4in.*

▲ *Grizzly bear: front foot 14 x 12.5cm/5¹/2 x 5in, rear foot 25 x 14cm /10 x 5¹/2in.*

Stalking animals

In order to get close enough to animals to hunt them, you will have to learn some techniques that enable you to catch them unawares. You won't have a high-powered rifle but a survival bow or throwing stick, and in order to get close enough to kill accurately with one of these, you'll need to approach to within 10–15m/33–50ft. This means you'll need to be able to move quietly and invisibly.

CREEPING LIKE A FOX
First of all, it is important to slow down and become more aware of your surroundings. You can achieve part of that by adopting the "fox walk".

The fox walk is a stalking style that would have been used by our ancestors. The idea is to take each step by leaving your weight on your standing leg, while you feel the ground with your free foot before putting it down. To do this, simply roll your foot from the outside of the foot to the inside, feeling what is beneath your sole. Once you are sure there is nothing sharp or noisy below your foot, you can put it down and move your weight on to your front leg. If there is anything painful or noisy

on the ground, lift the foot back up without putting your weight on it, and try another spot nearby. You need to be just as careful when lifting your feet as when putting them down to avoid cracking twigs or moving stones.

You will find that this method of walking is certainly very slow, but the main advantages are that you don't need to take your eyes off your surroundings to look down at the ground, it is very quiet, and you appear less of a threat to other animals because you are moving so slowly.

WIDE-ANGLED VISION
Animals usually see us before we see them. One reason for this is that we are so noisy and move quite fast. However, the other reason is that animals view their surroundings in a different way. Animals use wide-angled vision and this enables them to see all the movement around them.

The way we see the world is in a series of focused views. We take snapshots of our environment. This means there is a lot we never see at all, because we are focused on something else. However, we also have the ability

▲ *The throwing stick (*see page 104*) has the advantage that it is easy to pick up off the ground whenever you enter a survival situation. Carry it with you wherever you go in case you come across an animal that has not noticed you.*

to use our eyes in a less focused way, the way animals do. With practice you should be able to see all the movement that goes on around you, although everything will appear slightly blurred.

THE FOX WALK

1 Carefully lift the foot to be moved off the ground. Keep your balance on the leg that is taking your weight.

2 Move your free foot forward and gently bring it down, rolling it from the outside in over the ground.

3 If the ground is clear, lower your foot and shift your weight forward. Repeat, moving in a slow, fluid motion.

PRACTISING WIDE-ANGLED VISION

1 To learn to see all around you, go to a wide field or into a forest. Hold your hands out in front of you with your fingers pointing in, 30cm/1ft apart.

2 Look at both hands, but also at everything in between them. Slowly move your arms out to your sides, still looking at everything between them.

3 When your hands are at your sides wiggle your fingers, and you should see your hands again. While keeping this "view" slowly drop your hands.

4 Still in the same frame of vision, stretch out your arms again in front of you, but this time hold one hand below the other.

5 Move your arms apart again, one arm up and the other down, while seeing everything in between until you lose sight of your hands.

6 When you drop your arms, you should have a field of view about 180 degrees wide and 80 degrees high. You will instantly spot any movement.

A lot of people, when learning this technique, end up wandering around like zombies because they are trying so hard to retain their wide-angled vision.

Don't forget to move your head around – by doing this you can increase your total angle of view to 360 degrees. so you miss nothing. Then, as soon as you see some interesting movement, focus on it. If it turns out to be nothing of interest, go back into wide-angled vision and move on.

You will see a lot more wildlife on your walks through the wilderness this way, since every little movement will catch your eye.

A NEW WAY OF LISTENING

You can extend your listening skills in the same way as your vision. Follow the steps of the wide-angled vision practice in your head, but use your ears to try to hear everything, rather than just the most obvious sounds.

EXPERIENCING YOUR SURROUNDINGS

These techniques will make you far more aware of your surroundings, and will make it easier for you to spot any wildlife in the area. There is one more layer of awareness you can add to the three already discussed – feeling.

Become aware of the wind caressing your body, feel the muscles move in your legs. Feel the rain falling on your skin and clothes. When you put all these skills together successfully, you will become more attuned to your environment. Rather than just being aware, you will become part of your surroundings, allowing you to sense an animal almost before you see it.

Moving around like this in the wilderness will enable you to get much closer to the local wildlife. To get close enough to hunt them, however, you will need a few more skills: the skills of stalking and camouflage.

STALKING SLOWLY

The basic stalking technique is nearly the same as the fox walk – you feel the ground before you put your weight on it. This time, however, it is much slower. So slow in fact, that it is not noticeable that you are moving at all. An average step would take you about a minute. You might even try to disguise any further movement by moving only when your environment is "moving" – when leaves are rustling in the wind or trees are swaying back and forth. Not only does this method hide your movement, it may also cover up any sounds you make inadvertently. Try to keep your hands either in front of you or behind you to help break up the familiar human shape. In front is generally easier because you can hold your weapon there or use your hands to help lift up your leg.

The two stalks shown below are mainly used when there is plenty of concealing brush between you and the animal. A third method involves lying on the ground on your belly, with your hands beside your shoulders. Lift yourself about 10cm/4in off the ground on your toes and hands and move forward. Then slowly lower your body back down to the ground, move your hands and toes forward, and repeat the action. Any additional movements, such as standing, sitting, getting your weapon ready or swatting a fly, need to be done extremely slowly.

KEEPING YOUR BALANCE

A big problem when moving very slowly is balance. To avoid wobbling, bend your knees slightly while remaining upright. This enables you to keep a tight check on your balance. If you do lose it, try to correct it below the hip. If you correct with your upper body, the movement will surely alert any animals nearby.

STALKING ON ALL FOURS

1 Set out on all fours. Use your hands to feel for noisy material below you.

2 Place your knee exactly on the spot where you have just removed your hand.

3 Use this method to creep up when there is plenty of low brush.

MOVING SILENTLY

1 Make sure that any clothes you are wearing are well tucked in.

2 Ensure your body does not hook into any foliage.

3 Toes will catch in brush if you don't curl them when lifting your feet.

CAMOUFLAGE FOR STALKING

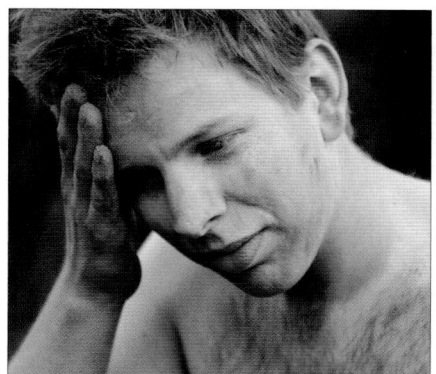

1 Rub white ash, from a cold campfire, into your skin to dull its shine. This will also help to de-scent you.

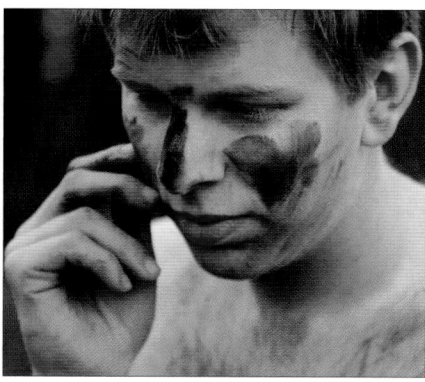

2 Apply charcoal on areas that would normally not be shadowed. Make the "pattern" as random as possible.

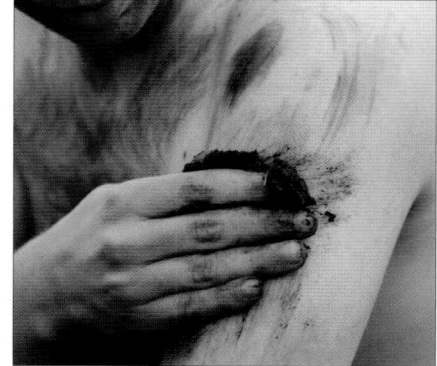

3 Break up your outline further using mud, again creating a random pattern of light and shade.

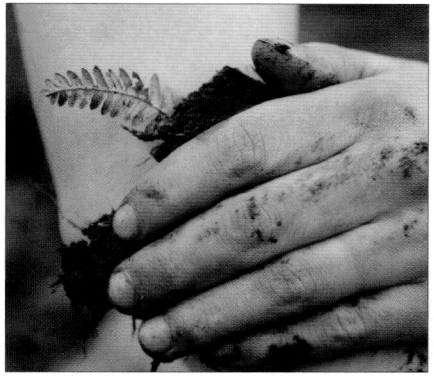

4 Use leaves growing in the area to "stamp" mud on to your skin.

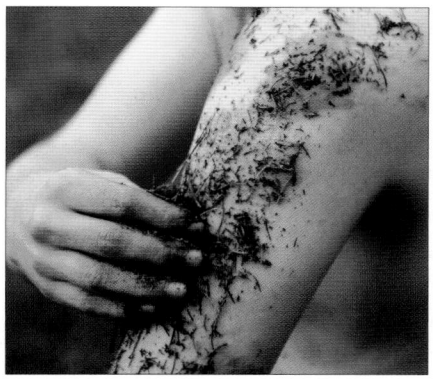

5 Sprinkle forest debris over the muddy patches while they are still sticky.

6 Try to cultivate a "quiet mind" as you get really close to your prey.

USING CAMOUFLAGE

Camouflage is not about hiding, it is about being "invisible" right out in the open, so you can approach your quarry. If you are hiding behind a tree, it will be hard to launch an arrow or a throwing stick at an animal.

There are two simple ways to camouflage yourself. One is to rub white wood ash all over your body and clothes, then use charcoal to break up your appearance. Apply it to areas that would normally be light, such as right below your eyes and on the bridge of your nose. Use mud to paint different colours on your body. You should finish by rolling through some forest debris to "fluff up" your appearance, breaking your shape up even further. Because you have covered yourself in wood ash, your smell will also be well camouflaged. The second method is a

lot easier. You simply roll in the mud, then in forest litter. Because your smell may not be adequately covered using this method, you may want to rub in some smelly plants. Use only species that grow in the area where you intend to hunt. If you use different plants your smell will still be obvious.

If you camouflage properly and apply good stalking and awareness, you should get almost within touching distance of most animals. To get really close, however, it is important to quieten your mind as well. Animals are very good at picking up your "vibe".

Mammals do not see colours, so even without camouflage you should be able to get close enough for a good shot, provided the animal doesn't smell you. That is, if there are no birds around. Birds do see colour, and birds are also the sentries of the wilderness.

▲ *It is important not to muddy yourself completely, as you will then be making the shape of your body more apparent. Instead, try to create a random pattern.*

Setting animal traps

Before you learn how to set traps, you need to know that it is illegal in most parts of the world to do this unless your life depends on it. This is because a trap can kill an endangered animal as easily as the most abundant species, not to mention the harm it could cause to bigger animals or even to humans.

The traps described here are simple to make, can be used in most situations and are designed to kill quickly and cleanly. There are many types of traps, but these are the most effective. Once you have set a trap, test it to make sure that you will not make an animal suffer unnecessarily. There is no excuse for an animal to limp away from a deadfall or choke to death on a snare.

When setting traps, try to disturb the area as little as possible so as not to warn any animals that something is up. You should also set your traps far apart, because when one is triggered, all animals in the vicinity will go on high alert. Make sure they are well camouflaged by using wood ash, mud and strong-smelling local plants.

THE FIGURE-4 DEADFALL TRAP
This trap is intended mainly for feeding areas. It is called a "deadfall" trap because it works on the principle that a heavy weight will fall on the head of the animal when it nibbles on the food you place on the bait stick.

The simple trap described here is made of three sticks and looks like a figure 4 when set up. The arrangement is kept in place by the weight, but will collapse when the baited end of the horizontal stick is pushed by the animal. The weight of the deadfall should be about twice the weight of the animal you are trying to catch –

enough to kill it, but not so heavy that the animal will be completely squashed. The trap shown below would be an appropriate size to kill a rabbit.

You can make the trap more effective by placing an "anvil" such as a flat stone underneath. Make sure that the weight does not extend over the upright stick. If it does, it may fall on top of the stick rather than the animal.

Bait the trap with the plant that, from your observation, the intended victim seems to enjoy most. Be wary of importing a plant for bait, as animals may be suspicious of a plant that does not naturally occur in the area.

To force the animal to come in from the right direction, so that it pushes the stick when it eats the bait, you can build some sort of fence around the structure, though it must look natural and not arouse suspicion.

SETTING A FIGURE-4 DEADFALL TRAP

1 Square off the central part of the vertical stick and carve the tip to a flat "screwdriver" shape.

2 Near the end of the horizontal (bait) stick carve an upward-pointing notch to take the end of the diagonal stick.

3 Carve a slot to hold the bait stick against the squared-off section of the upright, at 90 degrees from the notch.

4 Carve a notch in the diagonal stick to take the top of the upright and sharpen the end to fit in the bait stick.

5 To set the trap, apply pressure on the diagonal stick while using the other hand to put the notches into place.

6 Lean a weight (such as a log or rock) on top of the diagonal stick and bait the free end of the horizontal stick.

SETTING A TWO-HOOK SNARE TRAP

1 Carve a notch near the top of a stick and plant it securely in the ground.

2 The second stick, also notched, will be tied to a flexible branch overhead.

3 The loop the animal will walk into is also tied to the second stick.

4 Tie the second stick to the branch and hook the notches together. The fit should be secure but easy to set off.

5 Make sure the loop will slip easily and is the right size to fit over the animal's head as it walks through.

6 Rest the open loop on sticks or blades of strong grass, about two to four fingers' width above the ground.

THE TWO-HOOK SNARE TRAP

This snare trap is generally used on animal runs, though you can adapt it for use in feeding areas as well. It is important to ensure that the snare is strong enough to break the animal's neck and lift it high enough off the ground to prevent other animals getting at it before you do.

The trap consists of two sticks, each notched so they will hook into each other. One of the hooked sticks is planted firmly in the ground, while the other is tied with a length of cordage to a strong, flexible sapling or branch, which keeps the hooks together under tension. A slipknot loop is tied on to the hook attached to the string and placed over the run so that an animal walking into it will trigger the trap and be lifted up by the branch.

The height of the loop should be such that the animal will walk straight in. For a rabbit, for example, the correct height would be about a hand's width above the ground, while the loop should be about 12.5cm/5in in diameter. By varying the depth of the notches, you can change the sensitivity of the trap, depending on the size of the animal you are trying to catch. What you want to avoid is subjecting the animal to a slow death, so it's important to get the settings right.

Make sure you don't use green wood, since the two branches could fuse together – they can even freeze together during the night. You can increase the tension on the trap by using a number of saplings or branches in a row to compound their power. If there are no flexible branches near the run, you can make a lever and fulcrum by pounding a Y-shaped stick into the ground and tying a long branch over the top. Tie the string to one end of the lever and add a heavy weight to the other.

▼ *A lever and fulcrum can be made from sticks to support the two-hook snare trap when there is no suitable branch nearby.*

▼ *The two-hook trap can be adapted for fish by replacing the noose with fishing line. It must raise the fish well out of the water.*

Fishing techniques

If you are near water, fishing is an excellent way to obtain high-protein food. Fish can be netted, hooked, speared or snared, or even caught by hand. Setting a trap in a stream allows you to get on with other tasks while waiting for the fish to swim into it.

TRAPPING FISH

One of the easiest ways to catch fish is with a snare such as the two-hook trap described on page 101. You can adapt this by using fishing line in place of a noose, arranging it so that the fish is pulled well out of the water.

Another good method is to make a fish pen (*see below*): erect a curved fence to create an enclosure with only one opening facing upriver, then construct a funnel leading into the opening. If the stream is fast-flowing this may be enough to catch fish. In slower water, weave in flexible twigs so that they stick out towards the trap entrance. The sticks will bend aside as a fish swims in, but not when it tries to swim back out again. You can vary the size of fish the trap catches by adjusting the gaps between the fence poles.

MAKING A FISH SPEAR

If you want to catch larger fish and have enough time on your hands to be selective, making a fishing spear is the best option. The spear is made in two parts: a two-pronged spearhead is fitted into a notch in the end of a long, straight shaft. The reason for this is that if you miss the fish and hit the bottom of the stream, the spearhead will simply come out of the notch, whereas if the spear were made in one piece the prongs might break. The spearhead is loosely tied to the shaft so that it can be retrieved if it comes apart.

It is best to use green wood to make the spearhead as it has flexibility and will split without breaking. The stick should be completely straight and about 2.5cm/1in thick. It must be tightly wrapped with cord to stop it splitting too far, and the cord should be made of plant fibre, as sinew will loosen when it is immersed in water.

The prongs of the spear need to be sharp but strong, so that they will stand up to striking stones on the stream bed. On the inner surfaces of the prongs you will need to cut two small "shelves" to support barbs so that once speared the fish can't escape. The best materials for the barbs are sharp stones such as flint flakes or slivers of very hard wood. You can also easily make barbs from the bones of other animals. The barbs must be tied on tightly using fine cordage. If you know how to make pitch glue (*see page 128*) use it to make the joints between the barbs and wood more secure.

▲ *Spearing a fish requires clear water to spot your prey, stealth in stalking the fish then speed and accuracy in jabbing the spear.*

FISHING WITH A SPEAR

Look for a likely fishing spot – it could be on the outside of bends if it's cool, under shade on a hot, sunny day, in white water, or in shallows. Sit absolutely still, with the tip of the spear in the water, ready to stab a fish when it appears, or try stalking your prey. You'll need to experiment with different spots, times and styles until you are successful.

MAKING A FISH PEN

1 Erect a half-circle of sticks in fast-flowing water where fish are present, making sure the water flows into the opening in the "fence".

2 Create a funnel by planting more sticks to make two fences out to both banks of the stream, leaving a small opening where the fish can swim in.

3 In slower streams, weave some branches through the fences pointing towards the trap, so that the fish can swim in but not back out again.

MAKING A FISHING SPEAR

1 Find a straight stick about 30cm/1ft long and 2.5cm/1in in diameter and clean off any side-branches.

2 Wrap a length of cord made from plant fibre tightly around the central part of the stick.

3 Using a sharp stone, carefully split the stick. The binding will stop the split going further than the centre.

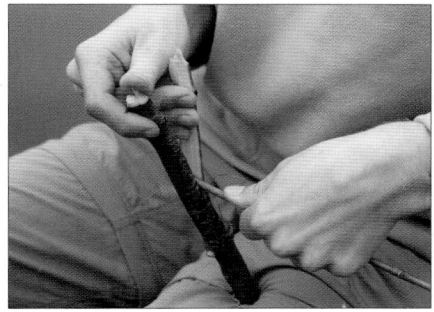

4 Wedge a small twig as far into the centre as possible to push the two "prongs" apart by 5–7.5cm/2–3in.

5 Use more cord to tie the wedge in place, to stop it popping out of the spear when the wood dries a little.

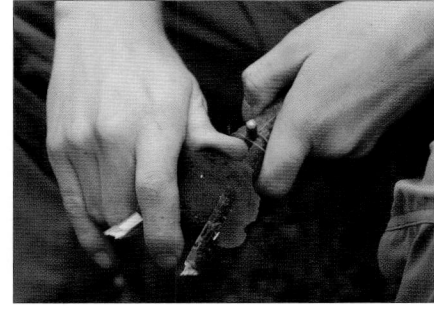

6 Using a knife or a sharp stone, carve the two prongs into long but sturdy points.

7 Carve a small "shelf" on the inside of each prong to support the barbs.

8 Use flint to produce two sharp flakes about 2.5cm/1in long for the barbs.

9 Using fine cordage, tie the barbs into place on the prongs.

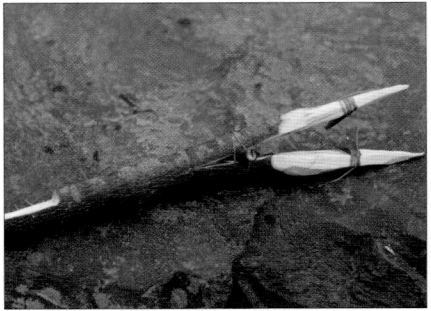

10 Carve the other end of the spearhead into a flat plank shape. This will fit into a notch in the spear shaft.

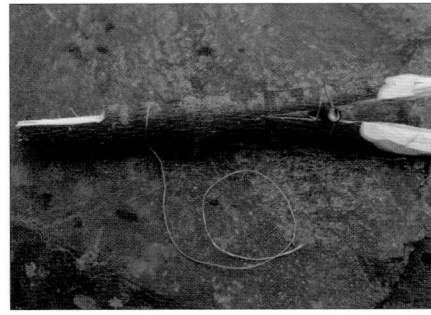

11 Tie a length of string to the spearhead and make a noose on the free end to tie around the spear shaft.

12 Carve a notch in the end of a straight pole 3–3.5m/9–12ft long and fit the spearhead on to the shaft.

Making and using a throwing stick

The first hunting tool you are likely to make and use in the wilderness is a throwing stick, which can be any sturdy stick you can find. It needs to be about 5–7.5cm/2–3in in diameter and about 60cm/2ft long. It can also be made into a quieter, faster weapon by carving the central section in the shape of a wing. You can even carve a non-returning boomerang, which may be accurately thrown over more than 100m/33yd. The principles are the same.

The throwing stick is mainly a tool for the opportunistic hunter. As soon as you are in a situation where food needs to be provided, you can simply pick up a suitable stick and carry it about with you wherever you go. It will be there when a curious animal pokes its head out of the bushes right in front of you. This way of hunting is particularly effective if you move around using the fox walk and wide-angled vision, as described on pages 96 and 97.

THROWING THE STICK

There are two common ways of throwing the throwing stick. The first method is overarm. Though there is less chance of hitting the animal, because the killing zone is only about 7.5cm/3in wide, this technique is very useful when there are many trees between you and the animal, or when you have to deal with high grass that

▲ *A throwing stick should be held so the butt end sits in the palm of your hand. It should not extend past your hand, as this could cause the stick to injure you, or the throw to go off course.*

would obstruct an underarm throw. One tip to remember is to give a flick with your wrist as you release the stick to give it extra revolutions, increasing the chance of hitting the target.

The second method is the underarm throw. The stick is held with its end in the hand in the same way as before.

▲ *Placing your thumb over the end of the stick ensures that it stays in the right spot in your hand. By holding the thumb like this, you can also achieve a throw in which the stick spins a lot while in the air.*

This time, however, you are standing sideways and the stick rotates horizontally through the air. This gives you a much better chance of killing the animal because the killing zone is about 60cm/2ft wide, but you can use it only when there is no grass or shrub to block the throw.

MAKING A THROWING STICK

1 Shaping the stick reduces the noise it makes in the air, and makes it fly faster. Find a sturdy but flexible piece of wood (yew in this instance).

2 Carve two sides of the stick, working it down to a wing-like shape. Try to orient any bend along the wing, so it does not affect the flight of the stick.

3 Leave more wood at the ends to provide some extra weight and so that you can easily sharpen the ends without the stick getting too weak.

USING A THROWING STICK OVERARM

1 If you are right-handed, place your left foot forward and hold the stick over your shoulder. Face the target.

2 You can use your elbow to aim roughly at your target. Start to throw the stick forward over your shoulder.

3 Just as you release the stick, give it a little flick with your wrist to produce extra revolutions in its flight.

USING A THROWING STICK UNDERARM

1 Stand sideways to the target, holding the stick at waist level.

2 Bring the stick behind you as you move your body forward.

3 Sink through your knees, resting your non-throwing hand on one knee.

4 Start to throw your hip into the throw as you crouch down.

5 Use your whole body to provide the power for the throw.

6 Flick your wrist just as you release the stick to give it spin.

Skinning and butchering an animal

Once you have managed to trap and dispatch an animal, it is important to hang and skin it as soon as possible. If the skin is left on for too long, the heat inside will spoil the meat rapidly. The internal organs should also be removed; they deteriorate quickly and any spillage of their contents will contaminate the meat.

If you are dealing with a large animal, such as a deer, hang it from a horizontal pole by its front legs and neck. If it is a small animal, such as a rabbit, lay it out on its back and tie all four legs to stakes so it is spread-eagled.

SKINNING THE ANIMAL

After making a small initial cut at the breastbone, insert your fingers to open it out so that there is no danger of puncturing the gut: from now on you can make sure your knife does not cut anything but skin. Push down under the skin with your fingers to create a

▼ If you are in the wilderness for a long period, a deer provides not only good meat but also buckskin to make warm clothes.

gap before cutting with your tool. Your cut should go all the way from the head to the reproductive organs.

With a large animal you should complete the skinning process before cutting into the flesh. If you have a small animal you can continue with the butchering, but if you decide to skin it fully now, make sure you are working on as clean a surface as you can prepare: it's amazing how forest debris always manages to get on to the carcass.

To continue the skinning, cut from the initial incision all the way up each leg, as far as you can go. Then finish off by cutting around the reproductive organs and the neck and by carefully cutting around the legs. (The leg tendons, or sinews, can be used in many ways. If you want to keep them, be very careful that you don't sever them when cutting around the legs.) With all cuts complete you can take off the skin. If the animal is spread-eagled, it is best to untie the legs at this point.

Try to avoid using your knife. In fact it is very easy to remove the skin entirely without using a knife, and this will prevent accidental cuts in the skin. If you don't use a knife, there will also be a lot less fat left on the skin, which will need to be removed if you intend to tan the hide. The easiest way is to pull the skin away from the animal with one hand, while you work the fingers of the other hand between the muscles and the skin.

BUTCHERING THE ANIMAL

Once the skin is removed you are ready for the next stage in the process. Carefully cut through the abdominal muscles, starting again at the breastbone. Make sure you do not puncture any internal organs at this point as this would spoil the meat.

Make this cut all the way to the reproductive organs. Now, you need to cut around the reproductive organs and the anus. This can be hard because the hips will be in the way. If you cut any tubes going to the reproductive organs or the anus, tie them off so they won't

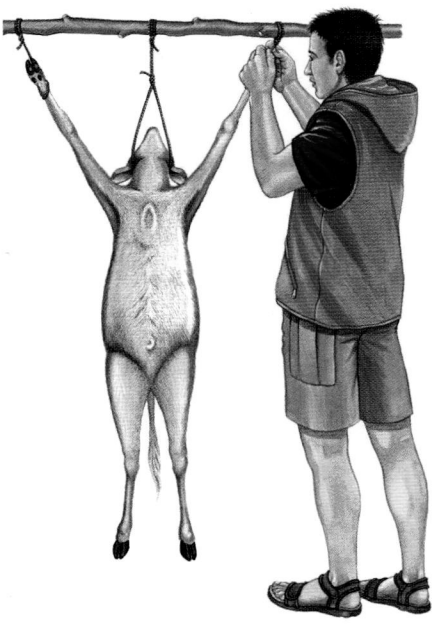

▲ Hang a large animal by its front legs and head so that when the innards are removed they fall between the legs, minimizing the danger of contaminating the meat.

leak into the meat. Now extend your cut all the way up to the windpipe. Once you reach it, cut through the windpipe and the gullet. If your animal is hanging by the front legs most of the internal organs should now fall out.

Now you can cut out the edible organs – the heart, liver, kidneys and lungs – and store them separately to avoid cross-contamination. Be careful not to puncture the gall bladder when removing the liver, as anything in contact with the gall will be spoiled.

WARNING

Ideally you should wear protective gloves when working with dead animals, as it is very easy to pick up an infection if bacteria from the meat get into small grazes or cuts on your hands. If you cannot get any kind of protection for your hands, try to make sure they are free of wounds and wash them at regular intervals, with soap or a disinfectant if possible.

HOW TO SKIN A DEER

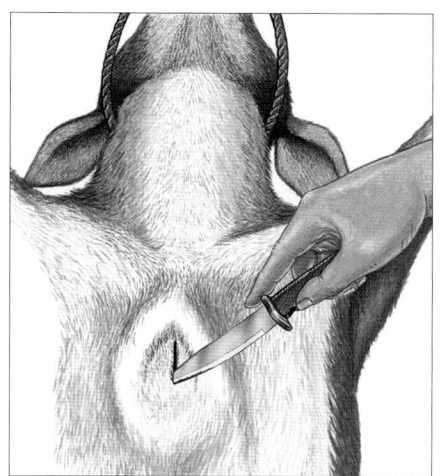

1 Start skinning by making a small, careful incision right over the breastbone to avoid piercing the gut.

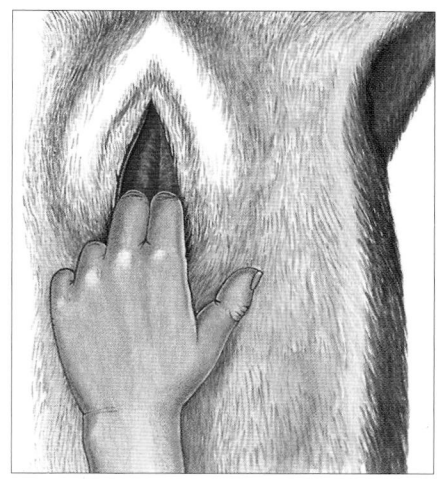

2 Insert two fingers, pointing down, into the incision to widen it and work the skin away from the flesh.

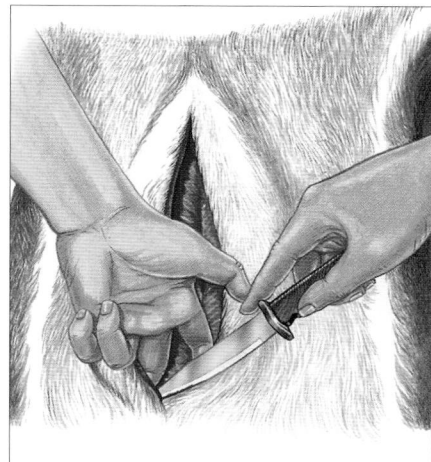

3 Insert your knife or cutting tool between your fingers, and slowly make your way down, cutting only the skin.

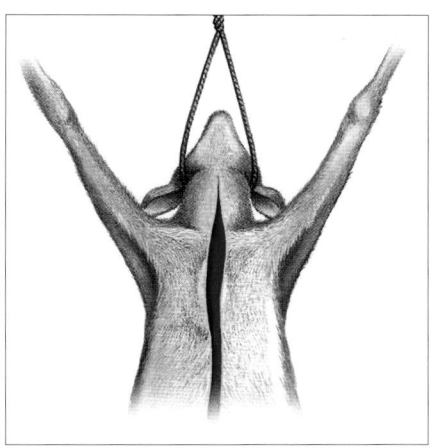

4 Stop at the reproductive organs, then do the same working upwards to the neck, starting from the initial cut.

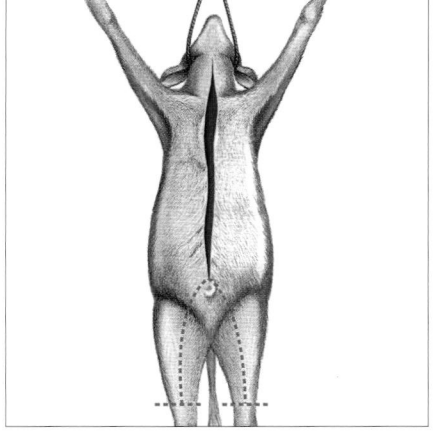

5 Cut through the skin around the hind legs, then cut down the fronts of the legs from the original incision.

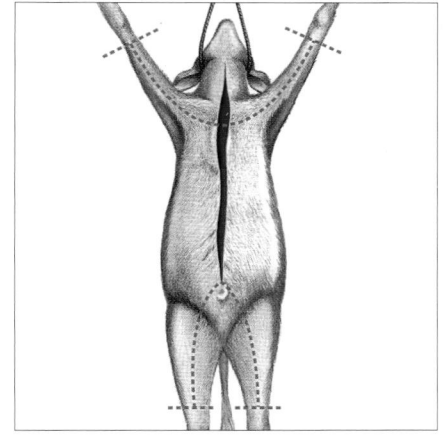

6 Do the same with the forelegs, cutting around the "wrists" and connecting these with the initial cut.

Check the whole carcass carefully for discoloration and other signs of spoilage. While you are working, you may find that a glaze seems to form over the meat. This is perfectly normal, and will even help to preserve it.

If you have not yet skinned a small animal, do so now. Otherwise, remove the legs and head and cook it as it is. For a larger animal, it is easier to cut off the meat while the carcass is hanging. Try to remove all the meat. Some parts, such as the ribs, have very little flesh, so it may be easier to cut the muscle between the ribs, break off the bones and fry them or put the whole ribs in a stew.

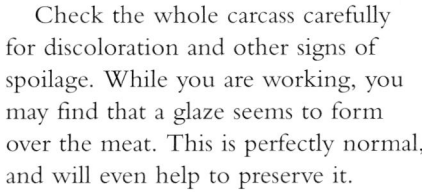

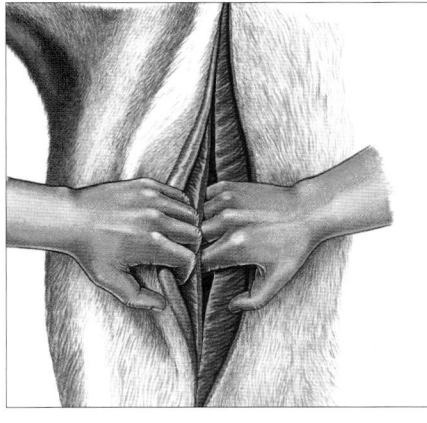

7 After cutting around the reproductive organs, anus and neck, you can pull off the skin. Next, deepen the cut on the breastbone until you hit bone.

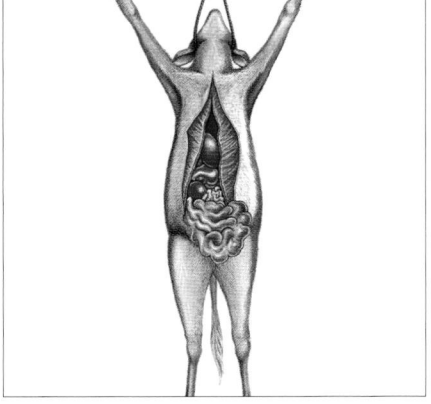

8 Follow the initial cut to open the body. Remove the edible organs and sever the windpipe, gullet and other connecting tubes to free the innards.

Preserving meat and other animal products

No part of an animal you have killed should be discarded. As well as providing fresh meat, the flesh of a large animal can be preserved for future meals, and the non–edible parts can be used to make clothes and tools.

USEFUL BODY PARTS

The intestines, stomach and bladder should be cleaned out immediately after butchering the animal, as they have many uses. The bundle of tendons should be carefully removed from each leg. Use a knife to open the bundle lengthways, then spread it out to dry.

The head of the animal contains lots of goodies. The liquid in the eyes makes a strong glue when mixed with resin. The tongue can be skinned and kept as meat. Keep the rest of the head intact for now. The brain can be eaten while fresh (within a day), but is better kept for tanning the hide later on.

Hooves should be kept as they can be boiled to make a strong glue. Skim the water they are boiling in to collect neatsfoot oil, used for softening hide.

DRYING MEAT

The easiest way to dry meat is in the sun or near a fire, but don't leave the meat too close to the fire, or it will fry, not dry. With bigger pieces of meat, you should remove any fat, which will go off quickly, then cut it into slices no

▲ *Antlers (if there are any) can be used for flint-knapping and other skills.*

▲ *The lower jaws of deer make great saws, though the teeth may loosen after a while.*

▲ *Clean and keep all animal bones because many of them can be made into tools.*

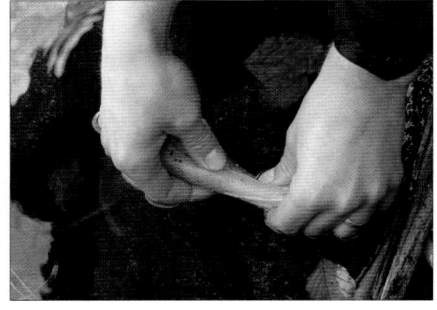

▲ *Either rinse animal bones well or bury them for a few weeks to clean them.*

more than 3mm/¹/₈in thick. Then you can hang these strips up around a fire or in the hot sun to dry. The meat must be fully dry before you store it. If it crumbles in your hands it may be a little too dry, but make sure that when

you bend the pieces of meat they crack. If they just bend without cracking, they are still too moist.

You can grind up this dried meat and store it for a long time in the intestines you cleaned earlier.

PRESERVING MEAT ON A TRIPOD

1 Find three poles about 120cm/4ft long and tie them together by wrapping cord loosely around the tops, then binding it tightly between them.

2 Place a number of horizontal poles around the frame you have made and bind them to the tripod at suitable heights to dry your strips of meat.

3 Cut the meat into strips as thin as you can get them. Place the tripod over the fire, making sure that the meat is not so close it cooks instead of drying.

Making buckskin for clothes

There is no material better suited to the outdoors than tanned buckskin. If you are to survive a long-term emergency, you may need to know how to make buckskin from animal hides so that you can make warm, durable clothing.

PREPARING THE HIDE

To start the process, make a framework that is about one and a half times larger all round than the hide you are going to treat. The framework should be strong and sturdy as the hide will be stretched on it. Two neighbouring trees make ideal verticals for the frame, and for the horizontals you can lash two strong poles across them.

Punch holes all round the hide so that you can tie it to the frame, but don't make them too close to the edge

as the cords will tear through the hide when it is stretched. Use strong cord for this, and check that the hide is taut.

You will need a sharp tool such as a knife or a sharp flake of stone to scrape the hide. Hold the tool so that the edge is at a right angle to the hide and draw it down while pressing into the surface. Make sure you are always scraping when pressing into the hide: if you stop the movement of the blade while maintaining pressure, you may punch through the hide.

SCRAPING

The purpose of scraping is to remove all the fat and the innermost layer of skin called the subcutaneous tissue (a layer of fat and connective tissue that houses larger blood vessels and nerves). Once the underside of the hide is

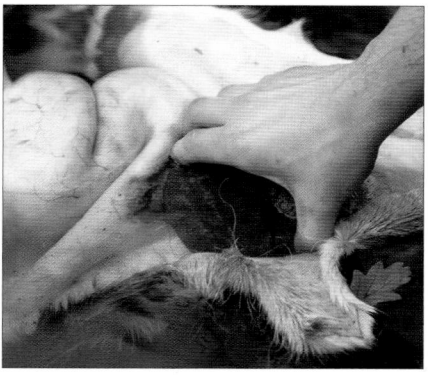

▲ *Leave the skin to soak in water mixed with charcoal, a tannic stream or a container of rainwater for a few days to loosen up the hair cuticles and any fatty tissue.*

scraped clean, start on the outer side and scrape off the hair and the outermost layer of skin (the epidermis). If the hair does not want to come off,

PREPARING AND SCRAPING AN ANIMAL HIDE

1 Tie two sturdy poles between two trees to make a frame one and a half times as long and wide as the hide.

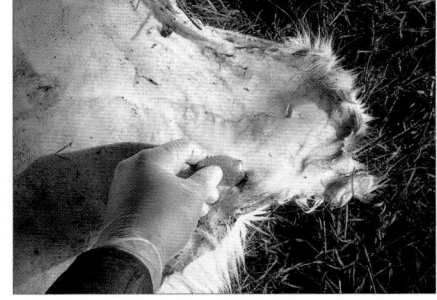

2 Puncture holes about 7.5cm–10cm/ 3–4in apart all round the skin, about 2.5cm/1in in from the edge.

3 Tie the skin on to the frame, using a separate cord in each hole so that you can tighten each one when necessary.

4 Using a stone with a straight but not too sharp edge, scrape off all the fatty tissue and remaining flesh from the underside of the hide.

5 Using a very sharp flint, scrape off all the hair. If the skin has been soaked in acidic water it should come off easily. Scrape off the top layer of skin as well.

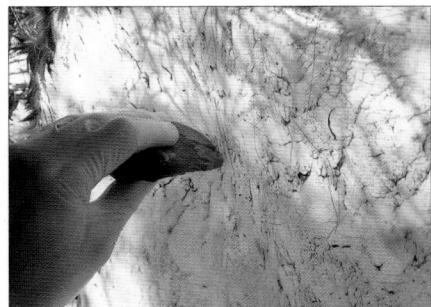

6 Scrape off any remaining fat on the underside of the hide and continue until the skin appears velvety. Leave the hide to dry out completely.

▲ *Part of the age-old process of making clothes from animal hides. When both sides have been scraped free of flesh, fat and hair, you are left with rawhide. To get buckskin for making clothes, the hide then needs to be tanned.*

then the skin may need to be soaked for a day or two in a stream or a container of water. Don't soak it for too long, or the hide may begin to rot.

When you have scraped both sides you are left with the dermis. Leave this stretched on the frame for a few days to dry out completely. At this point, you have created a fine grade of rawhide, which can be used for a multitude of purposes. To soften it for clothing, the hide needs to be tanned, and for this you can use the brains you saved when butchering the animal.

BRAIN-TANNING

Once the hide is dry, heat up some water and mix in the brains. Massage this mixture deeply into the hide. You can use egg-yolk for this job (if you have found birds' nests) as an alternative to brains, but in either case make sure the entire hide is saturated with the mixture. You can even take the hide off the rack, and soak it in the mixture in a container for a while.

The brains will stop the fibres binding back together to form rawhide, but only if the fibres are stretched apart while they dry. So the secret of soft buckskin is to stretch the fibres while the hide is drying. One way of doing this is to stake the hide out again and poke it with a rounded stick. Or you can hold it in your hands and stretch and pull it out until it is dry. If you can feel hard areas, you can try to give them some extra attention, though you may have to tan these sections again when the hide is completely dry. Once the whole hide is dry and soft, buff it over a tree trunk or a twisted cord to produce a material much like felt.

SMOKING THE HIDE

The next step is to smoke the hide. This is very important to stop your hide reverting to rawhide as soon as it gets wet. Sow the hide together to form a bag. Set a tripod above some embers and suspend the hide over it in such a way that the smoke has to travel through the hide. Now add smoky materials such as pine needles to the embers, and leave it for a few hours. Make sure the embers do not burst into flame, as this would ruin your hide. Once one side is fully smoked, turn the

BRAIN-TANNING AN ANIMAL HIDE

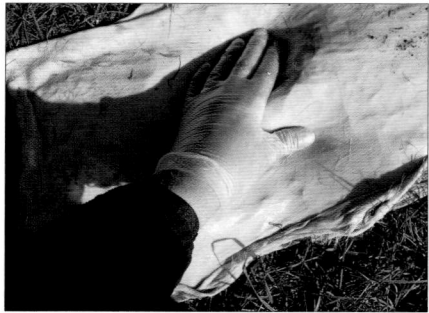

1 Having left the skin to dry completely, warm the animal's brains and massage them into the skin.

2 Pull the skin to stretch the fibres, continuing the process uninterrupted until the hide is completely dried out.

3 When the hide is dry and flexible you can soften it further by running it over a taut string or a branch.

bag inside out and smoke the other side. The finished product is buckskin, and is ready to be made into clothes.

You will need to re-smoke the hide once in a while to ensure it stays thoroughly oiled and prevent the fibres going hard again.

THE BENEFITS OF HIDE CLOTHING

Making clothes and other items from what is around you may be essential for long-term survival. Though it takes a lot of work to make a piece of soft buckskin, you will find that leather made this way is much stronger and more durable then modern leather. It is a natural product and therefore helps to mask your smell when stalking. It is also ultra-quiet and one of the best backgrounds for a camouflage pattern.

When making clothes, you can use various materials to sew hides together. Animal tendon could be used, though that would be more applicable in drier regions. You can also use cord made with plant fibres, though you may have to replace some of the seams from time to time. The easiest method is to tie the seams together using small strips of tanned hide made from offcuts. You can also use these for fringing, to help break up your outline in the bush. Make the fringing a little irregular and not too long, or it may snag in brush. The disadvantage of fringing is that it can show up your movements while stalking if you are not careful.

▼ *A small deerskin is easily big enough to make a pair of shoes following this pattern. If you have thick and thin skins, use the thicker skin for the soles.*

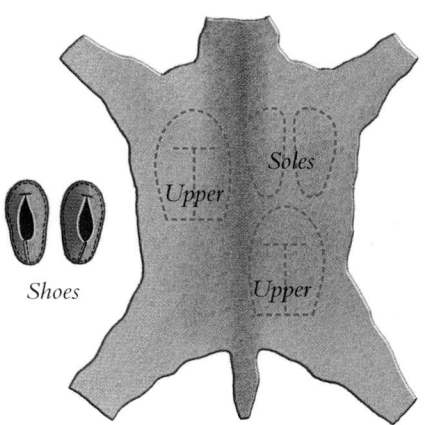

Shoes

TURNING SKINS INTO CLOTHING

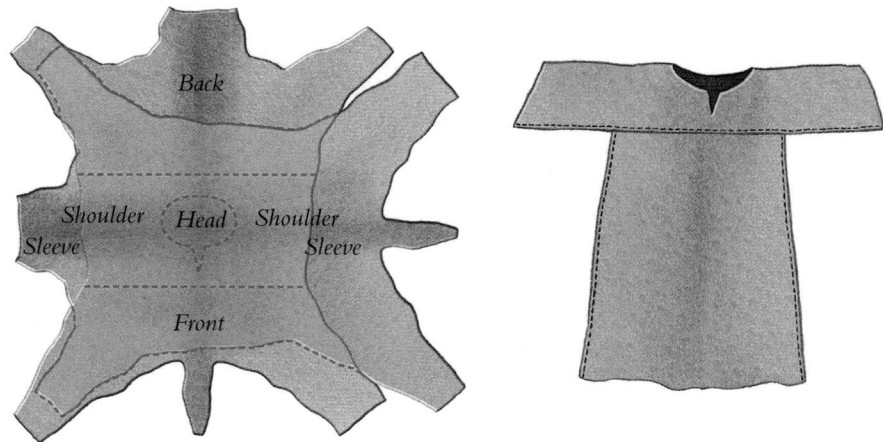

▲ *Two average skins can make an excellent shirt, using them as shown above. This design gives extra material on the shoulders, making the shirt stronger and warmer.*

▲ *This is what the shirt would look like when it is finished. You could add fringing to the sleeves and hems to make your shape less obvious when stalking game.*

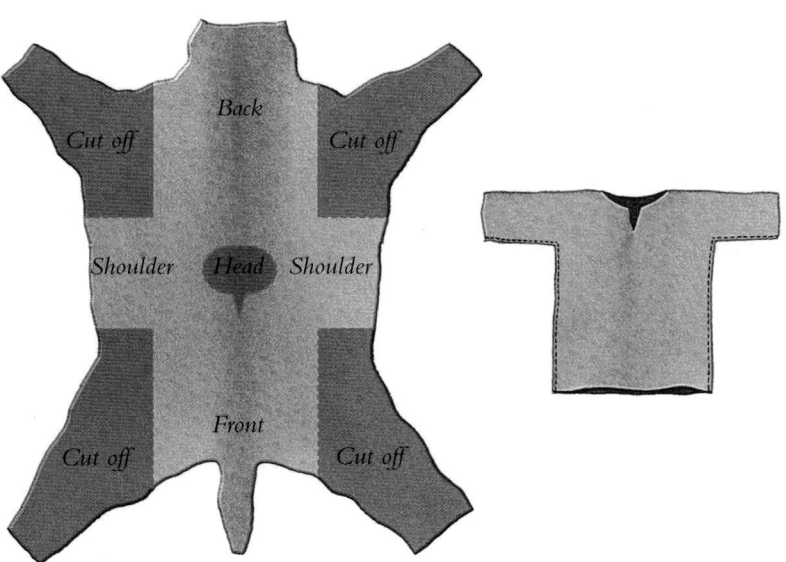

▲ *If you have a large hide, you can cut the whole shirt out in one piece, one half becoming the front and the other becoming the back. Simply fold it at the shoulders and sew up the sides and sleeves.*

▲ *This shirt might feel a little "square" due to the fact that the sleeves are not shaped. It is a good idea to make the shirt very roomy, allowing plenty of material under the arms so you can move in it easily.*

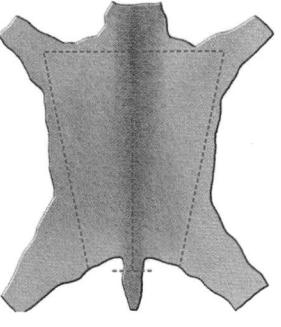

► *Basic trousers can be made by taking two hides, cutting out matching shapes according to the pattern shown here and sewing one on top of the other. Make the trousers roomy like the shirt above.*

TOOLS AND EQUIPMENT

One of the most satisfying aspects of survival in the wilderness is the making of tools and equipment. This often signals the end of sheer survival and the beginning of "living". Your existence is no longer a matter of primitive survival: many of the skills required to make tools from materials found in the wild are highly advanced techniques, which most modern people are not able to reproduce without re-learning and a lot of practice. These skills are truly a joy to learn, and many of them may lead you into a lifelong journey towards artistry and the perfection of, and even addiction to, wilderness survival skills.

Basic food bowls and containers

Using fire, you can very quickly turn out wooden bowls and spoons, simply by allowing an ember to burn into the wood in a controlled way.

To make a bowl, start with a thick log about 30cm/12in long (burn it to size if necessary). Split it in half then place an ember right in the centre of the flat side. By gently blowing on it, you can get the fire to spread slowly into the wood and also control the direction in which it burns. If you find you are getting too close to the side or bottom of the log, put some sand or clay over the spot to stop the ember

▼ *The stomach of an animal makes a watertight container and can be used to cook food and boil water in.*

▲ *Bark baskets are relatively easy to make, and can be used to hold a variety of items, such as equipment or edible plants.*

spreading that way. Scrape the surface clean of char regularly, as it will insulate the wood and make the burning process less efficient. If you want to speed up the process – and avoid hyperventilating – it is a good idea to use a straw made from a hollow stem such as elder, reed or bamboo, or the windpipe of an animal. You can use your burned-out bowl as it is, though you may find that food tastes better if you take time to scrape out all the char and sand the inside smooth.

Spoons can be made in exactly the same way as bowls, then carved to make them comfortable to eat with. Wooden utensils hold food particles in the fibres, however, so after washing them it is a good idea to hold them above a flame for a minute or two to sterilize them each time they are used.

▲ *Burning into wood is an easy way to produce containers, and has even been used to produce large items such as canoes.*

BARK CONTAINERS

Great containers can also be made from bark. Many different species, such as birch, cedar and elm, are suitable. Try to take it from trees that have fallen or are on their way out. If you have to take bark from a healthy tree, take a strip from only a third of its circumference to ensure that the tree survives. For best results, soak the bark in water for a few hours.

ANIMAL PRODUCTS

You can use the stomach of an animal to hold food or water. Clean it out, turn it inside out and suspend it from a tripod, or dig a hole in the ground and stake the edges around the pit. It can be used for boiling liquids by adding hot rocks. A bladder will work in the same way, though not for so long.

MAKING A SPOON

1 Light a good fire to make a large pile of embers. If necessary, shorten the stick you want to use in the fire.

2 Using tongs, place an ember on the flattened stick, on the point where you want your depression to form.

3 Hold the ember down and blow at it so that it burns into the wood. Sand out the depression and carve the spoon.

MAKING A BOWL

1 Make a sizeable fire in order to obtain plenty of embers for burning.

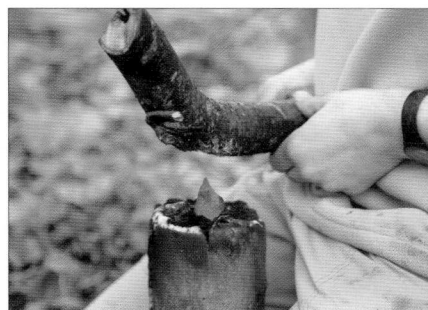

2 Split a log in half using a stone wedge and a sturdy branch hammer.

3 Place an ember on the wood, right in the centre of one half of the log.

4 Hold the ember down and blow on it gently. A depression will slowly form.

5 As the depression deepens, add more embers to burn the hole more quickly.

6 If you burn too close to one side, add clay to protect it from the fire.

MAKING A BARK BASKET

1 Select a strip of bark about 60cm/2ft long by 30cm/1ft wide.

2 Score an oval shape in the centre of the bark. Do not pierce the outer layer.

3 Using a sharp stone, punch holes all around the edges of the bark.

4 Bend the basket into shape and stitch the sides together tightly using cord.

5 To reinforce the basket, bind some stems into a ring to fit the rim.

6 Sew the ring into place using the holes you punctured earlier.

Weaving a basket

A basket can serve you in many useful ways, both for collecting and for storing food, and baskets can be made in a wide variety of forms, shapes and sizes. Once you have learned the technique you can use it to make containers of any size you need.

Basketwork allows air to circulate easily, so it is ideal for holding delicate wild foods such as berries and fungi, which deteriorate very quickly if they are carried in airtight containers. Baskets are also useful for storing wild greens or pieces of meat, or for gathering small-scale materials for kindling and tinder in the woods. A very loosely woven basket can also be used for trapping fish or to scoop small fish out of the water by hand.

MATERIALS FOR BASKETS

The function of each basket should dictate its size and shape, and may also influence the material you choose to make it from. Many different materials can be used to weave baskets, as long as they are flexible. The long, slender shoots of willow and hazel are traditionally used for basketry, and would be a very good source if they are growing in your vicinity, but there are plenty of other flexible materials that can also be used, such as pine or cedar shoots, spruce roots or cordage. Long shoots reduce the need to weave in new strands and make it easier to achieve a smooth, even finish.

▼ *A small collection of baskets of various sizes is useful for collecting food and keeping small items of all kinds safe.*

WEAVING A BASKET

1 Gather six flexible willow or hazel twigs to make the ribs of the basket.

3 Insert one of the other sticks into the split you have just created.

5 Push two strands of weaving material into the splits alongside the three ribs.

7 Weave the second strand under the first ribs, and over the second three.

2 Split one stick in the centre by inserting a cutting tool and twisting it.

4 Place two more split sticks beside the first, and insert the remaining sticks.

6 Tightly weave one of the strands over the first three ribs. Hold at the bottom.

8 Repeat to go around the centre three times. Make sure the weave is tight.

9 Now continue to weave between the individual ribs until you feel the base is big enough. Keep the shape circular.

10 Split each rib, right at the edge of the weave, twisting the tool as you bend it up to stop the rib breaking.

11 Repeat to bend all the ribs up, then place three weaving strands to the right side of one of the ribs.

12 Take the first strand and weave it over the first rib. Hold it in place at the bottom of the basket.

13 Weave the second strand under the first rib and over the second. Release the first strand and hold the second.

14 Weave the third strand under two ribs and over one rib. Release the previous strand and hold this one.

15 Continue weaving, following the last step, until the ribs are pointing upwards to your satisfaction.

16 When a strand runs out, lift it up and insert a new one in its place, so that it points in the same direction.

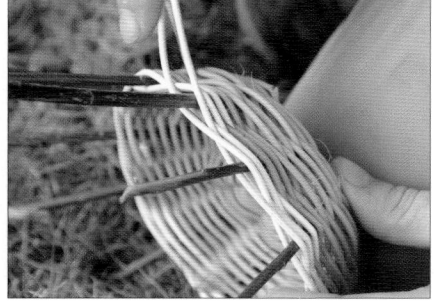

17 When the ribs are pointing up, continue using only two strands, following the weave used for the base.

18 When you have reached the height you want, tuck the ends of the strands into the previous rows.

19 Weave in the ribs if possible, or cut them off, leaving the ends protruding a little so that the weave doesn't slip off.

20 This weaving pattern will produce a strong basket of any size, even if its shape is not completely regular.

Crafting simple pottery

Pottery was the first craft to be developed in most human cultures, and serviceable pots are still made using natural river clay and the simplest of crafting and firing techniques. Your own containers may be crude but they will make effective utensils for cooking and eating.

FINDING THE CLAY

You won't have the luxury of buying ready-made clay in a survival situation but as it's an abundant natural material you should be able to find some to hand. Formed primarily by the weathering of granite, clay can be found all around us and the best way to look for pure, clean clay is by digging in a bend in a river, where the finest particles have settled.

PREPARING THE CLAY

Having gathered your clay, leave it to dry, then grind it to a powder so that you get rid of stones and any other impurities that would spoil the pottery. Once you have a fine clay powder, you should temper it by adding a little harder material, such as ground seashells, sand, powdered eggshells or

▼ *The thumb-pot technique can be used to make vessels such as bowls and lamps.*

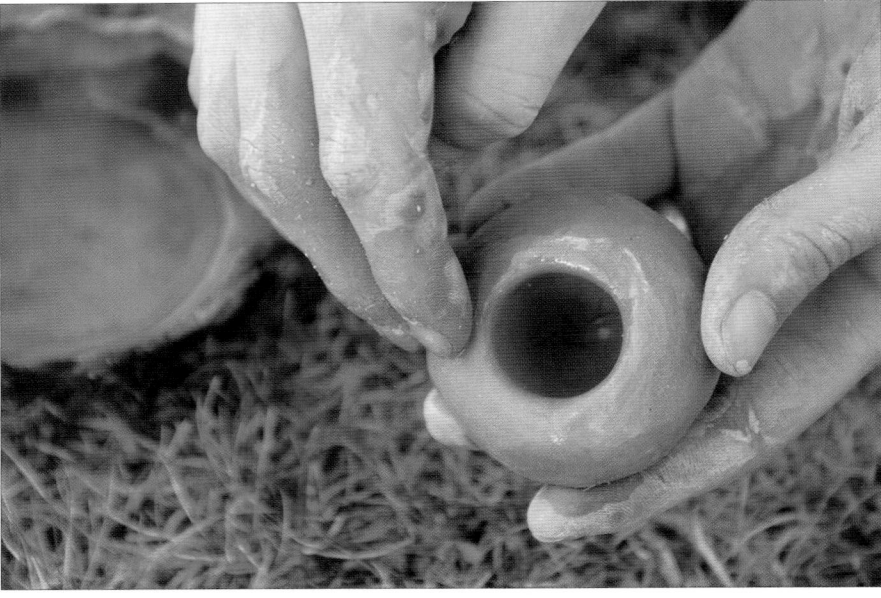

crushed pottery fragments. Tempering the clay will prevent the pottery shrinking too much during drying and firing, thereby helping to prevent it cracking. Once the temper is mixed in, you can add water.

Knead the clay thoroughly before you start to shape it to eliminate any air bubbles, which would expand during firing and break the pot. Try to get the consistency of the clay right before you start working with it. The clay should be soft enough for you to move but

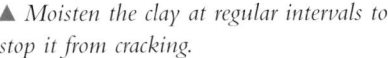

▲ *Moisten the clay at regular intervals to stop it from cracking.*

firm enough so that it does not stick to your hands. You'll soon get an idea of the sort of "give" you need to achieve in order to be able to craft simple pots.

FROM BALL TO BOWL

The pottery bowl described opposite uses a ball of clay about the size of an orange. It is simply shaped using your hands, using a pinching technique. Press in with your thumb as you turn it until you are about 6mm/^{1}/$_4$in from the bottom, then start pressing outward, working from the bottom up, to form a pot. If the pot gets too big, put it on a flat surface while you thin the sides to a uniform 6mm/^{1}/$_4$in. Once the pot is finished, leave it to dry for a few days.

Fire your pots after drying to make them more durable. The simplest form of firing, which is still practised by village potters in parts of the world today, is with open fires or with pits using a local source of fuel. The method used here is as basic as it comes. The firing temperature will be low, so your pots will eventually start to disintegrate, but you can easily make more to replace them.

MAKING A POTTERY BOWL

1 To make sure the clay is entirely pure, it is best to dry it and then pound it with a large stone.

2 You can then filter out any debris. Keep pounding until you have a fine clay powder.

3 Mix the powder with a small amount of temper such as crushed shell, adding about one part temper to ten parts clay.

4 Add just enough water to the powdered clay to make it hold together in a ball without breaking.

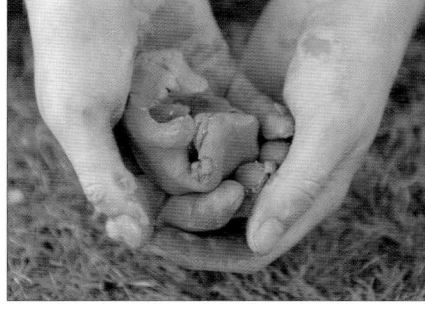

5 Knead the clay thoroughly, working it between your hands to smooth it and eliminate any air bubbles.

6 After kneading, shape the clay into a ball. For a small bowl you will need a ball about the size of an orange.

7 Press your thumb into the top of the ball, then turn it and repeat.

8 Keep turning and pressing, slowly widening the hole and shaping the pot.

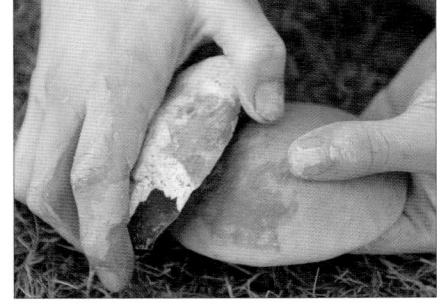

9 Dry for a few days, then burnish the pot with a stone to make it watertight.

10 To fire the clay, place the pot under a thick layer of soil and light a fire on top, or build a fire around the pot.

11 Make sure the flames are well away from the pot at first, and slowly get closer, so it doesn't heat up too quickly.

12 Once the pot is immersed in flames, add more wood and let the fire burn as hot as possible for about three hours.

Making a bow for hunting

A bow is a versatile hunting weapon that will allow you to stalk and kill mammals of any size. The bow described here is designed for short-term survival and is sometimes called a father-son bow, because it actually consists of two bows – a bigger bow with a smaller one tied on to the back. The reason for this construction is that the bow is made from green wood. Though this is easier to carve, it does not have the same strength as a bow made from properly seasoned wood. By adding a second stave, you can achieve a stronger bow with weaker wood.

WORKING WITH THE WOOD

To make the survival bow you will need a branch of a young tree without side branches or knots. The wood should be straight, about 150cm/5ft long with a diameter of 7.5cm/3in.

You will need to split the branch exactly down the centre of the wood as both halves will be used. If you don't manage to salvage two staves from the branch, cut another length and split it to obtain the second stave. In this case it need only be about 120cm/4ft long.

Once you have two staves, select the one that is going to become the "father" or main part of the bow. The side with the bark on will be the back of the bow, and this should never be touched with a knife. The other side, which will face you in the finished bow, is the belly. Measure off a handle

▲ *Though the "father-son" bow is made from green wood, which is weak, the two bows reinforce each other to give enough power for a kill.*

FLEXIBLE WOODS

The best woods for a bow are those that are flexible, such as hazel (although nearly all types of wood can be used for this survival bow). You can test the flexibility of wood by taking a small twig from a tree and bending its ends together. If it snaps cleanly, the wood might not be good for a bow. If it doesn't really snap, but breaks or bends with a lot of fibres, then you have a wood that will work well.

about 7.5cm/3in long in the centre of the bow, then carefully thin both limbs by carving until they start to bend evenly, forming a D-shape.

SHAPING AND TESTING THE BOW

At this point you can carve two notches at the end of each limb, and string a length of cordage between them. This is not the final string and doesn't have to be tight, but you can use it to pull the bow to see the result of your thinning more clearly.

The best way to do this is to make a "tillering-stick" about 75cm/30in long. Carve a notch on top of the stick and further notches every 12.5cm/5in. Sit the handle of the bow on the notch at the top and pull the string down to the first notch. Examine the bend of the bow. If it looks good, pull the string to the next notch. If you find spots that bend more then the rest, you need to thin the bow at either side of that weak spot so it bends evenly again. If parts of the limbs bend less than the rest, you'll need to thin those down a little more. Using this process to test the bow, keep thinning until you reach the last notch.

Now shorten the bowstring so that it is about 15cm/6in away from the handle when the bow is strung and

repeat the process until your bow has a draw of 63–70cm/25–28in. Use the same process to make the shorter bow, which needs a draw of 25–37cm/10–15in. The shorter bow will not need a handle. Once it is tied on to the back of the larger bow it should be "recurved" by pushing in two wedges on each side of the handle and tying them in place. Connect the limbs of the two bows and fit the string back on to the main bow. Each bow should bear a pull of 7–9kg/15–20lb.

FIRING THE BOW

Once you've made your arrows (*see following pages*) you can use your bow, though its performance will be greatly improved if it is left to dry out for a week or two. Don't expect instant success. Find some open ground (so that you don't lose your arrows), set up a target and start practising. Learn how to load, draw, aim and fire effectively from a range of distances. Once you are hitting the target with confidence it's time to go out and do it for real.

MAKING A SURVIVAL BOW

1 Gather two pieces of straight, flexible green wood, looking for poles without side branches or knots.

2 Split one branch in half using a stone wedge or other splitting tool. Always work away from the "back" of the bow.

3 Unless you have managed to split the branch exactly in half, repeat the procedure with the second stick.

4 The short bow should be about three-quarters the length of the main bow.

5 Carefully carve away to get an even bend along the stave.

6 With one stave completed, repeat for the second bow.

7 Carve two sets of notches in each end of the larger bow and one set of notches in each end of the smaller bow.

8 Tie the two bows together at the centre, with the belly of the smaller bow touching the back of the larger bow.

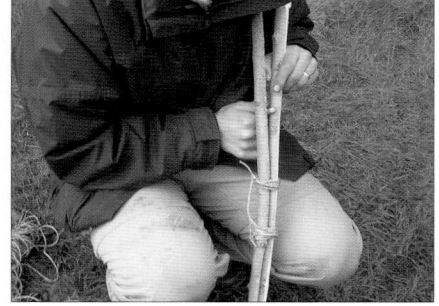

9 Insert wedges as close to each side of the handle as possible to "recurve" the smaller bow away from the larger bow.

10 Tie these wedges into place very securely to stop them popping out again when the bow is in use.

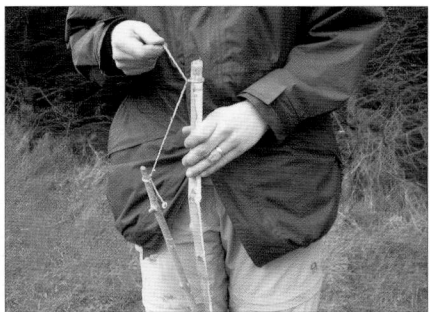

11 Tie the tips of the larger bow to those of the smaller bow. Make sure the connection is taut but not too tight.

12 Finally, string the main bow. The bowstring should be 10–12.5cm/4–5in shorter than the large bow stave.

Making arrows

It is best to make a number of arrows at a time, as they are easily broken or lost in use. Look for young shoots to make the shafts as they are firm and straight. Once the bark has been stripped off, the stems should be about 6–10mm/^{1}/$_4$–^{3}/$_8$in thick. Cut them to a length of about 70cm/28in. Shoots of hazel, willow and yew all work really well for survival arrows.

If the shafts needs straightening, you can do this by heating the wood over the fire until it is just too hot to touch, then bending it in the opposite direction and holding it in that position until the wood has cooled down. When you let go, the bend should be gone. If it is not, repeat the process.

If you do not have any feathers to use as fletching, you can fletch the arrows with tough leaves, or tie a bunch of pine needles on to the shaft.

STRENGTHENING THE TIP

If you need to use your arrows quickly, you can get away with carving the shaft to a point and fire-hardening the tip after you have finished the fletching. If you have a little time on your hands, it is better to strengthen the tip of an arrow by notching it and inserting an arrowhead. Simple arrowheads can be made of bone or very hard wood, but you can also make arrowheads from stone. In any case, the arrowhead should be tied on securely.

To make it extra strong, coat the arrowhead with pitch glue (*see page 128*) before you tie it on to the shaft. Now all you have to do is wrap just behind the arrowhead to prevent the shaft from splitting, and wrap the shaft just in front of the notch in the back to prevent the string from splitting the shaft when the arrow is fired.

▲ *A "primitive" arrow should be made as straight as any modern arrow, otherwise it may miss the mark.*

SHARPENING AND SHAPING A FLINT ARROWHEAD

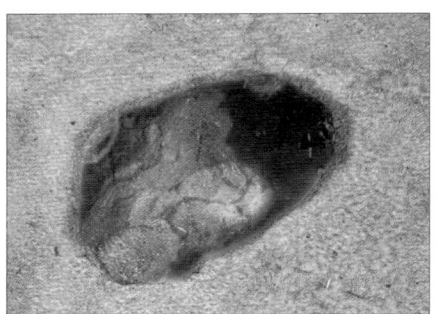

1 When you have found a suitable flake of material, imagine the arrowhead inside to help you shape the stone.

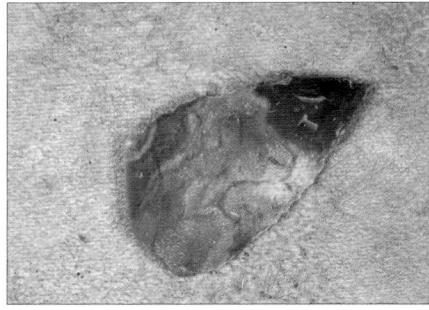

2 It is most important to thin the piece as much as possible while taking as little material as possible off the sides.

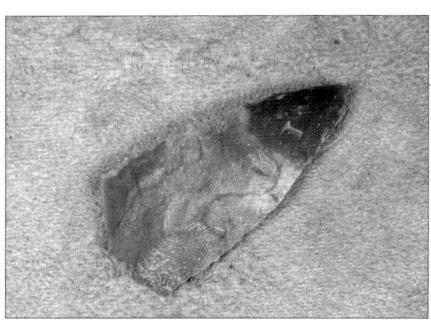

3 You should get to the required shape slowly but surely, so that a minimum of material loss is incurred.

4 When the piece is between 3–1.5mm/^{1}/$_8$–^{1}/$_{16}$in thick, it is thin enough for an arrowhead.

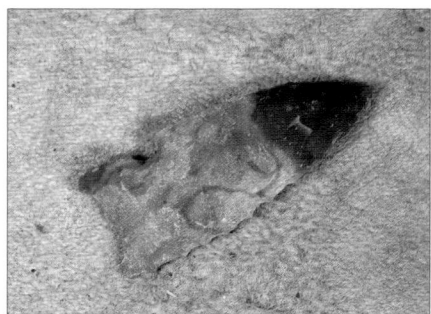

5 Small flakes are removed to create a notch. It is best to make the first notch on the most difficult side of the piece.

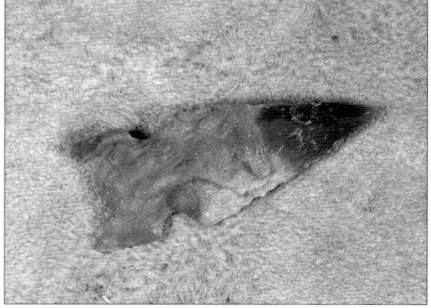

6 The second notch is made to match the first. After further sharpening and shaping, the arrowhead is ready for use.

MAKING AN ARROW

1 Find a young branch that is nearly perfectly straight with no side shoots.

2 Carefully strip off the bark. Don't cut into the wood, as that will weaken it.

3 Remove any bends by heating the wood and bending it the opposite way.

4 Cut a notch in one end to fit on to the bowstring, and a deeper notch in the other end to take the arrowhead.

5 To prepare deer sinew for binding the arrow, take a dried leg tendon and pull off long fibres.

6 Chew the fibres to make them supple and sticky: sinew sticks to itself when wet and shrinks and hardens as it dries.

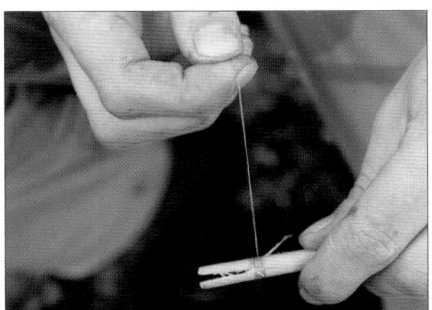

7 When the sinew is soaked through, use it to bind the shaft just behind the notch to prevent splitting.

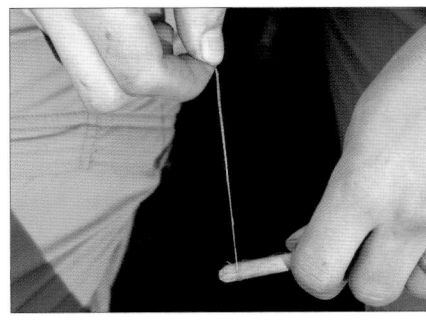

8 Repeat at the other end. Make sure the wrapping overlaps, because the sinew will stick only to itself.

9 Place a resin-soaked arrowhead in the notch, as deep as it will go. Make sure you orient it straight along the shaft.

10 Melt more pitch glue and mould it over the arrowhead so it "flows" into the shaft, to give smooth penetration.

11 When the glue has nearly set, wrap the arrowhead in place using more sinew to form an unbreakable bond.

12 Use sinew to bind on the fletching to balance the arrow – a half-stripped branch of spruce has been used here.

Making basic stone tools

Being able to make stone cutting tools is an important survival skill in this modern age. We are not allowed to carry knives on public transport, so after a crash, for example, you might find yourself in a survival situation without one. You may also want to learn the techniques out of interest, or as a way of connecting with the past.

The simplest way to produce a cutting tool is by "bipolar percussion". For this you need a rounded pebble about 7.5cm/3in long, preferably fine-grained or even glassy (coarse stone will not produce a sharp edge). Hold it on a stone anvil or pack sand around it to hold it upright. Now smash a heavy

rock with all your strength down on the pebble. If you hit it hard enough, the stone will fracture into long, sharp shards that can be used as emergency cutting tools.

KNAPPING STONE

For more refined tools, a technique called "knapping" is used. Creating a tool from a stone is very much like chess. You have to learn the individual moves and put them all together to remove the right flakes.

Because the flakes you are working on are extremely sharp (obsidian can be 400 times as sharp as surgical steel) it is vital to protect yourself. This means

▲ *Arrowheads come in all shapes and sizes, depending on the use of the arrow as well as the skill of the knapper, but their principle task is to reinforce arrows, so beauty comes last. Even a simple flake could do the job.*

FLINT KNAPPING PROCESSES

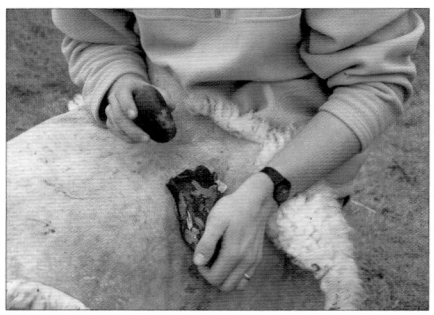

1 For large pieces of flint, "direct percussion" is used. The "core" is often held on the outside of the leg and the flake is struck off with a stone.

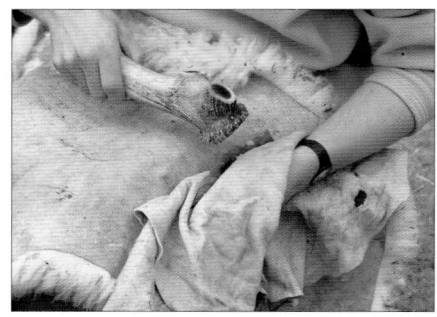

2 When large, thin flakes are needed a "soft hammer" (in this case a piece of antler) is used, and the blow is angled in the direction of the flake.

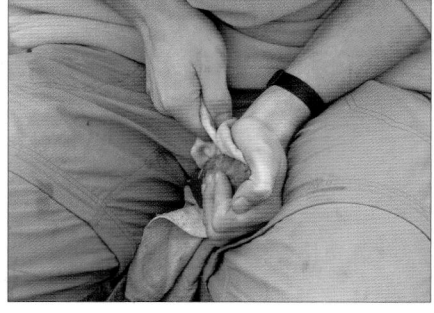

3 The final method, "pressure flaking", is used to remove small flakes with precision, pressing outwards with a fine piece of antler to push the flakes off,

MAKING A WORKABLE KNIFE FROM STONE

1 Select a fine-grained pebble roughly the size of an egg, and a solid hammer stone at least twice as heavy. Steady the pebble on a sturdy rock surface.

2 Keeping your fingers out of the way, or using sand to hold the pebble upright, strike it as hard as you can with the hammer stone.

3 Ideally the pebble will split into a number of sharp-edged flakes. Even if it does not, you will end up with at least one sharp piece, as here.

► *This hammer was produced by "pecking" a groove around a hard stone. A piece of hazel, shaped to fit the groove, forms a handle, which is strengthened with rawhide.*

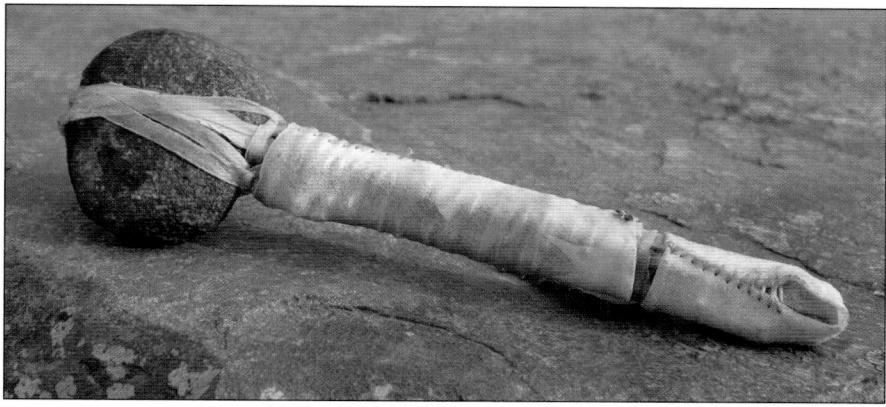

wearing gloves, and using sheepskin or a large pad of leather when working on your lap. You should also wear safety goggles when practising as splinters may fly towards your eyes. If you take up knapping on a regular basis, make sure you do it in a well-ventilated area, preferably outside. Put down a groundsheet and clean the floor and all surfaces well after knapping so that no sharp debris is left lying around.

From an archaeological point of view, you should dispose of your flakes and chips (known as "debitage") responsibly. Some people bury a glass bottle beneath them to show any future digs that the flakes are not prehistoric.

▼ *Stone tools and arrowheads can be made from different types of stone. The top arrowhead is made from English flint, while the bottom one is of porcelanite.*

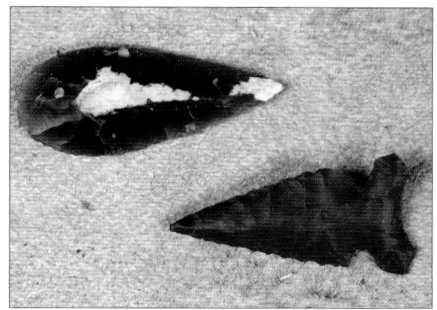

PREDICTING HOW STONE WILL FLAKE

There are five main "rules" to help you decide where flakes will come off a stone you are knapping:

- **The angle of the platform** The platform is the surface to which you are going to apply a force to detach a flake. An angle close to, but less than, 90 degrees in relation to the surface where the flake is to come off, gives the best result. An angle far less than this will result in a crushed edge, while more than this will produce nothing at all.
- **Every stone has an imaginary centre line** The centre line divides the mass of the stone in half. If a platform is above the centre line, it is very likely the stone will break when you apply a force. If the stone doesn't break, you could end up with a lopsided item. If it is on or

below the centre line, the flake should travel well without breaking the piece you are working on.

- **The angle of the force applied** With direct percussion the angle of the blow is more than 90 degrees in relation to the platform surface if a hard hammer is used (like a glancing blow). When using pressure flaking, or applying direct percussion with a soft hammer, the force is directed into the stone, following the direction of the flake you want to detach.
- **Flakes love to travel far over convex surfaces** They don't travel over concave surfaces, where they will just break off.
- **Flakes love to follow mass** They travel well along ridges and lumps on the stone.

MAKING A CHOPPER

1 Using a hard hammer, it is possible to create a rough tool such as a chopper in only three steps. Select a hammer stone and a flint nodule (the "core").

2 Flakes are removed by striking the edge of the core with sharp, forceful blows. The control of each blow is more important than its strength.

3 The rules described in the box above will help you predict where the flakes will come off, allowing you to shape the stone just as you want it.

Working with bones and sticks

Once your basic requirements of shelter, warmth, food and water are taken care of, you can use all the natural materials around you to create numerous other artefacts. If you are surviving in the wilderness for a long period you will want to make your life as comfortable as possible. You'll have time to develop your skills and to seek out the best materials for each task.

MAKING BONE TOOLS

The bones of any animals you kill for food should always be cleaned and saved for future use. Bone is soft enough to be shaped with stone, but hard enough to hold a sharp edge or point, so it can be turned into many useful tools, such as needles, fishing hooks, drills and punches. Large bones and antlers can be used for digging and hammering, or sharpened to make saws and knives.

Bones can be broken up easily by simply smashing them with a piece of rock, although the results may be unpredictable. If you want a specific shape, you can score bone in much the same way as glass to make it break in more predictable patterns. You can then give the bone its final shape using a fine abrading stone.

Bone tools can be extremely sharp. You can prepare an item such as a bone knife or arrowhead for sharpening by rubbing it with hot oil, then heating it in the fire. If you then sharpen the object much as you would sharpen a steel knife, you can get very sharp edges indeed.

BACKRESTS AND MATS

A simple backrest can make life a lot more comfortable, enabling you to relax in front of your fire or sit up in your shelter. You can make one quite easily using stout sticks arranged in a tripod. This will be easy to move around and stable on uneven ground.

You can make your backrest even more comfortable by weaving a grass mat to lay over it and sit on. You could also make a mattress to sleep on. For these you will need a lot of tall grass or long hollow reeds and a lot of cordage. Just keep adding more bundles of grass until you have a mat long enough for your needs. Its width will be decided by the length of the grass, though you can chop off the sides when you have finished if they are too long.

MAKING A KNIFE FROM BONE

1 Large bones, either found or harvested from an animal, can be broken up simply by smashing them with a rock to get shards.

2 Shape the resulting shards into whatever tool you need by using a large rough stone as an abrading block and rubbing the bone across it.

3 For greater precision, score the bone with a stone cutting tool in the rough shape of the object, then carefully "smash" it along the scored lines.

4 When the shaping of the knife is complete, rub hot oil into the bone, and heat the knife over the fire before sharpening the blade.

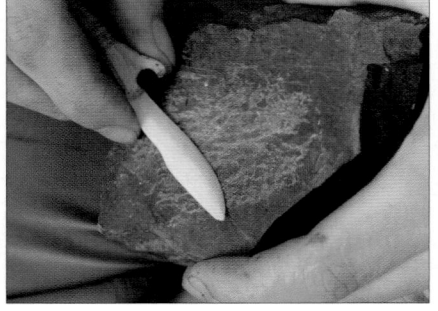

5 Sharpen the knife pretty much as you would a regular steel blade. Try to find a stone as smooth as possible for this sharpening process.

6 The bone blade can be bound into a notch in the end of another long, smooth bone or a piece of wood to create a handle.

MAKING A GRASS MATTRESS

1 Collect a large amount of long grass or hollow reeds. Start by making a bundle about 7.5cm/3in thick.

2 Split the bundle in half and turn one half over, so half the thicker ends are at each end, to keep the thickness even.

3 Tie the bundle using two or three long cords. Wrap the cord around itself three times to make each knot.

4 The knots provide a flat surface on which you can rest the next bundle. Tie this in using the same knots.

5 Repeat until the mat is the right size. The flat knots square off the bundles, eliminating gaps between them.

6 This method can be used to make mats of any size and shape you want. Trim the ends of the stems if you wish.

MAKING A BACKREST

1 Select three sturdy poles, each 90–120cm/3–4ft long. Make sure they are reasonably straight.

2 With the poles side by side, wrap a good length of cord fairly loosely around one end and knot it.

3 Wind the cord between the sticks to form a "cinch". This is the chance to tighten up your tie as much as possible.

4 When the top is tied securely, place the sticks upright, and bring the middle stick backwards.

5 Tease the two other sticks outwards to form a tripod. Adjust the distances between them to stabilize the structure.

6 Tie on some horizontal bars to give you a sturdy surface to lean against, and tie a grass mat over this frame.

Working with natural resins and oils

Both animal and vegetable products can be used to make glue, which has numerous uses in a survival situation. Apart from its use as food, animal fat is also useful as a lubricant, and can be used as fuel in lamps.

HIDE GLUE

Generally used to glue organic matter together, hide glue is the strongest glue known. The downside is that it stretches when wet, will not withstand heat, and will not glue materials such as stone. It is made from hide scrapings or pieces of rawhide, boiled until they dissolve into a thin liquid. You must use hide glue hot, as it sets fairly quickly on cooling. To reuse it, simply add a little water and heat it up slowly. However, it can be stored for only a few days before it goes off.

PITCH GLUE

The sap from conifers, chiefly spruce and pine, can be made into a good waterproof glue (it is used in the fishing spear project on pages 102–3). The resin seeps out of wounds on the trunks of trees, or can be found in blisters under the bark and scraped off with a stick.

Once you have a container full of resin, place it on the fire. As soon as it begins to melt, you will notice a strong turpentine smell: this is normal. Don't allow the resin to boil as that will reduce the quality of the glue. Make sure you have some sort of lid to hand as well, as it catches fire easily. If you have a large amount of resin, and require very clean glue, strain the liquid as quickly as possible, so it doesn't set while in the filter. For most outdoor projects, however, this is not necessary.

The resin on its own will simply revert to its natural state as it cools. In order to make it set hard and strong you need to add a "temper". Three different substances can be added, all with their own advantages. Powdered charcoal is most often used, because it's

MAKING HIDE GLUE

1 Place the scrapings from a hide in a fireproof container and pour on some water: you will need nine parts water to one part hide.

2 Put the container on the fire and allow it to boil. Fat may rise to the surface, and you should skim this off, but keep it safe.

3 Keep boiling, adding more water as required to stop all the moisture evaporating, until the hide has completely dissolved into a sticky glue.

MAKING PITCH GLUE

1 Collect a sufficient amount of spruce or pine resin in a fireproof container. Try to avoid getting too many little bits of debris mixed in with the resin.

2 Place the container on the fire and allow it to heat up. Keep stirring so that the heat is spread evenly and don't allow it to boil.

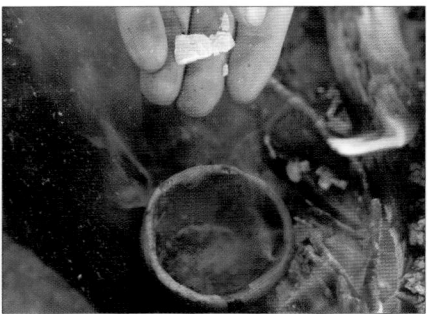

3 Mix in some powdered charcoal, wax or dried scat to make the glue set hard when it cools. Allow the liquid to set on sticks or in small clumps for storage.

MAKING AN OIL LANTERN

1 The container for an oil lantern can be made of many different materials. Pictured here are a simple clay bowl and a purpose-made lamp.

2 To render pieces of animal fat into usable lamp oil, heat it in a fireproof container on the fire, skimming off the liquid fat continually.

3 Pour this oil into the container you are using for your lantern. It is important you have rendered the oil well, so it remains liquid.

4 Make a "wick" for the lamp by braiding some plant fibres. The best fibres to use are from the resinous bark of trees such as red cedar and basswood.

5 Place the wick in the oil, making sure a little sticks out at the top. It is helpful to soak the entire wick in the oil for a minute or two to help it catch.

6 Now light the wick. The size of the flame can be adjusted to a certain extent by having more or less wick sticking out of the lamp.

easy to get. Charcoal works well for most purposes, though the glue may become brittle after a while. Beeswax creates a more flexible glue, though it is not so strong and tends to feel a little greasy. The glue also seems to be a little softer when set. A good temper is the dried scat of herbivores such as rabbits or deer, ground into a powder. This makes the strongest and longest-lasting glue, often referred to as "loaded" glue, though it is less hygienic – don't use it to waterproof a cup, for example.

It is hard to judge how much temper to add to the resin to make it set properly. Try about a tenth, then leave a little to set. If it sets hard, it's done. If it stays sticky and soft, add more. Once the temper is added, the glue must be used hot: it will set as it cools down.

It is best to divide the glue up into small portions containing just enough for each project. The reason is that the more times you re-heat the glue, the less strong and more brittle it becomes. There are many ways of dividing the glue into small portions, but the best is to create "pitch-sticks".

With a container filled with water to hand, take a small stick and dip it into the hot glue as you would dip a candle. Then place the stick with the blob of hot glue in the water to cool it down quickly. Briefly dip the stick into the glue again, so more glue is collected, and cool it again in the water. Keep repeating this until you have as much glue collected on the stick as you want. While the glue is still warm, you can mould it into raindrop or sausage shapes for easier storage.

When you wish to use the glue, you can either heat the object to be glued and touch the pitch-stick against it, or heat up the tip of the pitch-stick so that a drop of hot glue drips on to the surface of the object. You can improve the bond between the glue and the materials by pre-heating the surfaces to be glued.

OIL LANTERNS

The name would suggest that such lanterns use oil as a fuel. However, research into early societies has revealed that animal fat was often used for lighting. The oil lantern can be made from any container that will not burn. Clay containers are particularly good, because you can make them in any shape to suit your needs, easily creating a spout to support the wick.

The wick is best made from the bark of resinous trees such as red cedar and basswood. Alternatively, natural cordage made from nettles and other fibrous plants also works well. Simply melt the animal fat in the container and light the wick.

Making cordage

You will need cordage, or thread, of varying strengths and thicknesses, for many different purposes in a survival situation, from lashing together the timbers of your shelter to fishing and making snares. It can be made from both plant and animal fibres. The fibres of animal matter such as sinew (the leg tendons) are usually stronger, but plant fibres may be easier to find, and can withstand getting wet, while animal fibres stretch when wet, so your choice of materials will be governed by the jobs you need the cordage to do.

PLANT FIBRES

The inner part of a plant's stem is generally used for making cordage. The stinging nettle is a good plant to choose, but many other species with long, tough stems can be used. Find young, green stems and carefully remove the leaves without damaging the fibres (and without getting stung). Use gloves or a piece of leather to rub the hairs off the stalk, then split it open from on one side only and spread it out. Discard the woody pith from the inside and carefully scrape the outer part off the fibres. These parts of the stem add no strength, and may even make the finished product weaker. Gently roll the fibres between your hands for a while to make them supple.

SINEW AND RAWHIDE

For cordage that needs to have a lot of strength, sinew and rawhide will do the trick. The advantage of such animal matter is that it shrinks when it dries, enabling it to form a very tight binding. The downside is that it loosens up again when it gets wet.

You can use sinew as it comes from the animal, by ripping off fibres as you need them. This works well when making arrows. You don't even need to tie any knots. Wetting the sinew with saliva forms a sticky adhesive that will glue the sinew to itself when wrapped.

If you want to make a long cord out of sinew, you need to prepare it first by separating the fibres. You can do this by pounding the tendons on a wooden surface with a wooden anvil. If you use a stone or metal hammer, you will break the fibres. You may find that it takes a lot of hammering to loosen the fibres. Just try to get into a rhythm.

PREPARING PLANT FIBRES

1 Many different plants can be used to procure fibres for cord – this is blackberry. Pick a stem carefully, choosing the longest you can find.

2 Using a piece of buckskin or some leather gloves, rub up and down the stem to clean off the thorns as well as the leaves.

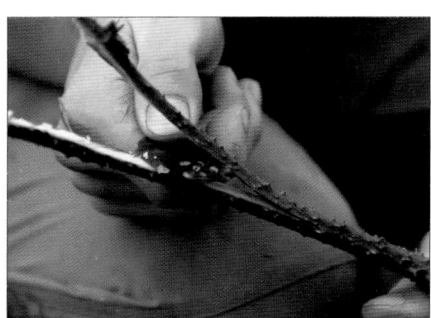

3 Split the stem in half lengthways (if it is very thick, you may even want to quarter it). Make sure the split goes right through the centre of the stem.

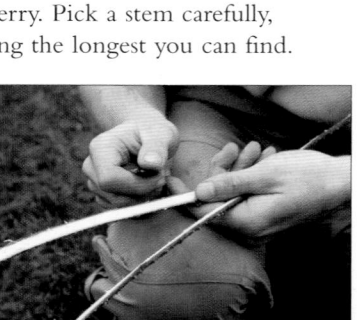

4 You will find a pithy substance inside, which should be scraped out (you can keep it to enlarge an ember when making fire by friction).

5 Break the stem outward. This will split the woody inner part from the bark. Follow this split all down the stem, breaking it again if necessary.

6 Strip off the outer bark by holding a sharp edge perpendicular to the fibre: the inner bark is the only part of the stem you want to use.

MAKING CORDAGE FROM PLANT OR ANIMAL FIBRES

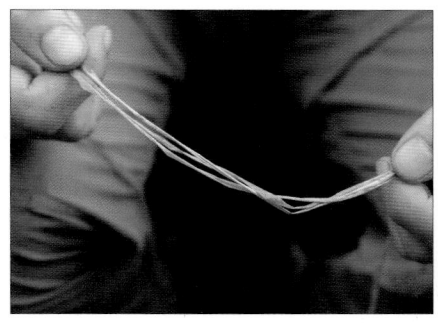

1 For long-lasting cord, it is best to use dried fibres, otherwise they will shrink later, leaving the cord loose.

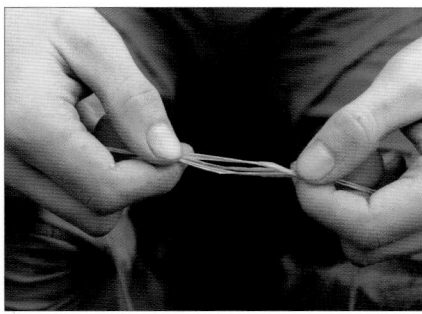

2 Hold the bunch of fibres between your thumbs and index fingers with your hands about 5cm/2in apart.

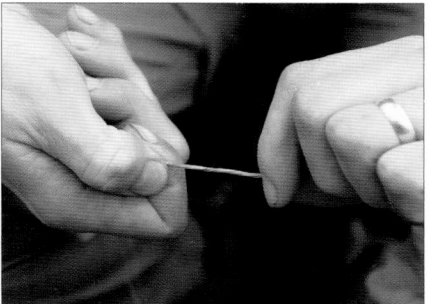

3 Twist the fibres away from you with your right hand. This will tighten the fibres together.

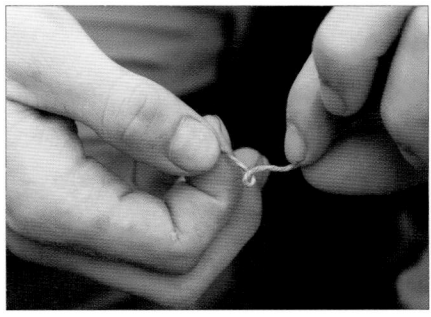

4 Keep twisting the fibres in your right hand until they form a loop or kink.

5 Grab the kink between your left thumb and finger.

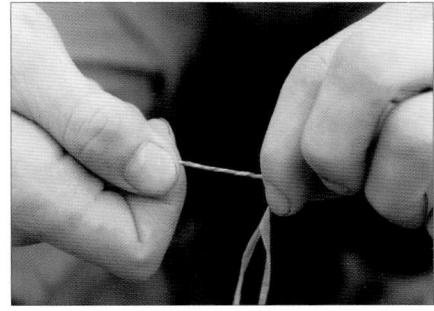

6 Twist the upper strand away from you; stop just before the fibres kink.

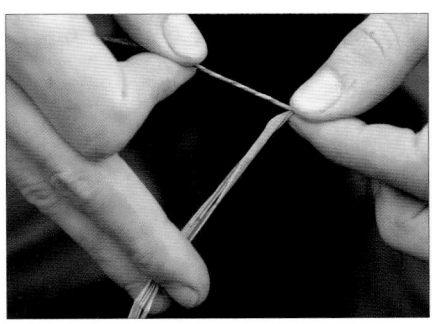

7 Still holding the twisted fibres in your right hand, grab the lower strand between your second and third fingers.

8 Twist your right hand towards you and slide your left hand up the cord to grab the fibres where the strands cross.

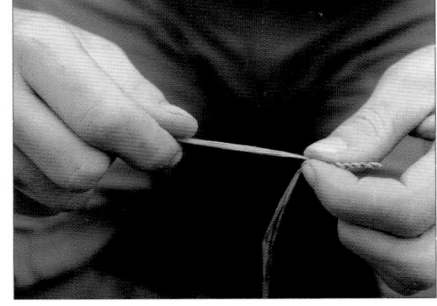

9 Release what is now the lower strand and grab the top strand. Twist it away from yourself as you did in step 6.

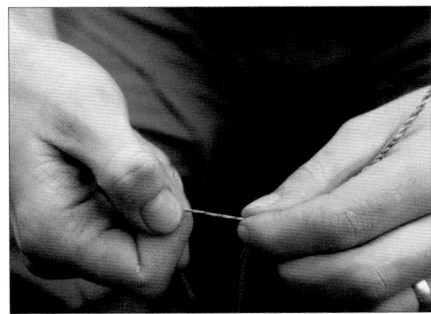

10 When it is rolled up tight, grab the lower strand again, and twist your hand over. Repeat until the cord is complete.

11 As the fibres run out, add another bundle to the ends of the old one, but avoid splicing both bundles at once.

12 To make a regular cord, ensure that both strands are equally thick, and remain constant in thickness.

SELF-DEFENCE IN THE URBAN JUNGLE

There are two key factors in surviving the hazards of modern urban life. One is to develop an awareness of your environment, establishing good habits in your daily routines and using common sense to minimize risks – for instance, avoiding a deserted underpass in which all the lights have been broken. The second basic rule of survival is that if you have to rely on self-defence "proper prior preparation prevents pathetically poor performance". In other words, success depends on correct mental and physical training.

Identifying the risk of attack

There are places in the urban landscape that it's obviously best to avoid at certain times, but if you have to be alone in a deserted area you should carry an alarm or a makeshift weapon such as an umbrella or dog lead. Sensible footwear is vital – don't wear shoes that will slip off or cause you to stumble if you need to run.

Prevention is better than cure, but if you do have to resort to self-defence remember that in potentially violent situations stress causes the body to release adrenaline, preparing you for flight or fight. However, this can make your movements less precise. It is only through training in a realistic way that you can learn to respond effectively when faced with danger.

The best way to develop effective skills is to join a martial arts school that concentrates on teaching methods of self-defence rather than developing competitors for sporting events. You need realistic training based on a genuine understanding of the demands of actual fighting, rather than visually impressive sports-based techniques.

AGGRESSIVE BEHAVIOUR

People are creatures of habit and in stressful situations habitual actions and movements tend to dominate. This is true of both attackers and defenders, and surveys of attacks show that various forms of aggressive behaviour can be identified and predicted.

Human predators are not that different from other hunters. Tactics used by aggressors, such as the use of stealth and surprise to isolate and then overpower a victim, often reflect the hunting habits of wild animals.

WHERE TO BE ON YOUR GUARD

▲ *In large car parks, numerous pillars and poorly lit areas make perfect cover for potential attackers, so maintain awareness in such places at all times, especially if they are deserted.*

▲ *Because you are facing a cash machine it's hard to know what's going on behind you. Glance around whenever possible, and put cash into an inside pocket or handbag immediately.*

▲ *In a queue it's normal to allow strangers closer proximity than usual. It is best to hold something in your hand, such as a rolled-up newspaper. Drunks can be a particular problem here.*

▲ *Pickpockets and gropers are the usual problems on public transport. Keep valuables in an inside pocket, ideally zipped. As for gropers, the best tactic is to shout to draw attention to them.*

▲ *A poorly lit, deserted underpass can be dangerous as there are few escape routes. If you must use it stay close to one wall and check around corners before you turn. Use your eyes and ears.*

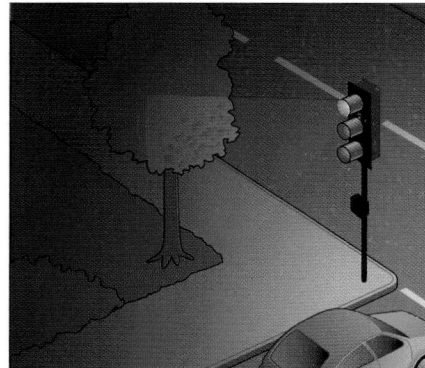

▲ *If you have to stop at lights in an unsafe area, keep the car doors locked and windows up. Look out for anyone approaching the car, and for missiles that could be used to smash a window.*

A TYPICAL ATTACK ON A MALE VICTIM

1 The attacker moves in close and attempts to intimidate his opponent by aggressive, loud, insulting language. Often a blank stare will accompany the use of threatening words and gestures.

2 The attacker pushes both hands into the chest, causing the victim to lose balance. He will usually try to push his victim over a chair or other object to increase the effectiveness of the attack.

3 The attacker next grabs his victim by the lapels and pushes him backwards again. By taking control of the victim's balance in this way he is making him vulnerable to further attack.

4 The attacker, now in full control, escalates the attack by delivering a blow to the victim's head with a bottle.

COMMON ATTACKS ON MEN

Studies show that when both assailant and victim are men, the ten most common forms of attack, in order of frequency, are:

1 A push to the chest followed by a punch to the head.

2 A swinging punch to the head.

3 A grab to the front clothing, one-handed, followed by a punch to the head.

4 A grab to the clothing with two hands, followed by a head butt.

5 A grab to the front clothing with two hands, followed by a knee to the groin.

6 A bottle, glass or ashtray to the head.

7 A lashing kick to the groin or lower legs.

8 A broken bottle or glass jabbed into the face.

9 A slash with a knife, usually a short-bladed lock knife or kitchen utility knife. (Hunting/combat-type knives tend to be used in gang violence and sexual assaults.)

10 A grappling-style head lock.

Attacks on women

There are a number of reasons why a woman might be attacked. As well as the obvious rape scenario, a woman could be attacked by a thief intent on taking something valuable, such as a mobile phone or a purse. In these circumstances it is not worth risking your health; let the thief take what they want and escape as quickly as possible. Only fight when the attack is directed at you rather than your property.

SEXUAL ASSAULTS

While strangers may seem to be the greatest threat, statistics prove that this is not the case. In fact most rapes occur in the home: 32 per cent of rape victims are attacked by their partners and another 22 per cent by men known to them.

From a self-defence point of view this means that the natural caution exercised among strangers is relaxed when in the company of friends, so reducing the opportunity for a fast, decisive response. However, it is important to react positively when a situation changes from one of normal affection or social interaction. Rape is an act of violence intended to degrade and humiliate the victim, and in police

▼ *Use your eyes to continuously scan for potential attackers or areas where an attack might come from. Stay away from dark doorways where an attacker could hide.*

interviews rapists often report that they commit the act as much for a sense of power and violence as for sex.

Submission to the rapist's demands is often thought of as a way to minimize the intensity of the attack, but in fact it may serve to encourage the attacker, who rationalizes that the victim is actually enjoying the activity and is, in fact, "asking for it".

The emotional effect of rape can include eating disorders, sleeping disorders, agoraphobia, depression, suicide attempts and sexual difficulties.

On pages 158 to 160 we cover other sexual assault issues including typical strategies employed by rapists. We also offer advice on how to fend off rapists in various street situations.

▲ *Badly lit car parks are high-risk areas for attacks. Always stay alert when approaching your vehicle and hold your keys ready in your dominant hand as a possible weapon.*

COMMON ATTACKS ON WOMEN

According to police records, these are the five most common forms of attack usd by men against women and girls:

1 The attacker approaches the victim displaying a weapon as a threat. The weapon is then hidden and the victim is led away, often by the attacker holding the victim's right upper arm.
2 The attacker pounces from behind, grabs the victim's head or neck in a lock and drags the victim away to a quiet place, often bushes or a deserted lane.
3 As with 2 above but the victim is grabbed around the waist and carried or dragged away.
4 The attacker pins the victim to a wall with a throat grab (often using the left hand). He issues a threat as in 1, and leads the victim away.
5 The attacker approaches from behind, grabs the victim's hair with his left hand and drags her away to a quiet place.

A TYPICAL ATTACK ON A FEMALE VICTIM

1 The attacker grabs the woman's right arm with his left hand. This initial assault is often accompanied by threatening instructions intended to frighten the victim into compliance.

2 In this case the threat is reinforced by the attacker brandishing a knife.

3 The knife might be partially hidden by being placed along the attacker's forearm. However, the victim can see it clearly, especially if the attacker pulls her in towards the blade.

DOMESTIC VIOLENCE

The victims of domestic violence, which accounts for almost a quarter of all the violent crime reported, are most likely to be women and children. Weapons are less likely to feature in domestic attacks: the victim is more likely to be injured from repeated blows with the hands and feet as well as being thrown into walls and furniture. Attempts at strangulation may also feature in this kind of situation.

Characteristically, this kind of attack is not a single incident, and on average a women will suffer 35 attacks from her partner before reporting the violence to the police. Domestic crime is the most under-reported type of violent crime, with about two-thirds of cases never coming to the authorities' attention.

Learning some basic survival strategies may minimize the chance of attack. On the physical level the ability to fight back will minimize the effects of an attack and may dissuade the attacker from using violence. Training can develop a level of self-esteem improving the victim's view of the world.

PERSONAL ALARMS

For well over a hundred years police officers carried the simplest form of personal alarm, a whistle, which could be heard over surprisingly long distances. Three strong blasts on it would bring speedy assistance.

Tiny modern key-ring whistles make useful personal alarms, but these days the more hi-tech, high-decibel, battery-powered alarm is more likely to be carried in a handbag or pocket. They emit a sound louder than that of a shotgun, and just above the pain threshold. The most practical type has

▲ *This tiny high-pitch siren alarm also has a built-in torch.*

a wrist cord connected to a small pin which, when sharply tugged free, allows a spring-loaded contact to complete an electrical circuit, triggering an ear-splitting siren. The second type, which may be little larger than a lipstick, is activated by pressing a button. This type of alarm is more discreet to carry in a pocket or bag, but it is just as effective.

◄ *A personal alarm can be clipped to a bag or belt hook and activated quickly if an attacker pounces.*

Learning to defend yourself

In a self-defence situation it is the training not only of the body but also of the mind and spirit that can give you an advantage.

TRAINING FOR IMPACT

Your strength and stamina can be improved by correct weight training, and the accuracy and impact of your strikes can be developed by hitting a target. It is best to train for impact without gloves as it is unlikely you will be wearing any protection on your hands if you are attacked. At first hit lightly, aiming for accuracy, but as you become used to the feeling of hitting you can increase the intensity of your blows. Learn to hit as hard as you can. If you ever have to fight for your life against a stronger, heavier opponent you may have only one opportunity to land a decisive strike. Learn how to do it properly.

By adapting to the stresses of training you are also improving your ability to face the shock of physical confrontation: without becoming masochistic about it, look on the knocks and bruises you receive in the gym as a good investment.

TRAINING WITH A PARTNER

If you train alone, a punch bag is a very useful tool to improve your striking skills, but training is more productive and fun if you have a partner. If you join a martial arts school you will have a ready supply of training partners, but you may be able to recruit a friend or relative who also wants to develop some self-defence skills.

A training partner is very useful if you train with a pair of specialized pads worn on the hands, usually known as focus pads or hook-and-jab pads. By moving the pads around, your partner can simulate an attacker moving in a random way, and you can learn how to hit a moving target. It is very important when training with a partner to hold back a little on the degree of power used in strikes, locks and chokes. It is very easy to injure someone inadvertently through over-enthusiasm or clumsiness. Begin slowly, adding power and speed as your levels of coordination and timing improve.

MARTIAL ARTS FOR SELF-DEFENCE

The best way to learn effective self-defence skills is to join a martial arts club. It is important to find a club that concentrates on training in self-defence methods rather than developing skills aimed at participation in tournaments. The traditions and customs of the martial arts exist to create safe training

IMPROVING YOUR PHYSICAL FITNESS

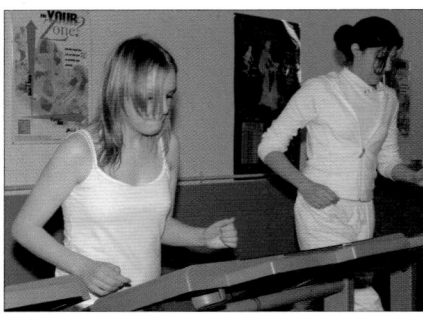

▲ *Cardiovascular conditioning is necessary to build up stamina and the ability to move quickly. Running outside or on a machine in the gym is an excellent way to develop stamina.*

▲ *Upper body strength is vital. By using a rowing machine grip strength can be improved, and the pulling action duplicates the movements used in grabbing an attacker's hair or flesh.*

▲ *The "pec deck", a piece of equipment found in many gymnasiums, is a useful way of training the muscles of the chest and shoulders.*

▲ *The bench press develops strength in the arms, chest and shoulders. Train as heavily as possible – the increase of strength not stamina is the intent.*

WEIGHT TRAINING

The easiest way to become physically strong is to join a weight training gym, and many sports centres have extensive facilities. If you are a total beginner join a class to learn how to do the exercises correctly and safely. As you gain experience you may want to train at home. As well as barbells and dumbbells you can try lifting heavy things such as large stones, bags of sand, buckets of water or car tyres.

MARTIAL ARTS TRAINING

• **Judo** is a very popular combat sport. Training is based on grappling and makes extensive use of throws and ground fighting. Since its introduction into the Olympics the stress in training has been towards competition skills, but its intensity means that the techniques can be most effective in self-defence. Being thrown hard into a wall, for example, deters most attackers.

• **Karate-do** is primarily a striking art, which concentrates on developing powerful structures and to develop the correct mental attitude towards the training. Each discipline stresses its own skills and approach.

punches, strikes and kicks. Some styles also make use of close-range knee and elbow strikes, throws and locks. Tae kwon do is the Korean version of karate, and specializes in kicking methods

• **Aikido** is a Japanese martial art. It makes use of circular movements, which are designed to intercept an attack, blend with the movement and throw the attacker. Advanced training in Aikido involves training with weapons such as the *jo* (stick). In a real self-defence situation these techniques can be applied to implements such as walking sticks or umbrellas.

• The term "**Kung-fu**" covers a wide range of Chinese martial arts. Some, such as T'ai Chi Ch'uan, are concerned mostly with health, while others such as the Wing Chun and Shaolin styles, are taught as combat methods.

• **Kick boxing** is a form of full-contact competiton fighting in a ring, but can also be very effective in self-defence situations. Tae kwon do also uses kick fighting (plus hand blocking and striking) for effective self-defence.

Finding a good club takes a little perseverance. If you know any martial artists you can ask them for their recommendations, explaining clearly what it is you are looking for. Then visit the club and watch the training in progress. Look carefully at the training methods and the way the instructors interact with the members. A bullying, militaristic atmosphere, where questions are not welcome, should be avoided. You may find that the training in this kind of club is not primarily about self-defence but is more a form of personal discipline.

Training methods and traditions in martial arts clubs are often derived from an oriental background, and as a beginner you may find features such as bowing or the wearing of white cotton training clothes a little exotic, but in essence these traditional elements are similar to the rituals found in Western fencing and boxing clubs.

LEARNING TO PUNCH

1 Practise with a focus pad to develop accuracy and impact. Hit with the big knuckles, keeping the wrist straight, and drive the fist in a straight line, as if you were trying to break an attacker's nose or jaw. Keep your balance and use your waist and hips to add drive to the blow, hitting through the target.

2 When you apply the punch, your intent should be to hit the fleshy parts rather than the bones, which could damage your hand. A fairly light punch to the throat will cause breathing problems to any attacker, but be careful in training as the neck and throat are very vulnerable to blows.

ELBOW STRIKE

1 Close in, an elbow strike can cause a lot of pain. In training, drive the elbow round and into the focus pad, aiming to land with the point of the elbow. Pull the other hand back to rotate the waist and simulate pulling an attacker into the strike.

2 The strike leaves the attacker's groin wide open for a follow-up kick or knee attack. Never rely on a single technique – be ready to exploit any weakness or hesitation on the attacker's part. Your survival may depend on this, especially if the attacker is bigger than you.

HAND SLAP

1 An open hand slap inflicts a surprising level of pain and shock. In training, focus on using the hand like a whip and slap down or sideways, hitting with the palm and not the fingers. Keeping the wrist a little loose gives a whiplash effect.

2 If the slap is aimed at the neck, try to hit in and slightly downwards to damage the throat. The best target for this kind of strike is the eyes. An assailant will almost certainly lift the hands to the face if the eyes have been heavily slapped. Take advantage of this to kick the attacker's groin or knees.

KNEE JERK

1 The knee is a very effective weapon, and is often used when an attacker has seized you and pulled you close. When training the knee on the focus pads, hold on to your training partner to simulate the correct range and the feeling of being close to an attacker.

2 The groin is a natural target, but many men will reflexively pull back if they sense an attack coming. By driving upwards it is often possible to hit the solar plexus. Other targets include the kidneys and the large muscles on the thighs. Try to augment the strike by gouging the eyes or biting the ear.

ROUNDHOUSE KICK

1 The roundhouse kick makes use of the whipping motion of the hips and the supporting leg. Use your instep to hit the groin, knees or thigh. With a lot of training this technique can even be used against the head, but in general it is safer to select a target from the waist downwards.

2 A very effective way to use a roundhouse kick is to strike against the back of an attacker's knee. As well as causing pain and slowing him down there is a strong possibility that this strike will cause him to stumble and fall. If this happens follow up your kick with a stamp to the ankle or groin.

GROIN KICK

1 A direct kick to the groin can drain an attacker of strength and aggression very quickly. Use the knee like a hinge and snap the lower leg directly to the target, aiming to hit with the instep of the foot. When practising this move, drive the kick upwards into the focus pad to develop maximum power and penetration. A male attacker who is kicked hard in the groin will usually bend forwards, covering his groin with his hands, leaving the eyes, throat and neck exposed to a powerful strike to any of those targets.

EFFECTIVE FIRST BLOWS

Ideally, the first blow should be decisive, allowing you to escape as quickly as possible. However, a number of factors could limit the effectiveness of your initial strike. The attacker may have been drinking alcohol or taking drugs, which will dull his response to pain. He may be wearing heavy clothing that absorbs some of the force of your blows, or your strike may be inaccurate.

It is therefore important to follow up as quickly as possible with a number of blows, all intended to cause as much pain and disorientation as possible. Aim at the eyes, groin, joints and other vulnerable parts. When training on a heavy bag try to keep going in bursts of 20–30 seconds; this will build stamina, fighting spirit and the skill to switch targets quickly. As soon as the attacker backs away, run towards somewhere safe.

Using improvised weapons

Because of the fear of attack some people habitually carry a knife or some other weapon. Although they may see it as a perfectly acceptable thing to do as they intend to use the weapon for self-defence only, the police in most countries would regard this as an illegal act, which could lead to arrest and punishment.

However, the law does accept that at times the use of force, even if it proves lethal, is justified if the action is reasonable in the prevention of an attack against yourself or another person. The key word is "reasonable". It would not be reasonable, for example, if having driven off an attacker you then pursued him and jammed your pen into his eye. On the other hand, if you performed the same act because you were being attacked and believed your life was in danger, it would probably be seen as reasonable, especially if your attacker was armed.

Within the boundaries set by the law it is perfectly possible to make use of items in your possession that are not usually thought of as weapons to defend yourself. These might include an umbrella or rolled newspaper, a bunch of keys, a belt or dog lead, the contents of a handbag – such as a comb (especially if it is made of steel or is pointed), credit cards, hairsprays and deodorants, a lighter, and pens and pencils – or the handbag iteslf, particularly if it is heavy.

IMPROVING YOUR STRIKES

As with all other aspects of effective self-defence it is important to practise your responses in order to develop efficient technique. If you make a target from a bundle of rolled-up newspapers taped together you can improve significantly your striking and targeting skills. Hang the bundle at about head height and practise delivering fast, hard and accurate blows at the centre line of the target.

NEWSPAPER OR MAGAZINE

1 A tightly rolled magazine or paper is surprisingly rigid and can be used to deliver powerful blows to the throat and face. The windpipe, eyes and mouth are especially vulnerable to this.

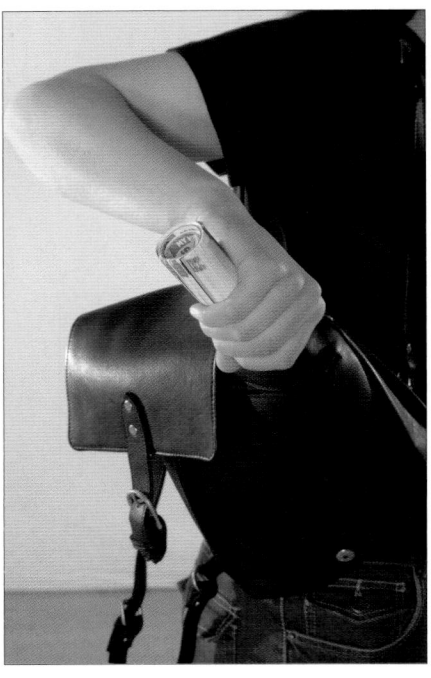

2 The magazine needs to be readily accessible, so it could be carried in the side of a bag, placed in such a way that the dominant hand (in this case the right hand) can grab it quickly.

3 Once the attacker has tried to take control of you as a victim, pull the magazine out of the bag and strike towards the attacker's neck or face.

4 Grab the hair or throat and pull the head towards the magazine as it moves up. Stab inwards, driving in with all the power of your shoulders and hips.

BUNCH OF KEYS

1 A bunch of keys can be used to deliver a very painful strike to the face. Keep the keys in the pocket nearest to your dominant hand, and if you feel you might be entering a dangerous place make sure that the pocket does not contain anything else that might prevent you getting to the keys quickly.

2 Pull the keys out and step backwards to create some space. This will also tend to unbalance the attacker if he has already made contact.

3 Drive the keys towards the attacker's eyes with a strong raking movement. A natural follow-up technique in this situation would be a knee to the groin.

UMBRELLAS

Umbrellas can be used in several different ways as an effective improvised weapon. A long rolled umbrella, held in either one or both hands, can be used to block someone attacking you with a weapon. Alternatively the tip can be rammed into the attacker's face with the intention of hitting the eyes, nose or teeth. Even a short umbrella, when open, can be used to distract an attacker while setting him up for a counter-attack such as a kick to the groin.

AEROSOL SPRAYS

Hair spray or deodorant can be used as an effective way to interfere with an attacker's vision. As with the rolled magazine and the keys, the aerosol needs to be carried in such a way that it can be brought into use quickly with the dominant hand. When transferring it to somewhere handy, make sure you remove its cap, if it has one, so that you don't lose the element of surprise by having to fumble with it at the crucial moment – speed and surprise are key in self-defence.

Once the attack begins, seize the initiative by stepping forwards and spraying into the attacker's eyes and mouth. Don't be afraid also to use the container as a striking weapon against the eyes, nose and mouth. The likelihood is that your attacker will recoil in pain or surprise, exposing his groin to attack from your knee or foot. Take the first opportunity to run to safety that you can.

Frontal attack

Most attacks from the front you will, by definition, see coming. That is to your advantage, giving you crucial moments to take in the situation and switch into survival mode.

Preparation for surviving a real attack must involve a physically vigorous approach. In training, the partner who is playing the part of an attacker must attempt to duplicate as closely as possible the actual situation likely to be faced to allow the defender to develop realistic responses. This is not simply about technique – a spirited attitude is very important. A man attacking a woman, for example, will generally be stronger and heavier than his intended victim. It is vital for the defender to respond with total

commitment and decisiveness and to keep on resisting, even if some pain is involved.

A study of victims of attempted rape found that those women who were used to engaging in a contact sport were better able to resist an attack and avoid being raped. This kind of habitual experience teaches that physical contact, even if it involves being hurt or knocked down, is not the worst thing that can happen, so it can be

▶ *Use a weapon of opportunity (in this case an umbrella) to continue your counter-attack. As soon as possible run away towards a well-lit area and report the attack to the police.*

TAKING CONTROL OF A FRONTAL ATTACK

1 The attacker makes his initial approach and contact by taking hold of the defender's right wrist.

2 The attacker raises his other hand as a threat. You should see this as an attempt to force your compliance by invading your personal space with a threatening gesture.

3 Break free from the attacker's grasp and slap his hand away to the side. Simultaneously, with your other hand grab his raised finger and bend it back with the aim of snapping it. If possible use a twisting action as you bend the finger back. Spitting in the assailant's eyes will also help to distract him momentarily.

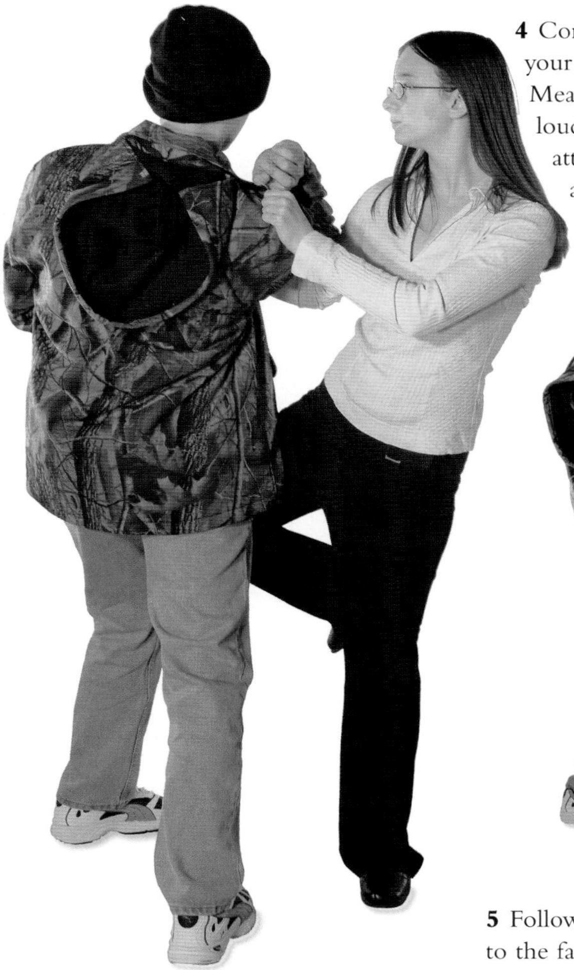

4 Continue the defence by driving your knee into his groin. Meanwhile, you should scream as loudly as possible to attract attention, intimidate the attacker and add strength to your attack.

NEVER GIVE UP

If your attacker proves stronger than you expected, don't give up. Continue to attack: bite, spit, gouge and use any chance to escape.

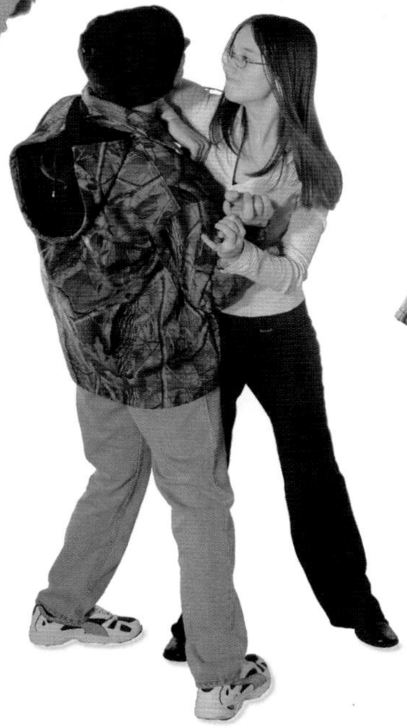

5 Follow through with a right elbow to the face, aiming at the nose, the throat or the temple.

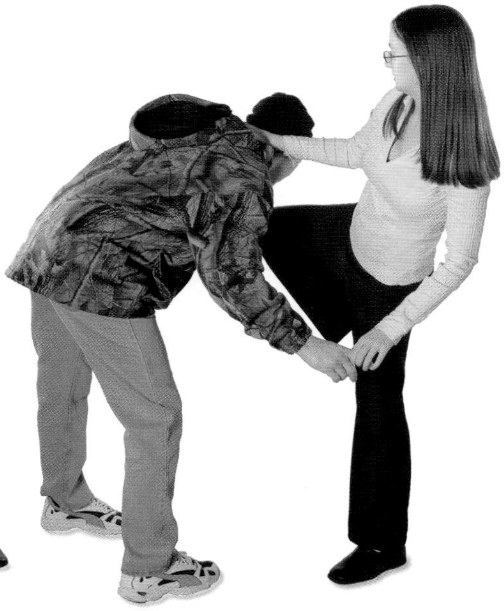

6 Step backwards and pull the attacker on to your rising right knee aimed at the face, throat or other target.

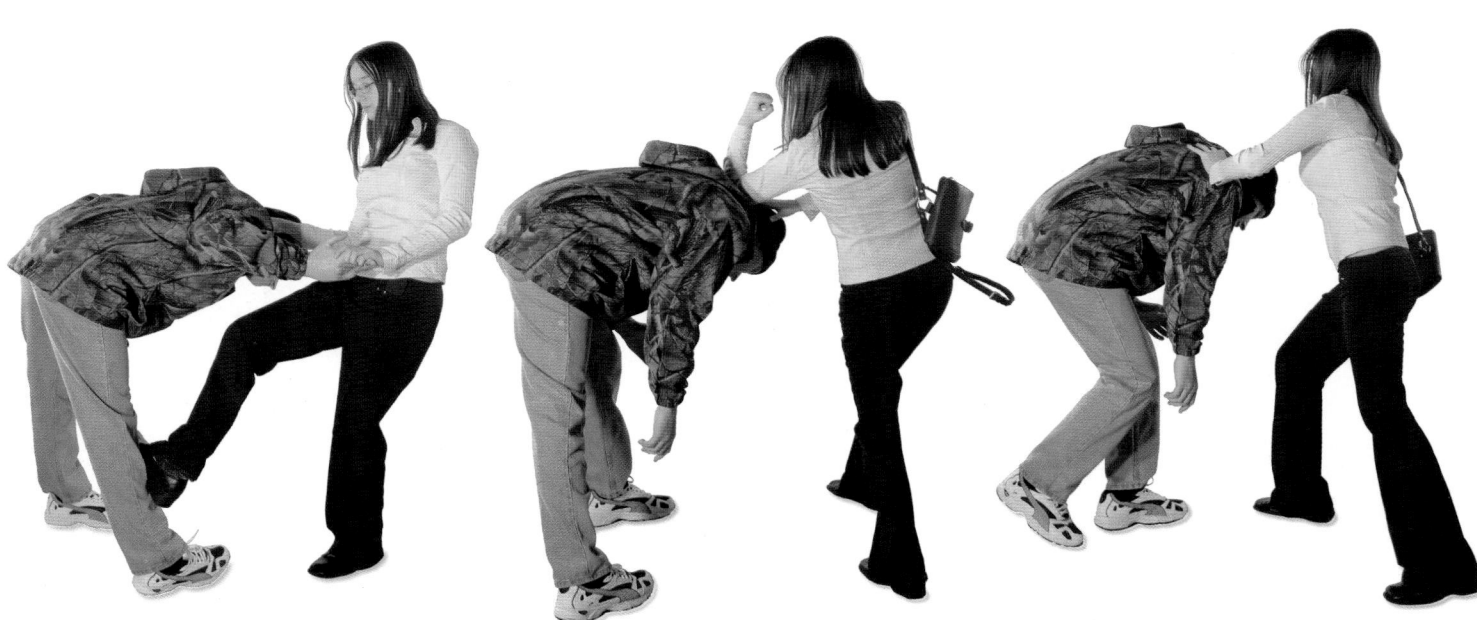

7 Continue to attack with your right foot, this time by stamping as hard as possible against the attacker's knee.

8 By now he may be doubled up. Step in and deliver a dropping elbow strike to the neck or face.

9 Drive the attacker into the ground to create space to escape, or hit him with an improvised weapon such as a bag.

Attack from behind

Any kind of attack from the rear is likely to be very successful as it makes the best use of surprise and the shock of impact and minimizes the possibility of the victim using the hands and feet in defence.

A person using a cash machine is in a situation where they are vulnerable to an attack from behind, and this approach is also often used by potential rapists targeting women and girls. As an attack from the rear is based on surprise the best defence is to stay alert to the possibility of such an attack. If you have to walk on your own along a poorly lit pavement at night, walk facing the traffic so a car cannot pull up behind you and catch you unawares. If you think someone is following you, cross the road more than once. If you are still afraid get to the nearest place where other people are – a take-away or somewhere with lights on – and call the police. Scan your surroundings continuously to minimize the possibility of an attacker approaching from a blind spot – even if it is unlikely to occur it is sensible to be aware.

Most attacks from behind will involve some grappling as the attacker is likely to wrap his arms around your upper body or grab and pull your hair.

It is important to maintain your balance and to try to destroy the attacker's balance while causing him pain. Tactics such as stamping on the foot or knee while clawing at his groin work well.

REACT INSTANTLY

Your training should prepare you to explode into your defence, going from rest to 100 per cent effort as quickly as possible, physically and mentally. Continue to exert forward pressure until the attacker is defeated or runs away.

COUNTERING A REAR ATTACK

2 Drive your elbow backwards into the attacker's ribs as hard as possible. As you make this strike you should feel as if you are trying to smash completely through the attacker's body in order to generate sufficient force.

3 With your left hand grab the opponent's left fingers, ideally the ring and little fingers. Bend the fingers backwards as far as you can, breaking them if possible.

1 The attacker attempts to grab you with a bear hug. At the moment of contact step forward as far as possible and lift your arms to minimize the attacker's advantage of strength.

▶ *If you can break the attacker's fingers you will make it virtually impossible for him to strike or grab you with his damaged hand. In addition, a relatively small slap to his broken fingers will cause intense pain.*

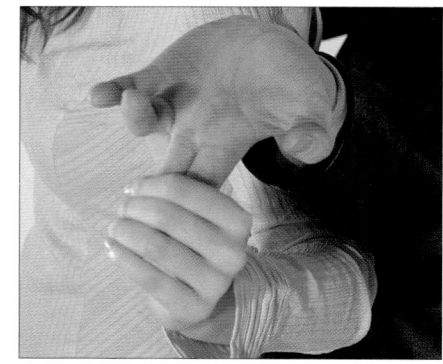

4 Step away from the attacker's right hand, pivoting at an angle to expose his centre line. Maintain the pressure on the fingers.

5 Push forwards using both hands to apply more leverage to the fingers; if possible apply a twisting, wrenching motion to the finger joints.

6 Reach with the right hand to grab the attacker's hair, and pull the head backwards and down while maintaining leverage on the fingers of the left hand.

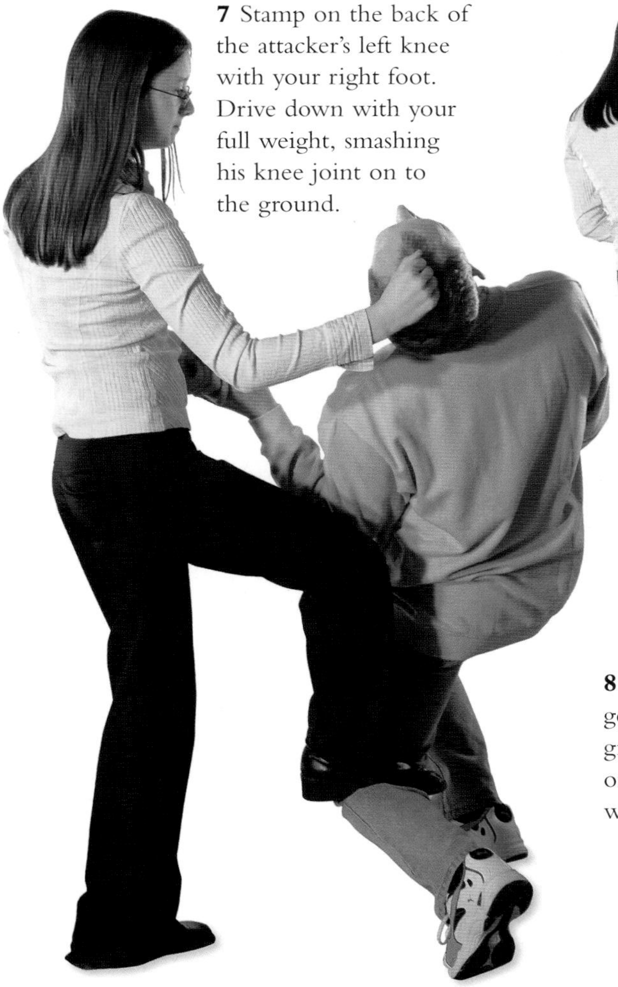

7 Stamp on the back of the attacker's left knee with your right foot. Drive down with your full weight, smashing his knee joint on to the ground.

8 Once you have succeeded in getting the attacker to the ground, maintain your holds on him as you shift your body weight forwards.

9 Now push the attacker away from you and down on to the ground. Escape as quickly as possible.

KEEPING THE ADVANTAGE

As you drive forwards take any opportunity that comes by to deliver strikes to the perpetrator's body.

Attacks with knives and other weapons

While a fist or foot can inflict lethal injuries, there is no doubt that the chance of being badly hurt or killed is greatly increased when an attacker makes use of a weapon. Many objects can be used as weapons but experience has shown that the most commonly carried weapon is a knife.

The number of attacks using knives has risen over the past few years, and some authorities believe that a knife culture is growing, particularly among young men. The claim is often made that they carry knives for self-defence, but it is also clear that blades can be and are used to attack anyone perceived as a danger or – more prevalent – as a target for theft or racial violence.

DEFENCE AGAINST AN EDGED WEAPON

Knives or broken bottles, glasses and ashtrays can cause horrific wounds. Certain arteries are more vulnerable to attack than others, because they are nearer the surface of the skin, or are not protected by clothing or equipment. It is important to protect these areas from attack – the neck, with its jugular vein and the carotid artery, is one such area.

The most frightening thing about a knife attack is knowing that you might be cut, stabbed or even killed. Such fear is potentially paralysing. In order to regain any degree of control over the situation, you need to accept that you might get hurt.

Trying to disarm a determined attacker is very difficult. But showing that you are not one to freeze with fear is enough to put some attackers sufficiently off-guard to enable you to escape. If you are forced to defend yourself, keep it simple – and whatever you do, don't rush a person with a knife. The most likely place you will be cut is across the face or abdomen. Keep circling your attacker and at a safe enough distance to avoid being slashed – keep sucking your stomach in. If you can, find something to use as a defensive weapon such as a chair. Grab a coat or belt to use as a striking, entangling device, or throw the loose change from your pocket directly at the attacker's eyes as hard as you can.

USING A KNIFE

Extreme circumstances might arise in which you are forced to wield an attacker's knife to save yourself or another victim in an attack. The heart or stomach are the best targets if they are unprotected. The psychological effect of receiving even a slight wound in the stomach is such that it is likely to throw an attacker into confusion.

If you are attacked in your own home, say by a burglar armed with a baseball bat, don't be tempted to pick up a kitchen knife and use it to threaten the attacker. You are just inviting the burglar to take it from you and to use it against you.

BLUNT WEAPONS

Weapons such as sticks, coshes, iron bars, hammers and similar objects can cause terrible injuries. A hammer smashed down on an arm can easily break it while the same blow to the head can fracture the skull and cause massive brain damage. Try to sway, duck and dodge out of the way. If you are knocked to the ground, keep rolling, shielding your skull with both hands and your ears with your wrists.

GUNS

The golden rule when faced by someone with a gun in a robbery is to do exactly what they tell you to do. If they say "Freeze," do just that. Many prospective robbers will carry a weapon precisely to scare you and may not even know how to use the gun properly. You are peripheral to their main plan, which is almost certainly to steal rather than murder. By remaining as inconspicuous as you can, you represent less of a threat and there is therefore less reason for them to escalate the crime. You also cannot guarantee whether they are a good shot or not and the last thing you want to do is panic your attacker into shooting.

▲ *A selection of combat knives designed to cause maximum injury. Always remember that a knife with a 7.5cm/3in blade is long enough to penetrate the heart. It is illegal in most countries to carry a knife as a weapon for self-defence so don't be tempted to do so, and it can always be turned against you.*

But what if this is nothing to do with theft and you are the intended victim? What if your attacker has been stalking you and is trying to force you into their car at gunpoint?

Some would argue that you should acquiesce on the basis that if you cooperate you might be able to talk the attacker round. Others say that you should play the odds and that the first few seconds of an attack offer you the greatest chance of escape and survival – by refusing to cooperate and making a scene you might just buy that crucial second that allows you to run.

If you do decide to run for your life, try to quickly put some distance between yourself and the attacker. Keep low and run in a zig-zag fashion to put them off their shot. If you can put some obstructions between you, such as a line of cars, trees or a fence then so much the better.

BEING ATTACKED WITH A KNIFE

1 If your attacker is armed the best defence is, of course, to run away as quickly as you can, but in some circumstances this may be impossible.

2 As the attacker slashes, sway back out of range, keeping your arms close to your body. Do not flap your arms wildly as they may be cut.

3 As the attacker slashes towards your face lift both arms to protect your face and neck. Do not expose the vulnerable inner wrists to the blade.

4 As you lift the arms to shield your face, don't raise them passively but smash them into the attacker's arm to cause injury or possibly loosen his grip on the knife.

5 When the slash has missed its target, grab the attacking arm strongly to put the weapon under control and drive your elbow into the attacker's ribs or face. Once you have established control over the knife arm do not give it up under any circumstances. This is your best protection against being cut.

6 Push the attacker's elbow straight up and push your weight into him to put him off balance. Turn the knife towards his ribs. Drive forward with all your weight to push the blade into his body. If he falls, back off as quickly as possible and escape.

DEFLECTING A STABBING ATTACK

1 The attacker has grabbed you with his left hand and raised the knife to stab down towards your head or neck.

2 Move inwards to intercept the stabbing arm and deflect the blade with your forearm.

3 Grab the wrist holding the knife and extend the arm while clawing at his eyes. Push him backwards off balance.

4 As you push him back, sweep his supporting leg away from under him with your foot, causing him to fall. Try not to lose control over the hand holding the knife.

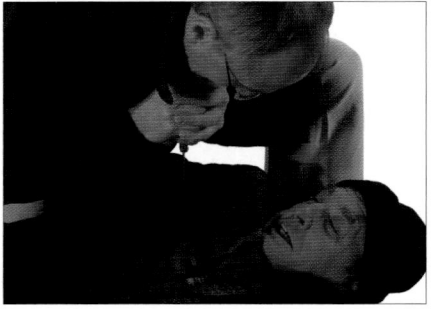

5 Use both hands to control the wrist holding the knife. Twist the point of the knife towards the attacker.

6 Drop your full weight on to the handle of the knife, forcing the blade into the attacker's chest. Escape as quickly as possible.

BEING THREATENED WITH A GUN

1 When faced with someone holding a gun the best piece of advice is to obey the attacker's instructions. If it is a robbery give him what he wants. Your life is worth more than a watch, money or a car.

2 If you are convinced that the attacker will shoot you whatever happens, you have no choice but to defend yourself. Sweep the gun to the side to get out of the way of the muzzle.

3 If the weapon goes off at this point you will be shocked by the noise, but you must hang on to either the weapon or the attacker's wrist.

4 Attack the elbow of the arm holding the gun.

5 Your aim is to get both hands controlling the arm holding the gun. Stamp-kick the attacker's knee as hard as you can to distract him as you make a move to get possession of the gun. Maintain forward momentum at all times to dominate the situation.

6 Pull the gun out of the attacker's hand, and back away as quickly as possible. At this point you might be tempted to use the weapon but you would almost certainly be found guilty of attempted murder, unless the attacker produced another weapon, such as a knife, in which case shooting him would be seen as reasonable.

Strangulation

Because the neck lacks any form of bony protection and contains the spinal cord, major blood vessels and the windpipe, it is extremely vulnerable to damage by being compressed. A victim will initially experience severe pain, quickly followed by unconsciousness and brain death. Pressure to the throat can affect blood flow to the brain and stop the heart beating. It takes only about 15kg/33lb of force to close the trachea; you can become unconscious in seconds. This form of attack is often directed by men against women and strangulation is frequently a feature of domestic abuse.

STRENGTHENING THE NECK

Weight training can be used to strengthen the muscles of the neck and shoulders, as can exercises such as shrugs and shoulder presses and those involving the head harness.

DEFENDING AGAINST STRANGULATION 1

1 The attacker attempts to grab your throat with the left hand, intending to throttle you.

2 Push down on the attacker's elbow joint as hard as possible while punching him in the throat with the other fist.

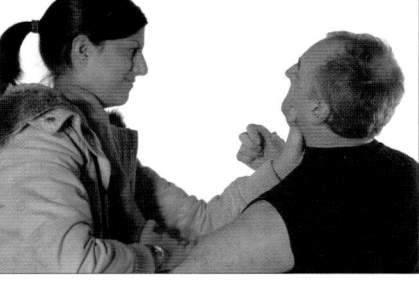

3 Spitting directly into the attacker's eyes will make him blink, leaving him vulnerable to further attack.

4 Drive the left hand upwards while grabbing the hair with the right hand to pull the head back strongly. Use a jerking action to damage the neck.

5 Stamp on the back of the attacker's leg, driving the knee into the ground. Commit your full weight to the stamp to do as much damage as possible.

6 Drive his head to the ground with your palm. If he begins to get up kick his groin or stamp on the back of his ankle. Escape as quickly as possible.

DEFENDING AGAINST STRANGULATION 2

1 The attacker reaches for your throat with his right hand.

2 Parry the attacker's hand and begin to apply upward pressure to his elbow.

3 Push the arm up and over to unbalance the attacker.

DEFENDING AGAINST STRANGULATION 3

THE COUNTER–ATTACK

Do not stamp on the attacker's face or head as it could be considered unreasonable force; a stamp to the arm or hand, or to the knee or ankle, is usually acceptable.

1 The attacker approaches with his right hand reaching towards the throat.

2 The attacker seizes your throat and starts to squeeze.

3 ◀ Pull your head a little to the side, drop your chin and then push forwards, simultaneously attacking with a punch, slap or grab to the groin, intended to force the attacker to back away.

4 ▶ Pivot to the outside, sliding your left forearm across the attacker's throat and pulling him off balance. Step backwards as quickly as possible while pulling the attacker to the ground. As soon as he is down you can use a stamp to prevent any further attack.

ATTEMPTED STRANGULATION FROM BEHIND

1 The attacker approaches from behind, giving him the advantage of surprise.

2 The attacker wraps his left arm around your throat and begins to apply pressure.

3 Lean forwards and pull the attacker's left arm down as hard as possible to reduce the pressure on the throat.

4 Maintaining control of the arm, pivot in a clockwise motion away from the attacker, wrenching his arm as hard as possible outwards.

5 Step in with your heel behind his nearer leg while delivering a strike to his face with your right hand. A strike with the heel of the hand to the jaw or throat is very effective, especially if it is accompanied with a clawing action directed at the attacker's eyes.

6 Push the attacker backwards over your leg to throw him off balance and drive him to the ground. Once he is down continue to counter-attack with a stamp to the body or groin. Don't assume that because the attacker is on the ground they have ceased to be a threat. Move away quickly so the perpetrator cannot reach out and grab your legs and pull you to the ground.

Head butt

A head butt can be a devastating form of attack if it lands on the nose, eye or cheekbone, and is often the favoured method of those skilled at heading a football. Its effect can be maximized by pulling the victim on to the strike, and the target area is stabilized by gripping the victim's clothing with both hands. If a head butt lands cleanly it can easily cause a knockout, concussion and damage to the soft tissues of the face. It can also lead to permanent eye damage or even brain damage.

Defending against a head butt requires fast reaction to the initial grab.

DEFENDING AGAINST A HEAD BUTT

1 The attacker has grabbed you to set you up for a head butt. Often the grab is so strong that the victim's head suffers a degree of whiplash. It is important to train the muscles of the neck to minimize the effects of being grabbed and jerked into a blow.

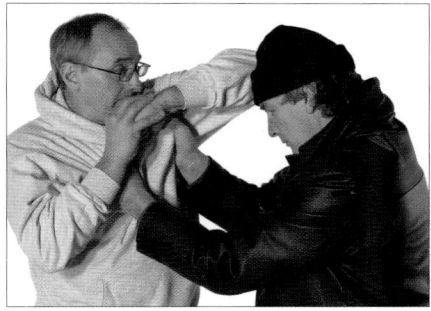

2 As the attacker drives his head forwards towards your face, lift your elbow in such a way that the point of the elbow meets the attacker's face. This will stop the head butt and cause some damage to the soft tissues of the attacker's face.

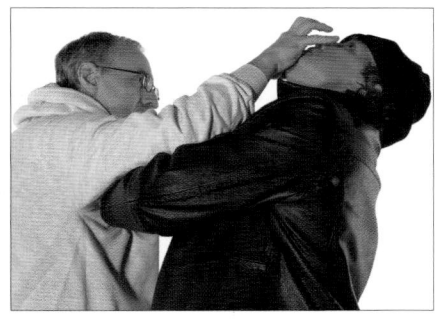

3 Drive the heel of your right hand directly into the attacker's jaw or throat, pushing the head backwards. A claw hand attack to the eyes can be delivered at the same time to further weaken and disorient the attacker.

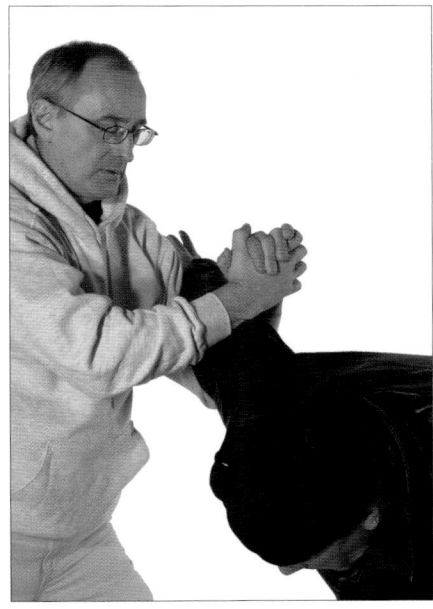

4 Drop your body weight and jerk the attacker's arm downwards as strongly as possible with the aim of damaging the elbow joint. If space permits you should step backwards or to the side to maximize the leverage you are exerting on the arm.

5 Twist the attacker's arm up and around, forcing it up his back and wrenching his shoulder. This will force his head downwards, where it is vulnerable to strikes with the knee or foot. If the attacker manages to retain his balance, ram him into a wall.

6 Grab the attacker's open fingers with both hands and pull sideways strongly to damage the joints of the hand. You do not need a lot of strength to do major damage in this way. The attacker will then be unable to use his hand to grab or strike you.

Bag snatching

A bag swinging on a long strap over the shoulder is an attractive proposition for an opportunistic thief. A safer and more discreet way to wear a bag is on a short strap under the arm, tight to the body – not that this will deter the determined mugger.

A common approach by bag snatchers is to move rapidly towards the victim from the rear, grab the bag and run away as quickly as possible. In some cases the thief will use force or the threat of force to obtain the bag. Some victims have been injured by the attacker pushing them to the ground or into a wall when the bag is grabbed. In the case of a frail victim, the consequences of the attack may far outweigh the value of the possessions that have been lost.

If an attacker makes a serious threatening gesture with a knife to intimidate you and force you to comply, let the bag go. It is not worth getting stabbed or slashed in order to keep your possessions. If possible back away while keeping your eyes on the attacker. Try to remember details of his build and appearance to report to the police later. Write down your impressions as soon as you can and get details of any witnesses.

To minimize the effect of having your bag stolen do not carry all your valuables in one place. If you

▶ *A thief intent on snatching a bag is likely to aproach from behind and simply grab it, catching the victim unawares.*

THEFT THROUGH A CAR WINDOW

1 If you see the attacker approaching the window turn on the engine. Ideally drive away, but if that is not possible, make sure the door is locked.

2 As the attacker reaches through the open window grab his arm with both hands and pull it into the car as hard as you can.

3 Try to pull on his arm with enough force to smash his face and neck against the door frame of the car. If possible twist the arm to maximize damage.

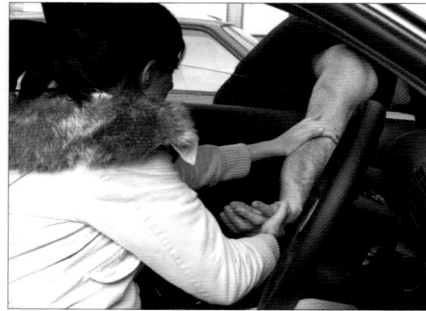

4 Throw your weight against his elbow joint, jamming his shoulder into the front of the window. Attack his fingers and twist or break as many as possible.

have to carry a large amount of cash, put most of the larger denomination notes in an inside pocket of your jacket. Do not display large amounts of money if shopping or taking money out of a cash dispenser; this will advertise to a bag snatcher that you are worth robbing.

If you become involved in a struggle with a bag snatcher, scream at the top of your voice. A street thief depends on speed and surprise so if you can slow him down or attract the attention of others he will be neutralized.

BAG SNATCHING FROM A CAR
Even if you are sitting in it, a stationary car with an open window is an open invitation to an opportunistic thief. Whether you are parked or stuck in a traffic queue, a thief can easily reach in and grab a bag on the seat, so get wise and keep valuables out of sight.

If you spot the thief's movements in time you may be able to take action by grabbing his arm. Meanwhile, sound your horn continuously to attract attention from passers-by. Other possible responses would be to use a demister aerosol as a spray into the attacker's face, or to use a pen or pencil as a spike to gouge his arm or hand.

DEALING WITH A STREET THIEF

1 The attacker approaches from behind and attempts to grab the handbag, which is worn in such a way that it cannot be released quickly.

2 As soon as you are aware of the attacker's intentions, pivot to the side and deflect his arm. Pull the arm to the side a little to disturb his balance and reach up and grab either his hair or the hood of his jacket.

COUNTER-ATTACK STRATEGIES

When there is a large difference in weight between attacker and victim it is very important to react with great speed and ferocity. Like a mongoose fighting a large snake, the victim has to rely on speed and counter-attacks to the vulnerable areas of the attacker's body. Punching the stomach or chest, for example, is less effective than clawing the eyes or landing a heavy strike on the testicles or throat.

Ideally, attack the knee joints to hamper the attacker's ability to move quickly. This will remove his advantages of weight and reach, and prevent him chasing you when you escape. A stamp on the back of the ankle should damage the Achilles tendon and prevent any fast movement with that leg.

3 Pull his head back while stamping on his knee joint.

4 Smash the attacker's knee on to the ground. While he is down move away as quickly as possible to a safe place.

Sexual assaults

Although anyone can be a target for a rapist, many victims are under the age of 18, and most rapists use physical force to intimidate and subdue their victims. Although there is a belief that rapes are mostly unplanned attacks committed by strangers, the great majority of rapists are known to their victims and the assault itself is a result of a plan worked out well in advance.

A group attack is possibly the most dangerous situation you could encounter. The most important thing is to maintain as much distance as possible. Ideally, run away as fast as you can to a well-lit, populated area.

RAPE STRATEGIES

A potential rapist will often use one of the following approaches:

• **Gaining the victim's confidence** Usually the rapist openly approaches the victim and asks for help in some way. Once within range he becomes more aggressive and threatening. An attacker using this approach may

pretend to be a police officer, a door-to door-salesman or a driver giving a lift to a hitch-hiker. This is the commonest tactic when the rapist is a stranger.

• **Sudden attack** The rapist hides in some kind of cover and suddenly attacks without warning.

• **Stealth attack** The rapist breaks into where the victim is sleeping.

Rapists try to control their victims through physical intimidation, verbal threats, the display of a weapon (usually a knife) and physical force. Often the victim is so frightened or shocked that little force is required to make them compliant. The rapist depends on this, so disrupt his plan by shouting and resisting his attack to attract attention.

Heavy drinking can make victims very vulnerable to attack. Their physical skills are impaired to such a point that it may be impossible to make use of either fight or flight, and the memory is so disrupted that it may be difficult to remember details that could help convict the attacker.

SEXUAL HARASSMENT

Though not usually as serious as rape, sexual harassment at work is a threat to your peace of mind and self-esteem and laws exist to protect employees from this kind of thing. It may take a variety of forms, from inappropriate comments about your appearance to a fellow employee trying to touch you in unwelcome ways. You should make it very clear that you do not welcome such comments or behaviour. Do not apologize for your reaction or try to present a friendly smiling exterior. Make it very clear from the outset, ideally in front of witnesses, that you will not accept any form of harassment.

If this does not work keep a record of all the incidents and report them to your employer. By law they have to take action against the offender. If, as a last resort, the continued behaviour necessitates physical action on your part, you may need to prove that your action was justified as the result of an unresolved situation.

FRONTAL ATTACK

1 Reach up and seize the attacker's clothing, or if he has long hair or earrings, pull on them forcefully.

2 As the attacker's head is moving down, drive your knee in an upward motion into his groin.

3 As the attacker falls forwards push his head backwards. Continue to counter-attack with a clawing action at the eyes.

SEXUAL ATTACK ON THE GROUND

1 When walking along a quiet lane, an attacker approaches from behind and quickly moves in to grab you.

2 He uses his weight and strength to push you to the ground, straddling you and pushing on your shoulders or arms.

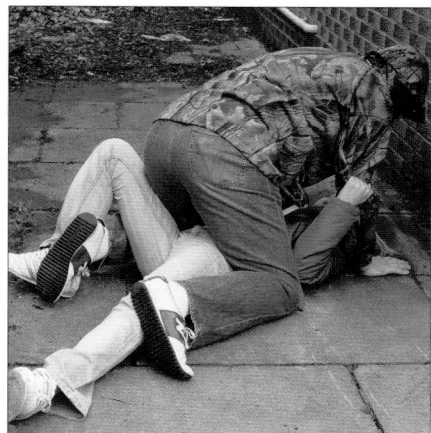

3 The attacker does not have control of your legs. Hook your foot around one of his ankles.

4 The ankle hook, seen here in close-up, gives the purchase you need to roll to the side, pushing hard with the arms and driving your leg against the ankle.

5 Once you have managed to dislodge the attacker, use your arms if possible to throw him into a wall to maximize the effect of the escape.

6 Drive your knee into the attacker's groin, then break free and run to a populated area. Contact the police as quickly as possible.

FENDING OFF A GROUP OF ATTACKERS

1 If confronted by a threatening group, shout as loudly as possible to attract attention and to show clearly that you will not simply accept the situation.

2 If the group persists and advances towards you, a belt with a heavy buckle, or a dog lead or chain, makes a useful weapon of opportunity.

3 A belt can be swung in fast arcs to keep attackers as far away as possible. Keep it in motion as they advance, while backing away as fast as you can.

ATTACK AGAINST A WALL

1 The attacker is hiding on a corner watching you as you approach.

2 He moves towards you quickly, pushing you back against a wall.

3 Respond instantly by driving a knee into his groin, stomach or thigh.

4 Move your head to one side and with all your weight and strength pull the attacker's face into the wall.

5 Push the attacker away from you on to his back. As he falls shout at the top of your voice and keep watching him.

6 Stamp on his groin and then run away as quickly as possible and move into a crowded area.

INAPPROPRIATE TOUCHING 1

1 Respond to the initial contact by trapping the attacker's hand to prevent further movement and raise your elbow in preparation for a response.

2 Drive the elbow directly into the attacker's face, aiming at the nose, lips, or eyes. Shout loudly to add power to the strike and inhibit the attacker.

3 Counter-attack by driving a knife hand into the attacker's groin. Stand up and move away, pushing the attacker as hard as possible in the other direction.

INAPPROPRIATE TOUCHING 2

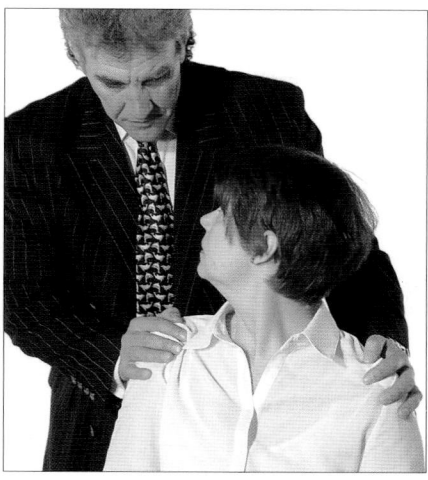

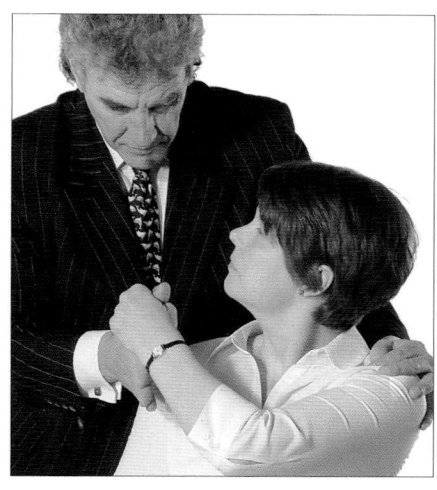

1 The attacker approaches from behind. Typically, this could be an approach to someone sitting at a desk.

2 He places his hands on the defender's shoulders and leans forward, as if he is about to speak quietly.

3 Respond by grabbing one or more of the attacker's fingers with your dominant hand (in this case the left).

4 Twist and pull the finger causing the attacker's head to drop and at the same time prepare a counter-attack with the other hand.

5 Slam the heel of your hand directly upwards into the attacker's chin, forcing his head back. This will create enough space for you to stand and move away.

SURVIVAL IN THE HOME

When did you last review the security of your home and its possessions? How would you guard against intruders in your house? Could you fall victim to a gas leak or carbon monoxide poisoning? Is your home a potential fire trap? If a fire did break out, would you know how to get everyone out safely? While you should know how to cope with such dangers in your home, it could also be your refuge in times of war, civil disturbance or terrorist attack. Have you considered how to make the best use of it in this context?

Guarding against break-ins

The best way to check how easy your home would be to break into is to imagine you have lost your keys and then try to find a way in, causing least damage and noise. You may be surprised at how easy it would be – and you can guarantee that a burglar will be better at it than you.

WINDOW LOCKS

For many burglaries windows are the primary point of entry, as even when locked they are often less secure than doors. Toughened glass or double glazing acts as a deterrent, as the last thing a thief needs is the sound of breaking glass to alert the neighbours, but of course if you don't bother to shut and lock every window in the house, a burglar won't even need to consider a forced entry.

On all but the most modern factory-made double-glazed units, a window is usually secured by just one central catch. Frequently, judicious use of a garden shovel in one corner is all that is needed to distort the frame enough to allow the burglar to release the latch.

▲ *A small safe, available from stationery chain stores, is a cheap and secure way of storing documents and valuables.*

IMPROVING YOUR HOME SECURITY

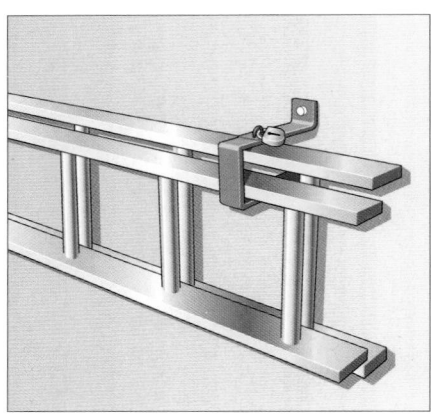

▲ *If you have to keep a ladder outside your home, secure it with a locking bracket to prevent thieves using it to gain access to your upper windows.*

▲ *Shut and lock all the upper floor windows when the house is empty, as your neighbours may not have secured their ladders even if you have.*

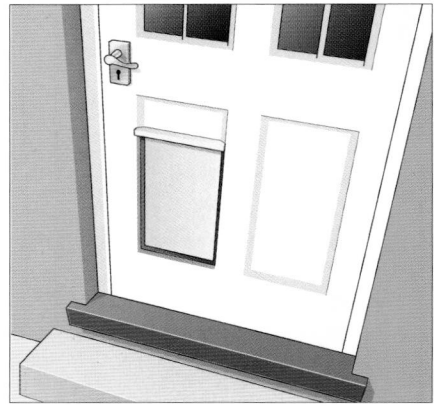

▲ *If you have a catflap in a door, you should be sure never to leave a key in the lock. An additional lock at the top of the door will improve security.*

▲ *The first two places a burglar will check are under the front doormat and under a nearby plant pot, just in case you have left a spare key there.*

▲ *If intruders should manage to break into your house, you will make their job very easy if you keep all your valuables and documents together.*

▲ *If you are going away, you can make the house look occupied by using time switches in a few rooms to turn lamps and radios on and off.*

▲ *A battery-powered alarm on the wall opposite the stairs will give you warning of intruders prowling downstairs at night.*

To counter this, cheap and simple surface-mounted secondary locks at the corners most likely to be pried open can be fitted by anyone who can wield a screwdriver. Incidentally, your home insurance company will probably give a discount if extra window locks are fitted, but they will only pay out if you actually keep them locked.

SECURING DOORS

The front door to the property is usually the most secure, and therefore is not such an inviting entry point for the burglar. However, if the door is secured only by a single latchkey lock, it becomes a more tempting target, as this can often be "sprung" from the outside using a flexible blade or possibly even a credit card. If the door is fitted with a secondary mortise lock, or a deadlock, the thief will think twice. Not only is it much more difficult – and noisy – to force this type of lock, but should a burglar get in through a window, it precludes the option of nonchalantly walking out of the front door with your valuables at the end of the job.

Rear or side doors, often less visible from the street, are usually an easier way in than the stout front door. As well as having less substantial locks, they are often part-glazed. As the family tends to use a secondary door frequently for access to the garden or garage, it may be left unlocked, or with

▲ *Even if you don't actually have a burglar alarm fitted, a dummy box on the front of your home can work as a deterrent.*

the key in the lock. Bolts may well be fitted top and bottom, but how many people bother to close them?

There are many ways of retrieving a key from the inside of a lock, but if a catflap is fitted the job is easy. Larger flaps, designed for dogs, can even be used by young or skinny burglars to access the property silently, unless they are fitted through thick walls rather than thin door panels. Even if the catflap in an outer door allows access only to a porch or conservatory, breaking into it can allow the burglar to get out of sight and earshot of neighbours and passers-by, and then to work at leisure in forcing locked doors or windows into the main building.

▼ *Some sliding glass doors can be lifted off their rails from outside, but fitting a secondary lock will prevent this.*

OUTBUILDINGS AND LADDERS

Even if you secure all your ground floor doors and windows, your home is vulnerable if you leave tools in an unlocked shed or garage, and have an unsecured ladder in the garage or garden. Would your neighbours question a "workman" or "window cleaner" working on your first-floor windows? Lock, and alarm, sheds and outhouses, and secure a ladder on a proper rack with a substantial padlock. These can be purchased very cheaply from good hardware stores.

DETERRING THE BURGLAR

Thieves will always go for the property of least resistance, so if a burglar alarm box is clearly visible, the side gate is padlocked to prevent anyone sneaking round the back, and there is flimsy trellis on top of the boundary wall, they will not waste time but will seek another target. They do not like gravel driveways either, as these make a silent approach very difficult. However, if you are stupid enough to leave a key under the doormat or an obvious plant pot, a burglar will be in and out in a trice.

Don't make the burglar's job any easier by leaving house or car keys openly visible from outside, as it takes only seconds to snatch them through a letterbox or prised window frame with a collapsible fishing rod. Your insurers probably won't pay up if you lose your car, or thieves break in, with keys that you obligingly left for them.

▼ *If a latch lock such as this is your only form of lock on external doors, add a mortise deadlock for extra security.*

Enhancing your security

Stout locks are likely to deflect a thief's attention away from your home, but at all times you should be aware of situations that make your home more vulnerable to intruders. There are also further steps you can take to protect your property, particularly at night, when a break-in could result in an attack on you or your family.

SECURITY LIGHTING

The careful positioning of security lights on the outside of the property, activated by movement sensors, will provide a great deterrent at night. For maximum effect, lights must be positioned to illuminate the most likely entry points, and they should not be mounted in such a way that they dazzle neighbours and passers-by while allowing the intruder to work unseen behind blinding light.

If you have a garden around your home, bushes that obscure doors and vulnerable windows from view are useful to the burglar. Chop them down. (Conversely, a thorny hedge on the boundary can be a good deterrent.)

PREPARING FOR THE WORST

If, in spite of your security measures, an intruder does manage to get in at night, bolts on the inside of your bedroom door will give you a few extra seconds to telephone for help; your mobile phone should be in the bedroom with you, rather than charging up in another room, in case the intruder cuts the telephone line.

You should also consider keeping a torch by your bedside, preferably a large, multiple-battery, police-style one that can double as a defensive weapon.

VULNERABLE SITUATIONS

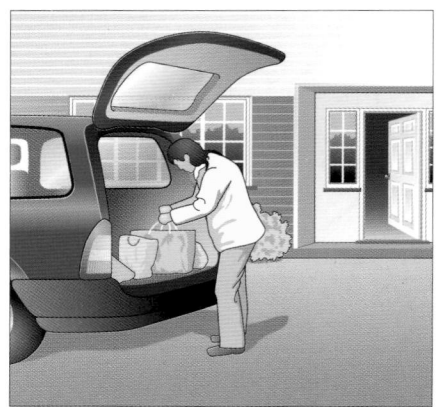

▲ *You are offering a sneak thief an open invitation if you leave the front door open while you return to your car to unload your shopping bags.*

▲ *An open garden door could allow your property to be burgled while your back is turned: and your insurers may refuse to settle your claim for any loss.*

▲ *Don't leave keys hanging neatly together where a burglar can help himself – especially if they include spare sets of keys for your neighbours' houses.*

▲ *Leafy shrubs growing too near your home can provide cover for a thief to hide behind while forcing an entry through a window or door.*

▲ *Window locks are only effective if you lock them and remove the key. If you leave windows open at night make sure they cannot be used to gain entry.*

▲ *Even if tools and ladders are not in full view, an experienced thief will know where to look and will use them if they are not locked up securely.*

▲ *Don't let in strangers at the door: use a spyhole or, failing that, a door chain to check the visitor's ID before you open the door.*

Levels of permissible force when dealing with intruders vary from country to country, so be aware of the law in this respect.

USING AN ALARM AT NIGHT

Finally, forewarned is forearmed. If you have a burglar alarm with a zone facility, set the downstairs circuit each evening when you go to bed. In addition to possibly scaring off the intruder, the alarm will alert you that somebody is prowling around on the ground floor and should give you time to telephone for help, get dressed, and prepare to confront an intruder who ventures upstairs.

A battery-operated stand-alone room alarm, positioned to cover the stairs, is a cheap alternative warning system if your house is not alarmed.

SECURITY CHECKLIST

Most burglaries are committed by opportunist thiefs when a house or flat is empty, more often during the evening or at night. Good security is about deflecting a thief's attention away from your house in the first place and reducing their chances of entry if they do decide to burgle you.

Around the home
- Install security lighting.
- Secure ladders, put away tools and keep garages and sheds locked.
- Don't make it easy for the intruder to slip into the garden – padlocked side gates, flimsy trellis and gravel drives are good deterrents.
- Trim back any plants or hedges near to the house that a burglar could hide behind.
- Never leave a spare key in a convenient hiding place outside – thieves know where to find them.

In the home
- Have a burglar alarm professionally installed and regularly serviced.
- Fit window locks to all downstairs windows and any others that are easy to reach. Keep them locked and their keys out of sight.
- Secure all outside doors with mortise deadlocks. Fit mortise bolts to the top and bottom of doors.
- Fit a door viewer and door chain

and use these every time someone calls. If you live in a flat, consider having a phone-entry system fitted to the main door of the building.
- Make sure that window and door frames are sufficiently strong to withstand forced entry.
- Keep your house keys safe and away from doors and windows.
- Rest easier at night by having a means of securing your bedroom door if you hear an intruder and your mobile phone and a defensive weapon to hand.

When you go away
- Keep curtains open during the day.
- Use timer switches to turn on some lights when it gets dark.
- Cancel newspapers and other deliveries when you go on holiday.
- Cut the grass before you go away.
- Ask a neighbour to keep an eye on your house – do the same for them when they go away.

If you are burgled
- If you return home and see or hear sounds of a break-in, don't go in – call the police immediately.
- If you are in the house and hear a prowler, phone the police if you can. You are allowed to use reasonable force to protect yourself or others from an intruder.

▲ *Put a bolt on your garden gate, and padlock it so that the thief can't use that route to remove larger valuables such as televisions and antiques.*

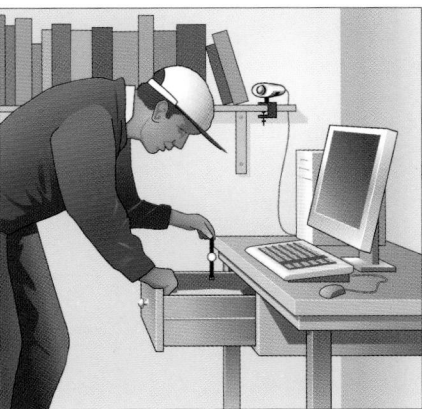

▲ *If a burglar does get into your home, a video camera connected to your computer can help identify him – but only if he doesn't steal the computer too.*

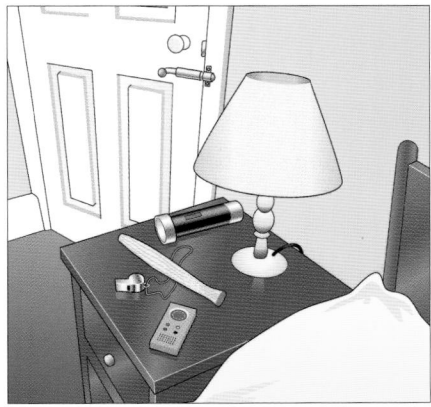

▲ *Keep a mobile phone, torch and other emergency aids handy in your bedroom. A bolt on the door could give you a breathing space if an intruder comes upstairs.*

Dealing with an intruder

The average burglar aims to sneak in and out of the home while the occupants are at work or on holiday, as confrontation leading to possible recognition is the last thing a thief wants. That said, if you return unexpectedly and surprise an intruder he is not likely to apologize, raise his hands, and wait quietly for the police to arrive. If you return home to find your window prised open or your front door damaged, never charge in alone or unprepared. Leave that to the police, who should be only a phone call away. You have no way of knowing if the intruder is still inside the building, or how many people are involved.

TYPES OF INTRUDER

If anything, you are more likely to encounter a sneak thief than a professional burglar. Opportunists, who are highly likely to be drug addicts looking for easy pickings to fund their habit, can be more dangerous than career burglars, as they are more desperate and therefore more likely to

---

REASONABLE FORCE

Should an intruder attack you in your home, you are likely to be within your rights if you pick up an item such as a frying pan, umbrella or golf club to defend yourself. Likewise if the attacker is wielding a hefty blade it is probably OK to parry this with a kitchen knife, but a court is unlikely to be sympathetic if you use more force than a court decides is necessary to deter the burglar or intruder.

---

take chances. Should the unsuspecting householder interrupt them in the act, they are just as likely to strike out in the hope that surprise is still on their side.

Of course, there are unscrupulous types who are prepared to bully and bluster their way into a home to commit their crime, usually picking on vulnerable members of society such as the elderly or infirm. The simple precaution of checking the identity cards of callers purporting to be from public utility companies, and making use of a stout safety chain fitted to the door when answering calls, should stop this type of intruder in his or her tracks. If they do become difficult or aggressive, a panic alarm carried in your pocket or mounted by the door can be used to attract the attention of passers-by and should be enough to deter such intruders. Unlike burglars, who are predominantly male, confidence tricksters can be of either gender, often hunt in pairs, and tend to rely on their smart appearance to talk their way into your home.

BREAK-INS AT NIGHT

The home is the place where people feel most relaxed, and therefore it is where they are probably at their most vulnerable and least ready to deal with a confrontational situation. At night, the householder is even more

---

▲ *If you find an unarmed intruder in the house, don't be the one to escalate the situation. Give him the opportunity to back off, while standing your ground and showing that you are prepared to defend yourself.*

vulnerable, especially if the intruder breaks or sneaks in while the occupants are asleep. Even if you are wearing nightclothes, you will still feel naked when confronted by a masked stranger, dressed in black and carrying a weapon. Should he walk into your bedroom armed with a gun or a knife, he will definitely have the upper hand. If this face-to-face meeting is in the dark, your fear will be heightened.

DECIDING HOW TO REACT

In such circumstances, many people assume that it is acceptable to use any means available to defend themselves, their family and their property, but in stable societies the law usually dictates that any force used has to be in proportion to the strength of the attack.

The official advice is to try to avoid a violent confrontation if you discover a burglar in your home, though in fact your basic instinct may be to lash out and drive the intruder out. If you do decide to tackle a burglar, you must be confident that you can win the fight and that you can do so without putting your own freedom in jeopardy.

One way of ensuring both is to prepare for the possibility of such a situation by joining a self-defence class. This way you will not only learn the necessary skills, but also build up your confidence in your own physical abilities. It is sometimes suggested that taking up a martial art can be useful, but these specialist skills can be lethal; always bear in mind that if you kill or seriously injure an intruder in this way, you could be punished for making unreasonable use of force.

If you decide to take the submissive route, particularly if you are female, the intruder may take violent advantage of this, whereas a show of bravado and confidence may well cause him to flee. Only you can make this split-second decision, based on your reading of the situation at the time. It is, however, worth bearing in mind that the

intruder does not know for sure what lies in store and how a householder will react if or when they discover him, so his nerves are going to be on edge. A sudden loud noise, such as the sound of a personal alarm, could be enough to frighten him off the premises. Likewise, if he has broken in at night, a burst of bright light from a high-powered torch shone in his eyes may temporarily blind and disorient him.

If a confrontation does develop, your positive mental attitude and confident body posture may well be enough to allow you regain control of the situation, but you should remember that if the attacker calls your bluff he is unlikely to fight clean. On the other hand, a screaming and pummelling woman with right on her side, however small and slight, can be enough to scare off a burly intruder twice her weight if

▲ *In self-defence, the palm strike is very effective. Cock your wrist and curl your fingers and thumb in. Aim for the jaw for maximum impact.*

he is unprepared for the onslaught. In many situations, the thief or assailant will simply try to escape if "caught on the job". Let him go. Property is replaceable, your life is not.

TACKLING A BURGLAR

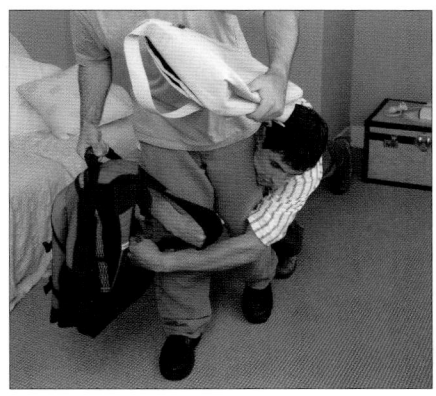

1 ◄ Remember, if you can avoid a fight do so because property is not worth risking a life for. But if you believe you or a family member are at risk then go for a lunge from behind.

2 ► A rugby-style tackle is an effective way to bring someone who is moving away from you to his knees.

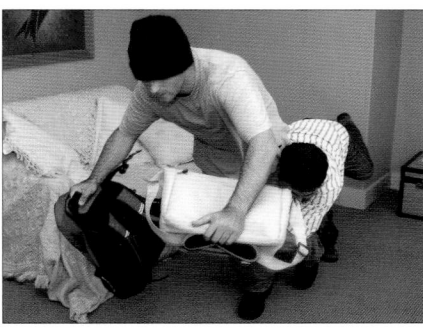

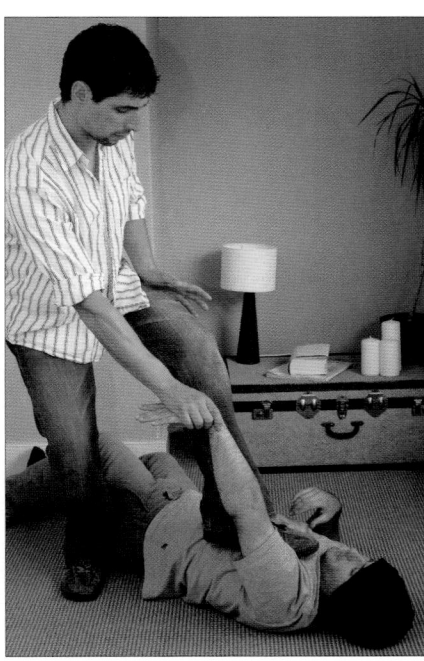

3 ▼ Drive your shoulder into the intruder's legs while gripping around his knees and squeezing until he falls. The intruder will quite possibly be disoriented by being tackled in such a decisive way.

4 ◄ Once on the ground you must immobilize the intruder and at the same time shout at the top of your voice for help if you haven't already done so.

5 ▼ Only confront the intruder with a weapon as a last resort.

Fire in the home

Although fire is the single greatest killer in the home environment, the vast majority of home fires would be easily avoided by taking some basic precautions. The kitchen is the most dangerous room in the house and is the seat of most daytime fires, but if a member of the household is a smoker, the chances of being involved in a night-time fire increase dramatically. Unguarded candles, the least technological way of lighting a room and a favourite in romantic or party settings, also pose a high risk of fire, as do the many electrical appliances used around the home. Awareness of potential fire risks is half the prevention battle, and most of the following advice is really just common sense.

SMOKE ALARMS

If a fire does break out, a functioning smoke alarm should give the occupants a few extra vital minutes to organize an escape, call the fire service, and possibly even attempt to bring the fire under control. At night, a smoke alarm will save lives, as smoke and gases produced by a fire can silently kill sleeping occupants before they become aware that their home is ablaze.

▼ *In less than 60 seconds a small fire can fill your home with smoke. Firemen have breathing apparatus – you don't so get out fast. If any closed door feels warm when touched, do not open it - the fire is on the other side. Go to the windows instead.*

Ceiling-mounted smoke alarms are cheap and easy to fit, though they are as much use as a chocolate fireguard if their batteries are not checked regularly.

AVOIDING FIRE

Prevention is always better than cure, so when deep frying, which is the largest single cause of kitchen fires, never fill the pan more than one third full, and never ever leave it unattended.

To extinguish a pan fire, turn off the heat source and throw a fire blanket, or a damp towel, over it to extinguish the flames. Never throw water on an oil fire, as that will make the flames flare up and spray burning oil outside the pan, igniting other combustibles. A small fire blanket, suitable for tackling most accidental fires in the kitchen, is an inexpensive necessity often overlooked. If you tackle a pan fire yourself, remember that cooking fat retains its temperature for a long time,

▲ *A domestic fire at night can be a killer, though it is usually the smoke rather than the flames that proves lethal.*

▼ *If someone's clothes catch fire, roll them on the floor and smother the flames using a blanket or rug or large coat. Keep low at all times as it's easier to breathe. Go to the window and wait for the fire brigade.*

▲ *Carbon monoxide is a silent killer – gas-fired central heating boilers and water heaters should be checked and serviced annually.*

and it may well reignite if you remove the blanket too soon. Vacate the premises and summon the fire service.

The easiest precaution to take against fires caused by cigarettes is to ban smoking completely inside the house. Unlike cooking fires, which flare up quickly, most cigarette fires start gradually, sometimes hours after a smouldering end has fallen unnoticed into upholstery or bedclothes.

The precautions needed to prevent electrical fires are simple: switch off and unplug appliances when not in use, and never overload wall sockets. Even when an appliance is switched off, it may still be drawing power from a live wall socket unless physically unplugged. Televisions left on standby mode and, to a lesser extent, video recorders and digital boxes

◀ *Pull, Aim, Squeeze, Sweep (PASS) is a good tip to remember. Aim low, point the extinguisher at the base of the fire and sweep from side to side.*

are all potential time bombs if they develop an electrical fault or there is a power surge during an electrical storm. Bad wiring or overloaded sockets, usually identifiable through the plugs being overly hot, should be remedied immediately. If you are not actually using a particular appliance, unplug it, and if you hear crackling, smell plastic burning or see lights flickering, find the cause. Make sure that any cables running on the floor do not get trapped or pinched by furniture, and that any long cables drawing a lot of power are not coiled, as both circumstances can cause wires to overheat and ignite out of the blue.

ESCAPING FROM A FIRE

If fire does break out, your first priority is to get everybody out as fast as possible. Do not stop to dress properly or collect valuables. Most fire deaths are caused by inhalation of smoke and noxious gases rather than burns. Furnishings, once ignited, burn with incredible intensity and very quickly produce dense toxic fumes. To survive this you not only have to get out very quickly, but you also need to stay as close to the floor as possible, as that is where any oxygen will be.

Do not assume that the air at head height is breathable if it is free of smoke, as some by-products of building fires are virtually clear. The first you will know about them is when they burn your throat and lungs, as you try to take your last gulping breaths. Burning plastics and upholstery rapidly

▼ *Blocking any gaps by the door helps to keep fumes out of the room you are in and may deprive a fire of oxygen.*

▲ *Smoke alarms are essential survival tools in the modern home, giving you precious time to escape. Battery life and location – at least one ceiling-mounted alarm on each floor – are critical.*

produce thick clouds of acrid smoke, and even at ground level you may find breathing difficult. A wet cloth over your mouth and nose will act as a temporary respirator; even a dry handkerchief or shirt tail may keep out larger toxic particles. You will need to remember the layout of the room to find your exit route, as even if it is not dark you will be blinded by the smoke.

Once clear of danger outside, alert any neighbours and call the fire service. Do not go back in. Material possessions can be replaced, but your life cannot.

▼ *If you have to escape from an upper floor try to find ways to lower yourself to safety rather than jumping, to reduce the height of your fall.*

Gas leaks

The most common cause of damage, injury and even death in the home is undoubtedly fire. However, gas incidents, though much less common, can be equally deadly. In most of the Western world, bottled or mains gas provides the fuel for the bulk of our heating and hot water systems, as it is more efficient and more ecologically sound than coal and oil. In the past, domestic gas was derived from coal and was a smelly substance, but modern natural gas is odourless and so has to have a smell added to alert us to leaks.

Gas, like water, will always find any leaks in pipes, joints and appliances. Unlike water, it is highly explosive, so it is imperative that you are both familiar with its artificial smell, and you attend to any leakage immediately. Do not try to repair a gas leak yourself, as this is a highly skilled job that can be very dangerous if tackled by a novice.

If you smell gas you should immediately open windows to vent the building and get outside as quickly as possible. The main supply valve, whether you are using bottled or mains gas, is usually located outside the building, next to the meter if you are on a mains supply, and should be turned off if at all possible. If you don't know where your gas valve is, go and check now!

Once you are clear of the building, hopefully having been able to vent it and turn off the supply, contact the service provider or the emergency services. Gas leaks can cause massive damage and those responsible for

▲ *Check your vents have not got clogged up with growing plants.*

prevention would much rather be called out before the explosion, even if it is a well-intentioned false alarm, than have to pick up the pieces afterwards.

CARBON MONOXIDE POISONING
It is not only the gas supply that can be potentially dangerous in a domestic situation. The by-products of combustion can also poison the occupants if gas appliances such as heaters and stoves are not working efficiently and properly vented.

Carbon monoxide is a silent killer that works by first inducing sleep before poisoning the body. Even if the poisoning is not fatal it can cause permanent neurological damage. The gas is odourless, tasteless and colourless, so a special detector is necessary to check for its presence.

To ensure that your home is safe, all gas appliances should be checked and serviced at least once a year, particularly after having lain unused for any length of time, and flues must never be blocked or obstructed. Birds' nests, and even ivy or other creeping plants growing on outside walls, can very easily block a flue during the summer months, turning the home into a death trap when the heating system is fired up again in the autumn.

The first signs of carbon monoxide poisoning are unexpected drowsiness and headache, and first aid for an unconscious victim is access to fresh air and artificial respiration.

DEALING WITH A GAS LEAK

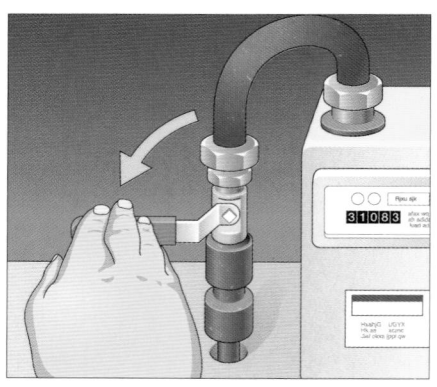

1 If you smell gas, turn off the mains supply by the valve near the meter.

2 Open all the windows to ventilate the building and disperse escaped gas.

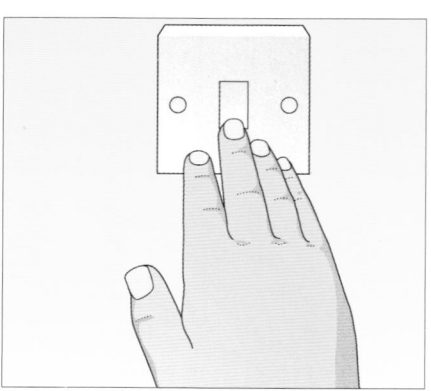

3 Do not switch on lights as this could create a spark and ignite the gas.

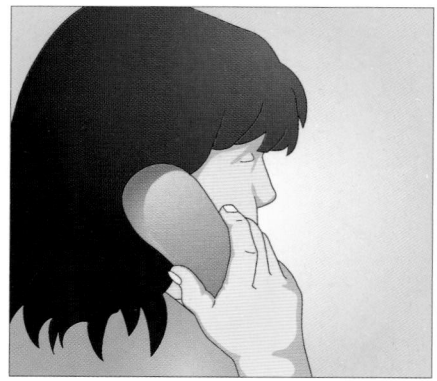

4 Report a leak immediately to the gas supplier or the emergency services.

Flooding

Water leaks in the home can cause untold damage. The primary causes are burst pipes during the thaw after a winter freeze, overflowing baths and faulty washing machines. Water spreads at an alarming rate and it does not take long for it to permeate into the fabric of a building. Burst mains pipes can be disastrous as the high flow rate can undermine foundations, but even an upstairs bath left overflowing for five minutes is likely to short-circuit the

▼ *If your home is prone to flooding, keep a supply of sandbags, ready-filled, with which to create barriers in front of doorways.*

electrical supply and damage the ceiling below to such an extent that a complete replacement is necessary.

NATURAL FLOODS

If you are one of those living in an area prone to natural flooding, the risks are of a totally different order. You should be alert to flood warnings and familiar with local plans for dealing with such a disaster. Simple precautions like having sandbags ready-filled and heavy duty

▼ *If you do not know where the main stopcock for your home's water supply is located, go and check it out right now.*

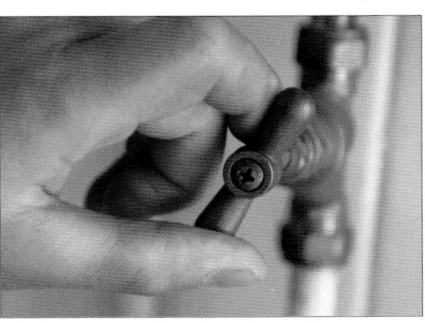

▲ *Freak weather can quickly cause flooding in low-lying residential areas: is your home in a vulnerable situation?*

plastic on hand to block doors may help, but if your home is subjected to a major flood, follow the advice of your local authority and emergency services.

If you have to leave your home, do not be tempted to walk through flowing flood water. Even if it does not appear to be very deep it may have a deceptively fast current that could sweep you off your feet, and there may well also be dangerous debris below the surface that could cause serious injury.

After drowning, electrocution is the second most common cause of death following a flood: stay well away from power cables and do not attempt to use electrical equipment that has been wet. You should also check for gas leaks in case the pipework has been damaged. A flood is likely to contaminate your water supply, so if you are at risk from flooding it is sensible to keep an emergency supply of bottled water.

Emergency escape

In a fire or gas emergency, it is imperative that you get yourself and any other occupants out of the building as quickly as possible. In a domestic situation you should be well aware of your primary escape route, but if fire is barring your way, you will need to seek an alternative. Despite what you may have seen in television dramas and on the cinema screen, the staircase is usually of sufficiently robust construction to survive the early stages of a house fire, and in most multiple occupancy buildings it will be reinforced and protected to afford a safe escape route. In some circumstances, however, especially if fire doors have been left open, use of the staircase may not be possible and you may need to use a window instead.

ESCAPING THROUGH A WINDOW

If window locks are fitted, the key should be kept in a place where it is easy to find, especially in the dark and when under duress. However, if you are in an unfamiliar room and cannot undo the catches, you may have no option but to break the glass. Double-glazed window units, or those with strengthened anti-burglar glass, will not break easily. (If you have windows of this kind, it might make sense to mount a safety hammer on the window frame in case the key cannot be found in an emergency.)

Be aware of glass shards, and wrap your arm with thick clothing for protection. If no hammer is available to break the glass, a small and heavy hard object, such as a bedside lamp or a metal ornament, can be used; if you

ESCAPING FROM A BUILDING

1 If you are trapped in a room and cannot open a window, put a heavy object in a pillowcase or a sock and use it as a hammer to shatter the glass.

2 To reduce the severity of injuries, the strongest person should lower the lighter occupants from upper windows, rather than letting them jump out.

3 As the last one out, you should lower yourself from the ledge to reduce your fall, remembering to bend the knees before impact then go into a roll.

1 If using an improvised rope to escape, such as knotted sheets or garments, tie it securely to an immovable object that will bear your weight.

2 If no structural anchor points are available, a strong bed frame can be effective as it is too large to be pulled through the window.

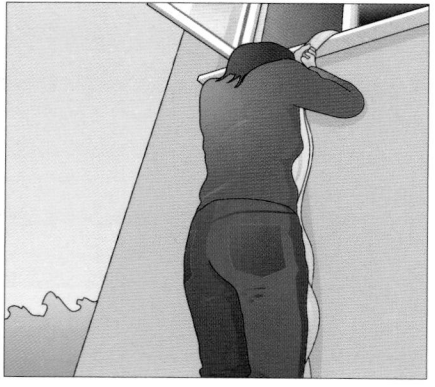

3 Grip the improvised rope between your insteps and use arm-over-arm movements to descend quickly – even a short rope will reduce your fall.

PARATROOPER ROLL

1 This roll was devised to prevent injury when hitting hard ground at speed, and it is easy to learn. The legs must be slightly bent at knees and hips.

2 As you hit the ground, absorb the initial impact through your bent legs then roll over on to your thigh and shoulder, swinging the legs over.

3 Keeping the knees and heels together and the lead arm tucked in will spread the impact of the fall throughout the body, saving your ankles and legs.

REVERSE BREAK ROLL

1 If you have no lateral speed, you will take the full-on impact with your legs. You must convert this force into rotational energy before it impacts your spine. Keep your legs bent before impact.

2 Immediately roll backwards as your legs compress, and strike the ground as hard as you can with your arms. This reduces the impact to your spine and adds to your rotational momentum.

3 Make sure you are rolling backwards and not simply falling flat on your back. Continue to roll over backwards.. This is the safest and least impactful way to absorb the energy of the fall.

put this inside a pillowcase and swing it around your head first, the striking power can be increased markedly.

Escape from ground floor room windows is pretty straightforward, and even from those on the floor above the drop should not kill you unless you fall on your head or land on sharp objects, such as spiked railings.

ESCAPING FROM UPPER FLOORS
Do not just stand on a ledge and jump, but try to find a way of lowering yourself gently. To break your fall, push a mattress out through the window if possible, followed by bedding and anything else that will cushion your fall. When it looks likely that staying in the room will be more hazardous than

risking the fall, drop children and the infirm out of the window, sliding them out feet first and lowering them as far as possible by the wrists before letting go directly over the improvised cushioning. If you have made enough noise, the neighbours may by now be there to catch or steady those dropped.

Ideally, a knotted escape rope or rope ladder should be available if the window is two or more storeys above ground floor, but few householders give much thought to providing these. An alternative would be to make an improvised rope by knotting sheets or other suitable items together to stretch from window to ground, but this is not a particularly quick fix. If you do have time to do it, make sure you tie the

rope to something that will bear your weight. If necessary, push the bed in front of the window: as it is wider than the frame, it should provide an anchor.

GETTING DOWN STAIRS
If escape through a window is not feasible, and the smoke-filled staircase is the only option, a well-soaked jacket with sleeves tied at the bottom will retain pockets of breathable air. Any remaining oxygen in the corridors and on staircases will be at ground level or close to the steps, so keep low and move slowly. Running fast and upright will probably cause you to inhale poisonous and damaging gases, but taking time without dallying will help conserve your breath.

Emergency home shelter

If a natural disaster hit your area, or your town was suddenly on the frontline of a combat zone, or if international terrorism unleashed a weapon of mass destruction on your doorstep, could you shelter and feed yourself and your family until normality returned?

An ordinary house will keep you safe from the elements in the depth of winter, but when shells and bombs start exploding all around, or if terrorists detonate a "dirty" bomb to contaminate your town, it won't hold up particularly well. However, if you had a strongpoint in the most structurally sound part of the house, and could retreat there with stocks of food and water, you and your loved ones might just make it through. Unless warring forces were to

▶ *Maintain a plentiful stock of candles and matches in case the power supply is cut off during an emergency.*

dig in for a battle of attrition, the fighting would probably pass you by quite quickly, and the contamination caused by a terrorist attack could be even shorter lived, so the ability to build a basic shelter and the availability of enough emergency supplies to last you just a few weeks, could enable you to survive.

SELECTING A SURVIVAL SPACE

In a conventional two- or three-floor urban home, the space beneath the stairs usually offers the best structural protection. In the case of a bombardment, this can be reinforced by removing the internal doors from their hinges and nailing them over the stair treads. The space under the stairs will be cramped and claustrophobic, but unless the house takes a direct hit, it should provide adequate shelter. Line the floor, and the walls where possible, with mattresses and you will have a snug refuge.

Apartment dwellers will probably not have the luxury of an under-stairs cupboard, so they will have to identify the room that seems structurally the strongest, preferably one without windows, in which to build a shelter. Tables sited in the

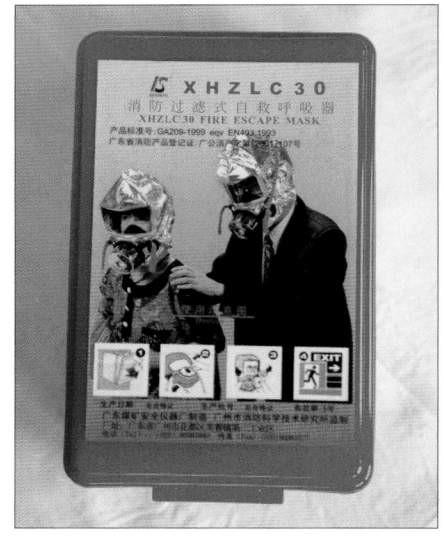

▲ *Terrorist attacks have led manufacturers to produce inexpensive emergency escape masks and smoke hoods for the general public.*

corner of the room, with doors and mattresses on top and on the open sides, can be used to construct a compact refuge, but only if the table legs are strong enough to take the weight. If they are not, lean the doors against the wall at an angle of more than 45 degrees to give a triangular shelter, and stack mattresses on top for additional protection.

IMPROVISED SHELTERS

▲ *The strongest part of many houses is the space under the stairs. It may be cramped and too small for long-term use, but it could save your life.*

▲ *A windowless bathroom can provide a safe retreat in a crisis and is easy to seal against gas attack. Fill the bath with water in case the supply is cut.*

▲ *Failing any other shelter, a mattress and doors stacked around a sturdy table make a survival capsule that offers some protection from explosion and shrapnel.*

▲ *Women's tights secured with a rubber band over the filter tap or stop-cock will act as a makeshift filter for some pollutants.*

EMERGENCY SUPPLIES

There is no point in having an emergency shelter in your home unless you also have the basics to support life for days, if not weeks. The one constraining factor in assembling your supplies will be storage space. If you are lucky enough to be using a large cellar as your shelter, stocking it with supplies for several weeks will not be a problem.

Water is the primary concern, as humans cannot live for much more than three or four days without water, but if the water is contaminated it could be a double-edged sword. It makes sense to keep at least a few days' supply in large sealed containers in your shelter all the time, with plenty of

▼ *Check the contents of your first-aid kit: you may want to add items you use regularly, such as basic painkillers.*

empty ones ready to be filled in times of crises and before the supply is cut off. Water filters and/or purification tablets should also be stocked in case the crisis lasts longer than expected. A "volcano" kettle in which to boil water efficiently will also come in handy, as will candles for light; candles also provide a little bit of warmth and can be used to heat tinned food. A wind-up radio and torch, which do not need batteries, are also useful to have in your shelter. In a civil defence scenario, radio will be used by the authorities as the primary method of broadcasting information about the emergency.

Adequate stocks of foodstuffs that don't deteriorate are also a necessity, in or close to your shelter. Tinned meat, fish and beans, which can be eaten without preparation, are far preferable to dried foodstuffs that will need scarce fuel and water for reconstitution, but dried soups are cheap and use up little storage space and they can perk up the spirits by providing a warm and nourishing drink when you are cold and downhearted.

If there is a threat of nuclear or biological contamination, temporarily tape up doors, windows and ventilators to the room in which your shelter is located, but remember that you will exhaust your air supply very quickly. When a candle flame starts to die, you will have to pull back the tape and take your chances.

▲ *In an emergency, the radio will be the primary method used by the authorities to inform the public: if you don't have a wind-up radio stock up with spare batteries.*

HOME SURVIVAL ESSENTIALS

- Drinking water
- Canned food, or other food that does not need cooking or refrigeration
- Can opener
- Candles
- Matches
- Cooker or kettle
- Wind-up radio
- Wind-up torch (flashlight)
- First-aid kit and any essential medication
- Covered bucket
- Clothing and blankets

▼ *Ordinary duct tape is adequate for sealing around doors and windows to protect against chemical or biological agents.*

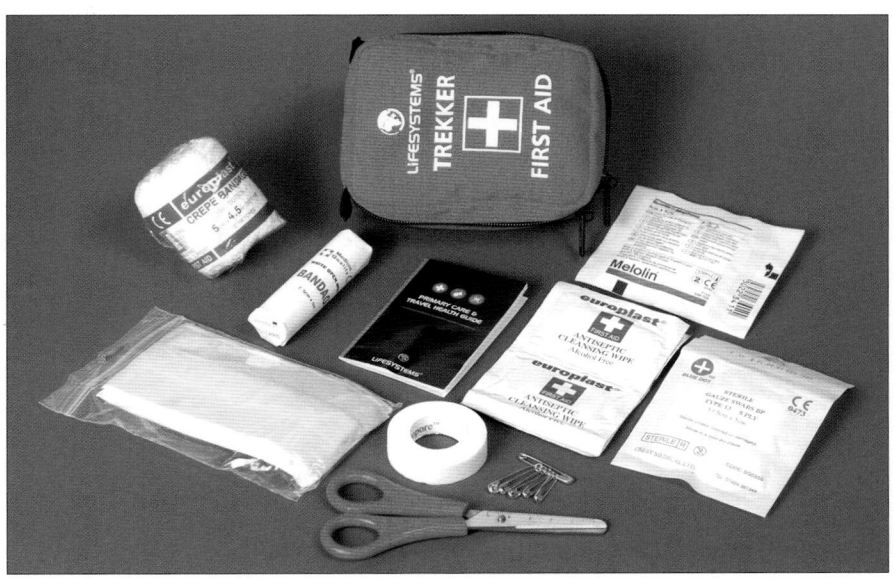

SURVIVING ON THE MOVE

We are often at our most vulnerable when travelling from one place to another. When walking, driving or cycling we can control the pace of our progress but need to be ready to cope with the careless actions of other road users, extreme weather or the mechanical failure of a vehicle. On public transport we must be watchful for our personal safety and that of our possessions, and cope with delays and diversions. World travel brings the remote yet awful possibilities of air crashes, shipwrecks and terrorist attack. Yet the spirit of adventure defies all these risks, and with the right approach and preparation we are right to regard travel as one of the greatest of life's experiences.

Safeguarding yourself and your possessions

There's an old adage that packing for a journey is not about what to take, but what to leave behind. Most irregular travellers have a lot of luggage, and this can be an enormous burden, not just in terms of weight, but as items to keep an eye on, to worry about losing, and to attract unwanted attention.

PROTECTING VALUABLES

Dress down when travelling, and do not flaunt money or wear jewellery, other than perhaps a wedding ring. Do not carry a laptop or camera in an obvious-looking bag. Use a money belt or a more obscure hiding place on your person for carrying money and documents while travelling. You should also carry medicines and other essentials on your person in case you lose your luggage.

If you are staying in a high-risk area it may be worth using a wire luggage protector to prevent anyone from slashing your bag in the street. Another common technique of street thieves is to cut the shoulder strap before grabbing the bag. This is very difficult to combat because the aggressor is holding a knife and is ready to use it. Make yourself look like a difficult target in everything you do, but if someone does take you on, let the bag go. It's just a bag.

▲ *Arriving in an unfamiliar city can be disorienting. For your first night, it's worth splashing out on a hotel in a central, safe location while you get your bearings.*

SECURING PERSONAL BELONGINGS

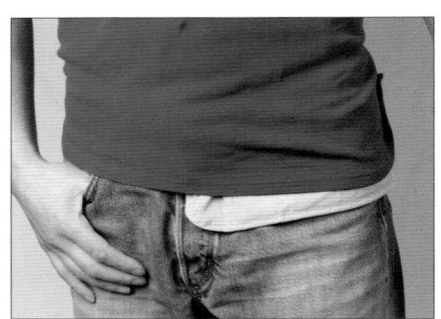

1 If you wear a money belt, it should not be visible in any way: keep it securely tucked under your clothing.

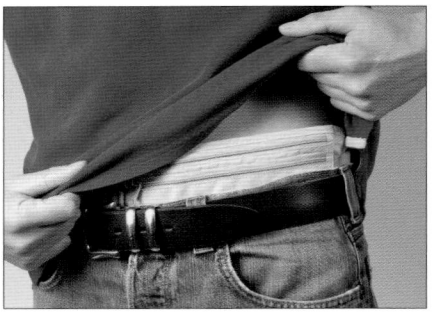

2 Put your trousers on over the belt, and tuck in your shirt. This way it will not be exposed by your movements.

1 In areas where luggage crime is rife, protect your baggage with a wire mesh cover like this one, which can be placed over the entire bag.

2 Close the mesh cover and secure it with a lock. You can then use the cable to fasten it either to your person or to an immovable object.

BAGS ON PUBLIC TRANSPORT

As well as the risk of theft, you should be wary of your luggage being tampered with for criminal purposes. Always lock your luggage or tie zips shut, and use labels that cannot be read by casual bystanders, allowing unwanted access to your identity. You might want to use a business address for added security.

Do not accept letters, parcels or gifts from strangers and do not leave your luggage unattended, even for a minute. If you see unattended luggage in an airport, train, or bus station, report it and then stay away from it.

For a small fee, many airports will shrink-wrap your bag in plastic. This not only prevents tampering but also saves wear and tear on your luggage.

FINDING SAFE ACCOMMODATION

What is safe? An expensive hotel, probably. But people come into such places to steal from the rich. Seek advice from travel agents, even if you do not plan to book with them, from people who have attempted a similar trip before, or better still from trusted locals. If you arrive somewhere by accident rather than design, ensure the provision of basic essentials like water, warmth and shade, then take time to consider what the local threats and opportunities might be before choosing somewhere to stay.

Surviving city streets

The greatest danger facing you as a road user, whether you are walking, cycling or driving, is everybody else. In a busy city street you may be preoccupied by the possible threat of malicious intent, but more prevalent than that is the danger of accidents.

As always, anticipation is the key. Keep an eye out for drivers nodding off at the wheel, reading maps while driving or using their phones. Be aware that cycles often go unseen by motorists, and that older and smaller cars often have poor levels of grip and limited braking ability. Avoid trouble by ensuring that your vehicle is in good condition and keeping your fuel topped up so that you don't have to stop where you might prefer not to. Keep a secret weapon (such as a rape alarm or pepper spray) in the door pocket.

ROAD RAGE

The phenomenon of road rage is increasingly common as roads become busier, and drivers unable to cope with daily pressures experience extreme stress and frustration when confronted by situations they cannot control. It is a serious problem because the affected driver is at the controls of an extremely dangerous projectile – a motor vehicle.

If you are an innocent victim of road rage you must protect yourself. Most importantly, do not make eye contact

▲ *Keeping safe on a busy street depends on staying alert, reacting quickly and anticipating the actions of other people.*

with an angry driver, but get away as quickly as possible. Take the next easy turn and choose an alternative route.

If an enraged driver follows you, do not go home: go straight to the police. If a driver gets out of his car and comes over, lock the doors and windows, and ignore him even if he attacks the car. It's far better that he should take his anger out on the car than on you.

CAR JACKING

With car security systems getting more sophisticated, thieves are turning to the weakest link in the system – the driver. Car jackings at traffic lights or in filling

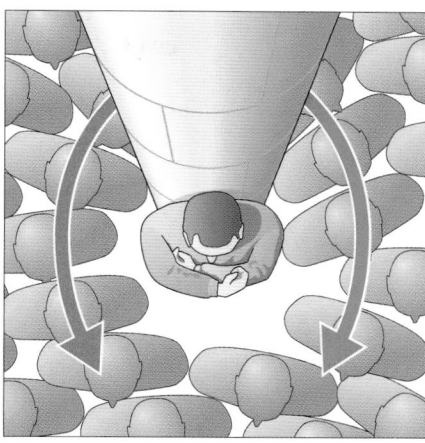

▲ *In the event of a crowd surge, say at an emergency exit, if you can find a pillar or similar structure seek refuge behind this.*

stations are increasingly common. If the car jacker's motivation is to steal your car, the best thing to do is let them. Don't resist, and get away safely. If they are trying to force you to drive, you are probably in less danger of personal injury as they need your cooperation and you have some degree of control.

HITCHHIKERS

There is a significant risk to a driver picking up any stranger, and those who look as though they really need a lift are sadly more likely to turn out to be difficult or dangerous. The safest course is simply not to pick up hitchers.

SURVIVING BEING HIT BY A CAR

1 When you realize a car is bound to hit you, jump just high enough to avoid the front of the car and land on the bonnet (hood).

2 Curl up on impact, drawing up your legs out of harm's way and protecting your head with your arms in case it hits the windshield or roof of the car.

3 Your secondary impact may be with the windshield or roof, or with the road, but in each case your injuries will probably be less than in a direct hit.

Coping with dangerous road situations

You can run into trouble on any road journey, and of course, you cannot influence when and where things could go wrong beyond ensuring adequate preparation and maintenance of your own vehicle and keeping the fuel tank topped up. Tell someone where you are going and when you expect to arrive, and always carry a mobile (cell) phone: the bane of modern life is also an invaluable lifesaver.

The number 112 is the international emergency telephone number and can be used in any country on any digital network. Due to the nature of cellular systems the success of such calls cannot be guaranteed, so you should also check for local emergency numbers. When you get through, if you are a woman travelling alone be sure to tell them so because rescue services give priority to women in this position.

MOTORWAYS

If you break down or have an accident on the motorway (freeway) and have to pull over, get out on the side away from the traffic and move away from your vehicle. It is quite common for inattentive drivers to crash into a stationary vehicle in this situation.

Telephone a recovery service or the emergency services as appropriate, but stay well away from the road while you wait for them to arrive.

BLIND BENDS

If you come to rest just around a blind bend there is the danger of a collision as other road users come around the corner. Alert other drivers by placing a warning device 150m/165yd up the road from your vehicle. Stay away from the vehicle. If you have no warning device, wait 150m/165yd up the road yourself, to warn drivers to slow down.

TUNNELS

If you break down inside a tunnel it is best to get out of the vehicle but you may feel there is no safe space where you can wait for rescue. Most tunnels, however, have alcoves in the walls at regular intervals that enable you to shelter from passing traffic. Make sure you are not wearing loose clothing that could snag on a passing vehicle.

There may be emergency phones in the tunnel, but if not you may have to walk out of it to summon help. Mobile phones often work in major tunnels because aerials have been installed in

the tunnel for that purpose. In any case, don't linger in a long tunnel or you may be overcome by heat or fumes.

INNER CITY BACKSTREETS

If you break down in a dangerous area there may be a threat from the local inhabitants. The best way to deal with an immediate threat is to stay in your

GETTING OUT OF A SUBMERGED CAR

1 Act immediately if your car ends up in water. Get out of the car by any means possible. Turn the lights on and try to escape via a window or sunroof.

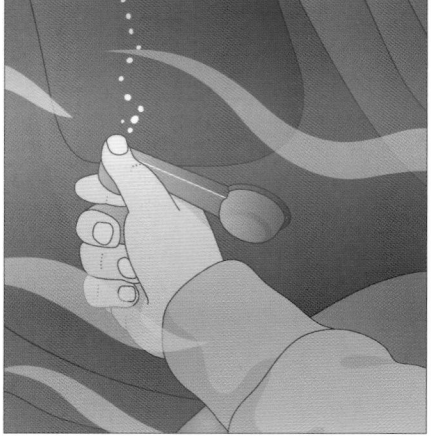

2 Wind down a side window in order to escape through it. If you have electric windows, they may well not be functioning – stay calm.

3 If you cannot open a side window by conventional means, try to smash it. Use a strong pointed object like a fire extinguisher or a wheel brace.

BREAKING DOWN ON A RAIL CROSSING

1 Don't tempt fate if your car becomes immobilized on the tracks. Assume that a train is approaching, even if you can't see or hear one.

2 Get any passengers out of the car immediately and make sure they retreat to a safe distance away from the crossing.

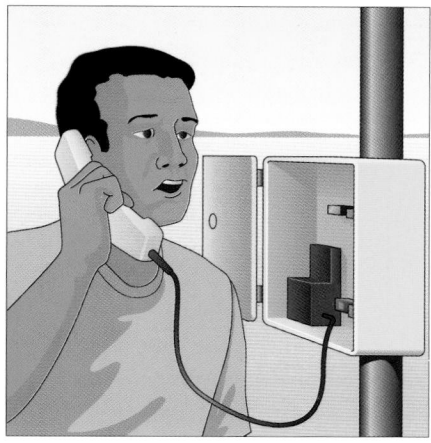

3 Use the emergency telephone by the crossing at once to inform the train operator or police that there is an obstruction on the line.

---

car and avoid eye contact or aggressive behaviour. If there is no immediate threat, lock the vehicle, leave all personal items out of sight, and make your way to safety, arranging for the recovery of the vehicle only when you have ensured your own personal safety.

REMOTE AREAS
If you break down in the middle of nowhere, you may be tempted to try to walk to safety. If you can positively

identify somewhere you know to be within range that will afford you safety and help, then do so – otherwise, you should stay with the vehicle and attempt to attract the attention of a passing motorist. Do not risk getting lost or injured or running out of food, water and energy by setting off on a hike that has no definite goal. Your vehicle will afford you excellent protection from most dangers in a wilderness area.

ON A BEACH OR NEAR WATER
If you are planning to leave your vehicle anywhere near water you must allow for the tidal variation. Just because others have parked by the sea does not mean the rising tide will not swamp your car – locals may be parking there only temporarily. Obtain a tide table or ask for advice before leaving the car for long.

Surface conditions can also change with the incoming tide. You may park on sand that seems solid enough to drive over, but as the sea approaches or recedes, the surface may become softer or more powdery, making it impossible to drive away.

CLIFFTOPS AND SLOPES
If you park on a clifftop, or on any slope, the security of your parking brake is paramount. You don't want your car to roll away, causing accident or injury or leaving you with no means of escape. Selecting "park" in an automatic vehicle or first gear with a manual transmission is an excellent precaution. However, if you have concerns about the brake, do not rely on the gearbox alone. Place chocks on the downhill side of the wheels, or if against a kerb or similar, turn the front wheels so that the vehicle will jam against it if it moves downhill.

4 If you can't smash the window, kick it as hard as you can, starting at the corners, the weakest spots. You could also try to kick out the windshield.

5 If all else fails, try to open a door. This will only be possible when the car is nearly full of water, with the inside and outside pressure almost equal.

Dealing with mechanical failure

Breaking down in a vehicle can leave you stranded and vulnerable, but a mechanical failure while you are driving can be very scary indeed, and you need to know what action to take to minimize the risks to yourself and others on the road.

FAILING BRAKES

When you make your regular inspection under your car before driving, always check to see if the brakes are leaking. It is tempting to carry on using a car with a poor hand (parking) brake, but you should keep it in good order as it's your best line of defence if the driving brakes fail.

In the event of catastrophic brake failure you can downshift to slow the car. Many steeply inclined roads have "escape lanes" for brake failure. If you are lucky enough to be on such a road then use the escape lane. If you have to stop urgently, the hand brake will do it, but be gentle and brake only while travelling in a straight line or you will spin. Other techniques to consider are slowing down using the friction of banks of snow, hedges or ditches against the side or underside of the vehicle, but unless you have practised this before

▲ *You can plug a hole caused by a nail using rubber plug material (available from tyre repair mechanics). Reinflate the tyre or spray latex foam tyre repair gunk (available from most auto shops) through the valve, which mends and reinflates it temporarily.*

the likely outcome is that you'll lose control or the car will turn over. If you are travelling in a convoy and can communicate with another driver, it is possible to get a vehicle ahead of you to slow you down using the power of their brakes. However, this technique is only to be tried by very calm and brave drivers.

CRUISE CONTROL FAILURE OR STUCK THROTTLE

If the engine will not slow down, *do not* press the clutch or select neutral unless your life depends on it, because

the vehicle may instantly over-rev and destroy the engine. Instead, switch off the ignition immediately. The car will decelerate straight away, if anything slightly more so than normal. Brakes and steering will still work normally. If extreme circumstances dictate that you need to accelerate again, turn the ignition back on.

Some older or diesel-powered cars may not respond to being switched off – in this case the brakes are all you have, but it is still worth trying to fight the motor with these before you admit defeat and trash the engine.

STEERING FAILURE

This typically happens in one of two ways. If the steering wheel pulls off its spline, you can try to jam it back on again – it doesn't matter in what position it goes on as long as it does. If this fails, or the steering rack under the car breaks or fails, you must try to stop as quickly as possible. If you do not have anti-lock brakes you can try to lock up all the wheels by braking too hard: this will make the car understeer instead of following the errant front wheels and in an extreme case you may decide that would be a safer option.

PUNCTURE

By far the most common failure to occur while driving is a tyre puncture. If this happens you will hear a muffled flapping sound, sense vibration through the steering, and possibly feel a change of attitude (the way the vehicle sits on the road). High-speed punctures can be extremely dangerous. Put your hazard lights on, brake and stop immediately – not at the next convenient place, but right now.

If you can bring the vehicle to a stop within a few seconds of the puncture happening, you should be able to change the tyre or even repair it. If you drive on it for any distance at all you'll probably damage the wheel itself. This means that when you do stop you may not be able to remove it from the hub to fit the spare.

WHAT TO DO IF YOUR BRAKES FAIL

1 Don't switch off the engine. Shift down through the gears if you can. This will slow the vehicle down considerably, while allowing you to maintain good grip and control.

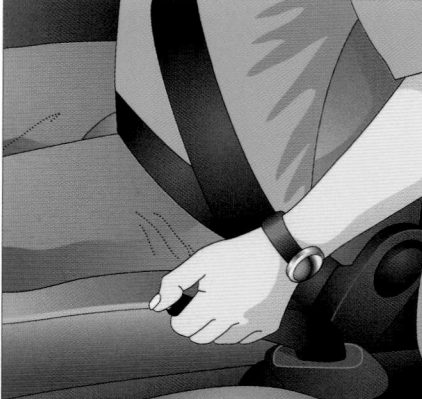

2 Once the car has slowed down to a speed of under 40kph/25mph try using the hand (parking) brake to bring it to a halt. Keep a tight grip on the steering wheel while applying the hand brake.

REINFLATING A TYRE

In extreme cases, you can reinflate a punctured tyre using lighter fuel and a match. If the tyre is still correctly seated, knock the "bead" (the stiff bit round the tyre edge that sits against the rim) off the rim on one side. For this you will need a lever such as a crowbar or very large screwdriver and a lot of strength. You could also use some sort of pipe to extend your leverage. If, on the other hand, the tyre has already peeled off the rim you need to lever it back on but make sure the bead on one side is unseated.

Squirt a small quantity (approximately half a cupful) of lighter fuel inside the tyre rim and spin the tyre to spread the fuel around inside. Ignite the fuel with a match or lighter, making sure that you keep your hands away from the rim so that your fingers don't get crushed. If it works there will be a loud explosion and the tyre will be inflated, possibly a little over-inflated. This technique can also be used to re-seat a tyre that has peeled off the rim.

Warning: This is an extremely dangerous procedure. Do this only in a life-threatening emergency.

▲ *In an extreme emergency you can reseat a tyre with lighter fuel and a lighter or match, but it is a dangerous procedure.*

JUMPSTARTING A VEHICLE

1 With the donor vehicle's engine running, connect a cable to the positive terminal of its battery. Keep the other end of the cable well away from the bodywork of the vehicle.

2 Connect the other end of this cable to the positive terminal on the vehicle you want to start. Connect the other cable to the negative terminal or another bare metal part (earth point).

3 Finally, connect the other end of the second cable to the donor car's negative terminal or an earth point. Turn on the engine, which should now start. Disconnect the cables in reverse order.

WHAT TO DO IF YOUR THROTTLE STICKS

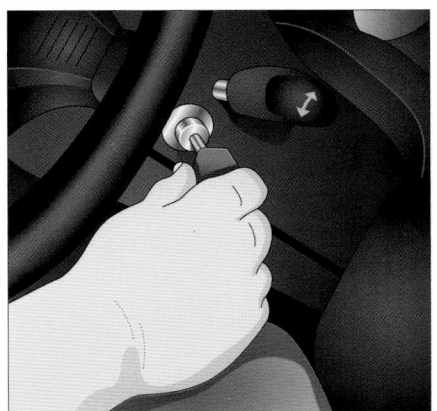

1 If your engine will not slow down you can control the car by turning the ignition off and on as required, but do not use the clutch if you have one as this could damage the engine.

2 If there is an escape lane or a safe run-off area, use it to get off the road and out of danger to yourself and other road users, and bring the vehicle to a halt.

3 You may be able to slow the vehicle down by friction against verges, hedges, snow banks or other soft objects, but beware bouncing off them into danger or turning the vehicle over.

Getting out of a skid

The secret of skid control is to practise. You can read and hear about it all you like, but you will not be able to do it adequately unless you have tried it before. However, a few attempts on a "skid pan" to acquaint yourself with the basics are enough to give you a good chance of controlling even extreme angles of slide.

The word "skid" is used to describe any kind of slide in which the wheels are not gripping the road, of which there are many. The most common are wheelspin and brakeslides, where excessive amounts of throttle or braking respectively have caused the wheels to lose traction. These do not necessarily cause any change of direction, however, and simply easing off the pedal will solve the problem. Cornering slides, which are more challenging to control, come in three main types.

UNDERSTEER

In an understeer (sometimes called push or scrub), the front wheels do not have enough grip and the car does not turn into the corner as much as is required. It can be caused by excessive speed or braking, and it is very difficult to stop a car understeering. You can jump on the power or ease off the steering – the former adds to your already excessive speed, the latter may take you off the road or into the path of oncoming traffic.

The most common accident caused by this happens when the driver continues to turn the steering in an attempt to make the car respond, and then the front wheels suddenly grip. The car then responds to the steering and may dart to the inside of the corner or make a sudden transition to an oversteer or even a spin.

HOW TO CONTROL A FRONT SKID

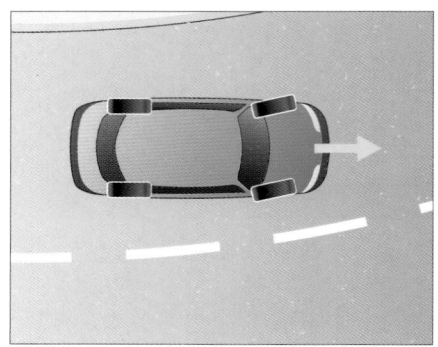

1 In an understeer, the front wheels of the car continue to plough straight ahead, so that the vehicle does not turn into the corner.

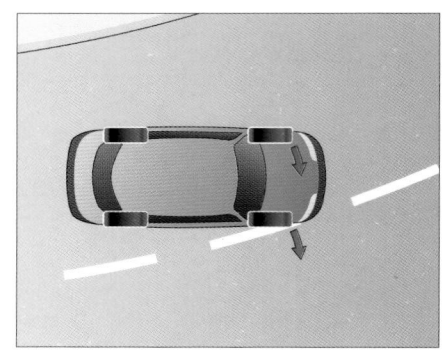

2 Reduce the amount you have turned the front wheels to regain grip and control. You will inevitably run wide of your desired path round the corner.

3 Once you have regained grip and control you can correct your course and turn the vehicle in the direction you originally intended to go.

HOW TO CONTROL A REAR SKID

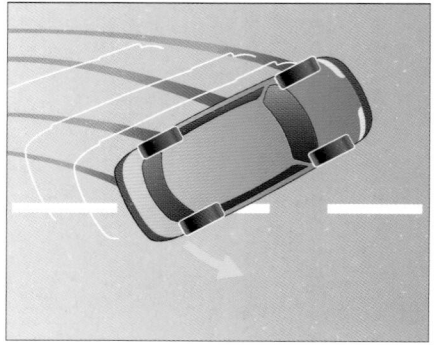

1 When the rear of the vehicle loses traction in a corner it will turn more than you intended, and could even spin right round.

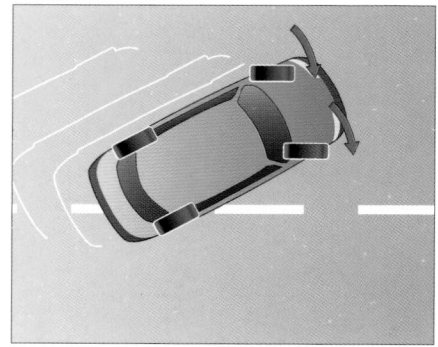

2 Turn the steering in the opposite direction (opposite lock) until the front of the car is back under your control, albeit at a rather extreme angle.

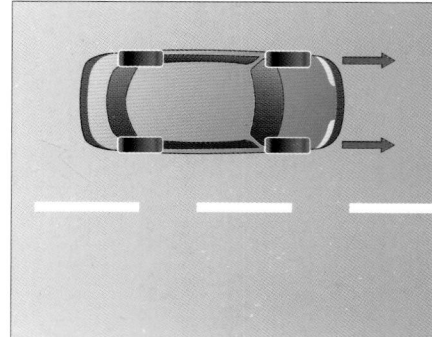

3 Bring the steering back smoothly to the centre as the car approaches the right direction: keep steering the front irrespective of what the back is doing.

OVERSTEER

This kind of skid occurs when the rear wheels lose traction in a corner. The rear of the vehicle will run wide, causing the car to turn more than the driver intended. In extreme cases it may spin right around. The cause is usually excessive power application in a rear-wheel drive car, but it can also occur due to overbraking while cornering and can be caused deliberately by applying the hand (parking) brake in mid-corner (when it is known as a hand-brake turn).

If oversteer occurs accidentally the remedy is to turn the steering wheel towards the outside of the bend. Ease off whichever pedal caused the offending slide. In extreme cases you will end up with the front wheels pointing the opposite way they do in a normal cornering situation. Turning the steering wheel the opposite way from normal cornering practice is called "opposite lock".

If your car has four-wheel drive or is exceptionally well balanced you can sometimes experience all four wheels sliding in a corner ("four-wheel drift"). The same basic rules apply: ease off the throttle or brake as applicable and apply opposite lock if necessary.

Most modern cars, especially those with front-wheel drive, are designed to have a slight tendency to understeer. This is because understeer is thought to be safer for drivers who do not have the necessary skills to control slides. Ironically, understeer is a nightmare for a skilful driver whereas oversteer is fairly controllable as long as it happens predictably.

SLIPPERY ROAD SURFACES

In ice or snow (or at very high speeds on other surfaces), the car will slide around no matter how well you drive. The trick here is to maintain a slight oversteer situation and never let the car understeer. To learn the various tricks to achieve this in different types of vehicle – front-, rear- and four-wheel drive – you may have to go on a specialist driving course. In snow, using chains or lowering your tyre pressures to about 0.7bar/10psi can really help, but you must be able to reinflate them subsequently for normal driving. On ice, narrow tyres are better, and studs or chains are best.

SWAYING TRAILERS

Trailers, caravans and horseboxes can cause all kinds of problems if you don't drive sympathetically. A trailer can cause snaking (swinging wildly from side to side) if you try to slow down too quickly, especially going downhill – the only solution is to accelerate slightly, which can be alarming to the uninitiated. At lower speeds, attempting to corner too quickly can cause the rig to jackknife and the trailer to roll over or hit the towing vehicle.

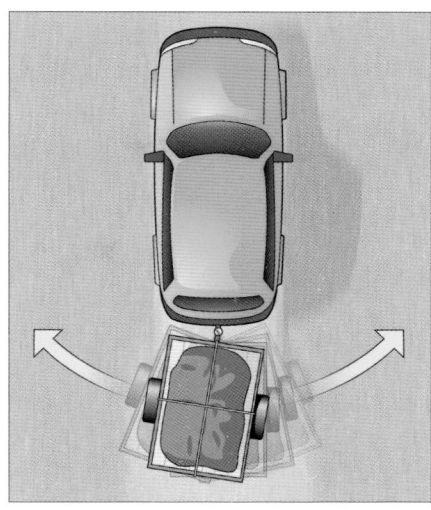

▲ *Too much weight at the back of a trailer may cause sway, which can lead to loss of control. In this case keep the steering straight – do not try to steer out of the slide.*

Even if you keep your tyres at the correct air pressure and check the treads and side walls regularly, there is always the chance of a blowout to one of your trailer's tyres. This is a highly dangerous situation, particularly if there is other traffic and you panic. Whatever you do, don't automatically slam on the brakes or try to stop suddenly. Apply the brakes gradually, and if the trailer tries to go sideways let off the brakes and accelerate a little. This will jerk the trailer back into line. Continue like this until you have slowed right down and it is safe for you to pull off the road.

ESCAPING FROM A CAR THAT IS UPSIDE DOWN

1 Push yourself up using your hands against the roof to take the weight off the seat belt buckle, otherwise you will not be able to release it.

2 If the doors won't open you may need to smash the nearest window with a heavy object. Use your arms to pull yourself through it.

3 Be aware of the danger of broken glass in the window frame, in the car and on the ground as you make your escape from the vehicle.

Fire in a vehicle

Most vehicle fires start either in the engine compartment (as a result of a fuel or oil leak), under the dashboard, or because a cigarette has fallen on to a seat. Many vehicles also catch fire when parked in tall grass and left while the engine is hot – this can ignite combustibles under the vehicle.

If you drive a motorhome or tow a caravan, you have to be doubly careful, because these vehicles contain propane tanks, which provide another source of fuel for fire. They are also prone to electrical fires because of their complex wiring harnesses. Make sure you have a smoke and/or gas detector.

USING A FIRE EXTINGUISHER

Different kinds of fire extinguishers are available, but an ABC (powder) extinguisher is the most versatile. Get a big, heavy one, to avoid the horror of the extinguisher running out, but also because it makes a very useful escape tool and weapon.

To put out a fire, sweep the extinguisher back and forth across the base of the fire until it is out. Don't spray at the flames – that won't put the fire out and will waste the contents of the extinguisher.

If you have a fire in a seat, put out the fire but then pull the seat out of the vehicle. The upholstery will probably still be smouldering: open it up to extinguish the fire, or discard the seat.

ENGINE FIRES

Fire may result from a fuel line leaking on to a hot manifold. Inspect fuel pipes frequently and replace them if they look cracked. If your engine is on fire, turn off the ignition immediately to shut down the fuel pump.

Putting out an engine fire safely takes two people, one to use the extinguisher, the other to open the bonnet (hood). It's important to get the bonnet open fast. Once the fire burns through the release cable there'll be no way to get it open. The fire will flare up as the fresh air hits it, so be ready to start spraying immediately. Don't try to put out an engine fire by spraying through the radiator or wheel arches – this won't work. You have to get at the source of the flames.

▲ *If your engine is on fire, try not to lift the bonnet (hood) more than necessary. Aim the extinguisher at the base of the fire.*

CONE OF DANGER

If you're fighting a vehicle fire, stay out of the cone-shaped danger zone, which is directly behind a vehicle with the fuel tank in the usual position at the back. If the tank explodes it sends a blast over this area that can be lethal for 15–30m/50–100ft. Some vehicles have the fuel tank at the front or side – don't assume the danger zone is the back.

Most danger is associated with petrol, not diesel fuel, which is difficult to ignite. Petrol will explode at the slightest exposure to heat, flame or sparks. So get everyone well away from a petrol-driven car.

WHAT TO DO WHEN A CAR IS ON FIRE

1 A dashboard fire can spread quickly into the engine or fuel system. Put it out at once or abandon the vehicle.

2 Prepare your fire extinguisher according to the instructions while you are standing safely outside the vehicle.

3 Reach into the car quickly and aim the extinguisher at the base of the fire. Spray until all the flames are out.

Drivers' survival strategies

If you break down in a remote area, or are stranded in severe weather, you may have to wait a long time for rescue. Your vehicle will give some protection from the elements, but in extreme cold keeping warm will be a priority.

MAKING A FIRE

Use a mirror or a car light reflector as a burning glass, or use a pair of glasses or binoculars to focus the sun's rays on to some tinder or dry leaves.

If there is no sun, use your car battery and jump leads, or any batteries and wire you have. If the batteries are small hold two together, positive to negative, and attach two pieces of wire to the positive and negative terminals at each end. Touch the free ends of wire to a bit of wire wool. It will spark up really well. If you have no wire wool touch the ends of the wires together to draw a spark. A small amount of fuel will help if your tinder isn't good.

If you have a petrol engine running and don't want to mess about, grip one of the plug leads with a gloved or well-insulated hand and pull it off the plug. Holding it near the plug or any metal part of the engine will make a big spark to light a handful of tinder. (If your insulation isn't good you'll get a very invigorating electric shock which will also warm you up.) Crucially, don't overlook the car's cigarette lighter.

DIGGING A CAR OUT OF SNOW

Dig the snow away from the vehicle's exhaust pipe before you start your engine, and dig through the snow to the middle of the underbody to allow any leaks from the exhaust system to vent. Without proper ventilation,

▲ *In extremely cold conditions you can light a small fire under a diesel engine to keep it warm if you are stranded. Never try this with a petrol vehicle, and be very careful the fire doesn't lick at wiring or rubber hoses or seals.*

deadly gases can quickly build up in the passenger compartment.

Clearing ice and snow from the windows and lights is a good start. Don't forget to clear snow from the bonnet and roof, or it will quickly blow on to your front and rear windows again.

If digging and spreading sand or gravel near the wheels doesn't give you enough grip to get moving, try rocking the car with quick movements forward and backwards. You can use the weight of the car to push it out of the icy depressions the tyres have settled in: be gentle with the throttle, ease forward, then rock back, until you are clear.

BEING SEEN

The colour of your vehicle may make it difficult to see: for instance, a white car in snow or a green one on grass. Put something brightly coloured on it such as a jumper or scarf so you will be seen and rescued.

◀ *Use blankets or coats to insulate your engine compartment to retain heat – either to keep you warm or to stop the engine freezing overnight.*

LONG JOURNEY ESSENTIALS

- Car/driving documents
- Map
- Mobile (cell) phone with emergency numbers
- Torch (flashlight)
- Extra batteries for torch
- First-aid kit
- Spare tyre, inflated to recommended pressure
- Jump leads
- Tow rope
- Road flares or warning triangles
- Ice scraper and de-icer
- Container for fuel
- Basic tool kit including adjustable spanners, cutters, some wire and duct tape
- Blanket or sleeping bag
- Waterproof clothing and gloves
- Extra washer fluid
- Bottled water/protein bars
- Shovel

Choosing a safe seat

Whenever you use public transport, whatever type of vehicle you are travelling in, your "What if?" survival attitude should equip you to choose the safest place to sit, based on experience and observation. Here are some tips to help you decide where and how to sit.

TRAINS AND BUSES

It is safer not to choose a seat at a table. In the event of a collision or a sudden stop, you could be severely injured by being thrown forward into the table, and you could also be hit by other passengers, or objects on the table, flying into you. It is safer to choose a seat where you are protected both ahead and behind by your own seat and the one in front of you. On the other hand, you need to bear in mind that on long journeys you are more at risk from discomfort – and in an extreme case from suffering deep-vein thrombosis (DVT) – than from being involved in an accident, so it may be more important to choose a comfortable seat with leg room and where you can get up and move around. If you have a choice of

forward- or rear-facing seats it is probably safer to be rear-facing, but this would depend on the nature of any accident and other factors may affect your decision.

A seat next to an emergency exit should always be your first choice. This is probably even better than being next to the main exit, since you will be in control of it, and first out of the door. Also, on aircraft and coaches such seats usually have more legroom than the rest of the seating. On airlines,

▲ *Public transport is statistically far safer than travel by car, with air travel being 27 times safer than cars in terms of fatalities.*

emergency exit row seats are allocated to passengers capable of operating the doors, which rules out the elderly and infirm and children. By contacting the airline, you might be able to secure an exit row seat in advance. If the airline policy is not to allocate them until the day of departure, arrive early and see if you can get transferred.

▼ *In a train with three cars, the middle one is probably the safest since it cannot be struck directly in a collision. In a longer train, consider being nearer the rear, though not in the last two cars.*

▶ *In a single-carriage train, sitting close to an exit will mean you are first in the queue for any quick escape needed.*

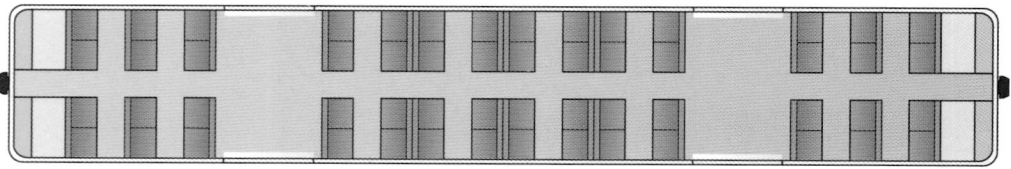

▶ *Take care when leaving a train on an open line – you could get hit by a passing train.*

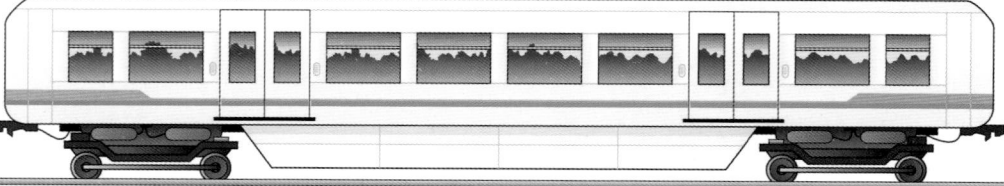

▲ *Before boarding many types of public transport your belongings may be searched or X-rayed. Be ready to demonstrate that drinks are harmless and electrical equipment is what it appears to be.*

SEAT BELTS AND RESTRAINT SYSTEMS

If there are seat belts, use them whenever you are in your seat. In an accident in any form of transport a seat belt can improve your chances of survival considerably.

Do not get up from your seat as soon as a vehicle comes to a halt. This is a common cause of injury – when a vehicle stops it will actually have moved forward on its suspension, especially if it has rubber tyres. A second or so later it will rock back. If

▼ *On a bus sit on the inside aisle so that you are able to make a quick escape and also are less likely to be hurt by flying glass.*

you get up too soon, you could be thrown forward or to the floor by the unexpected movement.

As with all survival considerations, the most important thing is to think at all times about the likely outcome of an accident. Some experienced travellers, when in Third World countries, prefer to travel on the roof of a bus rather than inside. They say this is safer in low-speed accidents (which are the most common), more comfortable and healthier than being crammed in with other travellers and their livestock; in addition, it enables them to keep an eye on their luggage, which is stored on the roof and may otherwise be stolen at bus stops. This way of travelling may not be for you, but extreme circumstances sometimes require extreme measures, so you should at least be open to such options.

STORING LUGGAGE SAFELY

Most people prefer to keep their luggage close by them for security and convenience, but it is also true to say that loose luggage can be a significant danger to passengers in the event of an impact. The overhead lockers or racks are the best places for items of hand luggage that you won't need during the journey, but don't try to stow very heavy items overhead as they could become dangerous missiles in a collision. Those items you would need in an emergency should be stored about your person as far as possible.

STRANGERS ON PUBLIC TRANSPORT

Other people are the bane or joy, depending on your attitude, of travel by public transport. You'll experience the full range of human behaviour, from the travelling companion who simply talks too much when you want to sleep or be alone to threatening, drunk or abusive passengers. It's also possible that they might try to steal from you. Try to appear confident but not aggressive when dealing with fellow passengers, using firm but non-threatening body language with open hand gestures.

Women in particular may be vulnerable to unwanted attention of a sexual nature, and this attention can become uncomfortable and/or escalate into confrontation or in extreme cases sexual assault. Rule number one is never to travel alone – but this is not much consolation if you have no choice. Try to keep within sight of other passengers or the driver, and form bonds with people you feel you can trust. Finally, keep a secret weapon handy, such as a rape alarm or pepper spray (but be certain that whatever you carry does not contravene local laws), to be used as a last resort.

▼ *In an aircraft, there is no evidence that any one part of the plane is safer in a crash, though being close to an emergency exit is clearly beneficial in terms of evacuation.*

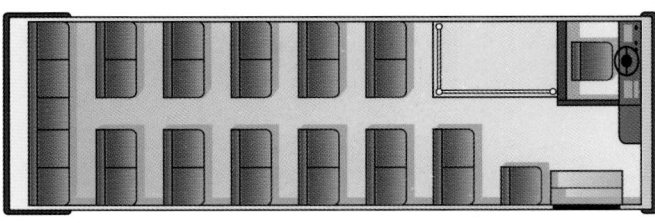

▼ *If you have to vacate a bus by a rear window be wary of passing traffic.*

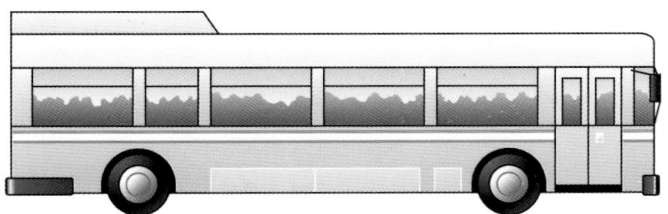

▼ *In a plane, the seats over the wing are the strongest and most stable but close to fuel tanks.*

▼ *The seats at the back are noisier and the plane moves more in turbulence.*

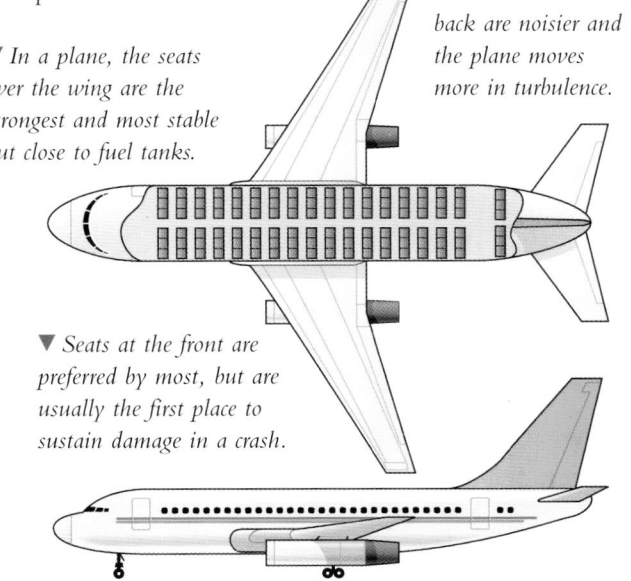

▼ *Seats at the front are preferred by most, but are usually the first place to sustain damage in a crash.*

Transport accidents on land

Accidents on buses or trains generally leave you in a less extreme type of environment than those in air or water, but unfortunately they are a lot more common. Many of us are likely to be involved in one or more during our lives, in particular when travelling by road. Preparation and premeditation is key, as in all survival scenarios.

Count the number of seat rows to the exits, familiarize yourself with the operation of emergency doors, and take note of the position and instructions for any glass-breaking devices supplied. Simple things like carrying a small torch (flashlight) and a mobile (cell) phone on your person, and considering your exit strategy from the moment you get on board, will always pay dividends if things go wrong.

ROAD TRAFFIC ACCIDENTS

The best protection you can have in a road accident is a seat belt. If the vehicle is fitted with them, wear one at all times, even when stationary. Once the vehicle has come to rest after an accident, release your seat belt and get yourself and others out and to safety as

▼ *Escalating congestion on the roads means that the chances of accidents and breakdowns are constantly increasing. We have to be prepared for any scenario.*

quickly as possible, unless you suspect someone has a serious spinal injury. Anyone injured in this way should not be moved until medical help arrives unless their life depends on it.

If you do not have a seat belt you should adopt the brace position – placing your hands on your head with your arms against the back of the seat in front of you – if you believe an accident is imminent. This will reduce the likelihood of injury.

ESCAPING FROM A VEHICLE

When you need to get out of a vehicle after an accident you may have to operate the doors yourself. The emergency exits may have releases on the inside, outside, or both. On some buses and trains they can simply be forced open by hand in the event of a power failure.

If you can't leave by a door you may need to break a window. Many public transport vehicles have small devices for breaking glass stowed at intervals along the passenger compartments. When you get on board, make sure you know where the nearest one to your seat is located, and read the instructions. The devices vary in type and operation and you won't be able to break the strong safety glass of the vehicle's windows by any other means.

▲ *Without their underground train systems, many of the world's capital cities would grind to a halt. Accidents on them are rare, but when they happen they present the rescue services with major problems in terms of access and communications.*

LEAVING A MOVING VEHICLE

If you realize you have to get out of a vehicle while it is still moving, keep to the following rules. Look in the direction of travel before you jump to make sure you aren't going to hit a lamp post or something similar. Aim to hit the ground as if running and then roll, protecting your head with your arms. If you have practised jumping off moving things such as swings, roundabouts, bicycles or skateboards you will do it better. Jumping off a vehicle travelling at more than about 50kph/30mph is probably not worth the risk of injury unless staying on board means almost certain death.

Warning: This is an extremely dangerous procedure. Do this only in a life-threatening emergency.

FIRE AND SMOKE

If there is a fire on a public transport vehicle the compartment will quickly fill with smoke from burning carpets, seat foam and plastic fixtures. Luckily, you counted the number of seat rows between you and the nearest exits, and

with the aid of your torch you can crawl to an exit along the floor beneath the worst of it. Wrapping a scarf around your face will help.

ELECTRIC TRAINS AND TRAMS

Having left the train you need to negotiate the tracks. These may be electrified, so do not touch them. Look out for any conductive debris that could also give you a shock. Some electric vehicles get their current from overhead wires. Look out for these, either on top of the vehicle, or brought down by the accident.

UNDERGROUND STATIONS

If you need to escape from an underground train you will arrive on the tracks in a tunnel. If trains are still running you are in great danger. There may be alcoves at intervals in the wall, in which you can shelter from passing trains. Face outwards and keep any loose clothing or hair under control. A passing train could suck items out of the alcove and snag them.

If you don't know the direction of the nearest station, see if there is a breeze in the tunnel. The nearer station is more likely to be downwind. Once in the station, get above ground and out of danger. If there has been a fire, do not use lifts (elevators) or escalators.

▲ *Standing too near the edge of a platform carries the twin dangers of trains passing at high speeds and the possibility of falling on to the live rail.*

It is usually better to use stairs anyway as fewer people may try this way. Those who habitually use a route are unlikely to shake off the habit in an emergency.

If you are already in a lift and it stops, force the doors manually to see if you are near enough to a floor to clamber out. If not, you may be able to escape through a hatch in the top and climb to a floor. Both actions are very dangerous, particularly if the lift starts again, so use the stop switch on the control panel before you try. Unless you are in immediate danger it is better to wait for rescue. Most lifts have a bell or phone with which to signal for help. This may not work after an electrical failure, but try it first. You can signal by shouting or banging metallic objects on the floor: this sound will carry a long way in a lift shaft.

BREAKING A SAFETY GLASS WINDOW

1 Follow the instructions to open the box containing the hammer – usually by smashing a glass cover. Use an object such as a book if possible.

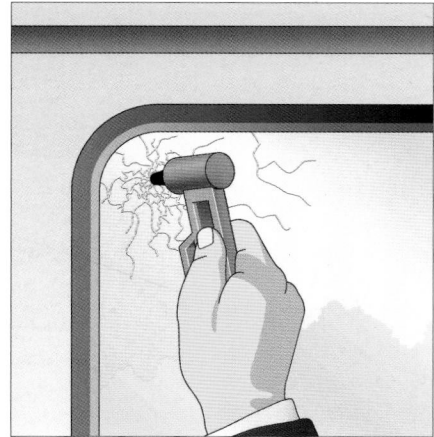

2 Remove the tool and tap it firmly against the window near the corner. Make sure you break both panes if the window is double-glazed.

3 Use a bag or coat to enlarge the hole until it is big enough to use as an escape route. Remove the glass to the bottom of the pane to avoid injuries.

When things go wrong in the air

Most people fear flying more than any other common form of transport, despite being perfectly aware that it is in fact one of the safest. This is partly due to lack of familiarity – you probably fly less often than you take a car, train or bus. But another factor is the lack of control you have over your environment. In almost no other mode of transport do you have so little influence – you don't get to choose when to travel or where to sit, and you are told what to do at every stage.

You can make yourself feel much better about flying simply by being proactive about the things you can control, and in doing so you can dramatically improve your chances of survival if the unthinkable did happen.

IN-FLIGHT BRIEFING AND SAFETY CARD

If you are apprehensive about flying, the safety briefing can make matters worse by putting in your mind the idea that you are likely to experience serious turbulence, loss of cabin pressure, a crash landing and being lost at sea – all of which are very unlikely to occur. Even so, you should listen to

▼ *Members of a fire crew carry a victim away from the scene of a serious accident. The foam from their chemical extinguishing equipment can be seen all around them.*

and concentrate on the safety briefing. It is important. Read the card that explains what to do in the case of an accident. Not only will this make any emergency action less of a shock to you but you will understand what everyone else is doing, and why.

The in-flight briefing and safety card will tell you where your lifejacket is stowed. It is usually under your seat – make sure you really understand how to access it. They will also explain how in the event of loss of cabin pressure, oxygen masks will drop down from the panel above you.

The ordinary person requires supplemental oxygen at altitudes above 3,000m/10,000ft, and either aircraft must have pressurized cabins or everyone must use oxygen masks. As a result, passenger aircraft must carry emergency oxygen supplied via masks in case the cabin pressurization system fails or the plane is punctured by accident. This supply provides the necessary time for the pilot(s) to descend safely to an altitude where supplemental oxygen is no longer needed. Loss of cabin pressurization by a bullet or other puncture isn't catastrophic, as portrayed in the movies, and the loss of a door or window does not destroy the aircraft.

▲ *This plane has veered off the runway at speed and the undercarriage has collapsed on the grass, but the passengers inside may have come to no harm at all.*

FAMILIARIZATION

When you board an aircraft, familiarize yourself with everything around you. In the event of an incident it is the cabin crew's job to open emergency exits and to deploy fire extinguishers, but it can't hurt for you to make sure you know how they work. The nearest crew member might be injured in the incident, or wrestling with a passenger who is less calm than yourself.

AIR RAGE

Extreme behaviour by unruly passengers, often called air rage, can put crew members and other passengers at risk. The reasons for such aggression could include excessive alcohol consumption, a ban on smoking, claustrophobia, the tedium of a long flight, psychological feelings of loss of control and problems with authority.

Cabin crews are trained to deal with this, but in the event that you become involved, maintain eye contact and passive, open body language and attempt to calm the troublemaker. Do not escalate the conflict.

TURBULENCE AND WIND SHEARS
Sometimes the aircraft can be jerked around violently by atmospheric conditions. The pilot will usually give you some warning of this but sometimes that isn't possible so it's a good idea to be prepared for it at any time during the flight.

Make sure that anything you put in the locker above you is correctly stowed and check that the locker is shut properly after each time it is opened. Minimize the chances of something falling on you.

Don't drink too much so that you need to go to the toilet frequently or at inconvenient times. Put your seat belt on whenever you are in the seat, not just when the seat belt light is on.

PREPARING FOR THE WORST
The worst-case scenario worth considering is that you have to exit the aircraft in an emergency. The trick here is to know how many rows of seats there are between you and each of the exits. Once you have found your seat, look around and identify the emergency exits, and count the number of seat-backs between your seat and each one of the exits. This knowledge could save your life in the case of smoke, fire or power outage, since you will be one of the minority of people who will be able to find the exits blind. Anything in your possession that would be absolutely essential for your continued well-being outside the aircraft (such as medication or an inhaler) should be carried in your pockets or otherwise on your person at all times. That way you won't need to stop to grab your carry-on luggage.

In the case of smoke or fire you need to be out of the plane within 90 seconds or you won't be capable of being proactive any more. Pulling some clothing across your face as a mask can help minimize inhalation problems, especially if you can wet it first.

▶ *On water the slides may be used to get passengers out, but afterwards they will be deployed as rafts. They remain tethered to the aircraft until all people and supplies are out, or the plane is in danger of sinking.*

DEEP VEIN THROMBOSIS
One danger you face on a commercial airliner is deep vein thrombosis (DVT), especially if you are overweight, unfit, drink too much alcohol, or have a history of vascular problems. Blood clots form, especially in the legs, and cause pain and swelling; they may later be life-threatening if they become dislodged and block a blood vessel in the lung. Contrary to urban myth the condition is not confined to flying, and can occur whenever you sit still for many hours at a time. To avoid it, just

▲ *In an emergency, escape slides are deployed from every exit and passengers are moved quickly away from the aircraft.*

go for a stroll up the aisle every hour, and do mild flexing exercises with your legs while seated.

Current medical thinking is that "flight socks" can reduce the risk, and these are available from airlines and travel stores. DVT is extremely rare and, while you should take precautions even if you're not in a high risk group, you shouldn't worry about it unduly.

Surviving an air emergency

If an emergency develops while you are on board an aircraft, make sure you have your jacket on with all essential items in your pockets. Any non-essential carry-on baggage should be left behind if you eventually have to evacuate the plane.

Ideally you should be wearing roomy, comfortable clothes that give you freedom of movement, and cover your arms and legs fully. Natural fibres give the best protection. Shoes should be low, with straps or laces to keep them on your feet in an emergency.

Fasten your seat belt and adopt the brace position. Make sure you have remembered how many rows of seats there are between you and each exit, and glance at all the passengers around you, to take in who is who and try to form an impression of how they will react if you have to get out.

EMERGENCY LANDING IN WATER
If the aircraft is forced to come down in the sea, do not inflate lifejackets or rafts until they are outside the plane. Get yourselves and all emergency equipment off the aircraft as soon as possible, remembering that fresh water is possibly the most important thing to have with you in a survival situation. Retain a line from the aircraft to the raft until everything you need is aboard

EMERGENCY IN THE AIR

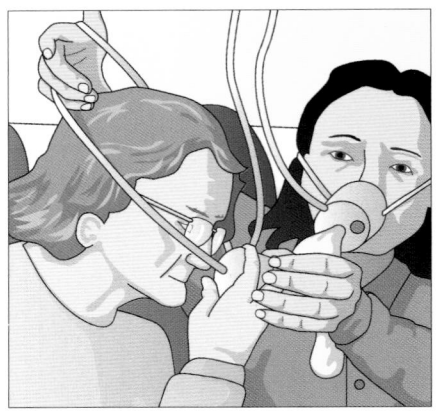

▲ *If the plane loses oxygen pressure, oxygen masks will drop down automatically. Secure your own mask so that you can breathe normally before helping others in difficulty.*

▲ *When you hear the words "Brace! Brace!" adopt the position shown here, with your hands on your head against the back of the seat in front of you.*

▲ *If fire breaks out after a crash landing, crawl beneath the smoke and fumes towards the nearest emergency exit, which you should have identified earlier.*

USING AN EMERGENCY EXIT

1 Emergency exits are opened by pulling a handle in the direction indicated. Do not attempt to operate it until the aircraft is stationary.

2 The door may open, or come right off. Make sure the way is clear before deploying a slide or other apparatus, and before attempting to make an exit.

3 Remove your shoes as they can damage slides. Jump into the centre of the slide, fold your arms across your chest and keep your feet together.

or the aircraft starts to sink – be ready to release the line and paddle away as the aircraft goes under.

If you have more than one life raft it helps to tie them together with 8–10m/25–30ft of line. If you can deal with it, linking swimmers together in this way is a good idea too.

If you need to search for missing people, think primarily about the wind direction and which way you, the aircraft and they might be blown by it. Any current is irrelevant because you are all in that, but wind affects different flotsam in differing ways.

Be careful about trimming and balancing your raft, but have a strategy for righting it and containing your important supplies if it should capsize for any reason.

The drier you are the better, as immersion can have adverse effects later on. If it is cold, think about ways to keep warm as soon as possible – if you deal with more pressing matters first and get cold you will probably not warm up again. If it is warm, you need to consider the consequences of sunburn or dehydration – get under cover or keep your skin covered. If you are swimming, face away from the sun or try to improvise some face covering with clothing. Obviously wear a hat and sunglasses if you have them.

Activate any rescue transmitters you may have as soon as possible. Try the radio as well if you have one. Remember that search aircraft and ships have difficulty spotting survivors, especially small rafts or swimmers. Do anything you can to increase your visibility. Keep mirrors handy, use the radio when you can, and be prepared to use the mirrors and/or marker dye if an aircraft or ship is sighted.

SURVIVING A CRASH LANDING

If fire breaks out in the aircraft after a crash landing, crawl beneath the smoke, following the floor lights if they still work and counting the seats to the exit, having identified the nearest one earlier. Go over or around anyone in your way. The chances are that some of these passengers will be lost, or just slow. That isn't your problem – don't wait in line.

If escape slides are being deployed, don't sit down to slide, just jump into the middle of the chute. Cross your arms across your chest to minimize the risk of snagging on something or injury to yourself or someone else.

Once you are out of the aircraft, stay well away from it until the engines are cooled and spilt fuel has evaporated. Check the injured and administer whatever help you can. Get out of the

wind or rain – improvise some kind of shelter as a priority. Make a fire if you need one, and make hot drinks if you can. Get communications equipment operative if possible and begin broadcasting. Having done this, relax, give yourselves a chance to get over the shock and leave any further planning and operations until later.

WAITING FOR RESCUE

After you have rested, recover all useful supplies and organize them. Remember that water is the most important thing. Determine your position as best you can and include it in any radio broadcast – if it is based on any assumptions, transmit those too.

If you bailed out of the aircraft, try to get back to it, as it will be found before you are. If it is cold you can use the aircraft for shelter while you try to build a better, warmer shelter outside. Do not cook inside the plane.

If it's hot, the plane will be too hot to use as a shelter. Instead, make a shade shelter outside using parachutes or blankets as an awning. Leave the lower edges 50cm/20in off the ground to allow the air to flow.

Conserve the power of any electrical equipment, and sweep the horizon with a signal mirror or light at regular intervals, even if you are broadcasting.

IN THE EVENT OF A CRASH LANDING

1 The pilot will attempt to make a survivable landing no matter how severe the situation: an ideal approach angle may not be achievable.

2 Whether the aircraft impacts nose or tail first there is a significant risk of the fuselage snapping, endangering the lives of the passengers.

3 The fuselage is most likely to break near the middle, and this may be accompanied almost immediately by fire in this and other areas.

Abandoning ship

Preparation is everything if you are to survive a shipwreck. Know where the lifesaving equipment is and know how to lay your hands on essential supplies: water is the most important, but also food, clothing and communications gear. If you do find yourself without a proper raft or life preserver you will need to seek out the largest floating item available, then try to transfer essential items to it.

Follow the instructions of the crew where possible. Once in the water, be rational about getting away from the ship. If it is not going to sink or explode immediately, stay with it, tethered if necessary, until all useful supplies have been recovered or it appears to be too dangerous to stay.

BURNING OIL

If fire breaks out and there is burning fuel on the surface of the water, try to make your way upwind. Burning oil is easily blown and does not spread upwind. It may be necessary to dive under narrow stretches of burning fuel, and you will need to deflate your life preserver to do this. If you have to surface among the flames, you can try to thrash your arms as you do so – this may make a break in the fire while you

get a breath, but you should regard this as a last resort as the fire will have extracted the oxygen from the affected area and the super-hot air inside a fire can burn your lungs and kill you.

You can breathe the air in a life-preserver if it was inflated by mouth. Although it is exhaled air, it still

▲ *Follow the instructions of the crew on when to abandon ship. If you are lucky, the rescue services may arrive in time.*

contains enough oxygen to breathe a couple more times. But beware automatically inflated vests – they are usually full of carbon dioxide.

IMPROVISING FLOTATION AIDS

▲ *Knot the ankles of a pair of trousers. Swing them by the waistband over your head then pull the waistband under water to trap air in each leg.*

▲ *Cushions and pillows can be used as flotation devices. Some of those found on board ship may be specifically designed for this purpose.*

▲ *If you have no flotation aids (don't take off the trousers you are wearing), try to tread water as little as possible to conserve your energy.*

SURVIVING IN THE WATER

Don't swim if you can help it. Float on your back using as much additional buoyancy (from a life preserver, or air trapped in clothes or cushions) as you can, and save your energy. Swim only if you can be certain from experience that you are capable of swimming to relative safety. Save energy by keeping your head submerged except when you need to breathe. Even if you are a strong swimmer you may find it very difficult in the sea. Previous practice swimming in rough seas is a great help.

Swimming, even gently, reduces your survival time, and strips the heat away from your body incredibly quickly. If you stay still you will warm up a thin layer of water around you, and particularly inside your clothes. Every time you move you exchange this warm water for cooler, and lose a bit more heat and hence energy. For this reason, keep as many clothes on as possible. If you have a bag (a bivvy bag or plastic survival bag, even a bin bag), getting inside this will trap water around you and dramatically improve your chances. Being a big orange blob is also a great deterrent to one of our greatest fears in the water – sharks (*see following pages*).

▲ *If there is burning oil on the water, swim upwind from it.*

◄ *The best place to be if your sailing craft is capsized or swamped is close to the boat so that rescuers can find you more easily.*

EVACUATION PROCEDURES

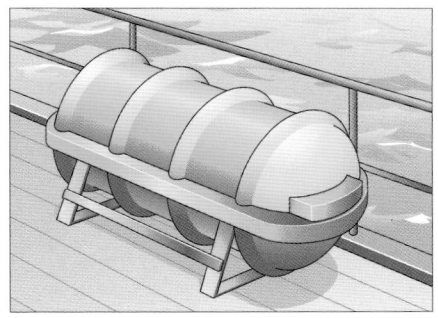

1 In addition to orthodox lifeboats, most ships have cylinder-shaped "throwover" life rafts complete with emergency survival kit.

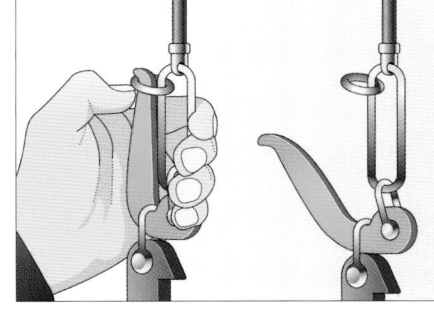

2 In order to launch the life raft, the lashings securing the two halves of the cylinder must first be released.

3 After securing the "painter" (the rope attached to the life raft) to a point on the boat, ensure all is clear below then throw the life raft overboard.

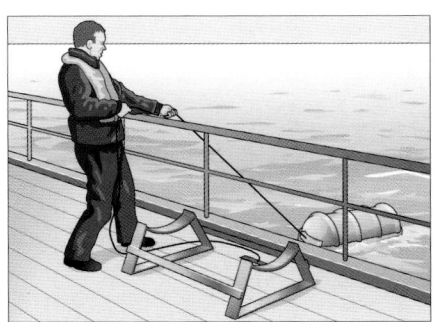

4 Pull out the entire length of the painter and then, when it is taut, give the painter a hard tug. This will start the inflation process.

5 Ideally bring the life raft alongside the boat and enter without getting wet, having first removed shoes and any sharp objects.

6 After everyone has boarded the raft, cut the painter, look for survivors who had to jump and paddle away from the sinking vessel.

Survival at sea

When you have to survive on minimal supplies you must first look after what you have – that means firstly your life raft. Any boat will stay drier with the weight near the centre, though it will pitch and roll less with the weight distributed. In rough conditions a sea anchor off the bow can help you stay stable and facing oncoming waves, but it also slows your downwind progress. In hot climates deflate the raft a little in the morning to stop it bursting.

FOOD AND WATER

Use any supplies wisely. You can go for weeks without food, but only days without water. Drink as little as you

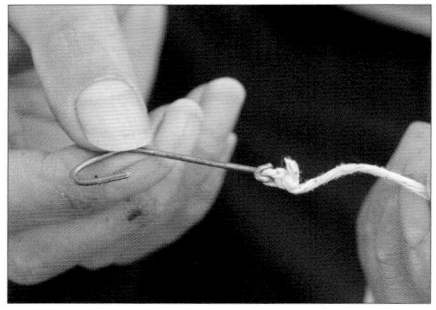

▲ *If you have some stiff wire you may be able to create a hook using any tools you have aboard. Tie the hook on to any thin string or line you can find. Try to bait the hook with something, but you may even be lucky with just a bare hook.*

can to keep yourself hydrated and if it is hot try to minimize perspiration by wetting your hair and clothes with sea water, provided this does not irritate your skin. Rain, old (bluish) ice, and the bodily fluids of sea creatures are all sources of water at sea. Do not drink salt water under any circumstances.

If you have no food, you'll have to catch some, and the primary food sources are fish, birds, and plankton. Plankton can be filtered from the sea with a cloth and are an excellent source of protein and carbohydrate if all spiny material and stinging tentacles can be removed, though you may ingest a lot of salt water with them and you should test them for toxicity.

It's easy to improvise hooks and line for small fish. Failing a line, you can

▲ *Sharks are greatly feared, but remember that only a few shark attacks are recorded around the world each year, and not all of those are fatal. You cannot swim anywhere near as fast as a shark, but they find it hard to stop or change direction quickly – especially large ones, so you may be able to get out of the way, especially downwards as the shark can't see ahead or below once it's jaws are open. If you are attacked and have a knife, go for the eyes or gills – the most sensitive areas – or gouge with your fingers. With a bit of luck it will be scared off.*

try to make a spear, but don't try to spear anything big. Birds are hard to catch but may be speared or lassoed after enticing them to land on the boat. Most seaweed is edible, while coral is always poisonous and inedible.

USING A DINGHY AS A LIFE RAFT

1 If possible attach a righting line running from gunwale to gunwale under the dinghy, which you can use to turn the boat if it capsizes.

2 Tie yourselves and your equipment into the boat if necessary, leaving your tethers long so that you will not be trapped under the boat if it capsizes.

3 You may be able to improvise a sail using a tarpaulin or even a shirt, which can move a small boat quite well and may also provide a little shade.

▲ *Sharks are careful hunters and will avoid what they see as a huge target with lots of limbs. If you group together, face outwards and stay calm, there is every chance that sharks will ignore you.*

To find out if something is okay to eat, you'll need to adapt the taste test outlined on page 90 as you won't have the means to cook the food.

SHARKS

If you're with a group of people and stranded in the sea near sharks, the best advice is to bunch together and face outward. Sharks are scared by strong, regular movements and loud noises so if one is close by try slapping the water with cupped hands.

If you are alone, try to float in a horizontal rather than a vertical position: this will slightly reduce the risk of attack because the shark may see you as a live target, not an easy sick or dead one. Swim rhythmically and don't panic. Sharks have highly developed

▲ *If you can see an attacking shark, you do have a good chance of defending yourself if it's not too big. Kick with your feet or punch with a stiff arm, using the heel of your hand to ward the shark off.*

senses of smell and can detect blood and waste matter from a great distance. Twilight is the most dangerous time, followed by darkness. Few attacks happen in full daylight. They rarely attack brightly coloured things but they see contrasts particularly well, even tan lines. Shiny objects can also look like a small fish-like target to a hungry shark.

OTHER HARMFUL CREATURES

Many species of fish have sharp defensive spines that can puncture your skin, and a small number of these are venomous. Any spines should be viewed with caution. Fish such as the stonefish and greater weaver hide on the seabed in shallow water and can be trodden on by the unwary. Other spiny fish can be accidentally hooked and

JELLYFISH

Jellyfish often have stinging tentacles, and in particular the Portuguese man-of-war and box jellyfish can cause death if the contact is prolonged and prolific. Jellyfish stings can be treated with vinegar except for a sub-group of the Portuguese man-of-war whose sting is made much worse by it, so it is safer not to use vinegar on man-of-war stings. Pluck off all the tentacles, apply vinegar if appropriate, and if possible treat with ice until the pain subsides.

sting you when you try to handle them. If in doubt, cut them loose as the venom can be fatal in some cases. If you are injured, remove the spines and flush the wound immediately. Apply very hot water and then hot compresses to try to kill the toxin with heat.

Although it is a small risk, some fish can give you a powerful electric shock if touched. These are electric rays, found at the bottom of temperate and tropical seas, and electric eels, found in tropical rivers. If you get close to one in water, a tingling sensation may warn you of the electrical energy.

Don't take any risks at all with snakes in or near water. There are thousands of different varieties, mostly harmless, but some are extremely venomous and fatal if they bite you.

CATCHING FOOD WITH A SEA ANCHOR

1 Tie a shirt or a similar piece of cloth over the mouth of a sea anchor to act as a sieve before deploying the anchor in the normal way.

2 While the sea anchor is in use the improvised sieve will collect plankton and other small creatures as well as fragments of seaweed.

3 Sort through the marine material you have collected each day and try it out for edibility adapting the taste test described on page 90.

Survival at the seashore

Many accidents and emergencies take place at the water's edge and it is as well to be familiar with the basic skills that can help you survive them, or to understand how your rescuers will act to help you.

There is a lot you can do to help yourself: you should be able to swim at least 50m/51.5yd in your underclothes, and to stay afloat indefinitely without wasting energy. You should also understand the basics of wave action, rip currents and tides.

▶ *The priority if you are in difficulty is to stay afloat, while alerting others to your predicament by waving and shouting.*

SWIMMER–SWIMMER RESCUE

1 A lifeguard or other strong swimmer may attempt a rescue by swimming if they are sure they won't get into the same predicament themselves.

2 The rescuer will swim to the victim as quickly as possible: this man is equipped with a towed float, which will not impede his movements.

3 The exhausted victim is carried ashore by two rescuers: the float has been tied round his waist to keep him afloat and aid the rescue.

CARRYING AN INJURED PERSON

1 Resuscitation is the priority but if rescuers suspect a spinal injury they will carry the victim ashore very carefully while supporting the neck and head.

2 The injured person is lowered to the ground as soon as the shore is reached so that resuscitation can be started in a safe environment.

3 Once breathing is restored the rescuers stabilize the victim to prevent movement and possible further injury until specialist help arrives.

LIFEGUARD RESCUE

1 A lifeguard may effect a rescue using a large, buoyant surfboard, enabling them to get to the victim quickly while maintaining good visual contact.

2 The victim can use the board as support while recovering while their state is assessed by the lifeguard, who stays on board to give stability.

3 The victim can be helped on to the board and paddled ashore by the lifeguard, which is quicker and easier than towing a swimmer.

4 If necessary the victim, who is probably exhausted, can be helped ashore by more rescuers.

5 The rescuers will check the victim over and make sure their condition is stable and not deteriorating.

6 If necessary the victim will be placed in the recovery position and checked for vital signs until medical help arrives.

RIP CURRENTS

1 When waves break on the shore a significant amount of water is pushed up the beach; as this falls back it may gradually build up a sandbar.

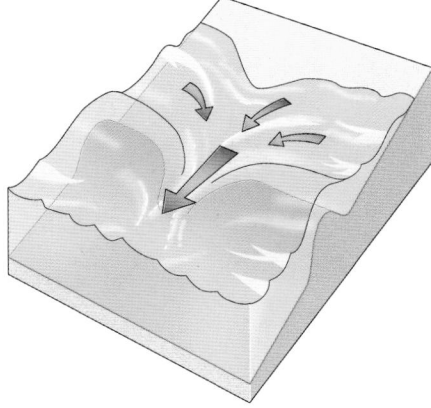

2 When the pressure of the returning water creates a channel through the sandbar, it all flows out in one spot. This powerful outflow is called a rip.

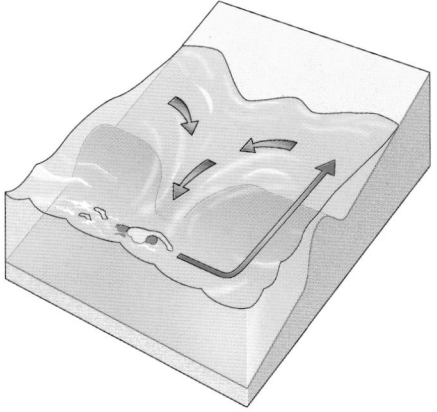

3 A distinct flattening of the waves often indicates a rip. Swim directly across it: don't try to make for the beach until you are out of the rip.

Travelling abroad

In spite of the fact that worldwide travel is now an essential part of so many people's lives, whether for leisure or business, there is still a widespread belief that abroad is inherently dangerous, and that a citizen cannot expect the same reasonable treatment from foreign locals that could be relied upon at home. In fact the opposite is more likely to be true.

The biggest danger you face when travelling abroad is probably your own disorientation and the difference between your preconceptions about a place and what is actually happening. You need to approach any situation with the same common sense you would utilize at home, without allowing your lack of knowledge of a foreign culture to flood your mind with irrational fears.

PASSPORTS AND VISAS

You need a passport to travel to most foreign countries and a visa to remain in many. Check on the restrictions before you even begin to arrange a trip, either with the embassy of your destination country or by consulting a professional travel service. You may, for example, need a passport that has at least six months left to run in order to enter certain countries.

On arrival in a foreign country, some travellers become paranoid about their passports, carrying them everywhere as if they were a lifeline. By carrying your passport you run the risk of losing it and having to go through a lot of bureaucracy to get a replacement. In some places foreign passports are quite sought after and you would not want to make yourself a target. Hotels in many countries require you to submit your passport when checking in: instead of arguing, hand it over – it will be more secure in

◄▲ *Legal self-defence sprays can shoot out a thick slimy goo that sticks to an attacker giving you time to react and escape. A bright difficult-to-remove UV dye helps identify the attacker days later. The rapid foaming spray (above) blocks an attacker's view and stains the face in a personal attack.*

▲ *As a visitor in a foreign city, you should not forget to take all the normal precautions you would at home to safeguard yourself and your possessions.*

the hotel safe. The exception to this rule is when your day's itinerary involves crossing a border – if you leave your passport behind you won't be able to complete your trip. This happens in many European ski resorts, for instance, so check before you go out for the day.

On the same note, e-tickets are much safer than paper travel documents, because you can't lose them. All you have to do is get yourself to your point of departure. Leave photocopies and details of any documents you do need to carry, such as air tickets, traveller's cheques and credit or debit cards, at home with a family member or a friend. Make additional copies for yourself and keep them separately from your documents. Consider setting up a web-based internet account and emailing such details to yourself so that you can access them from an internet café in extremis.

Make some effort to understand the monetary system in the country you are visiting, not just the currency and exchange rate with your own but the relative wealth of the local people. Carrying the equivalent of two years'

CHOOSING SAFE TRANSPORT

The safest mode of travel depends on where you are. In parts of many US cities, for instance, it is not safe to walk around, while in some parts of Europe driving is the most dangerous option. You'll see many people in Chinese and Indian cities riding bicycles, but it's not recommended for non-locals. In most countries air travel is advanced and safe, but there are still places you could be taking your life in your hands by getting on a plane. You should always accept expert advice and be prepared to adapt to the local conditions.

average salary around with you in case you need to buy a drink is a great way to get unwanted attention, even in fairly safe and civilized countries.

CULTURAL DIFFERENCES

It is amazing that you can get by knowing only the English language in so many places in the world. However, this is not a reason to be complacent if you are an English speaker. There are a

▼ *It's best to plan excursions in advance through reputable travel agencies or guides. Find out the duration of the excursion and how to get back to your accommodation on your return. Don't join an excursion if the transport looks dangerously overloaded.*

few language issues to consider whenever you visit a foreign country.
• Even if you stand no chance of being able to learn the language, knowing how to say "yes", "no", "please" and "thank you" goes a really long way.
• Consider whether the local language is going to be impossible to read as well as understand. If it is written in a non-Roman alphabet, you aren't even going to be able to read road signs and basic information unless you do some homework before you go.
• From the point of view of safety (or just comfort), differences in body language can be more important than the spoken word. In many ways people are the same the world over, and you

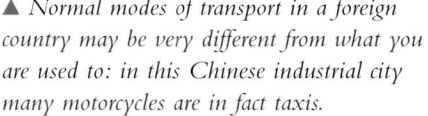

▲ *Normal modes of transport in a foreign country may be very different from what you are used to: in this Chinese industrial city many motorcycles are in fact taxis.*

will of course be able recognize something as basic as a threat or a smile. However, there can be major cultural differences and knowing about these can save you from causing offence or, at worst, from putting yourself at risk. Most good travel guides will give you the information you need on customs and cultural differences in the country you are visiting, so do your homework and find out about appropriate clothing before you go, whether any types of dress are compulsory or advisable (particularly if you are a woman) and whether certain behaviour is illegal or frowned upon.
• Knowing something about what is safe to eat is also a good idea. If the locals eat it, it's probably OK, but you may have a lower resistance to local toxins and bacteria than they do, so stick to food that has been well prepared and cooked.
• Many countries have specific local health problems that you might be vulnerable to. Malaria is a common example. While locals may not take any precautions at all, you need to check before you go whether you are at risk, and obtain the correct medication and inoculations from your doctor.

SURVIVING TERRORISM AND CONFLICT

The terrorist strikes out of the blue, when least expected, and almost invariably anonymously. He or she seldom wears a uniform and often takes the coward's way out by planting a bomb and sneaking away before either a timer or remote signal triggers devastation. Even more deadly and effective is the increasingly prevalent, fanatically driven suicide bomber, a development which calls for even more alertness and vigilance in public places and spaces.

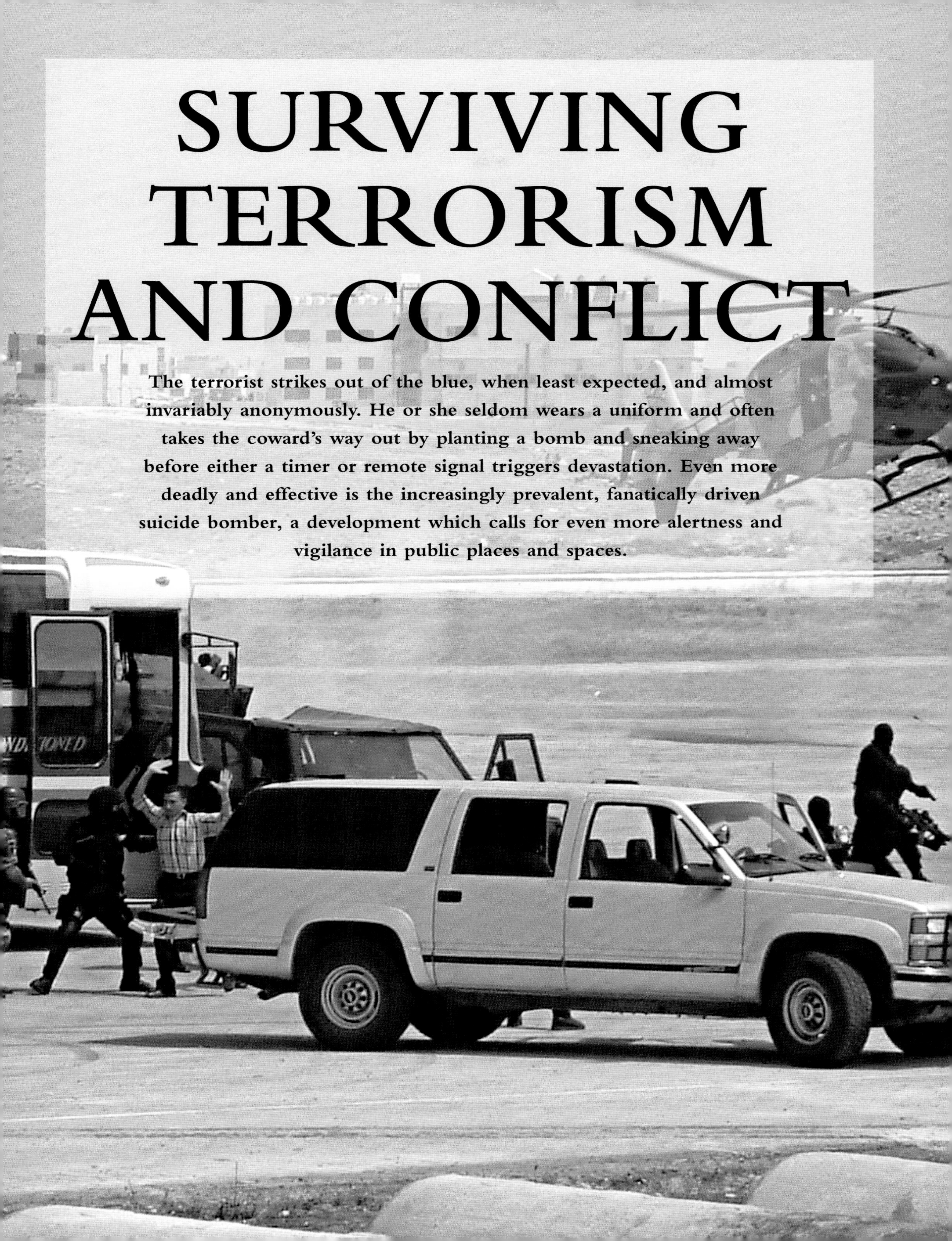

Being street smart

Terrorism is usually defined as being the unlawful use of, or the threatened use of, violence against the state or the general public as a politically motivated means of coercion. The 11 September 2001 terrorist attack by Al Qa'eda on the World Trade Center and Pentagon has had a marked affect on both American perceptions of international terrorism and the face of global politics, with the subsequent invasions of Afghanistan and Iraq being just the tip of the iceberg in what President George W. Bush labelled the "War Against Terror". Although 9/11 is seen as the ultimate terrorist act, terrorism is not of course a recent phenomenom. Countries such as Britain and Spain have been victim to prolonged and indiscriminate terror attacks arising respectively from the Northern Ireland "troubles" and the Basque separatist movement. Elsewhere around the globe over the last three or so decades, those seeking to overthrow the state in places as diverse as Zimbabwe, Sri Lanka, Lebanon, the Balkans, Peru, Chechnya and Sierra Leone, to name but a few, have used the bomb and gun as their political tool.

Inevitably, it is the innocent civilian who pays the price. Western holiday destination spots such as Bali and Egypt have also become bombers' targets and there are obvious considerations to be made when planning a vacation – not least checking with government alerts.

SUICIDE BOMBERS

While the United Nations tries to agree on a definition of "terrorism", city dwellers have to go on living with the real and present danger of the bomber strapped with explosives or carrying them in a backpack walking into the crowd, martyring themselves and taking countless innocent lives with them. Survival against this type of terrorist is not easy, should you be unlucky enough to cross their path, but if you have good powers of observation and are alert to the tell-tale signals, you may just survive.

Bombs, or to be more precise improvised explosive devices, are favoured methods of terror delivery. (Kidnappings and hostage-taking are also part of their arsenal and these are dealt with on later pages.) In times of heightened tension, government offices, military establishments, recruitment offices, power and water supply networks, airports and stations all become terrorist targets, and should be avoided where possible.

Anniversaries that are in some way related to the separatists' struggle are obvious magnets for those wishing to either heighten awareness of their

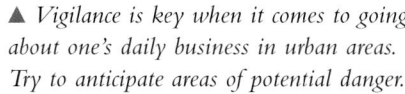

▲ *Vigilance is key when it comes to going about one's daily business in urban areas. Try to anticipate areas of potential danger.*

cause, or to create fear and outrage among the public; the 1987 IRA bomb attack on a Remembrance Sunday service in Enniskillen, which killed 11 and injured more than 60, being just one example of the latter. Through simply being aware of places where and times when the terrorist might be tempted to attack, and altering your plans to avoid these, you greatly reduce your chances of being caught up in such terrorist actions.

▲ *CCTV and identity cards will not stop the fanatical terrorist but they can help in the prevention of future outrages.*

▲ *Police around the world are armed now as a matter of routine which makes lethal outcomes more likely.*

▶ *Public spaces such as rail terminals are obvious targets for indiscriminate terrorist activity and you need to use your powers of observation to spot anything suspicious.*

PUBLIC AWARENESS

Could the Madrid railway bombings of March 2004 have been foreseen? With Spain's support for the Coalition invasion of Iraq in March 2003 and the chance to sway the result of forthcoming elections, the populace and the authorities should have been on heightened alert. More to the point, those in the carriages where the bombs were left unattended in luggage might have realized the potential danger and taken action before it was too late.

On 7 July 2005, after a four-year respite from terrorist bombings, due to the changed political climate in Northern Ireland, London was plunged back into chaos by a series of suicide bombs. This was a tactic never seen before in Britain – though it had been anticipated – and one that is harder to both detect and foil. This time the bombers did not leave unattended packages, but stayed with their lethal devices, dying themselves in the blast. They escaped detection by not standing out. Over 50 innocent civilians died after three bombs, carried in rucksacks, were detonated almost simultaneously in the cramped confines of underground railway carriages across the capital, and a fourth exploded on a city centre bus just under an hour later. At the time Britain was hosting the G8 international political summit, ensuring maximum attention for the terrorists' cause. Exactly two weeks later, an unsuccessful copy attack failed.

WHAT YOU CAN DO

Be street smart. Use your powers of deduction and observational skills to keep you alert to possible terrorist dangers, blending in with your surroundings. What police and military close-protection and undercover operatives dub "playing the grey man", is one of the most important skills to master. If the terrorist can neither single you as a potential target nor mark you out as deserving special

attention, your chances of survival increase dramatically. Don't stand out. Don't be the hero. Don't switch off to your surroundings. It is probably only you that holds the key to personal survival in a terrorism setting.

SEARCHING FOR CAR BOMBS

1 Check the wheel arches and around the underside where a sandwich box-sized device can be concealed. Memorize what the underside of your car looks like.

2 Check for signs of tampering – such as a forced door or marks or damage around the lock – and peek inside the interior for anything out of place.

3 A mirror on a pole (with a torch attached for checking in the dark), either improvised or a bought one, will help you see into vehicle recesses.

4 Do not assume that just because you cannot see a foreign object under your vehicle it is safe. Before opening the door, check the interior.

Being taken prisoner or hostage

The high profile cases of aid workers and contractors kidnapped in Iraq in 2005 and 2006 once again drew international attention to the methods used by terrorist groups to publicize their cause and how to protect foreign nationals in high-risk countries. To the committed terrorist, seizing an innocent charity worker is a sure way to attract the attention of the international media and in recent years terrorist organizations around the world have shown themselves to have very little or no regard for human life. If you are taken hostage by a terrorist group the situation is extremely grave.

A kidnap for ransom is big business for criminals with or without political leanings. To the gangster, a foreign businessman or engineer employed by a wealthy company can be just as tempting a target as someone who works for a bank vault.

Terrorists and criminals or, to be more specific, their foot soldiers, are not always the most logical or intelligent of people, so you do not need to belong to a high-risk group to be a potential kidnap victim. Mistakes of identity are easily made, or not even worried about, so it is essential that you try at the very least not to look like a

vulnerable target, and also that you take basic precautions to make it harder for kidnappers to seize you. Once again, become the grey man or woman so that you do not stand out from the crowd, and keep your wits about you for potential danger.

EARLIEST ESCAPE ESSENTIAL

If you are taken prisoner, you must attempt to escape at the earliest opportunity. The longer your captors have you, the less your chances are of getting away from them. During the initial lift, you will most likely be simply bundled into a vehicle by one

KIDNAP SCENARIO

1 Those who work with large sums of cash, such as bank employees and payroll staff, and their families, can be potential robbery kidnap victims.

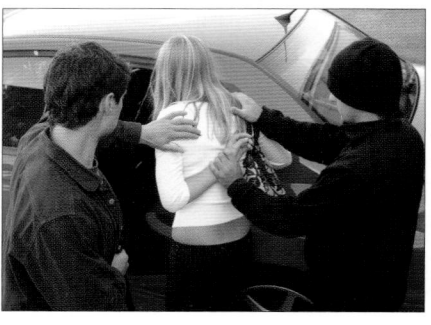

2 If kidnapped outside of the home, a get-away will be needed for the victim. Unless death or serious injury seems likely, try not to go quietly and easily.

3 The best time to escape captivity is immediately on capture while everything is still fluid and out in the open. Seize any opportunity you can.

4 If your captors are distracted, hit out and run. At this stage you are probably too valuable for them to seriously hurt you. Try to escape being incarcerated.

5 Once you know there is no chance of escape, try to befriend and take an interest in your captors. Such bonding might save your life.

6 When your captors are in total control, be submissive to survive; don't be confrontational. Bide your time until an escape plan presents itself.

or two assailants and driven speedily away. Unless you are very switched-on, this part of the operation will pass in a confusing blur, but it offers your first chance of escape. As they throw or drag you through one door, try to use your body's momentum and the power of your limbs to burst out of the opposite door – the chances are that they won't have locked it so that the team can make a quick escape if they run into trouble during the pick-up.

A van offers better rear-door options. Try to burst out through the rear doors as soon as you are lifted, as a broken shoulder and a few cracked ribs is probably a better option than weeks in captivity, or worse. Just try to work out which door of the two opens first before you hit the other one and find that it is secured in such a way that even an elephant would have trouble bursting out.

BUNDLED INTO THE BOOT
Up to now, we have assumed that you are conscious when thrown into the vehicle and that your captors are merely planning on hooding, gagging and binding you once they have you in the back. If they knock you out during the pick-up, the chances are that you will already be trussed up like a turkey by the time you come around, but if they merely throw you into the boot or trunk of a saloon, you may still have a chance. Your captors will have needed to use quite a large car for the boot to be big enough to fit an adult in speedily, and these days most large cars have a cable release to let the driver pop it open from the inside, so see if you can detect such a device running into the inner lock mechanism.

If there is no cable release, it may also be possible to spring the lock from the inside using a tyre lever or even the pressed metal stand for a warning triangle to pry the jaws apart. Chances are that either of these, which are carried as standard in many countries, could be stowed on brackets or in compartments to keep them out of the way and out of view when not needed. Hopefully your kidnappers have not spotted them either.

ESCAPING A LOCKED CAR

1 If you have to kick out a safety glass windscreen, remember the glass won't fall out or separate into pieces. It's held together by laminated plastic layers.

2 To kick out a broken windscreen in one piece brace yourself against the seat. Use a bag, coat or book to protect your feet as your legs strike through the glass.

3 Strike any of the other windows with a hard metal object near the edge of the glass. They will smash quite easily. Avert your eyes or cover them.

4 Clean off the broken shards from the edges of the frame with your chosen tool to avoid serious injury while you are making your escape.

JUMPING ON THE MOVE
If you really believe your life is in peril and the vehicle is speeding away, you will have to jump while travelling at speed. First try to pull the handbrake before opening the door suddenly and pushing yourself out at an angle away from the direction of the car. You will be moving at the same speed as the car so jump where you think you can hit grass or soft ground or undergrowth. Protect your head as much as possible by wrapping your arms around it and keep rolling away in a tucked-in position. (Try to adopt the Paratrooper Roll position shown on page 174.) If you have escaped injury get away fast to avoid re-capture by zig-zagging between any parked vehicles and buildings.

Warning: This is an extremely dangerous manoeuvre and should only be attempted in a truly life-threatening situation.

IF TAKEN HOSTAGE

- Keep calm – your captors will be in a highly emotional state and the situation will be very volatile.
- Don't become aggressive.
- Reassure others if they are showing signs of strain.
- Make yourself useful to your captors as much as possible by helping with other hostages.
- Get rid of any documents that may make the captors single you out.
- Keep your mind alert and look for chances to escape all the time.
- Listen to your captors grievances – don't try to argue politics.
- Talk about your family and show pictures if possible to make yourself more of an individual and less of a victim.

Survival in captivity

Once your captors have brought you to the place where they intend to hold you captive, possibly the first of many places that will be used, your chances of escape will diminish considerably. Here, unlike while they have you in transit, they will be in complete control of you and will no doubt have done their best to ensure that escape is difficult, if not impossible. That does not mean that they will not have made mistakes, and you will probably now have plenty of time to allow your brain to work out where they may have gone wrong, but unless you think that you are worth no more to them alive than dead, it is probably still well worth trying to make a run for it at the earliest opportunity.

EARLIEST ESCAPE ATTEMPT

By making an early escape attempt, you will not only test the resolve of your captors, but may well glean additional information for future attempts. On the other hand, you are likely to receive blows in return at best, or a severe beating at worst. Only you will know if you have the strength of will to take

▼ *When left on your own, explore all possible escape routes. Try to find a potential way out that can be concealed while you are working on it.*

▲ *Conventional handcuffs are not easy to escape from, but with practice you should be able to slip your hands over your posterior to bring them to the front of the body.*

this. Just remember that every bit of information that you gain on the routine of your captors and the layout outside your immediate prison, could affect how and when you eventually

▼ *Always check the obvious. Don't assume that just because a window has a lock, that it is functional, or that it cannot be forced to give a quiet and simple escape route.*

▲ *Make use of your observational skills to identify captor routines and spot potential escape routes or methods. Don't merely wait for rescue, as it may not come.*

escape. If the room outside your prison door is living accommodation for a large group of armed men, chances are that you will not be going out that way, but if there is only one guard sitting on a chair outside the door and you determine that there is a door or window to the outside world in the room or corridor, you could well be onto an escape route.

GAINING THEIR SYMPATHY

Let's assume that you are of some worth, be that political or financial, to your captors and that they have no reason to torture you for information or pleasure. Ideologically and culturally you could be worlds apart, but your jailers are still human beings, so you should try to find ways of gaining their sympathy and even bonding with them. Anything that will make your life in captivity easier or increase the chances of you escaping should be tried. Do not assume that your government or employer will pay a ransom or make political concessions to those holding you captive, as to do so would be seen as a sign of weakness and would just

These days, it is likely that your captor will use cable ties to bind you as they are light and easy to use. They bind the wrists and ankles tighter than cord, are near impossible to break, and cut into the skin if you struggle. You can loosen them by releasing the ratchet lock, but you'll need an accomplice to do so.

lead to more kidnappings. Do not bank on anyone coming to your rescue for a long time, if ever, as you will almost certainly be on your own.

MENTAL AND PHYSICAL TOOLS

Prepare yourself mentally for a long and boring wait, but use your time wisely to find a way out of your predicament. Remember that your mind is the one place that the kidnappers cannot see. To describe every potential way of escaping from a room would take a whole book, and most methods would be of little relevance to your particular situation. That you are reading this book suggests that you are intelligent enough to have read many books and newspaper reports where actual escapes were mentioned, and you are bound to have seen films where the hero breaks out from incarceration. Use your mind to draw parallels with your predicament and discover that chink in their armour that will rid you of your captors.

HOSTAGE SITUATIONS

Terrorism is usually behind most hostage situations, though occasionally a bank robbery may go wrong and the crooks decide to use those in the building as bargaining tools. Either way, if caught up in a situation like this you will be faced with dangerous and possibly unstable captors. As with a kidnapping, grab any opportunity to escape in the initial confusion, but if that is not possible you must try to keep alert.

If your captors are negotiating with the authorities for either political concessions or the opportunity to

escape themselves, there may be times when it is in their interest to release captives. The obvious ones in such a situation are children, women, the aged and the infirm. If you can, convince your captors that you are ill by feigning the symptoms of heart trouble or food poisoning or missing your medication – all can work in your favour. The last thing captors need if using hostages as a bargaining tool are dead or dying prisoners, so if you act convincingly you might just get away with it.

Play the sympathy card in terms of "understanding" their cause and listen to their grievances. It is often the best way of getting past their guard.

If your captors are terrorists and you belong to a religious or national grouping that they consider to be the enemy, you must try to mask this. Simple things like adopting a fake accent to hide your English or American one could be enough to throw them off the scent. It is the inconspicuous hostage that is most likely to survive.

BOUND AND TIED

1 If rope is used to secure your wrists, you have a good chance of loosening and untying it. Tense your fists to gain a degree of looseness.

2 Given time alone, and with your hands brought to the front for access, ropes can be loosened further and knots unpicked by using your teeth.

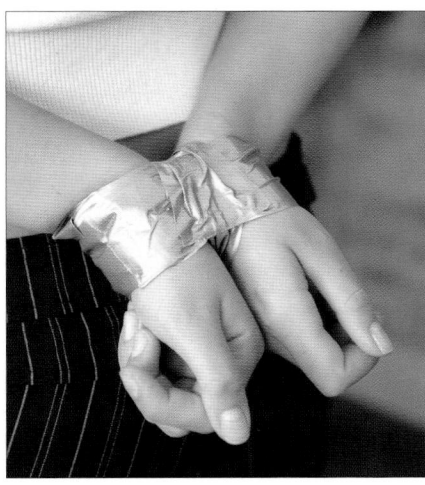

1 Broad fabric, electrical or gaffa tape is stronger than rope when in tension and if twisted, but carefully nick the edge first and you might tear it laterally.

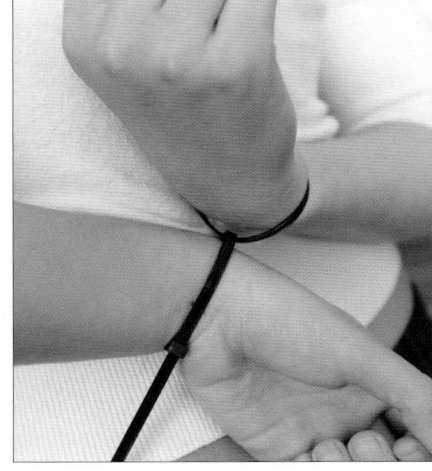

2 A pair of nylon ties is the worst wrist binding to escape from as the thin material cuts into the flesh when put under tension. They need to be cut.

Transport hijacks

Planes, coaches and trains pose an obvious target for terrorists as they provide large numbers of hostages packed into a small, mobile and controllable area. With the notable exception of the 9/11 attack on the World Trade Center and the Pentagon, where the terrorists killed themselves and everyone else on board the aircraft, almost every transport hijack has seen captives being taken primarily for publicity purposes, with most eventually being either released or rescued. However, with an increase in the use of suicide bombers by terrorist organizations, and the willingness of those bombers to take the lives of their captives at the same time, one can no longer afford to just sit back and wait for the men in black to come to the rescue. Any chance to escape must be seized if you want to survive.

SKYJACKING

Escape from an aircraft in flight is virtually impossible, so if it is clear that the hijackers intend taking your and their lives at some point, you have absolutely nothing to lose in attempting to overpower them. This is exactly what happened on Flight 93, the fourth aircraft hijacked on 11 September 2001, and although those who struck out against the terrorists did not succeed in turning the tables, their

heroic attempt did prevent the hijacked aircraft from reaching its intended target and taking countless more lives.

If you are caught up in such a situation, you will have to identify fellow passengers both mentally and physically fit enough to back you up and positioned in the aircraft where they can help you take out all captors at the same time. On many scheduled flights these days, there will be at least one sky marshal aboard, but the hijackers may well have identified and neutralized him or her, so don't bank on help from that direction.

▲ *High value performance cars and expensive 4x4 SUVs make attractive targets for thieves. The easiest way to steal one is to wait for the owner to appear with the keys.*

Unless you have smuggled your own self-defence weapon aboard, you will have to try to identify cabin fittings or items of passenger baggage that could be surreptitiously concealed for use as a weapon. Anything from handbag or camera straps, which could be used as garrottes, to bits of aircraft trim that could be turned into improvised stabbing or slashing weapons, should be

CARJACK ESCAPE

1 A hooded criminal with a weapon climbs into the passenger seat and attempts to carjack your car with you in the driving seat. Think quickly.

2 As the driver, you are actually in control. When travelling at a reasonable speed release his belt, if he is wearing one, and step violently on the brakes.

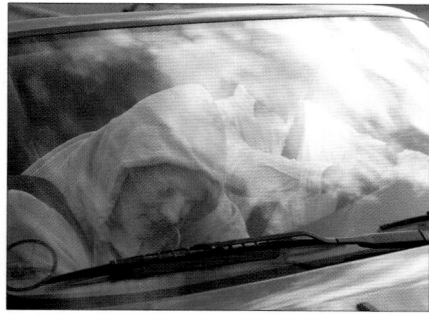

3 Taken by surprise, he should either hit the dashboard or be temporarily incapacitated by the air bag, and you can exit the vehicle quickly.

▲ *An evocative memorial near Shanksville, Pennsylvania, USA, where Flight 93 crashed on 11 September 2001. A National Memorial is being built there to honour the dead. The 40 passengers learned on mobile phones that they were one of four suicide attacks. They decided to fight and nearly succeeded in overcoming their captors.*

▲ *A "close protection" team practises ambush drills on a live-fire range. A high value business target or a contractor working in a conflict zone may need their services.*

▼ *In a "close protection" situation, your bodyguards will run you through possible scenarios and evasive action drills. Pay close attention if you wish to survive.*

identified; even that bottle of duty free spirits could become a cosh. In life or death situations like this, necessity is the mother of invention.

LIKELY SCENARIOS

In most cases the hijackers will gather all captives in one large group, usually at the back of the aircraft, coach or railway carriage, where they pose less threat of coming to the aid of the pilot or driver. Due to the close confines and high seat backs, this could work to your favour by allowing you to communicate with fellow plotters. When you are moved you may have the chance to secure an aisle seat from where you can launch your attempt to overpower the hijackers – assuming that you didn't get the chance to do so during the move itself. Try to stay alert at all times to any opportunities.

Once the aircraft is on the ground, or the coach or train is stationary, it makes sense to try to make a mad dash for freedom as soon as you can. Unless you have loved ones on board, make your move. If you can get to an emergency escape door and open it (instructions are on that aircraft seat pocket card that nobody bothers to read), a broken ankle or two caused by the jump to freedom might just save

your life, and if you roll under the aircraft fuselage when you hit the ground, the hijackers won't be able to shoot you. Escape from a coach or train can be easier, as a sharp hit on the glazing with an escape hammer or any other suitable heavy pointed implement, will give you instant access to the outside world – you just have to be quick and fit enough to take the opportunity when it presents itself.

The most dangerous time for hostages held captive in any mode of transport is the moment when the

security forces try to effect a release, as the smoke, stun bombs and panic bring on a tirade of lethal bullets, while the terrorists may also decide to trigger explosive devices.

If you see your captor is about to trigger explosives, tackling him or her might just be your only chance of survival. However, if this is not an apparent risk try to keep alert, look out for the security forces and their instructions, keep still and avoid any sudden movement that could attract shots in your direction.

Bombs and explosives

The bomb, be it placed in a car, a waste bin, an abandoned suitcase, or strapped to a fanatic's body, is the classic terrorist weapon. Unfortunately, if you happen to be at the wrong place at the wrong time and get caught up in an bomb attack, your survival will very much be determined by where you are sitting or standing at the time impact. Bombers usually strike with little or no warning, or worse, they give a warning that is actually intended to drive victims into the killing zone of the weapon of mass terror.

BEING FOREWARNED

The only ways to guarantee survival from bomb attacks are to be aware of potential targets and therefore avoid them, and to be constantly alert for suspicious packages and individuals. In Israel, where the constant strife between Palestinians and Israelis has seen countless suicide bomb attacks resulting in massive loss of life, police, soldiers and security guards are trained to watch for suspicious signs that could identify the bomber as he or she approaches. Either excess shiftiness and heavy sweating, or a state of euphoria, can betray the potential suicide vest wearer, but so too can the more obvious visual clues such as an excessively bulky torso when the rest of the person is conventionally proportioned. Many Israeli security personnel have lost their lives by spotting a bomber before they reached the intended target and forcing an early trigger, thereby saving countless other innocent lives by their sacrifice.

The suitcase or sports bag bomb, left in an airport, railway station, coach station or even aboard a railway train, is the classic low-risk but high-casualty weapon used by terrorists around the globe. Observation, and avoiding the places where such bombs may be left, are the keys to survival in such cases. If you see unattended luggage or a suspicious package on public transport or in airport or station terminal rest room, give it as wide a berth as possible

and report it to someone in authority. Never, ever, move it or open it to see what is inside, as the clued-up bomb maker will almost certainly have built in some form of anti-handling device.

MOVE ON TO SAFETY ZONES

We cannot avoid being in places that the terrorist may choose as a target, but we can certainly increase our chances of survival by passing through as quickly as possible. At airports, for example, check in early to avoid queues and the need to loiter on the public side. Once you have checked in your hold baggage, move straight through to the departure lounge, where all hand luggage will have been security screened and the chances of a terrorist incident are reduced.

THE DANGER OF FLYING GLASS

In a bomb blast away from the epicentre the vast majority of injuries are caused by flying shards of glass. If you have to spend any length of time in an area at high risk of bomb attack, try to keep well clear of windows and large glazed areas. Normally it is best to position yourself in a corner, facing entrances or doors, from where you can observe everything that is going on around you. However, if you feel exposed and vulnerable, particularly if there is a lot of glazing around, sit with

▲ *The UK has had considerable experience of dealing with modern terrorist attacks since the IRA campaigns in the 1970s.*

your back towards the potential threat area so that at least your eyes are protected, as they are the part of you most likely to be severely injured if on the periphery of the blast area.

▼ *A few sticks of explosive in a backpack – self-detonated or activated by a timing device – is all that is needed to bring a city to its knees and cause appalling injuries.*

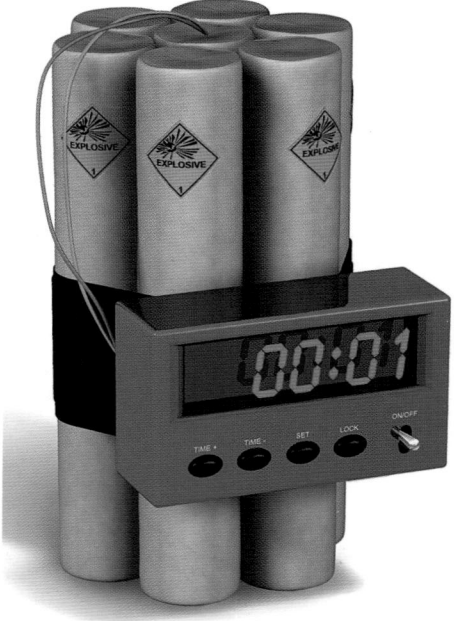

▶ *In the event of a blast, cover your mouth and nose as emergency protection and get out of the vicinity fast, as another blast might be detonated.*

▲ *Discreetly armoured cars like this Range Rover afford good protection against bullet and blast, but they cost as much as a small home.*

▲ *If you spot a suspicious package or case on a train, don't touch it. Call the authorities and don't be afraid to halt the service.*

SECONDARY DETONATIONS

Very often an initial bomb attack will be followed up with a second blast either to blow up security forces responding to the incident, or kill and maim those missed by the first bomb who are now gathered as a larger target in a muster area. Should you be caught up in a terrorist bomb attack, don't hang around on the periphery or allow yourself to be corralled into a holding area. Get as far away from the scene as you can, as fast as possible, keeping your wits about you and your eyes peeled for potential follow-up attacks.

▲ *The world's underground train systems are particularly vulnerable to terrorist attack. Stay alert and report anything unusual.*

IF A BOMB GOES OFF

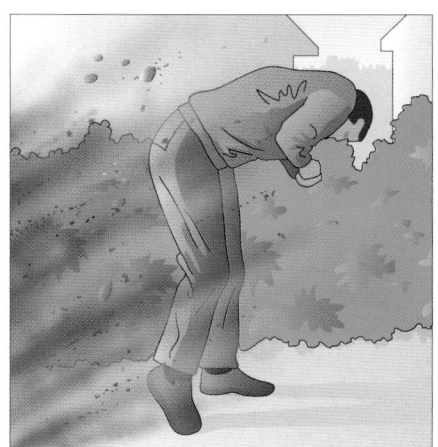

1 In the event of a blast away from the epicentre, turn away immediately to protect your eyes and vital organs from flying glass and shrapnel.

2 Throw yourself flat on the floor with your head away from the seat of the blast as shrapnel tends to spread out in an upwards direction.

3 Use your arms to protect your highly vulnerable ears and eyes (the aircraft safety position) if trapped in a confined space with a bomb.

Toxic gases and poisons

The spectre of Weapons of Mass Destruction (WMD) in Iraq has brought the subject of toxic gases, biochemical weapons and other poisons into the public eye, but these nasties have actually been around for the best part of a century. During World War I between 1914 and 1918, both sides used and suffered from poison gas attacks, but in the main these were not used against civilian targets. Then, in the late 1980s, when Saddam Hussein wiped out the population of a Kurdish town in a chemical attack, the topic came into the public eye. During the Iran–Iraq war in the 1980s, both sides had claimed that the other used chemical weapons on the battlefield but, just like with the war itself, few outside the region paid much attention.

It was only when Saddam invaded Kuwait in 1990 that the international community started to panic about the chemical and biological weapons that they believed he was capable of using. This fear rumbled on through the last decade of the 20th century, and when the predominantly Anglo-American

▼ Specialist decontamination units should eventually take care of any survivors, but it is only through your own efforts that you will be one of those survivors.

invasion of Iraq took place in 2003, it was the neutralizing of the WMD that was cited as being the driving force. It has now been admitted that no WMD have been found in Iraq, though the fear is that they or their constituent parts may have fallen into the hands of terrorists.

The same can be said for missing stocks of chemicals from the defunct Warsaw Pact days, and periodically the mass media in Europe and America

▲ Minute quantities of toxic, chemical or biological substances can contaminate thousands in minutes. In response, emergency respirators are now much more widely available

runs a scare story on this. The only major use of this type of weapon in a terror attack was when a Japanese religious sect released a quantity of sarin nerve gas on the Tokyo subway in 1995, killing 12 people and affecting over 5,000 others. The chemical used in this incident turned out to be an impure strain which the group had manufactured themselves.

DEADLY AND INVISIBLE AGENTS

Chemical and biological agents of the type likely to be used by terrorists cannot easily be detected before they affect you, and normally the first symptoms are breathing difficulties or vision problems. The one thing which might just save you is the immediate donning of a respirator when you see others beginning to be affected, but even then, there is no guarantee that your model will be proof against the threat, as each chemical or biological agent has its own individual characteristics and general purpose

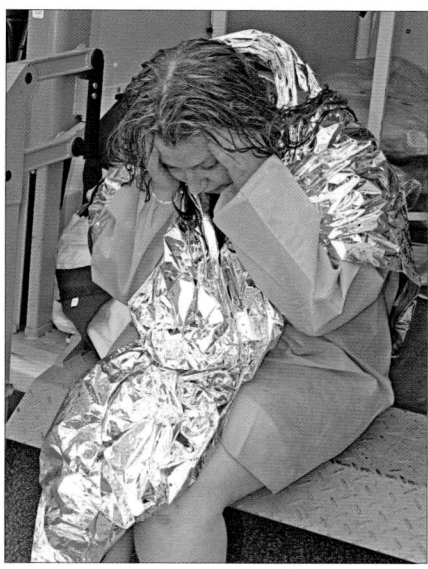

▲ *A decontamination team moves into action. The threat of chemical or biological attack by terrorists is very real.*

▲ *A trauma victim (role player) in the aftermath of a terrorist attack.*

masks can only guard against a limited range. However, any protection has to be better than none.

EMERGENCY RESPIRATORS

Since the outbreak of suspected anthrax attacks in the USA following the 9/11 terrorist outrage in New York, Washington and Pennsylvania, and a heightened awareness of how easily terrorists could obtain or manufacture basic chemical or biological weapons, relatively affordable pocket-sized emergency respirators have become available for civilian purchase. As competition kicks in their price is

dropping. If you are a regular passenger on mass transit systems, or if you frequent large public indoor events that could possibly be a tempting target for the terrorist, carrying one of these lightweight masks makes sense.

Some extremist political activist groups, seeking everything from regime change to the stopping of fur wearing or the performing of abortions, have turned away from the letter bomb to the chemical terror attack through the post. Usually some form of odourless powder is used, as sending liquids by mail is much harder. In almost every case, terrorist attacks like these turn out to be well-prepared hoaxes.

Government advice to anyone who may be a possible target for chemical attack, or who deals with mail in a

high-risk industry, is simply to be aware, to not disturb and to clean up afterwards. Awareness of suspicious packages is the first priority, followed by gently opening all mail, with an opener rather than fingers, in a manner that will not disturb the contents.

Once the package is open, preferably on a clear flat surface, it's important not to shake or pour out the contents, nor should one blow into the envelope, as airborne contamination can be the killer. Finally, it's important to clean your hands after dealing with mail, as the second most common form of chemical poisoning is ingestion through the skin.

▼ *Should you fall victim to a chemical or biological attack with no protection to wear, get out into the open as quickly as possible, and fight the urge to panic.*

▼ *By keeping upwind of others who have become contaminated, you will reduce the chances of inhaling or ingesting more poison. But a mask is a must to survive longer term.*

▼ *Attempting to wash off any contaminant – fire hoses are the obvious choice at public venues – will lessen its effects and prolong your chances of survival.*

War zones

Since the end of the Cold War, when the political balance between the American and Soviet superpowers broke down, the world has become a much more unstable place. Nowhere was this more noticeable than in the former Yugoslavia, right in the heart of Europe, where centuries-old hatred boiled to the surface and civil war pitted neighbours who had lived in harmony for nearly half a century against one another in the ultimate battle for survival. Most people think of war as being waged by one government upon another, but in reality it is more often ethnic or religious differences that bring about wars, many being civil wars rather than wars between nations.

WAR ZONE SURVIVAL
Survival in a war zone, where you not only have to avoid the enemy but also battle against mother nature when the infrastructure collapses around you, depends primarily on three basics:
• You must have the abilities to adapt as conditions deteriorate around you.

▼ *As thunder follows lightning, so a blast and shockwave will follow the initial explosive flash, so keep down and brace yourself.*

• You need to be able to construct a refuge that you and your loved ones can retreat to, certainly for days and maybe for weeks on end as the battlefront hopefully passes by.
• You have to build and maintain stocks of water, food and essentials to get you through the hardest times. The very fact that you are reading this book probably means that you are probably someone with a grasp of that first basic – the ability to adapt.

▲ *Ship and ferry hijacks are on the increase. Here Scandinavian and Dutch special forces recapture a hijacked ship during a maritime counter-terrorism exercise.*

WAR ON YOUR DOORSTEP
While there will be some who have the ideal base for a refuge in the form of a cellar, the vast majority of the population of the developed world are town or city dwellers and that will probably not be an option. In such circumstances it will be necessary to turn one room, preferably the one with the fewest outer walls and windows, into a refuge with both sleeping accommodation and emergency water and food stocks.

A survival cell should be constructed in one corner of the room, ideally the one farthest from outside walls and closest to a stairway where the structure will be stronger. You will need to improvise some overhead protection against falling rubble caused by nearby explosions, so under the stairs is a sensible option if there is sufficient space. The survival cell should be your main sleeping area, and it is also where your emergency water and medical supplies should be kept. If the fighting gets close, or if your locality is subject to bomb or artillery attack, you should retreat there immediately.

It is essential that adequate stocks of basic, non-perishable foodstuffs are stocked in your refuge, but stocks of drinking water are more important. The human body is remarkably resilient and can survive for weeks on little or no food, but without drinking water you will last only a few days.

In towns and cities, the two first major casualties of war tend to be power supplies and piped water, mainly because power stations are key targets for attackers, and the water supply relies on electricity to pump it out to homes and businesses. Limited emergency water can be kept in the bath, protected by a tarpaulin or board, but even if you seal around the plug with silicone before filling it to avoid any leakage, one bath of water is unlikely to last for long. As time passes you will have to use precious fuel supplies to boil the water to ensure it is still safe to drink. Maintaining stocks of bottled drinking water, preferably in 50-litre plastic containers or larger, is a good idea.

▼ *In addition to constantly training with each other police and military counter-terrorist teams regularly exchange information and techniques internationally.*

It is also sensible to maintain a large stock of basic long-life foodstuffs in your refuge, especially high-protein canned meat, fish and beans. Do not be tempted to store too much low-bulk dehydrated foodstuffs, or things like pasta and oats which require water for their preparation, as you will need to use valuable drinking water and fuel to make a meal. In peacetime cold beans or beef stew may not seem too appetizing, but if you are stuck in your survival cell for days at a time, as fighting rages all around, you will look forward with great anticipation to mealtimes of cold canned food.

▶ *Breathable, warm, windproof and waterproof gear is essential when the power supplies are cut off. A feather-down duvet will provide good insulation.*

▲ *Curfews are commonly set for dusk to dawn so security forces can keep a lid on terrorism or insurgency. You must not go outside at such times as you are putting yourself in unnecessary danger.*

Survival in the workplace

To the terrorist, the commercial world can sometimes be a better target than the civilian population. Society cannot easily function without bureaucracy, banks and big business, so the public servant, bank employee and business executive can easily find themselves in the front line. In recent years every "direct action" group, from animal rights activists and anarchists through to religious fundamentalists, has attacked businesses and the symbols of Western capitalism either to publicize their cause, to create a climate of fear in society at large, or to hammer home their political stance, so the laboratory technician, the office worker and even the counter assistant in the burger bar can also find themselves at risk.

If anarchists are attacking where you work, it is most likely to be during a public order crisis and the assault will probably be overt and aimed primarily at the premises, so your personal survival should not be too much of an issue. Just take off your work uniform and leave quietly by the side entrance. However, if political activists or religious fundamentalists pick on you, the attack is likely to be less overt.

LETTER BOMBS

The letter or parcel bomb and, to a lesser extent, hazardous substances such as toxins or biochemical agents, are the primary method of attack, and must be guarded against if you work for a high-risk commercial or government target.

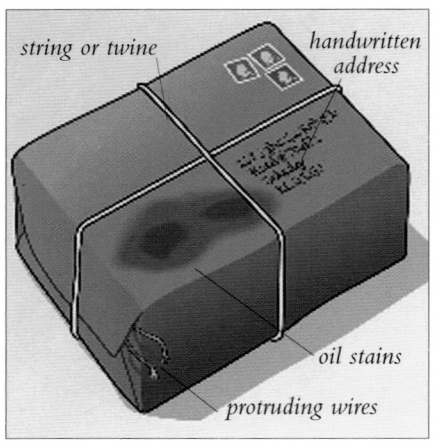

string or twine

handwritten address

oil stains

protruding wires

Usually, it will be the post-room worker or the secretarial assistant who falls victim to these devices, but if you open your own mail you must be aware of the potential threat.

Often bomb or hazardous-substance attacks against businesses involve carefully constructed hoax packages, as the fear of attack is often just as effective as the real thing, and the dangers of losing public sympathy by maiming or killing the wrong victim are less. Even so, the stress and trauma of opening a package and finding it contains a fake bomb or a mysterious powder along with a warning message is not a pleasant experience.

With the spread of the internet since the late 1990s, anyone with a grudge and the most basic technical skills can learn how to build a cheap and effective improvised explosive device from easily sourced components, so the threat has never been greater. To the anti-vivisectionist attacking pharmaceutical company employees, the political activist attempting to disrupt government departments or even the disgruntled former employee seeking revenge, the bomb delivered by

◀ *The parcel bomb has long been a method of attack for separatist and animal rights terrorists. Incorrectly addressed labels, twine bindings or odd bulges can be warning signs.*

▲ *The 6m/20ft tall cast iron "cross" found in the rubble of the World Trade Center was adopted by rescue workers as a symbol of faith.*

post is an anonymous and effective weapon. The last thing that most terrorists want is to be easily traced, so they will try to leave as few clues as possible on the packaging.

If the address is handwritten – and in most cases it will be as setting up computer-printed address labels can leave incriminating evidence – the writer will almost certainly try to disguise their handwriting, but the human eye and brain can usually easily spot this, so the first line of defence is to read the label. The device will also have been packaged so that it does not go off in transit and it is unlikely to be timer-driven due to the vagaries of the postal system, so handling it unopened should be safe. If it looks suspicious or feels suspicious, simply back off and call in the experts. It is better to be an embarrassed survivor than a dead fool!

LESSONS FROM 9/11

Since 9/11, businesses – especially in high-rise buildings – have taken risk assessment much more seriously with routine "major incident" evacuations and fire drills being timed and assessed. The 9/11 outrage was perpetrated by terrorists, but it could just as easily have been a terrible accident (after all, a B-25 bomber had crashed into the 78th floor of the Empire State Building on 28 July 1945) and it was one which was actually foreseen when the building was originally designed. Back in those days, wide-bodied jets had yet to take to the skies, so the designers underestimated the size of the aircraft that eventually tested their foresight, but even so they provided sufficient means of escape for all survivors beneath the impact-affected floors to escape. What they could not factor in was that some people failed to get out at the first sign of trouble, resulting in them perishing when the towers eventually collapsed.

The Twin Towers had already been the subject of a major bomb attack by the same group, which caused several deaths and badly damaged the

FREEFALL

You sometimes hear that you should jump immediately before an elevator crashes, so you would be "floating" at the second of impact. Chances are your freefall will be slowed by the compression of air at the bottom of the shaft as it fell (like a piston compresses air in a bicycle pump). The air pressure would slow the elevator down. Also many cable elevators have built-in shock absorbers at the bottom of the shaft – to cushion the impact. Either try to cling on to a ledge as shown or lie flat on the floor so that no single part of your body takes the brunt of the blow.

▲ *Check your company has fully implemented evacuation procedures in the event of a terrorist incident.*

lower floors, so people working there could have realized they were a potential terrorist target. When the first plane struck, with such devastating consequences and igniting several floors, many workers in both the neighbouring tower and on the lower, unaffected floors of the first tower, remained in their offices rather than following the well-documented emergency evacuation plans. Rather than looking to their personal survival, they waited either to be told what to do, or assumed that the emergency services would have the matter in hand.

OFFICE SAFETY

Remember that it is down to you as the individual to make your own risk assessment before trouble strikes, and have a plan to ensure your survival. Just in case that fateful day comes (and bear in mind that we could just as easily be talking of a building fire or a natural disaster as a terrorist attack), you should be well aware of how to get out by both the fastest route and by at least one secondary one should your first choice be unusable. In an emergency, you cannot count on the electricity and lighting supplies being maintained, as back-up systems could well be taken out by the incident, so make sure you know how to escape in the dark as well.

It makes sense to work as close to your emergency escape route as possible, so try to engineer this if at all possible. Time is precious in an emergency situation, and if you have to fight your way through a packed open-plan office with dozens of terrified workmates, you will already be at a disadvantage. If you have a say in the matter, opt for having your workplace near the emergency exit.

By their very nature, internal fire escapes tend to be the strongest parts of buildings, being either in the central core, or at the corners or ends of buildings where they form a self-standing structural feature. This is another good reason to have your workplace sited near them. If a vehicle bomb is used against the building, these are the areas most likely to suffer the least structural damage and subsequent collapse, thereby increasing your chances of survival.

Be aware that after blast trauma, flying glass presents the major injury hazard to most people. Even a bomb exploding several hundred metres away against a totally unrelated target will cause most windows in the vicinity to shatter, with terrifying results. It is tempting to sit near windows so that the view will break up the monotony of office life, but should the terrorist strike nearby, that view may well be the last thing you see.

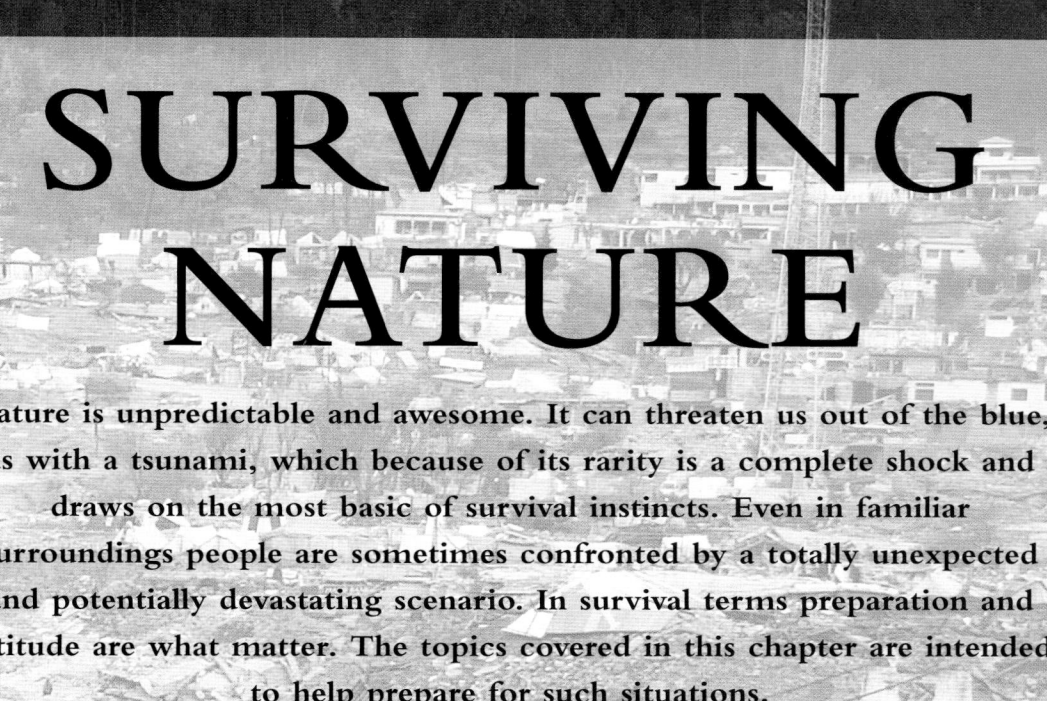

SURVIVING NATURE

Nature is unpredictable and awesome. It can threaten us out of the blue, as with a tsunami, which because of its rarity is a complete shock and draws on the most basic of survival instincts. Even in familiar surroundings people are sometimes confronted by a totally unexpected and potentially devastating scenario. In survival terms preparation and attitude are what matter. The topics covered in this chapter are intended to help prepare for such situations.

Surviving acts of nature

Being prepared for an earthquake or hurricane is the best way to survive one. Discuss the possibilities with your family and colleagues so you have a plan if disaster strikes. Always check radio and local area networks (internet) as well for disaster area advice.

EARTHQUAKE

If you are affected by an earthquake, stay calm. Don't run or panic. If you're indoors, stay there. If you are out of doors, remain outside. Most injuries occur as people are entering or exiting buildings. If possible take cover under something that will protect you from being hurt by falling masonry or other building materials or structures – under a table or upturned sofa, or next to a solid wall. Stay away from glass, windows or outside doors. Put out any fires and stay away from utility wires and anything overhead.

If you're in a car, stop carefully and stay in the vehicle until the shaking ceases. It's a good safe place to be. Do not stop on or under a bridge or flyover, nor under overhead cables or street lights. Look out for fallen debris.

▼ *Earthquakes can shatter constructed objects as easily as natural ones – don't think you are safe anywhere, but in particular avoid bridges and flyovers.*

▲ *Looking down into this volcano's crater we can see a low-energy eruption taking place. A column of steam rises high into the air, and hot ash is billowing out, but there is no sign of an explosion or pyroclastics.*

VOLCANO

Many volcanos are harmless, described by geologists as either extinct or dormant. However, an active volcano always has the potential to erupt and cause catastrophic damage. Most volcanic eruptions are slow affairs, quite unlike the ferocious explosion of Mount St Helens in Washington, USA, in 1980. Usually the eruption produces only slow-moving rivers of ash or lava and a variety of poisonous gases. That makes them extremely dangerous if you are in their path, but relatively easy to escape from. There is also a more insidious danger from vast quantities of odourless carbon monoxide which can collect in still valleys (or basements) and which can lull you into sleep, followed by oxygen deprivation and death.

Stay away from lava flows even if they seem to have cooled. Move directly away from the volcano and do

not shelter in low-lying areas. If a volcano explodes, the land for miles around can be devastated and all landmarks eradicated. You will find yourself stumbling around an unrecognizable, smoking landscape in incredibly severe heat, perhaps being bombed by a variety of pyroclastics (objects, often molten, launched high into the sky by volcanic eruptions).

The only real form of protection from the latter type of eruption is to have had enough warning not to be in the area when it happens.

▼ *Lava flows may be slow-flowing but they travel with molten intesity. Get well away from the locality.*

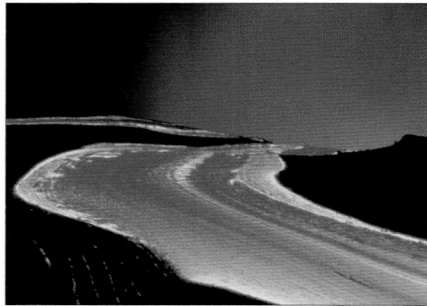

Volcanoes usually "grumble" for a long time before erupting, and science can warn of the danger. If you do find yourself there when it happens, all you can do is move directly away from the eruption as fast as possible, using far-away landmarks to help you navigate.

TSUNAMI

On 26 December 2004 an earthquake under the sea in Indonesia triggered a series of deadly waves which fanned out across the Indian Ocean and crashed on to shores – some as high as 20m/65ft – from Asia to Africa, killing over 140,000 people and leaving millions desititute. It brought to everyone's consciousness the word "tsunami", the Japanese word for tidal wave. They are not in fact caused by the tides but by earthquakes, landslides and volcanic eruptions – anything causing massive displacement of water. A tidal wave is not like an ordinary wave. It is more like a sudden increase in water level spilling across the ocean, and usually has several sequential wave fronts.

If you hear of an earthquake, a tidal wave might well be heading your way from the quake zone. Do not stay in low-lying coastal areas if this occurs. Sometimes the waters recede from the coast minutes before a tidal wave arrives. If this happens, put curiosity aside and run as fast as you can for high ground.

▲ *This tsunami sign warns of a risk. Heed the warning especially if the water suddenly recedes dramatically. Head inland and uphill.*

▲ *A tsunami can occur anywhere in an ocean that has undersea geological movement. The coastline affected might be calm or, as seen here, quite rough water.*

▲ *Before a tsunami the waters will often recede – this is the classic warning signal and the time to run for the hills, not to stroll on to the beach to pick up stranded fish.*

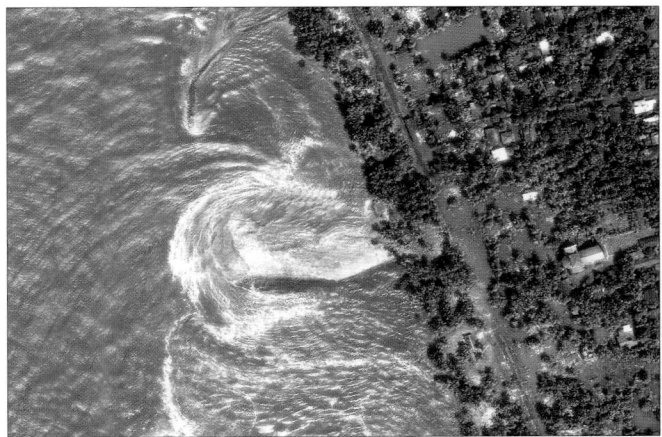

▲ *As the water surges back on to the shore a thousand tonnes of water crashes down on each metre of beach. In this whitewater zone the waves reached 10m/33ft.*

▲ *The water will continue to surge on to the land, moving much farther inshore than any normal tide, floods or storms, and demolishing almost everything in its path.*

FLASH FLOODS

It is important to know whether you are in an area that might be prone to flooding, and how high you are above typical flood levels, so that you are in a position to respond accordingly if a flood warning is issued.

If significant flooding is imminent, do not stack sandbags around the building to keep water out. Water beneath the ground may collect around the foundations and cause the entire building to "float" upwards causing structural damage. It is usually better to allow the flood water into the lower levels of the house. If you know it will flood anyway, consider deliberately flooding the basement to equalize the pressure inside and out.

• Switch off the electricity supply at the main distribution box.

• Store drinking water in clean, sealed containers since the water supply may be contaminated for some time to come.

• Disconnect any electrical appliances that cannot be moved, and decamp upstairs with any other possessions.

▼ *If you have to hang on to a tree or other fixed object in moving water, make sure you do it from the downstream side, as shown.*

▶ *If you have to, you can drive through flooded water. Work out where the shallowest water is — in this case it seems to be on the right, but it pays to check first.*

GROUP CROSSING A FLOODED RIVER

1 Find a place with anchor points (trees or rocks) and let a strong swimmer cross with two ropes. Check for any hidden dangers downstream or upstream.

2 Once across, tie a line between the two banks. The others can now haul their way across the water. A second, hand-held rope gives extra grip.

3 Equipment can be attached to the fixed rope with a karabiner and hauled across in a similar way. Make sure you keep both ends of the haul rope safely at either bank unless the river is narrow enough to throw the gear across.

4 The last member of the party can untie everything from the departure bank and be hauled across safely by the rest of the group. This is the most dangerous part, so this person should be strong and confident in the water.

▲ *Storms of any kind can cause trees or pylons to fall on to buildings, roads or cars. Avoid going out during a storm and keep an eye on vulnerable parts of your house.*

DRIVING THROUGH FLOODS

When driving through flood waters, put the car in low gear and drive very slowly. Try to avoid water splashing up into the engine area of petrol cars and affecting the ignition system. If practical, disconnect any electric cooling fan in the engine bay and remove any low-level mechanical one – this will stop the fans throwing water over the engine. Diesel vehicles are unaffected by water as long as water doesn't enter the engine through the air intake/air filter or the fuel tank through the filler or breather pipe. Be aware of these two. Remember brakes may not work well when wet.

Try to check the depth of water by having someone walk ahead tethered to a rope. A well-sealed car may begin to float in only 60cm/2ft of water – it could be very dangerous if the car starts floating away. Be certain the level is no higher than your knees or a car's wheels.

DEFENSIVE SWIMMING TECHNIQUES

If swimming in fast-moving water, maintain a defensive swimming posture with feet up and downstream (*see below*). Look ahead for obstructions. A current of 5–6.5kmh/3–4mph can pin you irrevocably to railings or fences causing almost certain drowning – be ready to swim out of the way of any such obstructions. Do not try to grab lamp posts or anything similar – you will just hurt yourself. If you're going to hit something try to fend off with your

▲ *You can get on to the roof of your house by going upstairs and pushing off some tiles from the inside – this will be much safer than going outside into the flood waters.*

feet and push around it to one side, whichever way more of the current is going. Wait for an opportunity to swim into an eddy or the safety of shallow water. Do not try to stand unless the water is under 30cm/12in deep.

If possible wear a buoyancy aid (personal flotation device). Do not enter buildings that may be damaged by flooding unless necessary. Do not approach people in trouble in the water until you have calmed them down and ensured that they won't endanger you. It is common for rescuers to be injured or even drowned by relieved victims climbing on them to get out of the water.

TACKLING THE CURRENT

▲ *You need a strong staff to give you triangular support – vital so you don't get carried away by the current.*

▲ *If you get caught in the current go feet-first and keep your head above the water with your feet and backside raised.*

▲ *You are only as secure as your weakest link so be extra vigilant if you use a human chain to pull partners across.*

HURRICANE

Fuelled by the ocean, hurricanes are extremely powerful winds generated by tropical storms moving up the coastline. They do not last long once they begin to swing inland, but they are immensely destructive in coastal areas. If you are living on high ground and have not been instructed to flee, stay indoors. Secure anything that might blow away and board up all windows. If there is a lull in the storm be aware that you might be in the eye of the hurricane and the severity might increase again. Away from home, do not shelter in your car. It would be better to lie in a ditch, but if there is nothing consider hiding under your car.

▲ *There is little you can do in the face of a hurricane except to hide from them. Don't stay inside a building that could be destroyed by one, such as this timber-built house.*

TORNADO

A tornado is a funnel-shaped storm capable of tremendous destruction with wind speeds of 400kph/250mph or more. Damage paths can extend to 1.6km/1 mile wide and 80km/50 miles long. If you see a tornado, try to move out of its way at right angles to the

▼ *The safest place in the wake of a tornado is underground in a tunnel or basement. Outside, get into a ditch or depression to shelter from the wind and flying debris.*

▲ *In any lightning storm keep away from hill brows, lone boulders, anything tall. Sit on any dry insulation such as rubber-soled shoes. A dry coil of rope is good insulation.*

direction it seems to be travelling. Cars, caravans and mobile homes are usually tossed around by tornadoes so head for a more solid shelter. If there is no escape, lie flat, sheltered in a ditch if possible. If you are indoors, follow the same rules as for hurricanes.

LIGHTNING

If caught in an electrical storm, get inside a large building or a vehicle with a metal roof. Don't touch any electrical items. If you can't get to safety, avoid being a vertical pinnacle, or being near to one. Stay low. Get away from open water. Put down objects like walking sticks or golf clubs. Stay away from small sheds or stuctures in open ground. If in a forest, find an area where the trees are small and close together.

If you are hopelessly exposed and feel a build up of energy, tingling spine or hair standing on end, drop to the ground and curl up. Those struck by lightning can be handled immediately. Quick resuscitation is essential – for further advice, see the chapter on life-saving first aid. Some people who seem unhurt may need attention later – check everyone for burns at the extremities and near to metal buckles or jewellery.

STORM ACTION

Abnormal weather conditions such as hurricanes and typhoons will be forecast on the radio, television and internet. Heed any advice – in coastal areas you might need to abandon your home and move inland to higher ground. Otherwise stay at home, bring in loose objects from the garden, barricade the windows, put away valuables, and gather together emergency supplies, including water. If the storm hits, head for the basement or under the stairs, or hide under furniture. Keep listening to the forecasts.

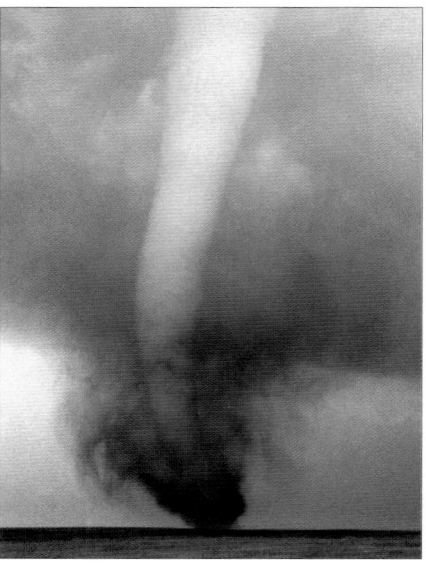

▲ *Lightning and trees don't mix — stay away from them. Make for low, level ground and jettison any metal objects on you.*

▲ *Get out of water fast if there is lightning. Anything wet reduces insulation. If you are trapped bend your head down and hug your knees to your chest.*

FOREST FIRES

In dry forests or brush, do not start any kind of fire or leave optical items like glasses anywhere that could magnify the sun's rays and start a fire. If you see or hear of a fire, try to stay upwind of it and get away.

Do not try to outrun a forest fire if it is close. Make for the nearest water and get into it, keeping yourself soaked and away from anything on shore that might burn. Rocks may become very hot and the water might warm up, but the water will not get hot enough to harm you unless it is a huge fire and a very shallow or stagnant stream or pond. Avoid smoke inhalation by making a mask from some clothing

▲ *Bushfires generate a lot of smoke and people can die from smoke inhalation before the fire front reaches them. It's safer to be in a building than in a vehicle or on foot, and though a building can burn down, cleared ground around the building may survive the passage of the flame front unscathed.*

or similar. The fire may deprive the area of oxygen so remain still and breathe normally to conserve it.

If you cannot get to water, you might try to clear an area around you of flammables. This will only save you in a small bushfire, not a huge forest fire where you need to run for safety. Remember also to stay outside and out of hollows and caves.

ESCAPING FOREST FIRES

1 Check the smoke to see the wind direction and run away from that. The flame front can travel at 8kph/5mph.

2 Head for any natural fire break such as a stream. Stay in the water, where you should be safe from leaping flames.

3 If the fire is getting really close and scorching, lie as low as you can in the stream and stay there for safety.

Surviving wild animal attacks

Most stories about the dangers of large mammals are sensationalized and very few people are threatened by them, even in the wilderness. However, most mammals will fight if cornered, threatened or protecting their young. Lone herd animals like elephants, rhinos and buffalo – perhaps self-exiled or driven away by their fellows – are unpredictable animals and may be inexplicably aggressive.

Always keep food items that might appeal to animals in sealed containers or away from you and out of harm's way (*see right*) since many incidents of attacks are associated with animals competing with us for food. Generally though, the greatest danger to humans comes from the smaller creatures that we might come into contact with accidentally – such as insects, spiders, snakes and scorpions.

BEARS

There are a number of different types of bear, and much of the received wisdom about the differences in their behaviour appears to be unreliable. It's wise therefore to consider all bears as very dangerous animals. Polar bears will

▼ *Never surprise a bear – on the trail let them know you're around by talking, singing or clapping loudly. If you do find one confronting you, let him know you know he's the alpha male. Don't look aggressive. If a bear is trying to intimidate you, be intimidated. Remain calm and unstressed, appear submissive, and make soothing noises if you can.*

MAKING A BEAR BAGGY

1 Throw your rope over a high branch of a solid tree, and get hold of both ends. It may help to weight the end of the rope or use a specialist throw line.

2 Tie your food stash to one end of the rope. Try to keep the package sealed to avoid unwelcome interest from fauna of all kinds.

3 Haul the bag until it is 4.5–6m/ 15–20ft off the ground. Stand to one side of the branch so you don't pull the rope off the end or get it snagged.

4 Tie off the loose end of the rope to the tree trunk using a reliable knot (*see page 251*) that won't come undone with tugging or other interference.

hunt and eat humans and are practically invincible unless you have a powerful firearm, but sometimes they will be scared off by loud noises. Other bears do not predate upon humans and will only attack if they feel threatened, or if they are competing for food. Therefore, don't have food or sweet-smelling items in the open in bear country, don't approach bears, and don't approach carcasses of other animals that a bear might regard as dinner.

If you are approached by a bear, remain calm and motionless and make soothing noises if you can. Don't ever try to outrun a bear as it can cover 50m/55yd in three seconds from standing. If it attacks, try to scare it off with loud noises or pepper spray if you have these options. Otherwise, curl up in a ball and wait for the bear to accept that you are no longer a threat. It may attack your prone form anyway, but play dead at all costs.

BEAR BAGGY VARIATION

1 You need about 15–20m/50–65ft of strong rope or nylon cord. Select two sturdy trees at least 3m/10ft apart from any vertical support and at least 3.5m/12ft tall. Tie one end of rope to a tree. The other end is for lowering/raising.

2 Tie a loop in the rope to connect the food bag securely. Then, with a rock or stone tied to the loose end, fling the rope over a branch of the second tree and pull. This will raise the food at least 3.5m/12ft off the ground.

DOGS AND OTHER CANINES

Canine animals come in many guises around the world, including dogs, wolves, hyenas, dingos and jackals. Their bites are generally infected with bacteria and parasites and they may carry rabies, which is usually fatal.

Despite what you may feel, these animals don't as a rule predate upon humans, but they do fight in defence of territory, their young, or their status. Their aim is to win a power game, not to inflict damage. The bites inflicted by canines under these circumstances are more like nips and lack the ferocity of a full-on attack. An appropriate reaction, like leaving the scene – which removes

the threat to their territory – will usually be enough to make them back off. An excessive reaction that threatens the life of the canine may cause an escalation of violence as the animal switches to full fight mode. It then applies as much force as it can with the only weapons it has, basically four small canine teeth driven by powerful jaws and strong neck muscles.

FIGHTING BACK

If any dog, particularly a hunting animal like a wolf, adopts a full fighting approach, your reaction must be extreme. If you attempt to flee the animal will bring you down, constantly improve its grip, and shake its head to inflict maximum pain and damage, until the trauma overcomes you.

Fight back aggressively. If it has your arm in its mouth, slam your arm to the back of its jaws. Use the gripping, squeezing technique shown left to inflict sufficient pain and stress on the animal to make it give up and retreat, allowing you to escape. If you don't do this with conviction, the wolf will quickly regrip, moving the bite to a more critical or damaging area. Finally, the wolf will begin to shake its head violently, causing more damage, blood loss, and ultimately death. It is therefore important that your grip on the animal is out of range of its jaws and very powerful. If it does have a part of you in its mouth, you should continue to try to squeeze and crush it.

CROCODILES AND ALLIGATORS

If you are attacked on land punch, kick and poke with anything to hand (including your fist) at the eyes and nose. Punching the nose might also get it to release its grip on you. In the water you must prevent it from rolling you over underwater and drowning you – its normal killer blow. Try to keep its mouth shut so it can't hold, shake or crush you, and try to pull away.

▼ *Canines are fast and aggressive, with sharp teeth. More often their approach is part of a complex power game and you can gain the upper hand without conflict.*

▲ *If you have to fight a wolf or aggressive dog, turn it around so you're grasping it across its back before squeezing its body as hard as you can with your arms and legs. If you do this aggressively it may switch from fight mode to flight.*

BIG CATS

Unlike canines, big cats have the additional weapons of dexterous and powerful limbs and claws, making them powerful predators. If a big cat were to attack you, you wouldn't stand a chance without a firearm or similar weapon. If you should meet a big cat on your travels do not run. Keep still, facing the animal, and make yourself as "big" and imposing as you can. Extend your arms and raise your jacket over your shoulders. If your size looks imposing this may deter the cat. Don't crouch or show fear as the cat will pick up your defencelessness.

HIPPOS

Stay away from hippos at all costs as they are far more dangerous than most of the scarier looking animals we all fear. They might not be predators but they are vicious fighters and commonly attack people, overturning boats, especially when with their young. They weigh up to 3,600kg/8,000lb and can gallop at 30kph/18mph, which is fast enough to catch you. The one consolation is that they can't jump, so that might give you some escape plan.

SNAKES

Most snakes are not venomous but all can inflict a nasty bite. In addition, some are powerful constrictors. No snake will go out of its way to hunt humans but most will fight if cornered or threatened. The usual cause of an

attack is when we stumble over them unawares. This can be avoided by making a noise to alert the snake of our presence and taking care not to disturb holes and trees where they might nest.

The striking distance of snakes is usually exaggerated – they can rarely manage more than half their length, less for a large snake. Even a 3.5m/12ft cobra will only strike over a 1m/3ft range. Although snakes have astonishing reflexes and lightning-quick strikes, they cannot outpace a running man.

SURVIVING A SNAKEBITE

Under half of all bites from poisonous snakes actually inject venom, but you should assume the worst. If possible, someone should kill the snake for later

▲ *Aggressive behaviour may simply be territorial defence if you're lucky. Back off slowly, facing the cat.*

identification. Try to keep the victim calm as this will slow the spread of venom more than anything. If you have one, attempt to suck out the poison with a venom pump, though opinion is divided over whether these actually work. Trying to suck out the venom orally is harmless to the person doing it but almost certainly ineffective. Don't cut the wound, which only exposes more blood vessels to the venom.

If, by the time you act, the victim has become envenomated (poison has spread through the bloodstream), he or she is likely to die unless medical attention is received. Tingling, facial numbness, cramp, palpitations or breathing problems are all indicators of possible envenomation – however, these could also be symptoms of the shock and anxiety associated with the attack.

The best chance of survival is to get the victim to hospital, ideally with the dead snake. A hospital may have the right antivenins, which are snake-specific and need to be refrigerated so are unavailable in the field.

Beware of snakes in cars. It is common for them to curl up in the engine bay or passenger compartment, then become startled by human intervention and respond aggressively. Always check for unwanted hitchers.

DEALING WITH SNAKEBITES

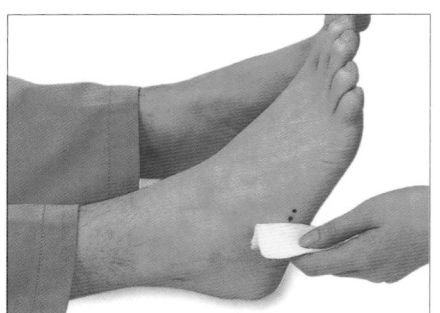

1 The distinctive twin pinholes of a snakebite. Angle the body so that the bite is below the victim's heart so that any venom has to travel "uphill".

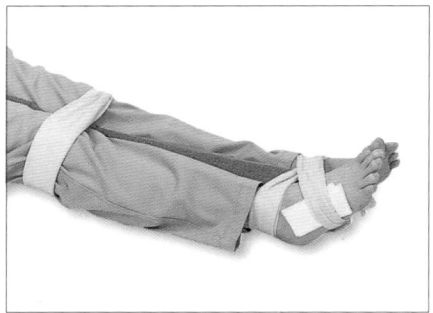

2 Assume it is venomous even if it isn't. Clean away any excess venom, and immobilize the affected area. If you can, take the victim to hospital.

▲ *Snakes will usually avoid you. If you encounter one, back off slowly and don't lunge at it. Most snakes will want to escape.*

▲ *Using a branch or long stick to thrash in front of you will flush out snakes in thickets. Watch where you put your hands.*

▲ *Although large tarantulas and bird-eating spiders are no threat to humans they do deliver a painful bite. There are, however, small spiders like the black widow that are extremely poisonous and can be fatal. These are found in tropical areas and in sub-tropical Australasia.*

INSECTS

Multiple stings from a swarm of bees, wasps or hornets can be fatal to humans, and even a single sting can in some people cause a massive and, if untreated, lethal allergic reaction (see anaphylactic shock, below). If you are being attacked, plunge through dense undergrowth or vegetation in order to brush away the insects. Bee stings break off in the wound and should be removed as soon as possible. Other types do not but this allows the insect to sting repeatedly.

Other dangerous stinging insects include some caterpillars that have stinging hair, and certain types of ant. Bulldog ants found mainly in Australasia have particularly nasty stings,

and a Tasmanian variety of these called the "Jackjumper" is known to cause potentially lethal allergic reactions in many people, even those not normally allergic to insect venom (see anaphylactic shock). African driver ants, known locally as "Siafu", do not have a sting but a vicious non-toxic bite, and swarms of them will attempt to eat almost any animal. Humans attacked by large numbers of them usually die by suffocation after their lungs have been invaded by thousands of ants. The best protection from ants is to drive them away with fire.

The stings of almost all insects can be treated with moist tobacco, ammonia or a paste of baking powder. These remedies also work for stings

from scorpions and other invertebrates. Scorpions have a sting in their tail and are quite aggressive. Most of them are fairly harmless, but some do have a powerful sting that can cause illness and even death. They are usually encountered hiding in shoes and clothing. Check carefully before putting these things on in scorpion-populated areas. The venom of scorpions can be sucked out more effectively than that of snakes. In the tropics, apply coconut meat to the infected area.

ANAPHYLACTIC SHOCK

Some bites or stings (such as wasp venom) can cause anaphylactic shock, a severe and sometimes fatal allergic reaction. The symptoms are breathing difficulties, fainting, itching, swelling of the throat or other mucous membranes and a sudden drop in blood pressure. These reactions are often so severe as to be fatal. Treatment is an appropriately dosed adrenaline (epinephrine) injection – if the casualty is prone to such attacks, he or she may be carrying an auto-injector.

▲ *If you are chased by a swarm put your shirt or jacket over your head as that's where they'll try to sting you. Run for cover.*

▲ *Do not jump into a pool or running water. The swarm will just hover and sting you as you surface.*

Surviving arctic conditions

If you travel or trek in arctic or alpine regions, as long as you are able to provide the basics of shelter, heat, water and food – as covered in previous chapters on bushcraft – you should be able to survive the extreme conditions for days or weeks at a time. Sometimes, though, things go wrong and that's often to do with the surface that you are travelling across giving way.

AVALANCHES

Around 95 per cent of people who are caught in avalanches are caught by a slide triggered by themselves or their group. Avalanches are more likely after recent heavy snow falls or after heavy rain. Be aware of your surroundings and take heed of the obvious warning signs – evidence of recent slides, signs of recent high winds or snow drifting, shooting cracks in the snow and snow collapsing around where you put your weight. If you do get caught out:

- Drop everything and run to one side of the advancing snow.
- Try to use a front crawl-style swimming stroke to keep above the snow as it carries you. Many survivors have said that being caught in an avalanche is similar to being caught in a large wave at the beach.
- Keep your mouth shut to avoid being suffocated.
- Just before you come to a halt, place

▲ *People on foot on a snow-covered glacier. Crevasses and other hazards abound so they are tied together in threes for optimal safety.*

your hands over your face and try to create an air pocket.

- If you are buried, the snow around you will probably be packed solid and you won't know which way up you are. If you can, dig a small hole in the snow around you and spit in it. The saliva should head downhill, showing you which direction is up. Then start digging your way out.
- Your best chance of survival comes if somebody has seen where you disappeared under the snow. Sniffer dogs and individual beacons are also effective aids.
- Avalanche beacons are built into a lot of winter sports equipment and

clothing. Make sure you have one if you are going off-piste or into the backcountry.

INJURIES IN ICY CONDITIONS

Blood loss is more severe in cold weather since the blood runs thinner and takes a long time to clot. Also, loss of blood is an even more serious matter since it is blood that carries heat around the body. You can bandage wounds to check the bleeding, but loosen these as soon as possible in case

▲ *If an avalanche overtakes you, swim with it just as though it were a surge of water, battling to stay near the surface at all times.*

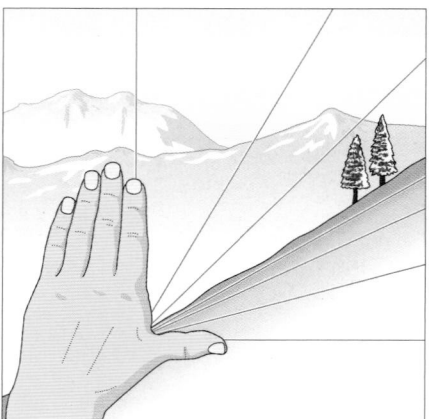

▲ *Beware of slopes of about 40 degrees. Snow does not gather on slopes steeper than 50 degrees while lesser slopes are more stable.*

▲ *Never ski off-piste without checking the local avalanche forecasts for your area, and never ski alone.*

of frostbite. If you can, elevate the wound and apply direct pressure to stop any bleeding. In extreme cases of bleeding from a limb, if you cannot stop the bleeding you must make the difficult decision to apply a tourniquet and accept that this may result in the loss of the limb due to frostbite and lack of blood.

Survivors in freezing conditions can become dehydrated just as easily as they do in hot ones. Although there is fresh water all around in the form of ice and snow, the obstacle is often the energy required to gather enough, or the lack of fuel to melt it. Do not simply eat handfuls of snow since this will cause further dehydration rather than curing

it. Any dark surface that absorbs solar heat can be used to melt ice and snow without using precious fuel. Try to arrange it so that the melt water drains into a container ready for use.

CROSSING ICE

Take care when crossing or walking on ice. That seasonally frozen-over lake or canal might appear strong and easily capable of taking your weight, but it only needs one weak spot for you to find yourself in bitterly cold water, which can knock the breath out of you, put you into a spasm and sap your strength within minutes. If things go wrong, follow the advice below.

▲ *If you fall into freezing water move as swiftly as you can for land. Roll on the ground to absorb the icy water. Change into several layers of dry kit.*

ESCAPING FROM ICE

1 If you fall through ice, you will be knocked out of breath and your body will curl up with shock. It's important to get your arms and chest out quickly.

2 If the ice is cracking, don't load one spot with your hands or elbows. Stretch your arms out wide, keep flat to the ice and try to roll out.

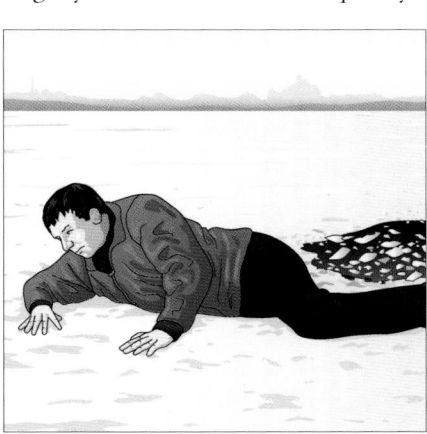

3 If you manage to free yourself, stay flat on the ice and drag yourself clear, making sure that you don't put too much weight on one spot.

4 If you can't free yourself, shout for help. You can survive for 15–20 minutes, so don't panic. Any rescue must be from the lake's edge.

DRESSING FOR EXTREMES

Don't run the risk of being underdressed in freezing or heavy snow conditions. If you find that you must go out, dress apropriately:

- Several thin layers of clothing is better than one thick layer since it allows you to control the temperature by adding or removing layers.
- Inner layers should be insulating materials, while outer layers should be wind- and waterproof.
- Do not wear tight base layers as these hamper blood circulation and reduce the amount of warm air that can be trapped next to the body.
- Wear a lot of socks. If your boots aren't big enough to allow this it might be better to improvise some footwear that does allow a lot of insulation to be worn.
- Keep clothes dry so that they can serve their intended purpose: to maintain body temperature by insulating it from the cold.
- Don't allow yourself to get too hot. If you sweat profusely you will get very cold as soon as you start to perspire.
- Keep your hands head and feet protected from the cold at all costs. Do not take off your hat, gloves or boots outside even if you feel warm enough.

LIFE-SAVING FIRST AID

Understanding first aid, and how to apply it, is a vital life skill for extreme survival and crucial in serious emergencies. If you know the basic techniques you can sustain a victim of an accident or sudden emergency until professional help arrives on the scene. At home or on a crowded street, the support you give can mean the difference between life and death, and if you are in a remote or dangerous environment you'll be much farther away from paramedics, so you really need to know what to do.

First-aid essentials and assessment

When someone has been injured, first aid is literally the very FIRST assistance you give. First aid help can cover an extremely varied range of scenarios – from simple reassurance after a small accident to dealing with a life-threatening emergency. In every case, a speedy response is crucial. Emergency workers refer to the first hour after an accident as the golden hour: the more help given within this period, the better the outcome will be for the injured person.

THE GOALS OF FIRST AID
- To keep the person alive. The ABC of life support – Airway, Breathing and Circulation – constitutes the absolute top priority of first aid.
- To stop the injured person's condition getting worse.
- To promote their recovery.
- To provide reassurance and comfort to the person.

In any emergency, the first essential is for you to stay calm. The second requirement is to assess the situation promptly and accurately. Once you

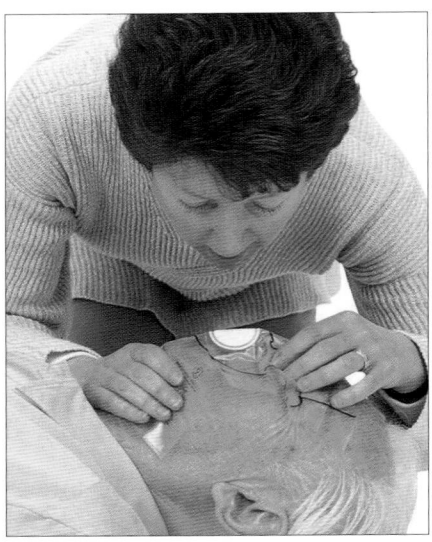

▲ *You can use a mouth shield to give mouth-to-mouth resuscitation. If you do not have one, placing a handkerchief over the person's mouth gives some protection.*

understand the problem you should follow the DRSABC sequence, which is designed to help you prioritize your actions and minimize risks to you and the injured person:

1 Danger: Your assessment should have alerted you to any potential hazards. Now you should:
- Keep yourself out of any danger.
- Keep bystanders out of danger.
- Make safe any hazards, if you can do so without endangering yourself or others. Only in extreme circumstances should you move the injured person away from danger.

2 Response: Try to establish the responsiveness level.
- If the person appears unconscious or semi-conscious, speak loudly to them – as in "Can you hear me?".
- If this fails to get a response, tap them firmly on the shoulders.

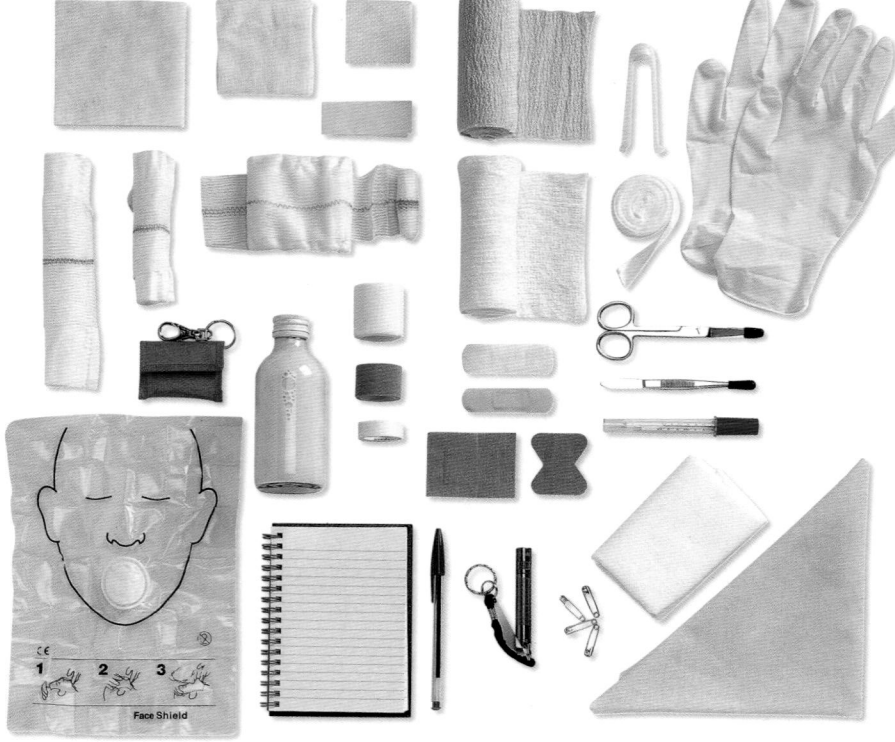

◀ *A first-aid kit, packed in a watertight box, should contain adhesive and sterile dressings in various sizes, gauze dressings and pads, tubular and roller bandages, safety pins, a thermometer, scissors and surgical gloves. Pen, paper and a torch are useful.*

3 Shout: If no response to step 2:
- Shout out loudly to anyone in the area for help with the situation.

4 Airway: Now determine whether the airway (the passage from the mouth to the lungs) is clear enough to allow proper breathing.
- Check the mouth and remove any visible obvious obstructions, such as food, at the front of the mouth only.
- Tilt the person's head back gently to prevent the tongue from falling back and blocking the airway. Place a hand on the forehead/top of head and two fingers under the jaw. Tilt back gently until a natural stop is reached.

5 Breathing: Is the person breathing?
- LOOK to see if the chest is moving.
- LISTEN for breathing sounds – put your ear against their mouth.

- FEEL for expired air by placing your cheek or ear close to their face.
- CHECK for other signs of life – body warmth, colour, ability to swallow.
- If these checks are negative, the casualty is probably not breathing. Now CALL THE EMERGENCY SERVICES. Ideally, get someone else to do this.
- Without delay, start artificial respiration procedures (giving two breaths): see next page.

6 Circulation: Look for signs of a working circulation.
- Check for breathing, coughing or any movement.
- Never waste time trying to find a pulse unless you are trained to do so.
- If there are no signs of a circulation, start cardiac massage (chest compressions) if trained to do so.

GETTING HELP

Phoning the emergency services is free on all kinds of phone. If the person is inside a building, ask someone to stand outside to guide the ambulance. If you are in a building and it's dark outside, switch on any outside lights. Tell the emergency services:
- Whether the person is conscious and breathing – information you will have if you have followed DRSABC.
- Your location and phone number.
- Your name.
- What the problem is and what time it happened.
- Number of victims, their sex and age.
- Report any hazards, such as ice on the road or hazardous substances.
- Don't hang up the telephone until the authorities tell you to do so.

FIRST-AID ASSESSMEMT

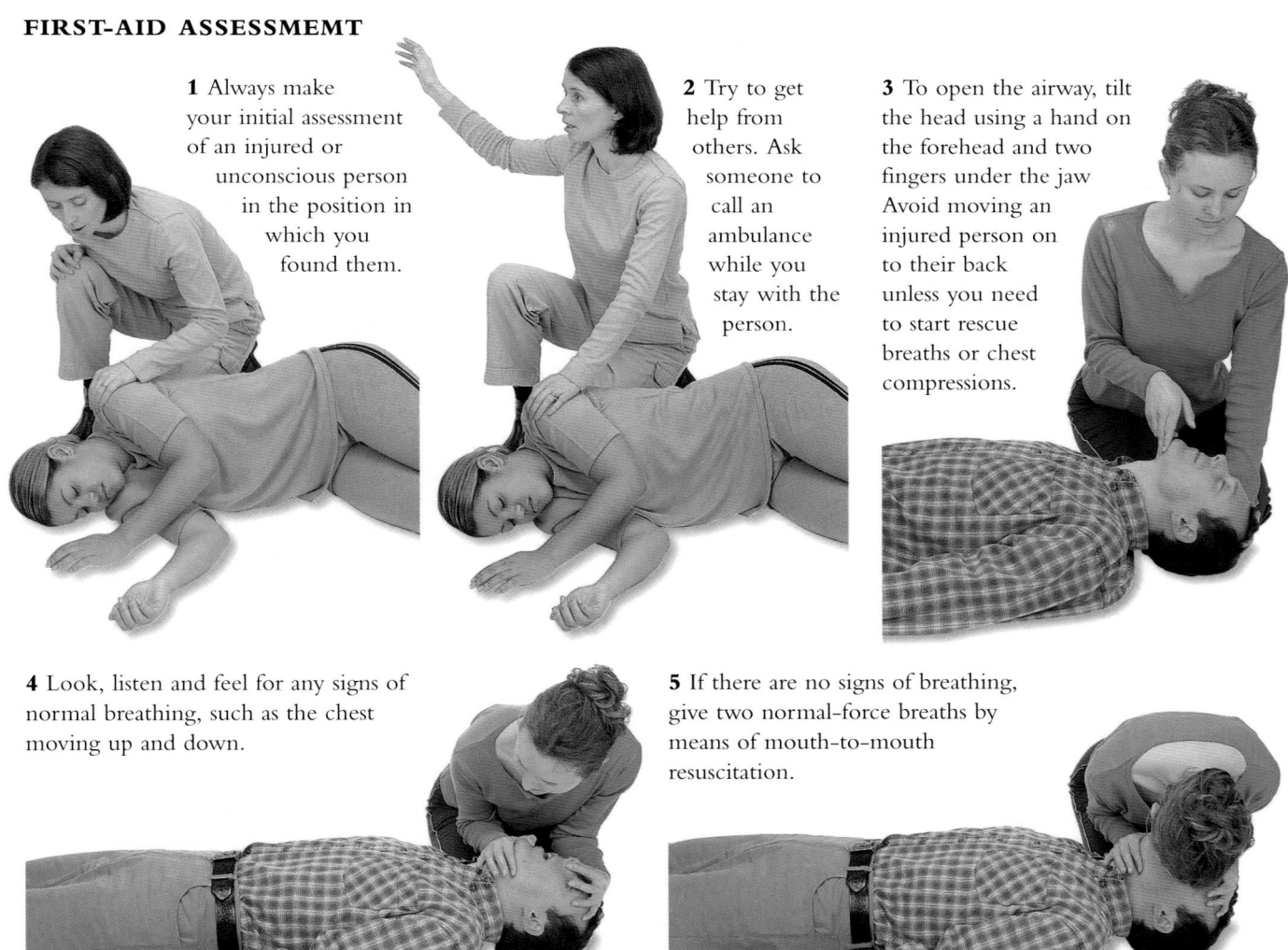

1 Always make your initial assessment of an injured or unconscious person in the position in which you found them.

2 Try to get help from others. Ask someone to call an ambulance while you stay with the person.

3 To open the airway, tilt the head using a hand on the forehead and two fingers under the jaw Avoid moving an injured person on to their back unless you need to start rescue breaths or chest compressions.

4 Look, listen and feel for any signs of normal breathing, such as the chest moving up and down.

5 If there are no signs of breathing, give two normal-force breaths by means of mouth-to-mouth resuscitation.

Moving an injured person

There are good reasons for leaving an injured person in place until more skilled personnel arrive. Injuries to the spine, especially to the neck, are possible after accidents and falls, and further movement can cause serious damage to the spinal cord. You may have to use some movement to deal with an injury, but the golden rule after an accident is not to move an injured person unless they are in danger, need to be resuscitated, or are unconscious and must be put into the recovery position.

EVALUATING RELATIVE RISKS

Never move an injured person if there is any chance that they could have a spinal injury, especially in the neck area. Sometimes, however, you will have no choice in the matter – the person may not be breathing and the airway must always take first priority. Very rarely, it may be vital to move

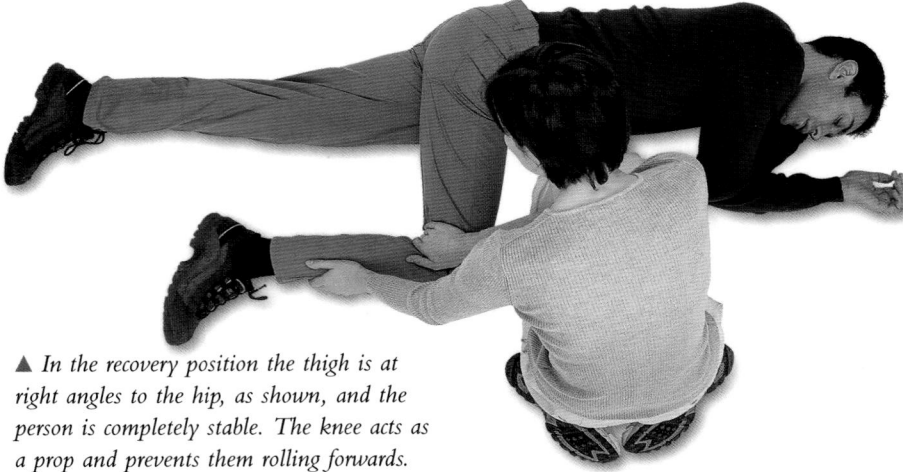

▲ *In the recovery position the thigh is at right angles to the hip, as shown, and the person is completely stable. The knee acts as a prop and prevents them rolling forwards.*

the injured person into a safer environment, perhaps because of fire or the danger of gunfire or explosion, or because they are in water and in danger of drowning.

If you have to move someone on your own, you must know how to move people without causing further

injury or endangering yourself, keeping your back straight and the weight close to your body. Otherwise, doing nothing may be wiser – it is a question of weighing up the relative perils. Also, think laterally: it may be easier to remove the danger from the person than the other way around. For instance, if an accident victim is lying in a busy street, park your vehicle so that others will drive around the incident area.

MOVING SOMEONE WITH HELP

It is much easier and less likely to cause further injury if two or more people help to move someone. If the injured person is unconscious or immobilized, you can try a fore and aft carry. This

▼ *Cradle carry. This method works particularly well with children and helps them to feel reassured and safe. Never attempt this lift on someone unless they are a great deal lighter than you, as you may damage your back; there is also the danger of dropping the person and causing further injury.*

▼ *Piggyback. Use this only in a severe emergency and if confident of your strength. With your back to the person, bend forward and get them to put both arms over your shoulders. Pull them on to your back and grasp their thighs. If you can, take hold of their hands. Try to keep your knees slightly bent while walking.*

▼ *Fore and aft carry. Lock your arms around the person's chest and move only when you are sure your helper is supporting their legs.*

▲ *Use the upturned hem of a jacket as an improvised sling for an injured arm. Leave the hand exposed to check circulation.*

can also be used if the person is conscious, but should be avoided if the arms, shoulders or ribs are injured. With an unconscious or immobile victim and two helpers, the stronger should take the upper body and the other the legs. Make sure you synchronize your actions and move in the same direction. Move slowly and carefully and watch out for any obstacles such as steps or stairs.

If there is an immediate risk to life, such as fire or water, that outweighs the danger of movement, very carefully roll the victim away from the danger with as many helpers as possible supporting and controlling the body to minimize damage. All helpers must act in sync when rolling the victim.

If four helpers are available and you have a blanket or piece of cloth, a blanket lift provides a safe, supportive method – except when spinal injury is suspected. With the injured person on their side, and the blanket edge rolled up lengthways, position the roll against their back. Move them over the rolled edge, on to their other side. Roll up the other long edge of the blanket. Two helpers on either side grasp the rolls firmly with both hands to lift the person, with head and neck supported.

THE RECOVERY POSITION
Placing an injured person in the recovery position means that they are in a secure pose that ensures an open airway and also allows any fluid to drain from their mouth.

Kneeling to one side of the person, straighten out the arms and legs. Place the lower arm nearest to you at right angles to their body, elbow bent with the palm uppermost. Bring the furthest arm up and over the chest, and place the person's hand against their face, with the palm facing outward. While holding this hand in place against their cheek, pull up their leg on the same side, so that the knee is bent and the foot is flat on the ground. Begin to pull this leg towards you.

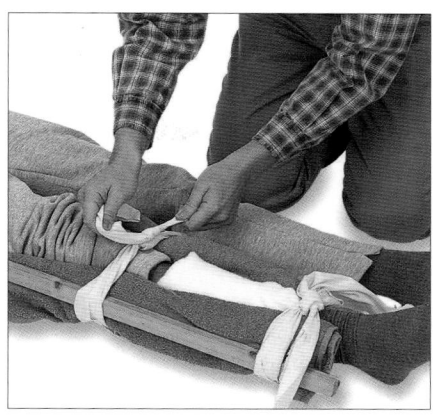

▲ *If you are in a very remote location and have to move someone with a fractured leg, you may need to splint it. Add extra padding around the limb and keep movement to a minimum.*

Continuing to support their hand against their face, pull them by the leg towards you, until their bent knee touches the ground. Check the airway, tilting their head back to keep it open. You may need to adjust the hand under their cheek, so that it is in the correct position to keep the airway open. Adjust the bent leg so that the thigh is at right angles to the hip and the position is completely stable. The knee acts as a prop to prevent the person rolling forward.

If you need to leave an injured person to get help, this is a safe position, but check on their breathing and circulation as soon as you return.

DEALING WITH A LOWER LEG FRACTURE

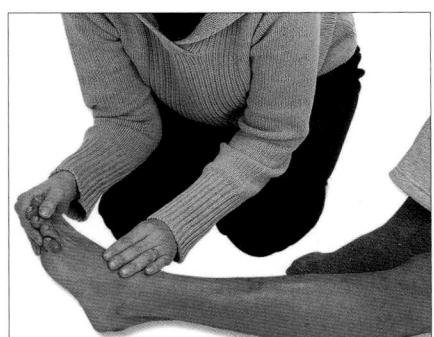

1 Help the person to lie down while supporting the injured leg. Feel the foot and leg for warmth and to check that the person can sense your touch.

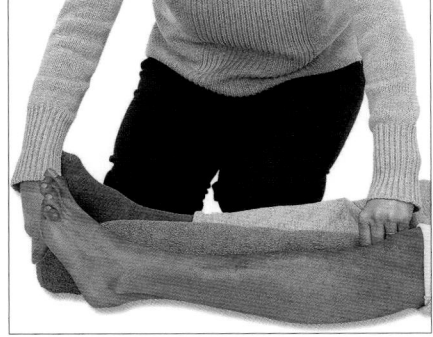

2 Place soft padding on both sides of the leg, extending well above the knees. Ensure that the foot is supported in the position found.

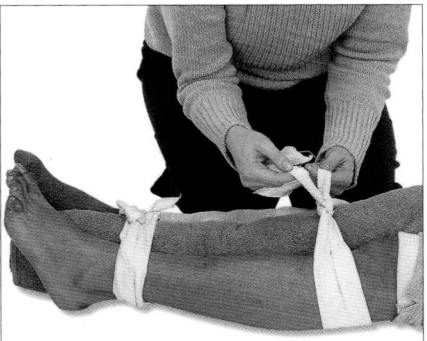

3 If help is delayed, splint the injured leg to the uninjured one. Place padding between the legs and tie bandages well above and below the fracture.

Rescue and resuscitation

Cardiopulmonary resuscitation (CPR) is the technique of providing basic life support using chest compressions and artificial ventilation (mouth-to-mouth respiration or rescue breathing). CPR is needed after a cardiac arrest: that is, when the heart suddenly stops beating and circulation ceases. A person who has had a cardiac arrest is unresponsive to voice or touch, is not breathing and has no pulse.

After only 3–4 minutes without oxygen, the brain can suffer irreversible damage and this can be fatal, so you should act swiftly. In most cases, a little knowledge and training can definitely save lives. If CPR is started within seconds of the cardiac arrest, the victim has a significantly improved chance of surviving.

In normal circulation, the heart pumps blood to the lungs where it absorbs oxygen and gives up carbon dioxide. The blood then returns to the heart, and the oxygenated blood is sent to all parts of the body, including the

brain. The brain controls all body functions, including those of the heart and lungs, and the working of these three organs is closely linked. If any one fails, it does not take long for the other two organs to fail too.

▲ *Never jump in the water when dealing with a potential drowning. Hand the person something to hold on to. If nothing is available, lie down and extend your arms so that they can haul themselves up to the safety of the bank.*

RESCUE BREATHING

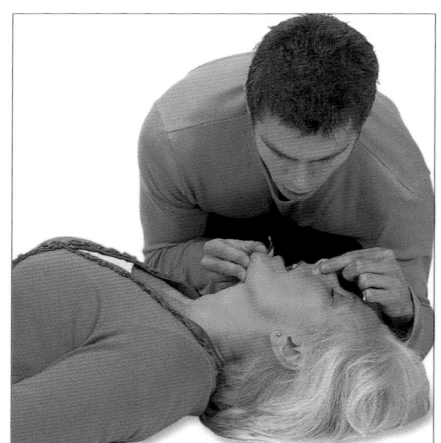

1 This is also known as mouth-to-mouth respiration. Maintaining the head tilt and pinching the nose, open your mouth wide and take a deep breath. Put your mouth against the injured person's mouth and make a tight seal with your lips around their mouth, so that when you breathe out no air escapes around the sides.

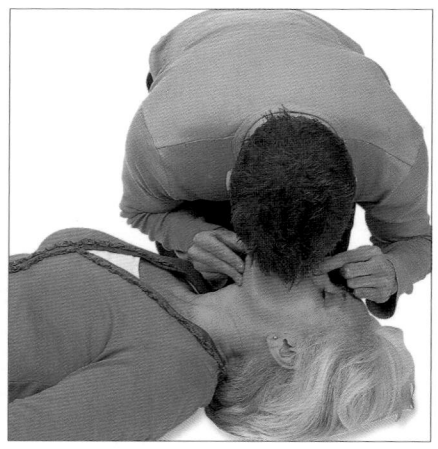

2 Breathe out steadily into the person's mouth, making this breath last for about 2 seconds. If you are in the correct position, you will see their chest rising as you breathe out. If you do not think you are getting air into their lungs on this first attempt, reposition the person's head, keeping the airway open, and try again.

3 Check for circulation signs: breathing, coughing or movement. If there are signs of circulation, continue giving rescue breaths until the paramedics arrive. Every 10 breaths (about once a minute), pause and spend a few seconds checking to see that there are still signs of a circulation. If there are no circulation signs, start cardiac compressions.

RESPONSIVENESS

You must assess an injured person's responsiveness before acting. Their level of consciousness may be anything from fully alert to a deep coma. If they have any level of response, they don't need to be resuscitated, but it is very important that their airway is kept clear and that you can see signs of breathing and circulation.

HOW CPR WORKS

Keeping the person's airway open, breathing for them and doing chest compressions means that an oxygenated blood supply will continue to reach their brain. This can "buy" really valuable time by keeping the brain alive until more specialized help becomes available to restore the circulation.

If someone has stopped breathing, their brain will soon be deprived of oxygen and there will be a build-up of toxic carbon dioxide in the blood. You can breathe for them by artificial ventilation, but if the heart has stopped as well, you must give chest compressions to help move the oxygenated blood around the body.

CHEST COMPRESSIONS

The blood is kept circulating by the use of external chest compressions. By pressing down on the breastbone, blood is forced out of the heart and into the rest of the body. When the pressure is released, the heart fills up with more blood, ready for the next compression. The procedure is done at a rate of 80–100 compressions per minute.

For cardiac compressions to be effective, the person should be lying flat on their back on a firm surface such as the floor or the ground. It's vital that you learn the correct technique from a trained first-aider. If done incorrectly heart massage may not work, and you may also cause damage to surrounding structures, such as the ribs or liver. Never practise compressions on conscious volunteers, as you may cause harm. Always use a first-aid dummy.

To find the compression site, run the fingers of the hand nearer the person's waist along the lower ribs until they meet the breastbone at the centre of the ribcage. Keeping your middle finger at this notch, place your index finger over the lower end of the breastbone. Place the heel of the other hand on the breastbone and slide it down to lie beside the index finger. The heel of your hand is now on the compression site.

DROWNING

Knowing what to do in a near-drowning incident can definitely save life: it is the third commonest cause of accidental death.

Drowning causes death by suffocation, usually because water enters the lungs and rapidly causes respiratory failure. "Dry drowning" occurs when a small amount of water makes the upper airways go into spasm.

Remember that the victim may have swallowed a lot of water as well as inhaling it. If they vomit, they may inhale the swallowed water into their lungs. To avoid this, try to keep their head lower than the rest of their body when you take them out of the water.

If the victim is not breathing, and the water is shallow enough for you to stand, start rescue breaths in the water. If their heart has stopped, remove them from the water and start CPR.

CHEST COMPRESSIONS

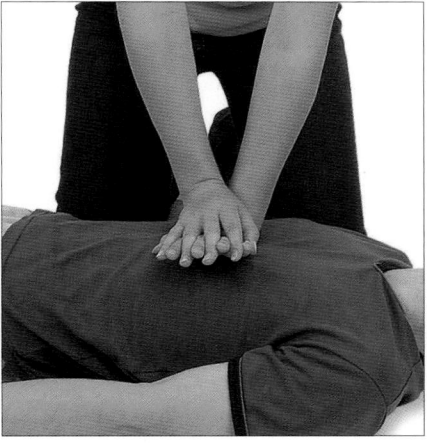

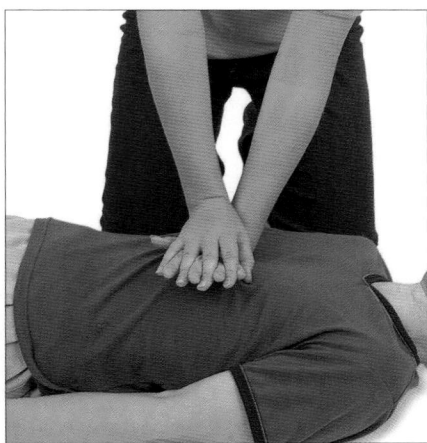

1 Adopt a position where you are kneeling at right angles to the person halfway between their shoulders and waist. Check for a circulation by looking for breathing, coughing or movement. If there are no signs of circulation, perform 15 chest compressions and then give two breaths via mouth-to-mouth.

2 Locate the compression site and place the heel of one hand over it. Place the heel of the other hand on top with fingers interlaced. Place your shoulders over your hands to concentrate pressure at the compression site. Compress the chest wall by 4–5cm/1^1/$_2$–2in. Release the pressure without lifting your hands or bending your elbows.

3 You must continue in cycles of two breaths to 15 chest compressions until expert aid arrives, because the person's circulation is unlikely to resume functioning without advanced techniques such as defibrillation – you are just keeping things going until help arrives with specialized equipment.

Dressing wounds

Even minor wounds can become infected and cause real problems with the victim's health. However, most bites, grazes and cuts heal without too much trouble and are easily treated. It is important that you are aware of the type of wound sustained so that you can carry out the appropriate first aid. Some wounds, such as puncture wounds, are more likely to cause damage to the underlying tissues and organs, and really need professional assessment by medical personnel.

TYPES OF WOUND

There are two main types of wound: closed and open. Closed wounds are usually caused by a blunt object, and vary from a small bruise to serious internal organ damage. A bruise the size of the injured person's fist would cause substantial blood loss.

Open wounds range from surface abrasions to deep puncture wounds. A laceration is a wound with jagged edges, which may cause heavy bleeding. As the object causing the wound may be very dirty, the risk of subsequent infection is high. Incisions are clean-edged cuts, such as those caused by a knife or broken glass, and may be deep. The wound may look relatively harmless, but there can be considerable damage to underlying tendons, nerves, blood vessels and even organs. Deep incisions may be

THE BASICS OF BANDAGING

- Make the injured person comfortable and offer reassurance. Work in front of them and start on the injured side.
- Make sure the injured part is supported while you work on it.
- Apply the bandage with a firm and even pressure, neither too tight nor too loose.
- Tie reef knots or secure with tape. Ensure all loose ends are tucked away.
- Check the circulation beyond the bandage and check on any bleeding.

life-threatening, especially if the injury is around the chest or abdomen, and bleeding from incisions can take some time to stop.

Puncture wounds can be tricky to assess, as the size of the external wound gives no clue to how deep it goes (and the extent of tissue damage). Professional assessment may be needed.

All bites carry a high risk of infection, with human bites almost invariably becoming infected – a doctor should see any human bite at all, in case antibiotics are needed.

Guns can inflict many types of wound, and bleeding can be external and internal. Handguns, low-calibre rifles and shotguns fire fairly low-velocity projectiles, which usually stay in the body, while high-velocity bullets from military weapons often leave entry and exit wounds. High-velocity bullets create powerful shock waves that can break bones and cause widespread damage.

The cutting or tearing off of body parts needs urgent help. Keep the severed part dry and cool and take it to hospital along with the person, as reattachment may be possible.

FIRST AID FOR MINOR WOUNDS

Avoid touching the wound, in order to prevent infection. Find out how and where the wound was caused. Wash it

BASIC FIRST AID FOR MAJOR WOUNDS

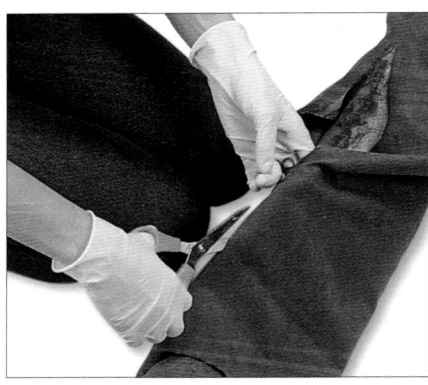

1 Expose the whole of the wound to assess the injury. Do not drag clothing over the wound, but cut or lift aside the clothing.

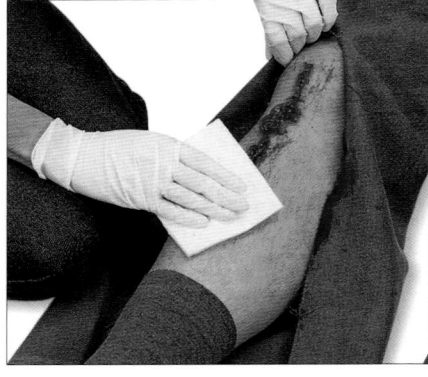

2 Using a gauze pad, clear the surface of the wound of any obvious debris such as large shards of glass, lumps of grit or mud.

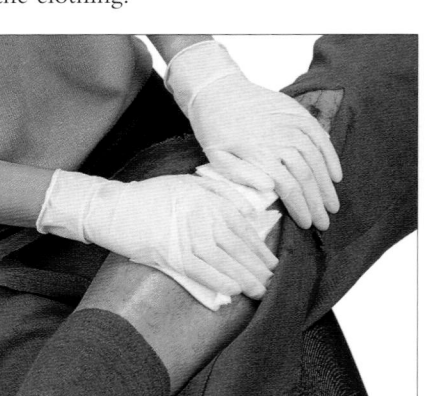

3 Control bleeding with direct pressure and then by elevating the limb.

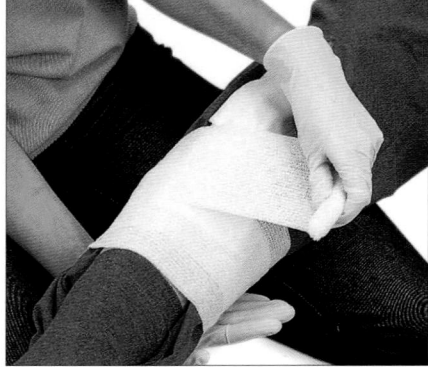

4 Once bleeding is controlled, apply a bandage to the wound.

BANDAGING A LIMB

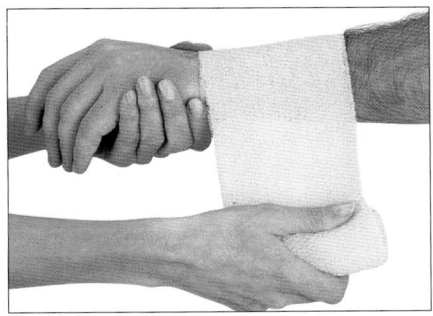

1 Place the tail of the bandage below the injury and work from the inside to the outside, and from the furthermost part to the nearest.

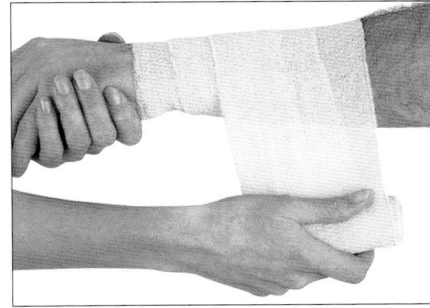

2 Roll the bandage around the limb and start with two overlapping turns. Cover two-thirds of each turn with the new one. Finish with two overlapping turns.

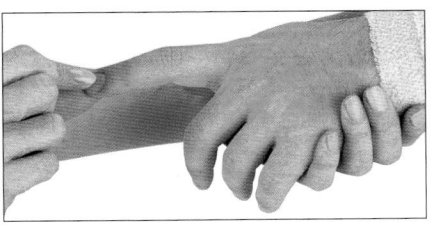

3 Once you've finished, check the circulation; if the bandage is too tight, unroll it and reapply it slightly looser.

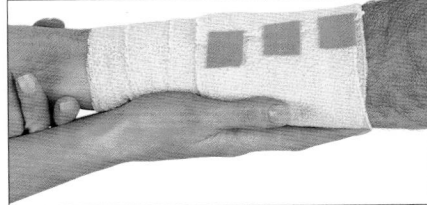

4 Secure the end with pieces of adhesive tape or tie the ends of the bandage using a reef knot.

---

under running water, or with bottled or boiled water. Dry the wound and apply a sterile adhesive dressing (plaster or Band-aid). For wounds that extend over a larger area, it may be better to use a non-adhesive dressing, sterile dressing and bandage. The wound must be kept clean and dry for the next few days.

A wound needs to stay fairly dry: wounds kept damp are more likely to become infected and can take longer to heal. If a dressing becomes wet, it should be changed for a dry one. Small wounds, grazes and blisters respond well to exposure to the air – provided dirt is unlikely to get into them.

INFECTED WOUNDS

Sometimes a wound becomes infected despite having been cleaned and dressed correctly. Some people are more vulnerable to infection, including those with diabetes, or with a compromised immune system.

You may notice the first signs of infection in and around a wound within hours, but it frequently takes longer to manifest itself. The infection may not surface until a day or two after the injury. Pain, redness, tenderness and swelling are all signs of infection. The person may also experience fever and notice pus oozing from the wound.

Infection may spread under the skin (cellulitis) and/or into the bloodstream (septicaemia). Suspect cellulitis if there is redness and swelling beyond the wound site. The glands in the armpits, neck or groins may be tender, and there may be a red line going up the limb towards the glands. Suspect septicaemia if the person feels unwell, with a fever, thirst, shivering and lethargy. These conditions require medical treatment. Tetanus can contaminate the tiniest of wounds, so immunization must be kept up to date.

Cover an infected wound with a sterile bandage. Leave the surrounding area visible, so that you can monitor signs of spreading infection. Elevate and support the area if possible and get medical help for the injured person as soon as possible.

DRESSING A WOUND WITH AN EMBEDDED OBJECT

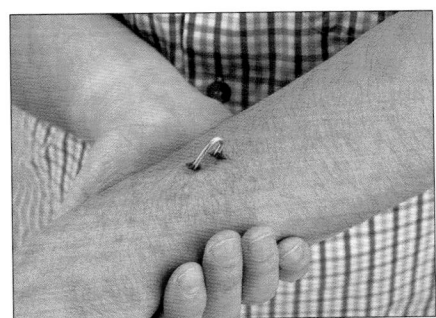

1 Do not try to remove this kind of embedded object as you may cause further damage. Your aim is to deal with bleeding and protect the area from infection, and to get aid promptly.

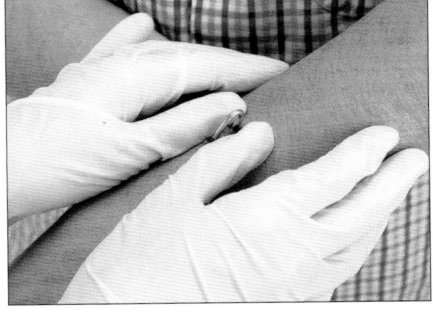

2 If the wound is bleeding, apply pressure to the surrounding area with your hands. Never apply pressure directly on to an embedded object. Elevating the wounded part will also help.

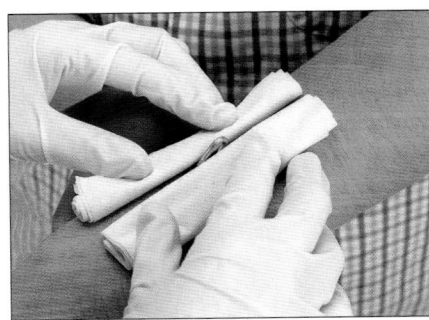

3 Place padding around the object. If possible, as it would be here, build this padding up until it is as high as the embedded object, ready to bandage over smoothly.

Burns, shock and extreme temperatures

Time is of the essence when giving first aid for burns. A major priority in all burn cases is to cool the skin. This not only eases the pain, but also reduces the amount of damage done to the skin, so that it will heal faster and scar less. However, be careful about making the person too cold and causing hypothermia. If in doubt, cover them with a coat or light blanket.

Run cold water over the burn site for at least 10 minutes, preferably from a gently running tap. If the burn is on a hand or arm, remove watches, rings, or bracelets, as the burn may cause swelling of tissues. Reassure the victim and phone the emergency service if necessary. If you think the burns are deep or cover a large proportion of the body, watch them carefully and be ready to deal with signs of further problems, such as shock.

Skin damage allows potential infection to enter, so burns must be covered. Dry dressings, even non-fluffy ones, tend to stick to burns, so the best

▲ *A large fire may cause life-threatening burns over a large part of the body, together with damage from inhalation of fumes.*

options are: wet sterile dressings or dampened clean handkerchiefs, clean plastic bags, or clear food wrap film.

WHAT NOT TO DO WITH BURNS
Here is a summary of major things to avoid when dealing with burns:
- Do not remove anything that is stuck to the burn – you may damage the skin further.
- Do not touch the wound and risk introducing infection.
- Do not put any fat, lotions, or ointments on a burn.
- Do not burst any blisters that form. While the skin is intact it continues to protect from infection, and provides an element of pain relief.
- Do not give anything to eat or drink if the burn is severe, unless you are a long way from hospital.

SHOCK
Physiological or circulatory shock is a serious condition caused by a sudden and dramatic drop in blood pressure, and without swift medical attention it can be life-threatening. It can be caused by any illness or injury that causes too little blood to circulate, depriving the body of oxygen, leading to the pale, cold, collapsed state that typifies shock. A common cause of

shock is excessive loss of body fluids, which may be due to blood loss after a serious accident or fluid loss caused by extensive burns. In reaction to the reduced circulation of blood, the body directs blood to vital areas such as the heart and lungs, and away from the skin. This makes the skin cold and pale. Adrenalin (epinephrine) is released as

▼ *Someone who appears confused or clumsy may be suffering from hypothermia. Get them into shelter and wrap them warmly.*

FIRST AID FOR SHOCK

- If the person is unconscious, check DRSABC. Start resuscitating, if necessary.
- If the person is unconscious but breathing, put them in the recovery position. Stop any heavy bleeding.
- If the person is conscious, lay them down and calm them.
- Call the emergency services.
- Check the body for fractures, wounds and burns. Deal with these as necessary; make sure any heavy bleeding is controlled.
- Unless you think the legs may be fractured, place them on a low, padded support so that the legs are higher than the heart.
- Cover the person with a blanket and try to keep them reassured.
- Do not give anything to eat or drink. Moisten an uncomfortably dry mouth with a wet cloth.

Basic principles

- Prevent further heat loss
- Get urgent help
- Rewarm the person – gradually
- Follow DRSABC

Keep movement of the person to a minimum, and be very gentle. Sudden movement can cause heart problems.

If outdoors

Keep the victim in shelter. Replace wet clothing with dry, ideally warmed (e.g. from dry, warm bystanders). Cover the person's head and insulate them against cold from the ground. Wrap them in something warm such as a sleeping bag or plastic bags (leave the face uncovered), or ideally a survival bag.

If indoors

Rewarm gradually in a generally warm room. Replace any cold, damp clothing. If the victim is alert enough to eat or drink, give hot, sweet fluids (no alcohol) and a little high-calorie food. Do not: heat up the body too fast, apply direct heat (hot-water bottles, sitting someone against a radiator), massage or rub the skin, or get the victim to exercise.

▼ *Give a shivering person who is still alert a warm drink, such as sweetened tea. Never offer alcohol to warm someone up.*

an emergency response and this causes a rapid pulse and sweating. As the blood flow weakens further, the brain begins to suffer from lack of oxygen, leading to nausea, dizziness, blurred vision, and confusion. If blood circulation is not restored rapidly, the person will start gasping for breath and will soon lose consciousness.

HYPOTHERMIA

Caused by cold, hypothermia occurs when the body's core temperature drops below 35°C/95°F. It commonly occurs in cold, exposed outdoor conditions, such as in mountainous regions, at the scene of traffic accidents, or as a result of immersion in cold water. Temperatures do not have to be freezing. It is more likely to occur in wet and windy conditions.

Diagnosis can be difficult, and unconscious sufferers may be mistaken for dead. However, due to the body's reduced need for oxygen when very cold, even prolonged resuscitation efforts have been successful.

HEAT EXHAUSTION

Due to excessive loss of water and salt from profuse sweating, heat exhaustion often occurs after heavy exertion and on hot days. If not treated promptly, heat exhaustion can prove fatal or develop into heatstroke.

HEATSTROKE

A very serious condition, heatstroke is often fatal. It may start as heat exhaustion, but if the body does not cool down, its heat-regulating mechanism fails, and body tissues start to heat up. Muscles and major organs begin to break down. Heatstroke tends to happen mainly in a very hot environment or with a fever.

Certain people are more vulnerable to heatstroke, such as the disabled and infirm, those with diabetes, the obese, and alcoholics. Some drugs, especially anti-depressants, diuretics, and sedatives, can increase susceptibility.

A person suffering from heatstroke needs urgent medical attention. While waiting for the emergency services, follow DRSABC, then move the

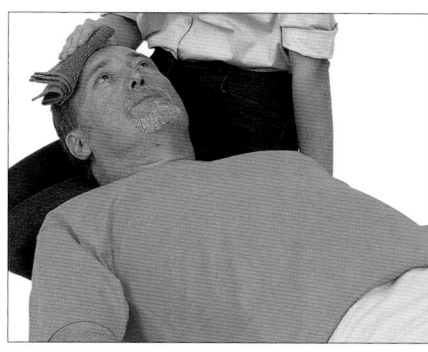

▲ *If someone is suffering from heatstroke, give frequent small sips of water and sponge the skin gently with tepid water.*

person out of the sun to a cool place. Remove excessive clothing. Lay them flat unless they have heart problems. In this case, sit them up. Watch for breathing problems.

To cool the person down, sponge the skin with cool water or spray with water and put them near a fan.

HEAT CRAMPS

These may happen after excessive exertion or exertion in very hot weather. They occur as a result of loss of salt and water from sweating. People may also feel sick and dizzy. First-aid treatment involves moving the sufferer to a cool place and giving them fluids with added sugar.

Follow DRSABC and call the emergency services if necessary or if the condition seems severe.

- Place the person in a cool place with a fan.
- Sponge the skin with tepid water.
- Give them cool water to drink.
- Do not give salt – this can cause dehydration if used incorrectly. A medical adviser will tell you what to give, or recommend an oral rehydration solution.
- If the person cannot drink because of nausea or vomiting, or there is no improvement after 1 hour, call a doctor or the emergency services.

Useful knots

These knots are useful survival tools so practise tying them until it becomes second nature. Relatively strong and secure, the hitch can be a lifesaver for securing a line to an anchorage or a rope to tree or post. It can even be used for towing a vehicle. The figure-of-eight is a quick and simple knot, a bit bulkier than a basic knot and easier to untie. The multi-purpose bowline is a non-slip knot that can be used to make a loop at the end of a rope, such as a waist loop for a climbing rope.

ROUND TURN AND TWO HALF HITCHES

1 Take the rope around the post, then around again. Bring the working end over and back under the standing end.

2 Now continue taking the rope through the loop you've formed. Add one more half hitch to make secure.

FIGURE-OF-EIGHT KNOT

1 Make a loop, carrying the working end first around, then behind the standing part. Now you have a figure-eight shape.

2 Begin to pull the working end through the loop from the top. Draw it right the way through.

3 To tighten, tug on both ends to remove any slack. Pull the standing end over and trap it against the knot top.

BOWLINE

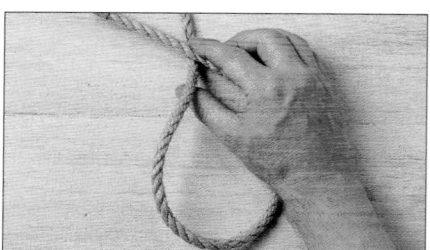  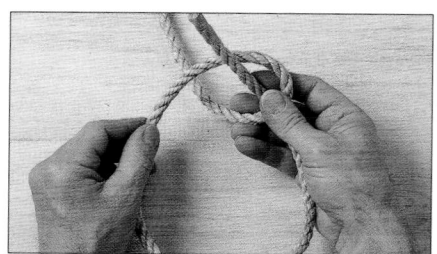

1 A non-slip knot that doesn't jam - bring the working end over for a loop.

2 Rotate the hand clockwise to produce a smaller loop.

3 Ensure the working end points upwards through the small loop.

4 Lead the end around behind the standing part of the rope.

5 Tuck it back down through the small loop, this time from front to back.

6 Complete the knot with a long end (longer than shown).

Survival resources

PUBLICATIONS

The following books are recommended for further reading on survival issues and acknowledged as reference sources.
• *Primitive Technology, a Book of Earth Skills* and *Primitive Technology II, Ancestral Skills* (David Westcott, Society of Primitive Technology)
• *The Science and Art of Tracking* and *Tom Brown's Wilderness Survival Field Guide* (Tom Brown jnr, Berkley Publishing Group)
• *The Traditional Bowyers Bible Vols 1–3* (Jim Hamm, Lyons Press)
• *Flintknapping: Making and Understanding Stone Tools* (John C. Whittaker, University of Texas Press)
• *Streetwise* (Peter Consterdine, Protection Publications)
• *Stopping Rape – Successful Survival Strategies* (Pauline Bart and Patricia O'Brien, Pergamon Press)
• *Principles of Personal Defense* (Jeff Cooper, Paladin Press)
• *Justifiable Force: The Practical Guide to the Law of Self Defence* (Robert Manning, Barry Rose Law Publishers)
• *US Armed Forces Survival Manual* (edited by John Boswell, Corgi)
• *SAS Survival Handbook* and *The Urban Survival Handbook* (Lofty Wiseman, HarperCollins)
• *The SAS Handbook of Living off the Land* (Chris McNab, Amber Books)
• *The Worst-Case Scenario Survival Handbook* (Piven & Borgenicht, Chronicle Books)
• *The Book of Survival* (Anthony Greenbank, Hatherleigh Press)

• *The Encyclopedia of Outdoor Survival* (Barry Davies, Virgin Books)
• *Combat And Survival Magazine* (Mai Publications, editor Bob Morrison, www.combatandsurvival.com)
• *Bushcraft and Survival Skills Magazine* www.bushcraftmagazine.co.uk/index.html

WEBSITES

The contributors recommend the following survival, self-defence and government travel advisory sites.
www.wildwoodsurvival.com
A good resource with well-documented skills
www.wild-live.org
Author's school where people can come and learn these skills and more
www.shomreihagan.org
A school in Israel where the ways of the desert can be learned
www.beyond2000bc.co.uk
A school in the UK run by Will Lord teaching flint knapping to its highest level
www.primitive.org
Non-profit organization dedicated to research, practice and teaching of primitive technology
www.survivalbox.co.uk
A product-based survival site
www.raymears.com
Acknowledged expert and TV popularizer of bushcraft skills
www.nookie.co.uk/rescue.html
Despite its name, an excellent equipment site
www.safetyforwomen.com
Does what it says on the address
www.kidshealth.org/teen/safety/safebasics/self_defense.html
Start them young
www.columbia.edu/cu/selfdefense/mind.html
Violent crime avoidance and prevention
www.microbiol.org/vl.martial.arts/selfdef.htm
Martial arts self-defence site
www.peterconsterdine.com
Good site on self-defence, practical martial arts, personal security, close protection and travel security books, dvds, courses
www.smartraveller.gov.au/index.html
The Australian Government's travel advisory and consular assistance service
www.canada.gc.ca/SSC/SSC_e.html

Official Canadian homeland security site
www.govt.nz/
New Zealand government's official site.
www.security.co.za
Definitive site on security in South Africa, with good links.
www.dhs.gov/dhspublic
Official US homeland security and disasters and emergencies website
www.bt.cdc.gov/disasters
US-based site on preparing against disasters from chain-saw injury to bioterrorism

SELF-DEFENCE COURSES

The following groups are recommended by the contributors:
• Seijinkai Karate-Do Association
Contact H. Cook, 3 Castle Hill House, Haltwhistle, Northumberland, England NE49 OEB, Seijinkaispider@aol.com
• iPhraya Pichai Muay Thai Boxing
Contact Bob Spour, www.phrayapichai.com/about_us.shtml
• British Combat Association
www.peterconsterdine.com

SURVIVAL RULES

Factors that help in survival
• Knowledge and training
• Determination to live
• Initiative and discipline
• A prepared plan of action

Factors that hinder survival
• Fear and anxiety
• Pain, illness and injury
• Cold, heat, thirst and hunger
• Fatigue and sleep deprivation
• Loneliness and boredom

Index

A-frame shelter 49
abroad, travelling 204-5
accommodation, finding safe 180
aerosol sprays 143
Aikido 139
air rage 194
aircraft 194-7
    choosing a safe seat 190, 191
    deep vein thrombosis (DVT) 195
    escape slides 196, 197
    hijacking of 214-15
    in-flight briefing and safety card 194
    oxygen masks 194
    preparing for the worst 195
    signalling to an 15
    surviving an air emergency 196-7
    using emergency exits 196
alder 57
anaphylactic shock 235
animal(s)
    avoiding dangerous 20
    bones 108, 126
    as food source 92-3
    footprints 94-5
    hides 109-11
    hunting and killing 89, 92, 94
    making containers from stomach of 114
    making cordage from fibres 130-1
    skinning and butchering 106-7
    sleeping and feeding areas 94
    stalking 96-9
    surviving attacks from 20, 232-5
    tracking 94-5
    trails 84, 94
    traps 100-1
ants 235
arctic conditions see cold environment
arctic fire 67
arrowheads 122, 124-5
arrows, making 122-3
attacks, animal 20, 232-5
attacks, human
    from behind 146-7
    frontal 144-5
    with knives and other weapons 148-51
    on men 134-5
    on women 136-7

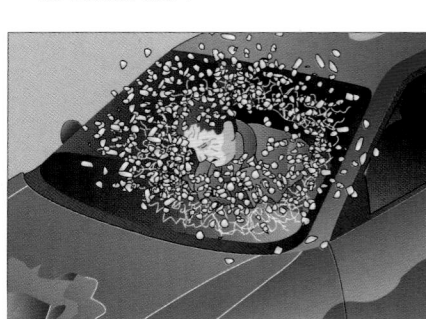

attitude 8-9
avalanches 236

backrest 126-7
bag snatching 156-7, 180
bamboo 48-9, 81
bandaging 246-7
baskets
    bark 114-15
    weaving 116-17
bear baggy 20, 232-3
bearings, finding your 16-17
bears 20, 232-3
bee stings 235
big cats 234
biological weapons 218-19
birch 24
birch sap 81
bites
    human 246
    insect 21, 235-6
    snake 234
blanket lift 243
bleach 82
bombs 216-17
    car 209
    letter 222
bone tools 108, 126
bow 120-1
    making arrows 122-3
bow drills 56-61
bowls
    pottery 118-19
    wooden 114-15
brace position 192, 196
brain-tanning 110
brakes, failing 184
breathing, and minimising fluid loss 77
buckskin 109-11
burdock 57
burglar alarms 167
burglars
    dealing with 168-9
    securing your home against 164-7
burning oil 198-9
burns 248
buses
    choosing a safe seat 190-1
    escaping from after an accident 192
    travelling on roof 191

cacti 81
calcium 89
calories 88
camouflage for stalking 99
candles 176-7
canines 233
captivity, survival in 212-13

car bombs 209
car jacking 181, 214
carbon monoxide poisoning 171-2
car(s)
    bag snatching from 156
    breaking down 182-3, 189
    dealing with mechanical failure 184-5
    digging out of snow 189
    drivers' survival strategies 189
    driving through floods 229
    escaping from an upside down 187
    escaping a locked 211
    failing brakes 184
    fire in 188
    getting out of a submerged 182-3
    jumping from a moving 192, 211
    jumpstarting 185
    skid control 186-7
    steering failure 184
    stuck throttle 184-5
    surviving being hit by 181
    tyre puncture and reinflating 184-5
caves 29, 44
    snow 38, 43
cedar 57
chemical attacks 218-19
chest compressions 245
cholera 78
chopper, making a 125
city streets, surviving 181
clay 118
clothes, making buckskin for 109-11
coconuts 81
    treatment of scorpion stings 235
cold environments
    avalanches 236
    dressing for 237
    drivers' survival strategies 189
    injuries in icy conditions 236-7
    making fire from ice 67
    snow shelters 38-43
    staying warm 40
    water from snow and ice 85
colds, alleviating symptoms 21
compass 17
condensation, collecting 84-5
cooking
    building a fire for 70-1

covered pit for 73
using hot rocks for 72
without utensils 70
cordage 130-1
coughs, plantain tea for 21
covered pit 73
CPR (cardiopulmonary resuscitation) 244-5
crabs 92
cradle carry 242
crocodile attacks 20, 233
crowd surge 181
cuts
natural remedies 21, 25
see also wounds

debris hut 30-1
debris wall, stacked 32-5
deep vein thrombosis (DVT) 195
dehydration 76-7, 237
desalinating sea water 83, 85
deserts 29
finding water 84-5
plants containing water 81
shelters 44-7
diapers 23
diarrhoea 21, 23
directions, finding 16-17
dogs, attacks from 233
dogwood 24
domestic violence 137
doors, securing 165, 167
drivers' survival strategies 189
drowning 245
DRSABC sequence 240-1
drying meat 108

earthquakes 226
eggs 89
elbow strike 140
elder 21, 57
electric eels/rays 201
elevators 193, 223
emergency escape 174-5
emergency home shelter 176-7, 220
emergency supplies 177, 221
emotional survival 12-13
escape slides (aircraft) 196-7
evacuation procedures (ships) 199
exploding rocks 53
"father-son" bow 120-1

fevers, alleviating symptoms 21
figure-4 deadfall trap 100
filter straw 84-5
filters, water 83, 177
fire 28, 51-73
building a 68
in a car 188
car breakdown and making a 189
clearing up a 53
for cooking 70-1
damping down a camp 69
dealing with in the home 170-1, 174-5
friction method of lighting 55-66
fuels and sources of wood 54-5, 57
lighting by using ice 67
making matches to carry 69
preparing a safe and efficient 53
on public transport 192-3
and signalling for help 14
siting of 52
tipi 68, 70
fire extinguishers 171, 188
fire piston 66
fire plough 56
fire pump 64-5
fire saw 66
fire thong 66
fireplace 34-5
first aid 239-51
assessment 241
bandaging 246-7
and burns 248
chest compressions 245
and drowning 245
DRSABC sequence 240-1
goals of 240
and heat exhaustion 249
and heatstroke 249
and hypothermia 249
lower leg fracture 243
mouth-to-mouth respiration 244
moving an injured person 242-3
recovery position 242-3
resuscitation 244-5
and shock 248-9
wound dressing 246-7
first-aid kits 177, 240
fish 92
grilling 70
gutting and filleting 93
harmful 201
fish pen 102
fish spear 102-3
fishing techniques 102-3
floods 173, 228-9
flotation aids 198
flying glass 216, 223
food 87-111
animal sources 92-101
balanced diet 88-9

calories needed 88
cooking of 70-3
edible plants 90-1
emergency stocks 177, 221
foraging for 93
preserving meat 108
survival at sea 200-1
footprints, animal 94, 95
fore and aft carry 242-3
forest fires 231
fox walk 96
freefall 233
friction method of lighting fires 55, 56-66
frogs 92
frontal attacks 144-5
fuels, fire 54-5
funghi 91
fuzz-stick 55

gas leaks 172
giardiasis 79
glue 128-9
grass mattress 126, 127
greater weaver 201
groin kick 141
group, survival in a 13
guns
being threatened with 148, 151
wounds inflicted by 246

haircare 25
hammock 37
hand drill 56, 62-3
hand slap 140
hand washing 18, 22
hazel 120
head butt 155
heat cramps 249
heat exhaustion 249
heat-stress index 45
heatstroke 45, 249
hepatitis A 78-9
hide glue 128
hides, animal 109-11
hijackings 214-15, 220
hippos 234
hitchhikers 181
home survival 163-77
dealing with intruders 168-9
emergency escape 174-5

emergency home shelter 176-7, 220
enhancing your security 164-7
and fire 170-1
flooding 173
gas leaks 172
hostage taking 210-11, 213
human waste, dealing with 22-3
hunting 92, 94
making a bow for 120-1
stalking 96-9
and throwing stick 104-5
tracking animals 94-5
hurricanes 230
hygiene 22-3
hypothermia 249

ice
crossing 237
escaping from 237
making fire from 67
water from 85
see also cold environments
igloos 38, 39
illnesses
caused by unclean water 78-9
natural remedies for 21
injuries
in icy conditions 236-7
preventing 18-19
see also first aid
insects 20, 235
as food sources 92-3
stings/bites from 21, 235-6
international emergency number (112) 182
iodine 82

'Jackjumper' 235
jellyfish 201
journeys, essentials for long 189
judo 139
jumping from a window 174-5
jumpstarting 185
jungle fire 66
jungles
getting water from plants 81
shelters 48-9

karate-do 139
keys, as improvised weapon 143
kick boxing 139

kidnapping 210-11
kindling 54, 55, 68
knapping stone 124-5
knives 18-19
making 124, 126
self-defence against attacks with 148-51
knots 250
'kung-fu' 139

latrine, digging a 22
leeches 20
leg fracture, dealing with lower 243
letter bombs 222
life rafts 197, 199, 200
lifeguard rescue 203
lifts 193, 223
lighting, security 166
lightning 230-1
locusts 88
London Bombings (2005) 209
luggage 180, 191
Lymes disease 20

Madrid railway bombings (2004) 209
magazine, as improvised weapon 142
mail
and chemical terror attacks 219
see also letter bombs
martial arts clubs 138-9
matches 69
mattress, grass 126, 127
meat
drying 108
preserving 108
menstrual care 23
mental survival 12-13
morning dew, collecting 80
mosquitoes 20-1, 93
moss
used in menstrual care 23
used as toilet paper 22
and wounds 21
motorways, breaking down on 182
mouth-to-mouth respiration 244
mouthwash, antiseptic 24-5
moving an injured person 242-3
moving vehicle, leaving a 192, 211
mullein stalks 57
mushrooms 91
mussels 92

nails, filing 24-5
nappies 23
natural disasters 176, 226-31
see floods; hurricanes; tornados; tsunamis;
volcano eruptions
natural remedies 21
nature, respecting of 19
newspaper, as improvised weapon 142
9/11 (2001) 208, 214-5, 222-3
north, finding 16-17
North Star 16-17
nuclear attacks 176-7

oak bark 21, 23, 25
obsidian 25
oil lanterns 129
Orion 16, 17
oxygen masks 194

palm leaves, covering a roof with 48-9
panic 12
paratrooper roll 175, 211
passports 204
personal alarms 137
personal belongings, securing 180
physical fitness, improving 138
pine needles, antiseptic mouthwash 24-5
pit shelters 46-7
pitch glue 128-9
pitcher plants 81
planes see aircraft
plankton 200
plantain 21
plants 89
edible 90-1
getting water from 81
making cordage from fibres 130-1
natural remedies using 21
taste test 90-1
poisons 218-19
polar bears 232
poplar 57
pottery 118-19
preserving meat 108
preventative measures 18-19
prisoner, being taken 210-13
protein 89
public transport
accidents 192-3
bags on 180
breaking safety glass windows 192-3
choosing a safe seat 190-1
fire on 192-3
seat belts and restraint systems 191
storing luggage safely 191
strangers on 191
punch, learning to 139
purifying water 79, 82-3, 85

quicksand, escaping 20
quinze shelters 38, 40-1

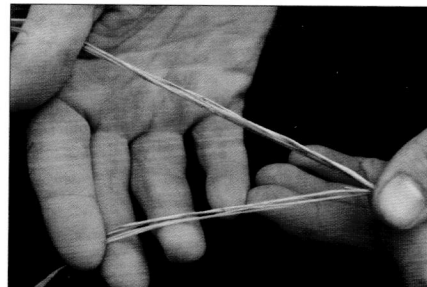

rabbits 94
radio 177
rail crossing, breaking down on a 183
rainwater 80
rape 136
    defending against 158-60
rawhide 130
recovery position 242-3
remote areas, breaking down in 183, 189
resins 128-9
respirators 218-19
resuscitation 244-5
reverse break roll 175
rip currents 203
rivers 16, 77-8
    crossing flooded 228
road rage 181
roads
    accidents 192-3
    coping with dangerous situations on 182-3
    slippery 187
rock wall shelter 46
rocks, cooking and hot 72
roundhouse kick 141
runs, animal 94

safety glass windows, breaking 192-3
salt 83
sanitary towels 23
scorpions 235
sea
    emergency landing of aircraft in 196-7
    parking car by 183
    survival at 199-201
sea anchor, catching food with 201
sea water, desalinating 83, 85
seashore, survival at 202-3
seat belts 191, 192
security, home see home survival
self-defence 133-61, 169
    attacks from behind 146-7
    attacks with knives and other weapons
        148-51
    attacks on men 135
    attacks on women 136-7
    bag snatching 156-7
    frontal attacks 144-5
    head butts 155
    identifying risk of attack 134-5
    martial arts clubs 138-9
    moves 139-41
    sexual assaults 136, 158-61
    strangulation 152-4
    training for impact 138
    using improvised weapons 142-3
self-defence sprays 204
septicaemia 247
sexual assaults 191
    defending against 136, 158-61
sexual harassment 158

shadow sticks 16
shampoo, making 25
sharks 200, 201
shellfish 92
shelters 27-49, 46-7, 197
    choosing a place 28-9
    debris hut 30-1
    desert 44-7
    emergency home 176-7, 220
    igloos 38, 39
    jungle 48-9
    long-term 34-7
    making after plane crash 197
    natural 28-9
    quinze 38, 40-1
    rock wall 46
    smoking out 36
    snow 38-43
    stacked debris wall 32-5
ship, abandoning 198
shock 248-9
signalling for help 14-15
signs, trail 14
sinew 130
skid control 186-7
slopes, parking on 183
smoke alarms 170-1
smoke hole 36-7
smoking out insects and bugs 36-7
snails 93
snakebites, dealing with 234
snakes 234-5
snow
    and avalanches 236
    digging a car out of 189
    shelters 38-43
    water from 85
    see also cold environments
snow caves ('drift caves') 38, 43
snow trench 42
soaps 23-4
solar still 85
south, finding 16
Southern Cross 16-17
spiders 93, 235
spoons 114
spruce roots 57
squaw wood 55, 68, 70
squirrels 92-3

stacked debris wall 32-5
stairs, survival cell under 176, 220
stalking animals 96-9
stars, direction-finding 16-17
steering failure 184
stinging nettles 57, 130
stone tools, making 124-5
stonefish 201
strangulation, defending against 152-4
suicide bombers 208, 214, 216
sun
    using to get bearings 16
    using to measure time 17
survival, keys to 9
survival kit 18
sweating 76-7
swimming, defensive techniques 229

taste test 90-1, 201
terrorism 9, 176, 207-23
    bombs and explosives 216-17
    hijackings 214-15, 220
    searching for car bombs 209
    and suicide bombers 208, 214, 216
    survival in the workplace 222-3
    taken prisoner or hostage 210-13
    toxic gases and poisons 218-19
    vigilance and public awareness 8, 208-9,
        216
    war zones 220-1
throat infections 21
throttle, sticking of 184-5
throwing stick 104-5
ticks 20, 93
time, using sun to measure 17
tinder 55, 68
tipi fire 68, 70
toilet facilities 22
toilet paper 22
toiletries, making 24-5
tools
    bone 108, 126
    stone 124-5
toothpaste, making 24
tornados 230
toxic gases 218-19
tracking animals 94-5
trail signs 14
trailers, swaying 187
trails, animal 84, 94
trains
    choosing a safe seat 190
    escaping from after an accident 192
    escaping from underground 193
transport see aircraft; buses; cars; public
    transport; trains
traps, animal 100-1
travelling abroad 204
tsunamis 227
tunnels, breaking down in 182

two-hook snare trap 101
tyre punctures 184-5

umbrellas, as improvised weapon 143
underground trains 193
underground water 84
upside down car, escaping from 187

valuables, protecting 180
vehicles see buses; cars; trains
visualization 7-8, 13
vitamins 88
volcano eruptions 226-7

war zones 220-1
water 75-85
    boiling 52, 72, 82
    building a shelter near 29
    checking for chemical pollutants 79
    collecting 79
    collecting condensation 84-5
    collecting morning dew 80
    conserving 77
    desalinating sea 83, 85
    effects of dehydration 76
    emergency supplies 177, 221
    filters 83, 177

    finding a safe supply 78-9
    from snow and ice 85
    from plants 81
    illnesses caused by unclean 78-9
    importance of 9, 76-7
    keeping fluid loss down 76-7
    locating underground 84
    natural sources of 80-1
    purifying 79, 82-3, 85, 177
    rainwater 80
    rationing 77
    signs of 77
water vines 81

weapons, using improvised 142-3
weapons of mass destruction (WMD) 218
weaving a basket 116-17
weight training 138
wide-angled vision 96-7
windchill factor 38-9
windows
    breaking safety glass 192-3
    jumping from 174-5
    locks for 164-5, 167
wood
    flexible 120
    for friction method of lighting a fire 56
    gathering 19
    ideal for fire 54-5, 57
    shaping with a knife 19
    testing for hardness 57
wooden bowls 114-15
workplace, survival in 222-3
worms 93
wounds 21
    dressing of 246-7
    in icy conditions 236-7
    infected 247
    oakbark compress for 21, 25

yucca-based soap 24

Acknowledgements

The publishers and contributors wish to thank the following people for their time, expertise and contributions to the book. We sincerely apologize if we have omitted any individual(s).
Debra Searle (Veal) MBE and her sister Hayley Barnard at SHOAL Projects Ltd for providing the introduction and photographs http://www.debrasearle.com.
Helen Metcalfe for planning and shooting the photography sequences and **Bill Mattos** for modelling and providing models on those shoots – and also for providing many of the props for free. Both Helen and Bill are at Nookie Xtreme Sports Equipment http://nookie.co.uk/rescue.html.
Tim Gundry for shooting the self-defense sequences: http://www.timgundry.co.uk/
Brian Turner and his wife at Kazan Budo Ltd (Martial Arts supplies - http://www.kazanbudo.com and Bellingham Fitness Centre for supplying the gym, models, props and lunches for the self-defence shoots.
Bob Morrison's Military Scene for the military and biological pictures http://www.combatandsurvival.com.
Peter Drake for supplying the charts and African bushcraft photographs.

Mika Kalakoski for his help on snow shelters as well as supplying the snow shelter images.
Rob Bicevskis for help on the images for making fire with a lens made of ice.
Tunde Morakinyo at the Iroko Foundation for supplying his jungle pictures.
Jean-Philippe Soulé at Around the World in a Viewfinder for the cahune palm shelter pictures – www.jpsviewfinder.com
With thanks to the following picture agencies for the photographs they provided.
iStockphoto p170tr, p171tr, p173bl, p189tr, p192bl, p194bl, p199tl, p208tr, p216tr, p216bt, p220bl, p221tr, p224/5, p227tr, p229tl, p230tl, tr, p231tr, p238/9.
Sciencephoto Library p218tr, p226bl, p227ml, mr, bl, bt, p228bl, p230b.
Alamy Images p9tl, p20tr, p194tr, p198tr, p209tr, p215tl, p222tr.

Patrick Mulrey for his invaluable survival step-by-steps and disaster scenario illustrations.
Peter Bull Arts Studios for the footprints, skining and tanning and hiding steps.
Sarah Ainley for her initial editorial setting up and input.

Anthonio Akkermans would like to dedicate his writing to Gillian and Reuben and to thank **Ofer Israeli** of Shomrei Hagan in Israel, who helped him with desert knowledge, guided him through the desert, and helped take the desert images.
Allan "Bow" Beauchamp: for some interesting discussions on primitive fire and also for images kindly supplied. **Tom Brown** and the instructors at the Tracker school for teaching these skills.
Harry Cook would like to thank Sheila Cook and the members of the **Hexham Seijinkai Karate-do Club** for giving up their free time to model: **Katie Khudarieh, Katy Cook, Sheila Cook, Catriona Moreland, Malcolm Wilson, Lucy Anne Donnelly.** Thanks are also due to **Lisa Henderson** for helping him to see the woman's point of view when discussing the requirements for effective self-defence.
Anness Publishing would also like to thank the following models for their time and effort under difficult and often treacherous conditions: **Garry and Loretta Harper, Matthew Harrison, Nikki Ball, Alastair Stewart, Paul Ross, Gabby Footner, Tattiana Cotts, S Atkins, Tim Denson, Alison Martin, Andy Parritt, Mike and Luke Waldock.**